Order without Design

Order without Design

How Markets Shape Cities

Alain Bertaud

The MIT Press
Cambridge, Massachusetts
London, England

This book was set in Palatino by Westchester Publishing Services. Printed and bound in the United States of America.

Library of Congress Cataloging-in-Publication Data

Names: Bertaud, Alain, author.
Title: Order without design : how markets shape cities / Alain Bertaud.
Description: Cambridge, MA : MIT Press, [2018] | Includes bibliographical references and index.
Identifiers: LCCN 2018008743 | ISBN 9780262038768 (hardcover : alk. paper)
Subjects: LCSH: Urban economics. | City planning.
Classification: LCC HT321 .B478 2018 | DDC 330.9173/2--dc23
LC record available at https://lccn.loc.gov/2018008743

10 9 8 7 6 5 4 3

To my wife, Marie-Agnes Roy Bertaud

Contents

Acknowledgments   ix

1   Economists and Urban Planners: Two Visions of Cities
That Need to Be Merged   1

2   Cities as Labor Markets   19

3   Formation of Urban Spatial Structures: Markets
versus Design   51

4   Spatial Distribution of Land Prices and Densities:
Models Developed by Economists   93

5   Mobility: Transport Is a Real Estate Issue—The Design
of Urban Roads and Transport Systems   143

6   Affordability: Household Incomes, Regulations,
and Land Supply   219

7   Alternative Urban Shapes and Utopias   307

8   Urban Planners and Urban Economists Have an Important Role
to Play If They Manage to Work Together   349

Notes   383
Index   395

Acknowledgments

The possibility to write this book on cities rested on a few favorable circumstances that allowed extensive travel during several years and many chance encounters with skilled and knowledgeable people. Some people contributed to this book with facts and case studies; some clarified theories and concepts; some helped focus the book on its essential message; some encouraged the writing process by their interest in the subject; some had the essential role of prodding me to keep writing; others, in the final writing phase, helped improved the clarity of ideas, language, and syntax.

I do not believe a book on cities can be written on a mountain top. It can only be written while immersed in its subject matter—a large city. The essence of cities is neither their buildings nor their streets but their people, who, in close proximity, constantly stimulate one another with new ideas and invent better ways of doing things. It is fitting, therefore, that the final phase of this book was completed in New York, a city of many encounters.

It is also in New York that I met by chance John Turner in 1970, just before leaving for Yemen. Turner's powerful ideas about the power of grassroots urban development, forcefully expressed in *Freedom to Build*, the book he later edited in 1972, have been constantly on my mind during my professional career.

New York is a city of these kinds of chance encounters. My wife and I were very lucky to meet Brent Brolin and his wife, Jean Richard, at an office party a few weeks after we had arrived in New York in 1968. We have remained close friends to this day. Brent is an architecture critic and historian and the author of several books. He believes that architecture and planning, but most particularly housing, should emerge and evolve from grassroots cultures, which make them better adapted to their user mores and to the environment. When we first met Brent, his ideas went completely against the zeitgeist that promoted an international style pretending to be derived from a universal logic to be applied worldwide. His advocacy of grassroots solutions has greatly influenced me since. Some of the positive housing policies and outcomes in China and Indonesia, which I describe in chapter 6, are a direct illustration of Brent Brolin's ideas.

It was also in 1968 that we met Rosalie Siegel in a French bookstore in Manhattan. Rosalie was a bilingual literary agent, immersed in the world of book publishing her entire life. Years later, she convinced me to write this book and have it published formally, instead of pursuing my first idea of just disseminating these chapters in the form of online blog posts. Rosalie and her husband Evan Wolarsky have remained close friends to this day. Meeting John Turner, Brent Brolin, and Rosalie Siegel by chance in New York, and how they subsequently contributed in different ways to this book, are a vivid example of the spillover effects that can occur in a large city, as I describe it more theoretically in chapter 2.

Favorable Circumstances: Living and Working in Many Cities

To write a book on cities, it is necessary to know many of them. Cities are like people—they all share a similar physiology but have very different personalities that have been formed by their history and their environment. Urban planners very rarely create new cities from a tabula rasa, although many dream of being able to do so. Planners must work in existing cities with long histories. Their job is to improve the way cities function and eventually help them adapt to changing circumstances. The job of an urban planner is in many ways like that of a family doctor who tries to heal the illness of patients and to advise them on how to maintain a healthy life in the future. Nobody would trust a doctor who has treated only one patient. In the same way, to contribute to the knowledge and management of cities, an urban planner should know many cities. Serious working knowledge of cities' physiology and pathologies cannot be acquired by just visiting them while collecting data. To acquire the necessary urban knowledge, an urban planner must live a nomadic life for an extended time. The possibility to live this nomadic life over several years was the first favorable circumstance that allowed me to write this book.

The credit for allowing this favorable circumstance to happen is due largely to my wife, Marie-Agnes, whose enthusiasm for change and travel allowed us to move from city to city during our first 15 years of marriage. The observations made at close range during this period of our life established this book's empirical foundation.

Marie-Agnes and I were married in Oran, Algeria in 1965. For the next 15 years, we kept moving with our growing family, following the happenstance of new assignments, driven by our curiosity for new professional experiences. From Oran, we moved successively to Tlemcen, Paris, New York, Sana'a, Port-au-Prince, Washington, DC, San Salvador, back to Washington, then to Bangkok, and finally we settled in Washington, DC, in 1980. This nomadic life, changing countries and cities 10 times over 15 years, was essential to the gestations of many ideas presented in the chapters in this book. Marie-Agnes, therefore, deserves the first and more important credit for this book. Our three children—Yann, Veronique, and Marion-Xochitl—each born in a different country, accompanied us also in this initial itinerant life.

Marie-Agnes not only created and maintained a new home in successive cities as we kept moving, she also shared my passion for understanding the hidden mechanisms that make cities work. Her experience as a woman working in series of constantly changing cultures provided many insights, which contributed to forming our ideas about how cities function and evolve. In addition, on the job, she developed strong skills in surveying, mapping, and geographical information systems that she used either independently as a consultant to international organizations or as a partner contributing to my own work and to some graphs and maps appearing in this book.

International Organizations as Collectors and Disseminators of Ideas

The other favorable circumstance that allowed me to write this book was the possibility of working for international organizations, first the United Nations Development Programme, then the World Bank, and finally as a freelance consultant. Working as a consultant for these organizations for the first 15 years allowed me to live a nomadic life, accumulating observations and urban knowledge. Later, joining the staff of the World Bank gave me the chance to work with an international select team of urban economists—Solly Angel, Patricia Annez-Clarke, Robert Buckley, Man Cho, Larry Hannah, Kim Kyung-Hwan, Steve Malpezzi, Steve Mayo, Bertrand Renaud, and Jim Wright—all widely traveled, sharing my passion for understanding how cities function, and finding out which policies work and which do not. While during the 15 years of nomadic life I accumulated empirical knowledge, during my years as Bank staff, I was able to relate my field experience to urban economic theory due to the conversations, debates, and work with my urban colleagues. Many of the concepts developed in this book came from this interchange.

An added benefit of working for the World Bank Urban Department was extensive travel to some of the major cities of the world, where I was able to participate in their development. The identification, appraisal, and supervision of large urban infrastructure projects and housing policy reforms allowed me to work with local professionals over a period several years in the same cities. I gained enormously from this team work with people who had an intimate knowledge of the potential and the limitations of their own city. Many of these professionals met during my fieldwork deeply influenced my understanding of cities. I credit particularly Madame Bai in Tianjin, Cai Jianmin and Guo Jifu in Beijing, Ronald Contreras and Alberto Harth in San Salvador, Bimal Patel in Ahmedabad, Vidyadhar Phatak in Mumbai, Hendropranoto Suselo in Jakarta, Sidhijai Thanpipat in Bangkok, and Wu Zheng Tong in Shanghai.

The World Bank also gave me an opportunity to meet eminent urban economists whose books I had read and who had contributed to a better theoretical understanding of field observations. Meeting in person scholars like Jan Brueckner, Paul Cheshire, Richard Green, and Edwin Mills was a privilege.

During the 1990s, working in Russia was a new learning experience. While the former Soviet Union was certainly not a model of good urban management, my Russian colleagues, Michael Berezin, Sergei Istomin, Olga Kaganova, and Leonid Limonov, demonstrated that the failure of the system was not due to mediocre human capital but to the rigid Leninist ideology that did not allow brilliant professionals any initiative. The major failure of Western liberal democracies in dealing with the former Soviet Union was a failure to recognize that extremely capable people could be found in failing political systems. The massive technical assistance directed to former command economies was too often paternalistic, irrelevant, and humiliating for the local professionals and managers, who could have carried out the reforms from the inside but were submitted to the "tyranny of experts" as my New York University colleague William Easterly has argued in a book.

The role of international organizations is often misunderstood, often even by themselves. Their main role is not to transfer knowledge or resources from rich countries to poor ones, or from "advanced" to "less advanced." The record shows that they are notoriously inefficient at doing so. Their usefulness is their possibility to acquire knowledge from all the countries where they operate and disseminate it widely. They play an indispensable role, like pollinating insects. Insects do not create pollen, they just carry it randomly from plant to plant. Cities, like plants, are not mobile, they need an agent that transmits ideas from city to city. This includes documenting and disseminating successful innovations as well as documenting failed ones. In a modest way, this book aims at disseminating further the knowledge accumulated while working in these organizations.

The Marron Institute

Finally, when we moved back to the New York area after leaving the World Bank, another favorable circumstance presented itself. I met the economist Paul Romer, nearly by chance, through Bob Buckley. Paul had recently moved from Palo Alto, California, to New York, intending to dedicate his vast talent and imagination to urban development. Within the academic structure of New York University, he created and became the director of the Marron Institute, an institute dedicated to improving the performance of cities, their spatial development and also their health, safety, mobility, and inclusiveness. He generously asked me to join the staff, with the understanding that one of my main tasks would be to finish writing this book. In the small but select staff of the Marron Institute, I found a stimulating intellectual environment composed of people sharing the same passion: developing a better understanding of how cities work, and how they could be improved through key infrastructure investments and better regulations. Under the stimulating direction of Paul Romer and the management of Brandon Fuller, the focus of the Marron Institute has been operational, relying on the development of quantitative indicators in the context of a solid theoretical framework.

In the Institute, most of my contacts were with the Urban Expansion project, led by Solly (Shlomo) Angel. I was happy to work with Solly again. We had first met in Bangkok in the late 1970s. Years later, we worked together again in Russia in the 1990s, keeping in loose contact in between. Although we spent several years without seeing each other, Solly's urban ideas and mine ended up converging into one concept: cities should be allowed to expand as they develop and become wealthier. The main objective of the planner should be to maintain mobility and housing affordability as a city's population increases and it diversifies its activities. Efforts to coerce a city's shape into an arbitrary predetermined form or an arbitrarily set density would always result in adverse consequences for mobility and affordability.

Marie-Agnes and I soon immersed ourselves in the debates and conferences organized by the Marron Institute. I found among my new colleagues the same intense intellectual stimulant that I had found earlier in the urban group at the World Bank. I am grateful for the exchange and feedback that they gave me when I gave talks about the main ideas behind the different chapters of this book. I particularly thank Nicolas Galarza, Eric Goldwyn, Achilles Kallergis, Patrick Lamson-Hall, and Jonathan Stewart for the time they spent with me clarifying many of the topics found in the following chapters. In addition, Jonathan played a particularly important role in reviewing the early chapters of the book and providing his insights as an economist.

Eventually, when the writing of this book was sufficiently advanced, I was asked to teach a course to New York University students. The course, called "Markets, Design, and the City," followed the sequence of the book's chapters. It was a good way to test its content on the critical minds of NYU graduate students. It became an occasion for further exchanges of ideas and perspectives, as the students came from many different countries. We still meet regularly with some of them, who by now are pursuing careers in urban planning: Eduard Cabré-Romans, Javier

Garciadiego Ruiz, Hannah Kates, Simon Lim, Jwanah Qudsi, and Amalia Toro Restrepo. Marie-Agnes and I find these regular reunions with the younger generation particularly rewarding. We feel privileged to be able to exchange ideas with some of the new crop of urban professionals who are soon going to influence the development of the cities of tomorrow.

The Final Phase: Editing and Publishing

Ideas are not enough; a book must be written and published for ideas to be of any use. I therefore must give credit to the people who encouraged me to start and to keep writing. Discussing the early drafts with me, they kept me focused on the story. Marie-Agnes, Robert Buckley, Paul Romer, and my colleagues at the Marron Institute played this important role with competence and tenacity. Their obstinate and friendly interest made it impossible for me to give up half way, despite the difficulties and the periodic self-doubts. Again, without their friendly prodding and advice, this book would never have been finished.

During the writing stage, Laura Fox edited the many drafts of this book. She was the first person to read all the chapters. Laura's understanding of urban economics and her familiarity with many cities in the world made her exceptionally competent as an editor. Laura looked at each chapter's structure with a critical eye and underlined with severity any logical inconsistency; she also corrected with patience the recurring Gallicisms, and removed any redundant text like a gardener prunes a fruit tree. She further scrutinized the numerous graphs and maps, suggesting changes when she saw inconsistencies between graphs and text, or a lack of clarity. I am particularly grateful for this last task. As a former student at the École des Beaux-Arts, I often reproach economists for their neglect of the language of graphs. I was glad that Laura was not affected by this bias and did not hesitate to spend a large amount of time reviewing the quality of the maps and the graphs contained in this book.

Finally, I must thank MIT Press for having agreed to publish this book with no hesitations and no red tape. Jane Macdonald established the first contact at a conference at NYU and reviewed the first three chapters. As the writing progressed, Emily Taber took over from Jane and finalized the agreement to publish with MIT Press. Emily provided further guidance on putting the manuscript in its final phase. I thank Emily for giving friendly, quick, and clear answers to all the questions, possibly naive, coming from an author publishing his first book. I also thank the four anonymous reviewers who provided very useful comments that improved the final version of the manuscript.

1 Economists and Urban Planners: Two Visions of Cities That Need to Be Merged

Nations stumble upon establishments, which are indeed the result of human action, but not the execution of any human design.
—Adam Ferguson, *An Essay on the History of Civil Science*, 1782

Order generated without design can far outstrip plans men consciously contrive.
—Friedrich Hayek, *The Fatal Conceit*, 1988

Markets and Design

This book is about the observed interaction between economic markets and design in the development of a few cities around the world. Markets are impersonal, transactional mechanisms resulting from human action (e.g., exchanges of value, movement of goods) but not from human design, as expressed by the Enlightenment-era Scottish philosopher Adam Ferguson. Indeed, markets create an order generated without design, as argued by Frederick Hayek, an Austrian-British economist and philosopher who taught at the London School of Economics, the University of Chicago, and the University of Freiburg in the middle of the twentieth century. The order created by markets manifests itself in the shape of cities. Markets transmit through prices the information generating the spatial order. When prices are distorted, so is the order generated by markets.

Urban planners—on behalf of politicians—aim to modify that order through design. These design interventions implemented by planners consist mostly of regulations and the building of infrastructure and public spaces. The objective of planning regulations is to modify the outcome of unconstrained markets to increase the welfare of citizens. What is the extent of the modification of market outcome achieved by planners? It varies from only slight modification in a city like Houston, Texas, to complete obliteration in a city like Brasília, Brazil, and in some cities of the former Soviet Union.

We are facing a strangely paradoxical situation in the way cities are managed: the professionals in charge of modifying market outcomes through regulations (planners) know very little about markets, and the professionals who understand markets (urban economists) are seldom involved in the design of regulations aimed at restraining these markets. It is not surprising that the lack of interaction between the two professions causes serious dysfunction in the development of cities. It is the story of the blind and the paralytic going their own ways: The planners are blind; they act without seeing. The economists are paralyzed; they see but do not act.

The main objective of this book is to improve operational urban planning, as practiced in municipal planning departments, by applying urban economists' knowledge (and models) to the design and planning of regulations and infrastructure. Urban economists understand the functioning of markets, while planners are often baffled by them. Unfortunately, the very valuable knowledge that has accumulated in urban economics literature has not had much impact on operational urban planning. My aim is not to develop a new urban theory but to introduce already existing urban economics knowledge into urban planning practices.

Urban Planning versus Urban Economics

Urban planning is a craft learned through practice. Planners must make rapid decisions that have an immediate impact on the ground. The width of streets, the minimum size of land parcels, and the heights of buildings are usually based on planners' decisions. Urban planners are "normative," that is, they base their decisions on best professional practices that usually rely on rules of thumb transmitted from generation to generation. Urban planners use expressions that are often more qualitative than quantitative. They like to use adjectives like "sustainable," "livable," "compact," "resilient," and "equitable" to characterize their planning objectives. However, planners seldom feel the need to link these qualitative objectives to measurable indicators. It is therefore impossible to know if the planning strategies used are indeed "sustainable" or "livable." In the absence of quantitative indicators, one might conclude that these terms are only labels that provide a kind of moral high ground to whatever urban plan is proposed.

By contrast, urban economics is a quantitative science, based on theories, models, and empirical evidence that are developed mostly in academic settings. Papers published in academic journals are the primary output of urban economists, and urban economists mostly exchange ideas with other urban economists. They seldom have direct contact with people in planning departments who make decisions on zoning or on the alignment of a new subway line. Economists' contacts with cities are usually indirect, consisting mostly of obtaining databases that they analyze with great skill. There is no obligation to give feedback to the planners.

I believe that applying the theories of urban economics to the practice of urban planning would greatly improve the productivity of cities and the welfare of urban citizens; I have seen the benefits of this approach in my own practice as well as for a small subset of planners. In addition, convincing urban economists to participate directly in the day-to-day work of municipal planning departments might, as an added benefit, focus academic research on current crucial urban development issues. Cities generate a large amount of data, often recorded in urban departments, but it remains unused; planners, busy with their day-to-day operational responsibilities, lack the time and the theoretical background to fully use the data to guide their decision making. New technologies are creating an abundance of new sources of urban data. Starting in the 1980s, the availability of satellite imagery allows year-by-year monitoring of the development of cities; NASA night light imagery provides a useful proxy for urban economic development; and data from GPS-enabled phones permits measurement of traffic congestion and commuting times at any time of the day. The usefulness and significance of these new data sources have seldom been explored. Economists working in urban departments should be able to make good use of the data available. This would rapidly increase our understanding of cities for the greatest benefits of their citizens.

A Personal Journey of Discovery
This book is largely based on my personal experience as a practicing urban planner and on what I learned from urban economists on the job. Urban planning is a craft learned mostly in the field. I worked in many cities and many countries during a professional career of about 55 years. Every new project and every new city contributed to my experience and knowledge. I have been a resident urban planner for seven cities and consulted for more than fifty cities. I'm now working at New York University, where I teach planners and urban economists from around the world. I try to reflect this experience throughout this book.

Some readers might deplore the fact that I do not devote much space to a critical review of urban planning theory. Indeed, in this book I do not refer often to academic debates about the nature of urban planning, or to the urban planning literature. By contrast, I often quote academic urban economists, precisely because this discipline appears to me more relevant to understanding the problem at hand. In writing this book, I have been inspired by the approach used by Albert Hirschman when confronted with world development economics. Hirschman's method was to observe reality on the ground, analyze the facts, and then develop a theory. He had a marked skepticism for imported theories and expert opinion. One of his major books, aptly named *Development Projects Observed*,[1] is entirely based on a field survey of development projects around the world. He summarizes his field method this way: "Immersion in the particular proved, as usual, essential for the catching of anything general."

Three major events significantly improved my understanding of cities. The first was in 1965, when I became, by chance, responsible for authorizing building permits for the city of Tlemcen in Algeria. I then discovered how arbitrary and harmful some urban regulations could be, no matter how well intentioned their original objective had been.

The second major event was in 1974, when for the first time I had the opportunity to work with an urban economist on a specific project in Haiti—the master plan of Port-au-Prince. I discovered there that there were economic theories that explained some of the empirical observations I had made about cities.

The third event came much later, in 1983 in China and in 1991 in Russia, when I had the opportunity to work in countries that were just transitioning from command economies to markets. By then, I already knew the indispensable role that land prices and rents played in shaping the spatial structure of cities. In China and Russia, I witnessed for the first time the absurdity resulting from planners having to allocate land among users without the help of land prices, the primary driver of urban markets.

The experience of working in the 1980s and 1990s in China and Russia was particularly valuable and unique. Large command economies have now disappeared. The cities of the last two command economies in the world, North Korea and Cuba, are seldom analyzed. Command economies have never been very open about sharing data. Unfortunately, the memory of the poor outcomes created by the command economy experience in the development of cities seems to have been lost. In this book I will occasionally remind the reader of the outcomes of the utopian system I personally witnessed, not only the Marxist experiment in urban planning, but also other equally utopian ideas based on the design of inspired planners like Le Corbusier, Lúcio Costa, or Oscar Niemeyer. I sometimes meet younger colleagues or students taking my course on Market and Design at New York University who are tempted by the idea of cities designed entirely by planners without the guidance— they would say hindrance—of land prices. I hope this book will convince them that there is no need to repeat this costly utopia.

Approving and Rejecting Building Permits in Tlemcen, Algeria

In 1965, I had not yet completed my architectural and planning studies in Paris. At that time France still had a military draft, and my student deferment period had expired. I was lucky enough to spend the last year of my military service in Algeria as a civilian technical assistant, a sort of French version of the Peace Corps. Algeria had been independent for only 2 years after a bitter war to free itself from colonial rule. At the time, there were so few Algerian urban planners that the government appointed me *"Inspecteur de l'Urbanisme"* or "Urban Inspector" for Tlemcen, a city of about 80,000 people in the Western part of Algeria. My job consisted of preparing new land development plans, but mostly it required spending the majority of my mornings deciding the fate of building permit applications.

A very experienced administrative assistant, many years my senior, reviewed the building permit applications the day before I had to make the final decisions. She prepared letters addressed to the applicants that approved or rejected their applications. I had only to sign the letters. The decision to approve or reject building permits was based on whether the plans provided by the applicant conformed to the rules contained in the *Code de l'urbanisme.* The huge book that contained the rules, norms, and regulations for land development and construction looked like a family bible. It certainly had the authority of a Holy Book for urban planners and for the employees working in the urban planning department. Because independence was so recent, the Algerian administration had to rely on the regulations previously imposed by the colonial power. Therefore, the provisions of the *Code de l'urbanisme* reflected the practices and norms of France, a country very different from Algeria in terms of income, culture, traditions, and climate.

On my first day on the job, to my dismay, about eight out of ten residential building permits were to be refused. The letters of rejection were already typed in their final form, including references to the articles of the "code" that were violated by the plans attached to the request. Most of the violations had to do with inadequate setbacks as well as window sizes and locations.

The violations of the code were easy to explain from an economic and cultural point of view. In the cities of newly independent Algeria, vacant lots facing a formal street were rare and expensive. The price of land was such that lots tended to be small in order to remain affordable. Traditional houses in the old medina of Tlemcen were designed around a central courtyard, while the building surrounding the courtyard occupied the entire lot up to the property lines. Because privacy was highly valued, there were few windows opening onto streets, and these windows were narrow and placed high on the walls to prevent any direct view from the street into the house. The applicants for building permits were trying to design a house as close as possible to their preferred model, but the regulations were designed to produce a suburban detached house like the ones found in the suburbs of Paris. The small size of the lots the applicants could afford combined with the generous setbacks demanded by the regulations made the floor size of the prospective house much smaller than they would have been if regulations had allowed them to build a house, with a central courtyard, that occupied the entire lot. In addition, the requirement of large windows opening onto the streets was a direct violation of their cultural norms.

I had traveled extensively in the Middle East as a student and was well aware of the cultural differences between the design of houses in the Southern and Eastern part of the Mediterranean and those of continental Western Europe. I had also visited some of the elegant houses in the old medina of Tlemcen and found them, not surprisingly, much better adapted to the climate and mores of Algeria than were detached French suburban homes.

During my first 3 days on the job, I reluctantly signed the letters prepared by my administrative assistant, but with a guilty conscience. By enforcing the regulations, I was forcing on local people an inadequate design and an inefficient use of scarce land in the name of abstract norms established long ago in a distant land with a different climate and culture. I was also aware that by rejecting building permit applications I was slowing down and increasing the cost of construction of new dwellings that Algerians desperately needed. Most of the new immigrants moving from the countryside to Tlemcen could not afford a formal house, so they built whatever they could afford in the informal settlements surrounding the city. By rejecting building permits, I was likely to further increase the growth of informal settlements. With the end of the war, people were moving to cities from rural areas in great numbers. They formed tightly packed informal settlements filling vacant land around cities. These settlements lacked running water, sewer, and electricity, but the new settlers found their location close to a city more desirable than the isolation of the scattered villages and hamlets of the countryside.

On the fourth day, I did not sign the letters but went to see the prefect of the region. The prefect was the representative of the central government in Tlemcen and had authority over all the functionaries of the state, including me. I explained the problem to him: by enforcing the law I was decreasing the welfare of the inhabitants of the region. As an architect, I asked him for permission to use my own professional judgment and common sense in providing building permits, even when some norms were at variance with the code. The prefect was a young military officer who had fought in the armies of the National Liberation Front and, like me, was a little puzzled by all the administrative rules that he was supposed to enforce. He heartily gave me permission to use common sense. In any other circumstances, giving permission to ignore the law would have been a crime, but in the frontier atmosphere of newly independent Algeria, we both got away with it.

Poor Regulations Are Still Common
This episode in my early professional life gave me a healthy skepticism toward urban regulations that are based on norms whose rationale is seldom challenged. The dimensional norms that I was supposed to apply were imposed by the code solely to impose a preset design on residential areas. They were conceived for the sole purpose of preventing a deviation from the design that was predominant in

the suburbs of French cities. The regulations had nothing to do with safety or sanitation—I would not have doubted the wisdom of these types of regulations without expert evidence.

In this case, the circumstances were exceptional. Algeria's urban regulations had been imposed by a colonial power, and there had not yet been time to modify them. My current experience, more than 50 years later, makes me fear that the same regulations are still on the books in Algeria. To this day, when working in India, I am still stumbling on some remnants of the British Town and Country Planning Act passed in 1932, causing similar welfare reductions in India as the *Code de l'urbanisme* did in Algeria in 1965.

I do not deny the necessity of urban regulations. But their impact should be regularly audited to weed out those regulations that have become irrelevant or even noxious. The original objectives of urban regulations are often lost and therefore are difficult to question. Urban rules are often transmitted through generations as traditional wisdom that is seldom challenged. However, circumstances change, and rules, specifically urban rules, must be adapted to these new circumstances.

At the time I revolted against the regulations applied to Algeria, I was not yet aware that the urban economics literature had an abundance of papers that evaluated the costs and benefits of urban regulations. Unfortunately, to this day the knowledge accumulated in this economic literature seldom percolates into urban operational planning practices, and urban regulations detrimental to the welfare of citizens still survive unchallenged. The inadequacy of poorly designed urban regulations is not an idiosyncrasy of a recently independent Algeria. In a recent report, Edward Glaeser,[2] a prominent American urban economist at Harvard University, writes about US urban regulations:

Arguably, land use controls have a more widespread impact on the lives of ordinary Americans than any other regulation. These controls, typically imposed by localities, make housing more expensive and restrict the growth of America's most successful metropolitan areas. These regulations have accreted over time with virtually no cost-benefit analysis.

Although Glaeser is writing about US land use regulations, based on my worldwide professional experience, his comments also apply to the urban regulations of most world cities.

I want to make clear that I do not advocate "deregulation" as an ideological doctrine. Some urban regulations are indispensable. I only advocate periodically auditing urban regulations to eliminate the ones that are irrelevant or malignant. This is an exercise that every urban planner should do on a regular basis. Auditing urban regulations is like periodically pruning a tree: the objective is not to cut branches but to allow the tree to develop fully.

The Fortuitous Encounter of an Economist and an Urban Planner in a Capital City of the Caribbean

My first encounter with an urban economist took place in Port-au-Prince, Haiti, in 1974. That year, I was going to be the lead urban planner of a multinational team assembled to prepare the master plan of Port-au-Prince, a project financed by the United Nations Development Programme. In the preceding years I had worked as resident urban planner in several cities around the world, including Chandigarh, India; Tlemcen, Algeria; Sana'a, Yemen; and Karachi, Pakistan. My experience in those cities had been purely operational, setting standards for new areas to be developed, designing low-income housing, and planning new public transport routes. In addition, I had worked for 2 years in New York City for the Urban Planning Commission, where I had been conducting some research on the possible redevelopment of air rights over Park Avenue in Harlem.

I was considered experienced enough by my employers—the United Nations and a Washington-based US consulting firm for which I worked—to lead the preparation of a master plan for a capital city; a project that would require 2½ years of residence at Port-au-Prince. Among the team members that I met in Port-Au-Prince when we assembled there for the first time was Jim Wright, a 30-year-old American urban economist who had graduated from Georgetown University and who had already worked in Zambia and Bolivia in the Peace Corps.

It was my first encounter with an economist, despite my several years of urban planning practice. My degree in architecture and urban planning from the École des Beaux-Arts in Paris had taught me that a city was to be designed just like a building—only the scale varied. Urban problems could be solved through good design. I did not have a clear view of what urban economists did. Like most urban planners, I did not even make a clear distinction between an urban economist's job and that of a financial analyst or even an accountant. In 2017, I still often encounter urban planners who do not have a clear view of the difference between economics and accounting. In their view, an economist is someone who will add up the costs of an urban project they propose and probably will argue that the costs are too high despite their "good design."

During my professional practice, I had observed patterns in the way cities were spontaneously organized. Land prices decreased as one got farther away from city centers. When land prices were high, households and firms consumed less land, and as a consequence, population density increased. While the objective of urban planning regulations was nearly always to limit densities, I noticed that they had very little success in doing so when the price of land was high compared to household income.

These were personal observations on the relationships between densities and prices. I did not know that a rich theoretical and empirical literature on the subject helped explain, with the help of mathematical models, why those patterns emerge spontaneously. Using simple models, economists could predict in which directions densities were likely to change with changes in variables like income, price of transport, or price of agricultural land.

Some readers might think that I may have been an exceptionally ignorant urban planner. I do not think that I was exceptional: I was rather typical in my ignorance. In the planning profession, high land prices are often deplored but are usually thought to be caused by speculators. To this day, few planners make a connection between land prices and rents, and the supply of land and floor space. That is why planners who design regulations that severely limit the extension of cities (e.g., through measures such as green-belts, designations between urban and agricultural land, etc. explored in chapter 4) are often surprised by increasing land prices and attribute them to external factors for which they were not responsible.

The Port-au-Prince Experience

Because of the very open personality of Jim Wright, his enthusiasm, and his competence in his field, I soon learned that urban economics could provide a theoretical framework and solid empirical evidence to explain facts that I had observed but could not explain. I was like somebody who, after spending years observing the planets, has suddenly gained access to Newton's law of gravitation.

Our first professional exchange concerned the population growth of Port-au-Prince. Both the Haitian government and some "experts" sent by the United Nations had declared that the growth of Port-au-Prince—636,000 inhabitants in 1973, growing at about 5 percent a year—should be stopped and that the government policy should be to divert migration toward smaller towns. Jim and I thought this policy absurd, but for different reasons.

I had three main arguments against policy limiting the growth of Port-au-Prince. The first was that no known urban planning instrument could prevent people from migrating to large cities, even under the dictatorship of Jean-Claude Duvalier, who was then Haiti's "President for Life."

The second was that I knew that people moved to large cities to find jobs. They had other choices as well—like migrating to smaller cities or staying in their villages—but most did not make those decisions. Instead, they moved into the dense slums of Port-au-Prince, where living conditions were terrible. This decision was motivated by the living conditions in the rural areas from which they came, which were even worse.

The fact that, after moving to Port-au-Prince, migrants survived and remained in the city demonstrated that they could support their families by the income from their work in the informal or the formal sector. Haiti was not a welfare state, and their mere survival proved their ingenuity at integrating into the urban economy. I had often talked to slum dwellers in India, Algeria, and Yemen, and always found them very practical and full of common sense. We planners had to trust that migrants moving to the big city had knowledge that we did not have about living conditions in the city slums compared to those in the countryside.

Finally, I believe in democracy. In Haiti, under Jean-Claude Duvalier's dictatorship, people could not express themselves through the ballot box, but at least they could vote with their feet by moving to the place that would enhance their welfare. This form of primitive democracy had to be respected. The size of cities should be decided by the inhabitants themselves; cities will stop growing only when the misery of urban slums becomes greater than that of the countryside. Only migrants themselves can make this assessment.

At that time, planners were debating about the optimum size of cities, usually advocating for a size between half a million and a million people. I was firmly convinced that the size and growth rate of cities could not be modified by expert opinion, no matter how scholarly that opinion was. However, I had to recognize that my strong conviction was only based on personal observations and anecdotal evidence collected during a short professional career.

A conversation about the size of cities with Jim Wright, the first economist I had ever met, was enough to make me aware of a vast economic literature about the efficiency of large labor markets. I realized that the field of urban economics complemented urban planning. Jim Wright shared my opinion about the absurdity of planning Port-au-Prince assuming a constant or even decreasing future population. However, he could back up his opinion with a large body of economic literature, based on both theoretical and empirical evidence. Jim then patiently explained to me the concept of scale economy, knowledge spillovers, and why large labor markets were often more productive than smaller ones.

Our professional exchange was not only one way, however. To do his job as an economist, Jim needed data on Port-au-Prince, and except for the census and a set of recently taken aerial photographs, very little data were available. Jim had never worked with an urban planner before. It was my turn to explain to him that I could rapidly produce data on densities, housing prices and rents, and time and cost of transport from different parts of the city just by measuring and interpreting aerial photographs, and superimposing on the photographs census tracts drawn on tracing paper.

While we were in Yemen, my wife Marie-Agnes, who is also a planner, and I had developed a set of survey techniques based on the interpretation of aerial photographs associated with stratified sampling that required only rapid field surveys. Using these techniques, we could generate credible urban spatial data in a short time. There was no GIS at that time. Calculations were done using slide rules, and areas had to be measured on paper maps using a mechanical planimeter. It was a lengthy and tedious process, but the information that emerged justified the effort.

As planners, we were using the data generated by our surveys to project the need for infrastructure and social services per neighborhood, and we could link these services to the ability to pay for them based on an evaluation of household income, rents, and house values in each neighborhood. But our measures were static: We did not have models to predict trends in population densities.

Jim, of course, was delighted to learn that he would soon have access to spatial data, and he was planning to use the data for much more sophisticated analysis and projections than we had done so far for infrastructure and services. This is when we decided that our two fields were indeed complementary and that by working together—an economist and an urban planner—we could rapidly produce the evidence that would convince the Haitian government and the United Nations that a larger city could also become more affluent if we could plan and implement the minimum physical and social infrastructure that would accommodate the rapid spatial extension of Port-au-Prince. Jim and I became not only close professional partners but also good friends, and we have maintained our close friendship ever since.

Cities without Land and Labor Markets: China 1983, Russia 1991

Planners believe in norms. They happily regulate minimum lot sizes, minimum dwelling floor sizes, maximum heights of buildings, minimum street widths, and so forth. However, when trying to enforce these regulations, they often run into the harsh reality of land prices. What should be done when many households cannot afford the minimum regulatory lot size because of high land prices? Planners see land prices as the main obstacle to affordability. If a government were to replace land markets with design based on norms, the major obstacle to housing affordability—and to good planning in general—would be solved. Additionally, land could be allocated in sufficient quantity to low-, middle-, and high-income housing on a map. To this day, this is the essence of most master plans.

This urban planner's dream—where designed norms replace markets for allocating land—existed in the Soviet Union from 1922 to 1991, and from 1947 to around 2000 in the People's Republic of China. I had the chance to work in China and in Russia before land markets were reintroduced, and I could observe from the inside how a planner's dream could transform itself into a terribly wasteful utopia.

My first trip to China was in 1983. I was part of a World Bank team that was appraising, for prospective financing, a major sewer project in Shanghai. My job consisted of assessing population densities, spatial urban structures, and development trends to ensure that the sewer system financed by the World Bank maximized economic rate of return for the city and would benefit a large number of low-income households. I was also asked to collect data on housing conditions in China to explore the possibility of housing reform, as the Chinese government had shown a tentative interest in the subject.

Observing the inner workings of a command economy was an incredible opportunity to see a live experiment of what happens to a city when prices are not used to allocate resources. Urban planners have few opportunities to experiment on the real world. Economists may build mathematical models mimicking command economies, but observing first hand the impact of an economic system so different from anything we had seen before was fascinating for the entire team. Nothing provides a better understanding of markets than observing a city where market forces do not apply.

Brain surgeons greatly improved their understanding of the functioning of the brain when they had to treat victims of accidents and wars who had severe brain injuries. In the same way, planners and economists, familiar with the functioning of market economies, who worked in China in the 1980s and Russia in the 1990s, improved their understanding of markets by observing on the ground the spatial outcome of this gigantic social experiment.

Cities without Land Markets

In 1983, China had already started some reforms, but the country was still largely a command economy. Housing was provided by state-owned companies. Housing was not considered a commodity to be bought and sold but a factor of production owned by enterprises that provided housing to their workers practically rent free.

Salaries were set for each economic sector by the central government. There was no real labor market, as employees were expected to have lifelong employment in the same state firm. While changing jobs was theoretically possible, it usually had to be initiated by the state employer. Salaries appeared incredibly low to outsiders. My urban planners' colleagues were paid about US$25 monthly. This was not their real income, though. In a command economy, the state collects about 90 percent of the value that a worker produces and gives only "pocket money" in cash to the worker. Most of a worker's income is distributed in kind in the form of housing, food in the enterprise cafeteria, and heavily subsidized clothing and other consumer items available at nominal prices in each enterprise's commissary. Even vacations were usually provided by the work unit. Of course, as everything was either free or heavily subsidized, rationing and shortages were the only way to balance supply and demand.

For a planner, the absence of land markets created a striking difference in land use between Chinese cities and market economies' cities. According to the Chinese constitution, land belonged to the "people" and could not be sold or bought.

However, the right to use land was allocated to firms, and sometimes households, by the Land and Planning Bureau. In the absence of land prices, the quantity of land to be allocated to different activities was based on norms established by architects and engineers. These norms were often originally developed in the Soviet Union in the 1950s and eventually passed on to the People's Republic of China. I had an occasion to discuss norms with my Chinese colleagues, and they were curious to compare their norms with Western ones. I remember a discussion about the number and size of barber shops that should be planned per 1,000 people in residential neighborhoods. I had to use the favorite response of economists to answer the question from my Chinese counterpart on planning barber shops norms in the United States: "It all depends!"

Cities without Markets Are an Urban Planner's Dream ...

The allocation of urban land following design norms without taking land prices into account is of course an urban planner's dream. But for planners working in market economies, it remained a dream, while in China it was the daily reality. Planners and engineers like to reason in terms of "needs," while urban economists think in terms of scarce resource allocation. Asked to provide an opinion on the optimum density of a residential area, a planner will usually provide a number, say, 150 people per hectare. This estimate would be based on norms—for instance, the density required if the walking distance to a primary school of optimum size should be less than 15 minutes, or the optimum density to be able to operate a network of public transport buses that arrive every 15 minutes. Asked the same question, an urban economist would answer, and rightly so, "it all depends." This answer will infuriate urban planners. However, it is obviously correct. Urban land is a scarce resource, and its price indicates how scarce it is in a specific location. Therefore, depending on its price, land should be used parsimoniously where the price is high, resulting in high density, and more lavishly where it is cheap, resulting in lower densities. From an economist's point of view, there is no optimum population density, as density, which is a land consumption indicator, depends on several variables whose values change over time even for the same location.

But Norms Are Unable to Allocate Land among Multiple Users

The absence of land prices in China and Russia had an important impact on the structure of their cities. Because the land occupied by a firm was not recognized to have value per se, it could not be recycled for another use or passed to another user, who, in a market economy, would have been bidding for it. As Chinese cities expanded, there were pockets of industrial land located close to the city center that could not be reconverted for other uses, because no mechanism existed to do so.

In a market economy, when the potential rent of a lot is higher than for its current use, the owner of the lot has a strong incentive to sell or redevelop the land for a more profitable use. In this way, low-rise buildings are transformed into high-rise buildings, and warehouses into office buildings. The increased price of the land under the new use pays for the demolition and relocation of the obsolete building. The land use transformation process is triggered by land prices. There is no need for a planner's intervention to initiate land use change. The dynamic of market prices is so powerful that often planners impose land use regulations to slow down the transformation triggered by the land market.

In a command economy, there are no price signals, so an obsolete land use is likely to remain in effect for a very long time. Let us take the example of a factory built long ago near a city's central business district, on what would now be a very desirable piece of land for a department store or an office building because of its accessibility. The state firm owning the land use rights cannot move its factory to a different part of town that would be more convenient for operating a factory, because the land occupied by the factory has no market value. The firm can only request the government to provide a new parcel of land in a new location, while probably also requesting funds to cover the cost of relocating the factory. As one can imagine, this is not likely to happen often. In a command economy, a land use change always appears as a cost without any direct apparent benefit either to the owner of the land use right or to the government department that will have to authorize the change and pay for it. Even the loss of productivity due to a poor location will not appear in obvious ways to the managers of an enterprise, as prices for production are established by the central government independently of the cost of inputs.

This has consequences for the structure of cities in command economies. The newest buildings are always found in areas newly developed in the suburbs. In Russia, for instance, factories built in the nineteenth century or in the first half of the twentieth century found themselves located in what is now the downtown area. High-rise residential buildings are found on the periphery of cities, while low-rise buildings are found closer to the center. High population densities are found in the suburbs, where land values would be the lowest if located in a market economy, and low densities are found close to the city center, where land values would be the highest. One of my colleagues, an economist from the World Bank named Bertrand Renaud, and I wrote a paper titled "Cities without Land Markets,"[3] which summarized our observations of the impact of the absence of prices on land use in Russian cities.

Does this difference of urban spatial outcome between command and market economies matter? A Russian colleague, head of a construction *kombinat*,[4] once told me, "The Soviet Union had a wonderful system; we just ran out of money!"

This was precisely the point. The inefficiencies of urban spatial structure, the lack of labor market mobility, the inability of an economy based on norms to adjust to evolving technology and to changing demand for land, contributed to the economic collapse of the Soviet Union, despite its very well educated and skilled urban population and its abundant natural resources.

In cities of market economies, urban planners still tend to prefer norms to prices when allocating land and floor space. In the cities where they are successful, they may waste land in a way that resembles what happened in the Soviet Union.

The system allocating resources in the former Soviet Union was so inefficient that its economy collapsed suddenly. There was not much time to ensure a smooth transition from one system to another. It resulted in a rapid and opaque privatization of many state enterprises that produced oligopolies that only remotely resemble markets. Some Russian cities have real land market; in others the system of land allocation is less clear.

Under Deng Xiaoping, China chose a different path. It gradually reformed its system until it made a progressive, orderly transition from a command to a market economy. However, the shift of the system in China was not due to an ideological conversion. As Ronald Coase and Ning Wang explained in their book on China's reform, "China became capitalist while it was trying to modernize socialism."[5] Indeed, the Chinese government allowed cities to experiment with small-scale labor and land market liberalization before expanding successful experiments to the entire country. It was only in 2013 that the Central Committee of the Chinese Communist Party declared that:

The basic economic system should evolve on the decisive role of the market in resource allocation.[6]

Urban planners, who still dream about the wonderful cities that they could design without the hindrance of land markets, should get acquainted with the experiments made by the Communist Party of China, whose results drove them to decide that using market prices was a good way to allocate resources. The Chinese now advocate adopting market mechanism to allocate land because:

• it sends strong signals through prices when land is underused or the use is unsuitable for its location;

• it provides a strong incentive to users to use as little land as possible in areas where there is strong demand, in particular in areas well served by transport networks; and

• it stimulates innovation in construction: without land prices, there would have been no skyscrapers, no steel frame structures, and no elevators.

A Channel of Communication Is Needed between
Urban Planners and Urban Economists

Do I exaggerate the knowledge gap that exists between urban planning practices and urban economics? Even today, a first encounter at mid-career between an experienced urban planner and an economist could still happen. But unfortunately, most of the time the economist and the planner are likely to talk past each other, because they are not familiar with the vocabulary and professional jargon specific to the other's field.

I think that, worldwide, the unfamiliarity with basic urban economic concepts by those in charge of managing cities is one of the major problems of our time. This is a serious issue at a time when cities are the major engines of economic growth, and living in cities is the only hope of escaping poverty for billions of people. The constraints put on the supply of urban land and floor space by restrictive regulations, which have nothing to do with preserving the environment, are causing severe urban dysfunctions, which I explore in depth in the following chapters. In poor countries, these supply constraints are responsible for the severe hardships imposed on households living in informal settlements. In richer countries, they are responsible for a lack of mobility of poorer households toward the cities, where they would be the most productive.

Urban Planners Usually Have a Deep Knowledge of Their Own City

Although, in the following chapters I will at times be critical of the planning profession, I think that urban planners are often very competent in managing the day-to-day operations of the city they work in. They usually know their city in great detail, including the history behind the complex features of the built environment. They work under great pressure because a city is constantly transforming itself, and this constant evolution cannot be delayed by asking for more time for reflection or further studies. They are also subject to pressure from various interest groups that have a stake in the changes affecting cities. Some pressure groups would like the city to stay still; other groups would prefer to accelerate changes. Each of these groups has a valid point to make. In many cases urban economics could help provide a solution based on quantitative reasoning rather than on an arbitrary normative preference.

Finally, urban planners are also subject to pressure from elected officials, who want to get things done or at least want to show that they are doing something in the short time frame of their terms. Land use decisions are, and should be, political, because there is no scientific way to know what is best for the future. However, mayors and planners who design the regulations that modify the outcome of their land markets would greatly benefit from better knowledge of the way markets function. This understanding would be more likely to help them develop regulations that result in an implementation of their objectives.

Urban Planners Are Usually Unfamiliar with Basic Urban Economics

Some urban planners are indeed familiar with urban economics, and they might regularly contribute papers to economic journals. I know a few of them, for instance, V. K. Phatak, a Mumbai urbanist, who over the years has relentlessly pushed to introduce economic thinking into the reform of Mumbai land use regulatory system. But I am afraid they are not numerous. I have worked in many cities during my years as Principal Urban Planner of the World Bank, and later as an independent consultant working directly for municipalities all over the world. I have found that many urban planners, even in the very affluent cities of Western Europe, North America, and East Asia, not only seldom understand how markets work, but are proud to pretend to ignore them. I have heard mayors and planners complain that their city had too low density, while simultaneously complaining that land prices were far too high.

Over the past few years I have reviewed many new master plans for cities located in various parts of the world. None of them mentioned real estate markets, land prices, transportation costs, commuting times, or basic supply and demand concepts. All of them recommended specific densities in various locations. These densities were selected as if densities were generated by planners' design and not by the laws of supply and demand for land and floor space.

In chapter 4, I give an example of a master plan recently prepared for the city of Hanoi by a reputable international consulting firm. This urban development plan, typical of many other plans prepared by planners and infrastructure engineers, never uses the words "markets," "land prices," or even "household incomes." As I was taught nearly 55 years ago, it seems that urban planning is all about design and "needs."

Urban Economists Are Too Removed from Day-to-Day Operations of Cities

Urban economists are not innocent, either. They certainly strive for rigor in their reasoning, and they constantly try to better understand how cities function and operate. But they seem to avoid being involved in the day-to-day decisions made in urban planning departments. Possibly they are not given the opportunity, because they speak a different language, unintelligible to urban planners. Most of their analytical work, whether theoretical or empirical, is aimed at their academic peers; the products of their efforts are papers published in prestigious peer-reviewed journals. I have not seen many efforts to make the results of urban economic research operational for cities, framed to have a direct impact on decisions made in the day-to-day operations of a city.

Of course, I am not the first urban professional to raise the alarm over the impact of poorly conceived urban regulations that ignore basic urban economic concepts. Many economists have certainly attempted to influence how decisions are made by cities. For instance, in the United Kingdom, the work of Kate Barker, Paul Cheshire, and Alan Evans, among others, has shown convincingly how urban regulations can have an adverse impact on land prices and housing supply if poorly conceived. In the United States, Jan Brueckner, William A. Fischel, Edward Glaeser, and Stephen Malpezzi, among others, have also looked at the costs and benefits of urban regulations. Many urban economists have contributed to shaping the policies of the US Department of Housing and Urban Department (HUD) at the federal level. Many economists have testified in front of municipal planning boards and city councils. But the ones who have raised the alarm about the lack of theoretical and empirical evidence justifying many urban regulations have always been economists who do not directly participate in the design of these regulations. No matter how eloquent and convincing their papers are, they have no way to change a practice in which they do not directly participate. I have never met an urban economist working as a team member in a planning department at the time land use regulations were being designed. In this sense, my working experience in Port-au-Prince with Jim Wright was rather unique.

The Purpose of This Book
I wrote this book with two objectives in mind. First, to familiarize those urban planners who have not yet met an urban economist with basic urban economic concepts and how these concepts apply to issues encountered in a municipal urban planning office. Second, to generate an interest among urban economists in working in the trenches, side by side with urban planners. In this way, they could provide economic input to the design of urban regulations, infrastructure, and urban development strategies when they are conceived, not after they have been approved by the mayor and city council.

I would like to convince some economists to participate directly in the decision making of an urban planning department. For this to happen, urban economists and urban planners should speak the same language and understand each other's jargon. It is impossible to avoid jargon when practicing a profession. Jargon is a short cut for specialized concepts. Avoiding it may be possible in a newspaper article aimed at a mass audience, but rarely in professional communication.

I hope that this book will contribute to the communication between urban economists and planners by familiarizing planners with concepts like negative externalities and opportunity costs, and helping urban economist learn about the different ways of calculating a floor area ratio or population density.

2 Cities as Labor Markets

The Efficiency of Large Labor Markets Is the Main Cause of Ever-Growing Cities

Cities Are Primarily Labor Markets

Cities are primarily labor markets. This claim may seem terribly reductionist to the many among us who love cities. Certainly, the attractions offered by the amenities of a large city cannot be reduced such that the whole is seen merely as a place where firms are looking for labor and people are looking for jobs.

During the French "cultural revolution" of May 1968, students were deriding a life reduced to only three activities: "Metro, boulot, dodo," which can be roughly translated by "commuting, working, sleeping." This became one of the most ubiquitous tags on Paris walls. The students were revolting against what I, more pedantically, call an urban labor market. They had a strong point: I have seen such reduced forms of urban life in many malfunctioning cities with dysfunctional labor markets. Better land use and transport improve the way that labor markets function, allowing for the core indispensable values of urban life beyond "Metro, boulot, dodo":

- a commute short enough that one has time for leisure activities,

- an open job market that allows one to change jobs and—through trial and error—find a job that best suits, and

- a residence from which access to social life or nature is quick and easy.

So even though I am not implying that a city's only purpose is as a labor market-place, I am arguing that without a functioning labor market, there is no city. Try thinking of an alternative explanation for the existence of very large cities. A city nucleus might have been created originally as a commercial port, a trading post, an administrative center, a military stronghold, or a center of religious pilgrimage, but over the years, the growth of a diversified labor force would be the only possible cause for the expansion of the original urban nucleus. While most cities offer a lot more than job opportunities, it is important to recognize that the expansion of job markets makes everything else possible. A well-functioning labor market brings together people with varied but complementary knowledge and skills—the preconditions for innovation. A well-functioning labor market makes possible every other urban attraction—symphonic orchestra, museums, art galleries, public libraries, well-designed public spaces, and great restaurants, among many others. In turn, these typically urban amenities require additional specialized jobs and attract an even more diverse population, which becomes the source of future innovations and a more interesting urban life.

Usually when a city's population is growing, it means that its labor market is growing. But a segment of any urban population (usually between 35 and 50 percent) does not participate directly in the labor market. Statisticians rightly call the nonactive segment the "dependent" population. Its members—including retired people, infants, students, and prison inmates—are not part of the labor market and participate in the urban economy only as consumers.[1]

People migrating from other cities once they have reached retirement age may be the cause of the growth of a few cities whose growth is more driven by consumer markets than by labor markets. These types of cities might become more common in the twenty-first century with the projected aging of the world population. The retiree population of these cities is expected to consume a lot of services in health care facilities, restaurants, and entertainment venues. The growth of these "retiree" cities would then be caused by the dual effect of both the retirees' migration and that of additional workers to staff the services required by the retirees. These retiree cities would not require spatial concentration and are unlikely to create much economic dynamism. The eventual growth of retiree cities is the only exception to growth created by the efficiency of large labor markets. And, of course, the retirement income of retirees will have been generated by efficiently working labor markets in other large cities.

Large Labor Markets Are More Productive Than Small Ones

Economists have convincingly demonstrated the productivity advantage of larger cities over smaller ones. Large cities generate economies of scale that allow enterprises to reduce their costs by increasing output, thereby reducing costs per unit. Economies of scale are only possible in cities with a large labor market. When many related activities are located in close proximity, they generate what economists call "knowledge spillovers." New ways of doing things in one firm are soon imitated by other firms and eventually by other sectors as a result of the proximity and close contact among workers of different firms and sectors in the urban economy.

For instance, the first users of electronic spreadsheets on microcomputers (in the early 1980s) were mostly accountants and financial analysts. The use of spreadsheets soon became common in all sectors of the economy, but the spillover occurred first in large cities, spreading from MIT in Cambridge, Massachusetts, where it was originally invented. Knowledge spillovers are responsible for agglomeration economies (i.e., economies that increase productivity due to the rapid dissemination of new ideas because of large numbers of workers in close contact).[2] Agglomeration economies also result from a lowering of transaction costs in larger cities because of the proximity of competing suppliers and consumers.

Economic literature linking the wealth of cities to spatial concentration is quite abundant and is no longer controversial in academic circles. National accounts show that the output share of large cities is always much higher than their share of the national population. The 2009 World Bank Development Report "Reshaping Economic Geography," and the report of the Commission on Growth and Development "Urbanization and Growth" (published the same year) exhaustively summarize and document the theoretical and empirical arguments justifying the economic advantage provided by the spatial concentration of economic activities in large cities.

But if larger cities are more productive than smaller ones, why are large cities not growing faster than small ones? And why do many households and firms choose to remain in or even move to smaller cities when they could instead settle in the more productive environment provided by larger cities?

The Proportion of Smaller Cities to Larger Ones Stays Constant over Time: On Average, All Grow at about the Same Rate

Data on city size distribution by country or by region show that the proportion of small to medium and large cities stays roughly constant over time. When households decide to migrate and firms decide to select a location for a new enterprise, they are as likely to choose a small city as a larger one.

The Canadian economist Vernon Henderson, who pioneered work on the growth rate and size distribution of cities in various countries, shows the regularities found in the distribution of city size across countries except for anomalies in the former Soviet Union and China. In his book *Planet of Cities*, Shlomo Angel summarizes previous studies on the subject and addresses the issue of worldwide city size distribution.[3] Angel based his analysis on a reliable worldwide database. His conclusions confirm previous, less exhaustive studies.

Planet of Cities proves that on average, large cities are growing at about the same rate as medium and small cities in the same countries or regions. It seems that cities' growth rates follow Gibrat's law of proportionate effect, which states that the size of a city is not an indicator of its future growth rate—that is, cities' growth rates are random, with the same average expected growth rate and same variance. In any given region, the distribution of cities of various sizes therefore remains stable. The population of larger cities keeps growing, but on average, so do smaller cities. This seems paradoxical, given that larger cities are more productive than smaller ones. However, larger cities do not play the same economic role as smaller ones do. They complement each other's activities. The increased productivity of larger cities is therefore linked to the existence and growth of smaller cities. In turn, smaller cities' economic growth is dependent on larger cities' innovations and inventions.

Some Cities Keep Growing, While Others Don't
The rate of population growth is determined by economic opportunity, which in turn is largely determined by the comparative advantage of a city's location and its population's capacity for innovation. But the economic advantage provided by location is not necessarily permanent; it may increase, decrease, or even vanish with technological change. Being close to an obsidian mine might have been a decisive advantage for the early Middle Eastern cities like Çatalhöyük described by Jane Jacobs,[4] but that advantage disappeared when obsidian ceased to be the preferred material for tools and weapons. The Anatolian cities, whose economies had not been able to diversify into activities other than obsidian's craft and trade, inevitably shrank and eventually disappeared. The dominance of New York as the United States' main eastern seaport was made possible by the comparative advantage provided by the Erie Canal. By the time railways made waterway transport obsolete, New York's population had accumulated such a high level of diversified, specialized skills that it continued to thrive without having to rely on the advantage conferred by proximity to the canal.

The history of the world's cities is full of examples of large cities dominating their regions for a time and then shrinking back to a smaller size or even into oblivion. In 1050, Cordoba, in the south of Spain, was the largest city in Europe with 450,000 inhabitants, followed by Palermo, Sicily, with a population of 350,000. By the middle of the fourteenth century, the population of both cities had shrunk to 60,000 and 50,000, respectively, because their respective locations had become less important to eastbound trade routes. In the eleventh century, Kaifeng in China was probably the largest city in the world, with 700,000 people, while Shenzhen was not even on the map. Today, Shenzhen has 10 million people, and over the past 10 centuries, Kaifeng's population has barely increased to 800,000 people—a stasis determined by the economic center and political capital having moved to other cities in later dynasties.

Why Don't Households and Firms All Migrate to Larger Cities, Where Productivity and Salaries Are Higher?

In spite of the prospect of higher productivities, only some types of firms can benefit from moving to a larger city. Firms established in larger cities require greater capital and higher operation and maintenance costs than those located in smaller cities. Land and rents are more expensive in larger cities than in smaller ones. Distances traveled are longer, and the "congestion tax" is higher. In addition, not every enterprise can benefit from economies of scale or agglomeration economies.

Moving to a smaller city where land is cheaper and salaries are lower makes economic sense for firms whose activities require a lot of land and labor that is not particularly specialized. For instance, activities like furniture making require a lot of land and easy truck access to transport the bulky materials necessary for the finished product. They require skilled, but not particularly specialized, labor. Furniture manufacturers therefore have no reason to relocate to a large city, where land and labor would be expensive and where moving bulky raw materials and finished products in and out of the factory would be inefficient and costly. These types of firms tend to locate their manufacturing activities in smaller cities. However, furniture makers may require innovative designers, who may not be found in smaller cities. In such cases, these businesses may need to subcontract the design of furniture to a firm located in a large city, where talented designers are more likely to be found and where agglomeration economies and idea spillover, both important for a design firm, are also more likely to occur. Such firms as furniture makers can carry out their highly specialized and innovative activities—design and marketing, for instance—in large cities. Their repetitive and land-intensive activities (manufacturing) can be carried out in smaller cities. In this way, they can enjoy the advantages of both a large city (innovation, specialized labor) and a smaller one (low land and labor costs).

Speedier and cheaper communication over the past 20 years, including widespread adoption of the Internet, has contributed to the splitting up of large firms into various departments located in cities of different sizes. Specialized tasks (e.g., design, marketing, export promotion) can take place in larger cities, where the requisite innovators and specialized labor force are more likely to be found, while more routine manufacturing can take place in smaller cities. In addition, large firms increasingly subcontract tasks to smaller firms that are often located in different areas. The same factors have likely led to the growth of both large and small cities, allowing them to specialize in what they do best.

For instance, the corporate headquarters of Herman Miller, a company specializing in office furniture of high design quality, is based in Zeeland, Michigan, a town of about 5,500 people. However, it recently advertised for a creative director to be located in its New York City office. By splitting the location where manufacturing and design take place, Herman Miller is taking advantage of the cheap land and labor in Zeeland, and of the innovative environment of New York. In this case the economies of both cities benefit. A similar rationale could be applied by workers who prefer either to remain in large cities or to migrate to smaller cities: the latter have lower salaries but also lower rents, lower commuting costs, and often a better natural environment.

Some services are likely to thrive in both large and small cities and are thus not dependent on the advantage provided by location. Fast food restaurants, barber shops, and laundry services, for instance, follow the labor force of more specialized firms wherever they locate, contributing to the even growth rate of small and larger cities.

The Planners' Anti-Big-City Bias and Their Attempts to Balance Growth

Cities grow when their labor markets expand. This economic expansion is usually the result of a comparative advantage gained from location or an exceptional concentration of skilled workers. The rate of a city's population growth cannot be attributed to advance planning. Instead it is due to a combination of exogenous and endogenous circumstances. To the chagrin of urban planners, a city's growth rate over the mid or long term is largely unpredictable, and it is futile to pretend it is the result of careful planning.

Planners and city managers have traditionally been concerned about the unplanned growth of large cities because of the complexity involved in managing them, the difficulty integrating poor migrants from rural areas into city life, and an instinctive aversion to anything that seems "undesigned." Planners have even described the growth of large, dominant cities like Paris or Mexico City as "cancerous."

The aversion to unplanned or to asymmetrical spatial patterns is quite apparent in most urban planners' approach. Some planners look at a country's map and observe that some regions contain many cities while others have only a few. They incorrectly conclude that this "imbalance" represents an inequity due to parasitic urban activities or to other market failures. In their view, it then becomes the responsibility of the government to modify the imbalance and to remove this regional inequity through national spatial planning, with the declared objective of restoring a regional symmetry in the spatial distribution of cities. However, the assumption that national spatial planning can modify the distribution of urban populations in order to reach a new, planner-designed spatial equilibrium is false.

Cities that have a decisive comparative advantage, either because of their location or because of their large specialized and innovative labor pool, are likely to grow. People migrate toward cities where economic and social opportunities are best, from their point of view. The idea that a city's economic and demographic growth rate is due to parasitic activities occurring to the detriment of other cities is fanciful—unless, of course, piracy, smuggling, or other unlawful or predatory activities are its main cause.

The assumption that the preparation of national or regional plans would result in a predictable urban growth rate for each individual city in a region is also demonstrably false. Unfortunately, in many countries this common planning conceit has resulted in misallocated public investments and regulatory impediments that have decreased cities' productivity. In reality, planners have very little influence on city size distribution and city growth rates, unless they take active, targeted measures to destroy the urban economies of the cities that have grown "too large." The Khmer Rouge's urban policy applied to Cambodia in the late 1970s was an extreme and brutal example of planners' temporarily successful attempt to manage city size by forcefully reallocating urban population to rural areas.

As a consequence of the planners' hubris about the necessity of managing city size, many regional plans designed in the second half of the twentieth century have promoted regulatory limits on the growth of large cities. These were combined with planned infrastructure investment aimed at stimulating the growth of smaller cities, which were deemed more manageable. A seminal and influential paper published in 1947, calling for a national plan for the spatial development of France, was titled "Paris and the French Desert," implying that the growth of Paris had occurred at the expense of the French provincial towns. Anyone familiar with French provincial towns would recognize their comparison to a barren desert as a slightly comical but gross exaggeration. While it is possible that the centralizing tendency of successive governments since the French Revolution of 1789 contributed to Paris's rapid growth, the problem, if it exists, lies with the political system. Preventing investments in the capital while directing large resources toward provincial towns is unlikely to change a city size hierarchy caused by an idiosyncratic political system whose reforms fail to allow for more decentralized decisions.

In 1956, the Indian government adopted a policy dictating that new industries should locate in "backward areas." At the same time, it prevented further development of manufacturing in large cities.[5] Through this policy, the government committed itself to correcting regional imbalance and to preventing further industrial growth in cities of more than 500,000. In 1988, the negative impact of the policy was compounded by an interdiction that new industries locate less than 50 kilometers from cities with a population of more than 2.5 million and within 30 kilometers of cities with a population between 1.5 million and 2.5 million. As one can easily imagine, the latter policy didn't prevent the growth of industries in successful cities like Mumbai or Bangalore with a population significantly bigger than 2.5 million;

it just made it more expensive for these industries to expand there. More tragically, it diverted scarce government infrastructure resources to regions with weak potential while starving large metropolitan areas of desperately needed investment, *even though the latter areas were where most people were migrating*. The current poor performance of public infrastructure—roads, transport, sewer, drainage, and power—in major Indian cities is in part the result of misguided national spatial policy conducted over the past 50 years.

If planners are unable to control the growth rate of cities, how can we explain the successful growth of entirely planned cities like St. Petersburg; Brasília, Brazil; or Shenzhen, created ex nihilo by powerful rulers as diverse as Peter the Great, Juscelino Kubitschek, and Deng Xiaoping? These planned cities became large and successful as the result of two major factors:

• First, each city's location was selected because of a geopolitical necessity[6] and not because of an abstract planning concept.
• Second, each city had the strong political and financial support of a powerful ruler of a very large country. This support allowed these cities to sink large amounts of money into infrastructure investment without having to borrow and tax their own initially fledgling economies.

Other examples of this abound. Politicians created new capital cities like Washington, DC (United States), Canberra (Australia), Islamabad (Pakistan), Abuja (Nigeria), and Naypyidaw (Myanmar). All are capitals of large countries and were initially without economic base beyond the national government bureaucracy. The "cost is no object" concept presided over their construction and ensured their initial survival, as they were financed by taxes paid by the rest of the country, and they constituted a captive labor market composed of government employees. Eventually, a more diversified labor market grafted itself onto the government activities.

During the 70 years of the Soviet Union, planners decided which cities should grow and which should not. No city could grow without supporting resources allocated from the Gosplan,[7] a specialized ministry in Moscow. The government had the means to enforce the movement of people, and migrations toward selected locations in the Soviet Union's vast hinterland were often involuntary. Many new cities were created for various political or perceived economic reasons, but none of these cities was the result of voluntary migration of firms and people toward areas that represented better opportunities.

In 2010, traveling to Moscow as a consultant, I was asked by the ministry of construction to provide advice on how to proceed for the "closing" of 60 cities that the Russian government had identified as no longer viable. The government could not continue to support social services and infrastructure in cities that had been abandoned by the large monopolistic industries that were originally their raison d'être. The labor market had disappeared, but the laborers were still there; closing down these cities would entail another forced migration of several million people. Apartments that had recently privatized represented most people's only asset; however, because the apartments had become worthless, their owners were unable to move. The closing of cities in Russia is an extreme illustration of the danger of creating cities based on so-called planning criteria without an economic base and of using forced migrations or heavy subsidies to promote urban growth.

Why Planners Should Not Try to Alter the Distribution of City Sizes

In countries and regions, a natural equilibrium is reached between the size of the population and the firms choosing to settle in small, medium, and large cities. This equilibrium is created by the accumulated decisions of firms and households to "vote with their feet," thereby selecting to move to the cities that will grow and to leave the cities or villages that have less potential. The spontaneous spatial equilibrium created by the sum of uncoordinated, individual decisions illustrates the principle of *Order without Design* that will be further developed in this book.

With the exception of the few geopolitical examples mentioned above, planners have no credible rationale for intervening directly in the location and growth rate of cities. Planners should no more "encourage"—a favorite word in the planning literature—the growth of large cities at the expense of smaller cities than they should discourage that growth. History has shown that these types of planner initiatives are bound to fail or, worse, to create serious diseconomies, making a country poorer. The size of a city does not make it automatically more productive—large, dense refugee camps are less productive than small towns, although they may provide shelter to several hundred thousand inhabitants. To increase productivity, a city must have certain preconditions:

1. Firms and households have the freedom to stay put or migrate at will,
2. Travel within the city remains fast and cheap, and
3. Real estate is sufficiently affordable that it does not distort the allocation of labor.

I will review each of these preconditions in the following sections. For each, because households and firms have the most invested in the successful outcomes of their moves, we have to trust that the majority of them have enough information to justify their choices. Planners, in contrast, lack the information about the economy of individual firms and households that would be necessary to make informed decisions about the advantages and disadvantages of locating in a small, medium, or large city.

We will see below that planners' "optimum design" hubris is not limited to the size and location of cities. Within cities, too, they attempt to regulate both where households and firms should locate and the quantity of land and floor space they should consume. As we will also see, planners do have a crucial role to play in the development of cities, in particular in the development of their infrastructure. However, it must be clear that allocating land and floor space in specific locations is not their role.

A City's Productivity Depends on Its Ability to Maintain Mobility as Its Built-Up Area Grows

Mobility, which I would argue is the centerpiece of our national productivity, is neither highly valued nor understood among public officials.
—Alan Pisarski, *Commuting in America III: The Third National Report on Commuting Patterns and Trends*, 2006

Good management can therefore increase indefinitely the "optimal" size of a city.
—Rémy Prud'homme and Chang-Woon Lee, *Size, Sprawl, Speed and the Efficiency of Cities*, 1998

Larger labor markets are made possible by an increase in the mobility of people and goods. Advances in urban transport technology have improved the mobility of people and goods, which in turn has contributed to the growth of large cities during the past 150 years. Improvements to transport technology have also made possible the spatial concentration of both people and fixed capital. Economists describe *fixed capital* as factories, office buildings, houses, apartment buildings, community facilities, and infrastructure. In the past 50 years, increasing returns to scale in agglomeration economies as a result of this spatial concentration have led to the emergence of megacities.

The potential economic advantages of large cities are reaped only if workers, consumers, and suppliers are able to exchange labor, goods, and ideas with minimum friction and to multiply face-to-face contacts with minimum time commitments and cost. As a city grows, it is important to monitor mobility by comparing how average travel times and transport costs vary over time, as productivity cannot increase without fast and cheap travel (see chapter 5 for a full discussion of travel times and transport costs).

The Daily Human Tide: The Challenge of Moving People and Goods
The necessity of managing urban growth rather than to trying to slow it down is finally being understood by mayors, city managers, and urban planners. An increase in city size is not the only condition necessary to increase productivity.

Productivity increases with city size only if the transportation network is able to connect workers with firms and providers of goods and services with consumers. This connectivity is difficult to achieve in large cities as it requires consistency among a number of factors: land use and investments for transport networks; pricing decisions for road use, parking, and transit fares; and collection of local taxes and user fees. In their 2009 book, aptly titled *Mobility First*, Sam Staley and Adrian Moore describe in detail the cross-disciplinary reforms in road and urban transport design and in road pricing, among other things, that would be required to maintain mobility in cities in the twenty-first century.[8]

Failure to manage urban transportation in a manner that maintains mobility results in congestion. Congestion decreases labor mobility and productivity and is in fact avoidable in large cities. Its presence represents a failure on the part of city managers. Congestion has a dual negative effect: It acts as a tax on productivity by tying down people and goods, and it degrades the environment and increases greenhouse gas emissions. It is conceivable that in the future, some mismanaged large cities may reach a level of congestion and pollution whose combined negative effects could offset the economic advantage of spatial concentration. These cities would then stop growing, and the economic advantage of spatial concentration would be taxed away by congestion and an unsafe environment.

Given this potential scenario, the positive economic effect of agglomeration must be very powerful in cities like Bangkok and Jakarta, where urban productivity continues to offset the price of chronic congestion. It is difficult to assess a city's productivity just by visiting, but traffic congestion is clearly apparent even on a short visit to either city. But even the spectacular and semi-permanent traffic congestion in these economic powerhouses (or in Beijing as well) does not cancel the productivity advantage of their large population concentrations.

Maintaining mobility while a city's built-up area and its population are growing is not easy. For centuries of urban development, walking was an adequate means of urban transportation. At the beginning of the industrial era, one could walk from the periphery to the center of each of the largest European and American cities in less than an hour. In the 1830s, the area occupied by each of the three largest cities in the Western world—Moscow, London, and Paris—was less than 60 square kilometers. By contrast, the built-up areas of today's largest cities cover several thousand square kilometers each. In large modern cities, mobility can be maintained only with an elaborate system of transport, usually combining private and public modes of travel. The frequency of face-to-face contact among the millions of people living in large cities depends entirely on the efficiency of a motorized urban transport system.

The Spatial Pattern of Labor Mobility

Every day in urban areas, the millions of people who constitute the active population leave their homes to travel to their places of work, usually located in parts of the metropolitan area other than the ones in which they live. Every evening these same people come back home. In between, they may drop off their children at school, stop to buy groceries, or meet friends at a coffee shop. These daily trips originate and terminate at people's homes but also include their workplaces and any number of amenities—restaurants, museums, supermarkets, cinemas, and the like. The commute constitutes a daily tide moving back and forth in a predictable manner, with peak hours and ebb times, from home to workplace and amenities and back.

In addition to trips by commuters and consumers originating in residential areas, economic activities generate freight trips between firms' locations and increasingly, with the growth of e-commerce, from firms directly to their consumers in residential locations. Firms in large cities need to be constantly supplied both with merchandise to be sold in shops and with the materials and parts to be used in manufacturing. These freight trips do not follow the same patterns as commuting trips and are often ignored by planners. In a typical city in an OECD[9] country, freight trips may represent 10–15 percent of the total vehicle kilometers traveled. When roads are congested, the tax on productivity affects both labor and freight mobility.

A city's economy is therefore dependent on the repetitive flow of commuting and freight trips. If by chance a snowstorm, a flood, or a public transport strike forces these trips to be canceled, the city's economy freezes immediately and remains frozen until the daily commuting tide resumes.

Commuting Time and Commuting Cost Limit the Size of Labor Markets

Obviously, the money and time that workers are willing to spend on commuting are limited. These limits impose a constraint on the commuting distance, and as a consequence, on the size of the urban labor market. For very-low-income workers—whose income is nearly entirely devoted to food and shelter—the cost of commuting is a more binding constraint than the time spent commuting. As a household's disposable income increases, the cost of transport becomes a smaller fraction of income (typically less than 15 percent), and the time spent commuting becomes the major constraint for workers, limiting the size of the labor market. Because the time spent commuting is a dead loss for both individuals and employers, the size and efficiency of a labor market depends on how short, cheap, and comfortable the commute is. The maximum cost in time and cash that workers are willing to spend commuting will therefore dictate the size of the labor market and, by extension, the productivity of a city.

Urban commuting surveys indicate that the median travel time across cities and countries is, and for a long time has been, remarkably stable, with an approximate mean of 30 minutes each way. Only a small percentage of commuters in large cities have a total commuting time of more than 1 hour per day. In 2009, the mean travel time in US metropolitan areas was 26 minutes; however, in New York, the largest US metropolitan area, with 19 million people, it was 35 minutes.

Figure 2.1 compares the distribution of commuting travel time (one way) between an average of US metropolitan areas; the Paris metropolitan area; and Gauteng, the South African metropolitan area that includes Johannesburg and Pretoria (12.3 million people in 2011). Gauteng has one of the worst dispersions of population and jobs that I have ever encountered. This dispersion is caused by the legacy of apartheid that will take many more years to cure, and by an unfortunate housing policy that is discussed in chapter 6.

In spite of the difference in their economies, urban structures, cultures, and topographies, approximately a third of commuters in Gauteng, Paris, and US cities spend 15–29 minutes on travel time one way. The percentage of commuters who spend less than 15 minutes on travel time is significantly higher in the US cities, and the percentage who spend either 30–59 minutes or more than 60 minutes is significantly higher in Gauteng. In addition, Gauteng has an unemployment rate of 25 percent in 2014. It is possible that, given Gauteng's population dispersion, the poorer workers living in dense but remote townships cannot afford the cost of commuting to those jobs that are farthest away from their homes. If they were able to afford the trip cost, their commuting time would probably increase the number of commuters in the more-than-60 minutes category.

The distribution of commuting time for metropolitan areas around the world is unfortunately not often measured outside major OECD cities. It is, however, important data for assessing the effective size of labor markets. The distribution of US city commuting times represents probably one of the best in the world (this assertion may seem surprising to some; it will be discussed in detail in chapter 5). From my own experience, Gauteng must represent one of the worst commuting-time distributions in the world. If this is true, then the graph shown on Figure 2.1 shows a good approximation of the variations in commuting time distribution in large metropolitan areas at the beginning of the twentieth century. The goal of urban planning should be to reduce the commuting time of the worst performers by improving the speed of transport and decreasing the regulatory constraints that tend to disperse population artificially.

In the following chapters, I will consider that an hour's commute (one way) is the absolute limit when defining the spatial extent of a labor market. For a worker, the number of jobs that can be reached within a travel time of less than 1 hour defines the size of his labor market.

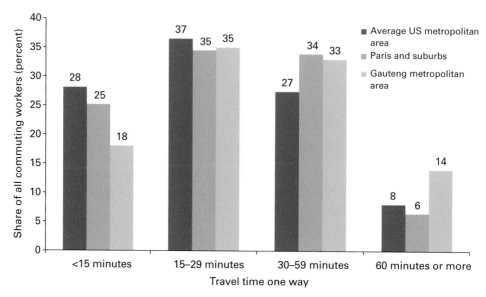

Figure 2.1
Distribution of commuting times in US cities, Paris, and in Gauteng, South Africa. *Sources*: United States: US Census Bureau, 2010 American Community Survey, tables S0802 and B08303; South Africa: Statistics South Africa, Department of Transport Gauteng Households Travel Survey, figure 3.10, Pretoria, South Africa, 2009; Paris: Direction des statistiques démographiques et sociales, "Enquête nationale transport et déplacements 2007–2008," Institut national de la statistique et des études économiques, Paris, 2011.

One could argue that the number of jobs for which a particular worker would be qualified or in which he would be interested would be much smaller than the total number of jobs accessible within an hour of his home. This is true, but increasingly specialized jobs have led to a greater dependence on the physical proximity of people with other specialties and skills. In the service industry in particular, which constitutes a large portion of the jobs in large cities, wide varieties of skills are needed in close proximity. For instance, a lawyer who specializes in European agriculture regulations would not be very productive if she were surrounded only by people with the same skills. To be effective, she will have to be in close contact with other specialists in taxation and import tariffs, and she will need to engage the services of workers who will fix her computer, clean her office, deliver coffee to the board room, and prepare and serve the food that she will eat at lunch. In the same way, an unskilled industrial worker is likely to work in a factory requiring a large array of workers specialized in electronics, mechanics, labor law, insurance, and so on.

The idea that a lawyer needs to access only areas where lawyers are likely to work while an industrial worker needs to access only industrial areas no longer corresponds to the reality of job distribution in a large modern city. Our European agriculture regulations specialist may only be interested in a few jobs, and these few jobs are likely to be randomly distributed among many other jobs. For this reason, the larger the total number of jobs is, the greater will be the chances that a few highly specialized jobs are among them. In addition, the larger the number of jobs accessible within an hour's commute, the better will be the ability to change jobs when desired. This type of labor mobility—the ability to change jobs in different economic sectors—benefits both individual workers and the city economy by redistributing labor where it will provide the most benefits.

The Effective Size of the Labor Market Depends on Travel Time and the Spatial Distribution of Jobs

The impact of travel time, size of labor markets, and spatial distribution of jobs on urban productivity has been convincingly demonstrated for European and Korean cities by Prud'homme and Lee[10] and for US cities by Melo, Graham, Levinston, and Aarabi.[11] Prud'homme and Lee's paper, titled "Size, Sprawl, Speed and the Efficiency of Cities," shows that productivity per worker is closely correlated to the average number of jobs per worker that are reachable in less than 60 minutes. In Korean cities, a 10 percent increase in the number of jobs accessible per worker corresponds to a 2.4 percent increase in workers' productivity. Additionally, for 25 French cities, a 10 percent increase in average commuting speed, all other things remaining constant, increases the size of the labor market by 15–18 percent. In the United States, Melo et al. show that the productivity effect of accessibility, measured by an increase in wages, is correlated to the number of jobs per worker accessible within a 60-minute commuting range. Productivity increases as accessibility does due to the following: when individuals are able to optimize individual labor decisions, firms have the most productive people in jobs, and aggregate output increases. Beyond 20 minutes of travel time, worker productivity still increases, but its rate decays and practically disappears beyond 60 minutes.

Both papers demonstrate that workers' mobility—their ability to reach a large number of potential jobs in as short a travel time as possible—is a key factor in increasing the productivity of large cities and the welfare of their workers. Large agglomerations of workers do not ensure high productivity in the absence of worker mobility. Therefore the time spent commuting should be a key indicator in assessing the way large cities are managed.

As Prud'homme and Lee write in their paper (p. 2), "the benefits associated with city size are only potential, they are contingent on the quality of management. City size would therefore define an efficiency frontier, with effective efficiency often significantly below this frontier." The "quality of management" as defined by Prud'homme and Lee in large part is the ability of the local government to adapt the transport system to the spatial structure so that workers can access a maximum number of jobs in less than 60 minutes of one-way-trip travel time.

The effective size of a city's labor market is, therefore, not necessarily equal to the number of jobs available in its metropolitan area but to the average number of jobs per worker accessible in a 1-hour commute. Depending on the speed of the transport system, the effective size of the labor market could be equal to the total number of jobs available in a city or to only a fraction of it. The location of workers' residences relative to their jobs and the commute time will determine the effective size of a labor market and, therefore, the additional productivity that could be gained by the economies of scale and agglomeration described earlier.

I will illustrate the relationship between speed of transport, effective size of labor market, and spatial distribution of jobs by using a schematic representation of a city as shown in figure 2.2. Imagine a linear city, where workers' residences are spread evenly between *a* and *e*. Jobs are concentrated in only three locations *b*, *c*, and *d*. Each location contains 1/3 of all jobs. The speed of transport is uniform within the city and is represented by the arrows showing travel times between different points. It takes 2 hours to travel from *a* to *e*, which are on opposite outer edges of the hypothetical city.

Workers living between *b* and *d* can reach 100 percent of the jobs in less than 1 hour, but workers living between *a* and *b* can reach only the jobs located in *b* and *c* in less than 1 hour; jobs located in *d* are out of reach for workers living between *a* and *b*. Similarly, workers living between *d* and *e* can reach only the jobs located in *c* and *d*; the jobs located in *b* are out of reach. As a consequence, 50 percent of the workers (those living between *b* and *d*) have access to 100 percent of the jobs in less than 1 hour of travel time, while the other 50 percent (those living between *a* and *b* and between *d* and *e*) only have access to 2/3 of all the jobs. Therefore, the effective size of the labor market represented in figure 2.2 is only 83 percent of all the jobs available in the city: (50 percent × 3/3) + (50 percent × 2/3) = 83.3 percent. If the speed of transport could be increased so that one could travel from *a* to *d* and from *e* to *b* within 1 hour, rather than the 90 minutes each trip currently takes, then the effective size of the job market would be 100 percent of all jobs available (100 percent × 3/3 = 100 percent).

The effective size of a labor market depends on commuting travel speeds and the relative location of workers' residences to their jobs. This dependence may be illustrated in a less abstract way by representing a city as a two-dimensional object (rather than the one-dimensional linear representation of figure 2.2) and by showing alternative arrangements for travel speeds and job locations.

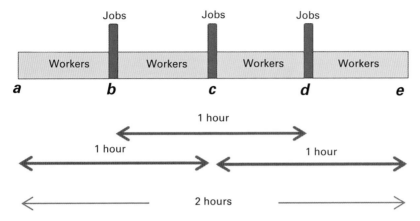

Figure 2.2
Distribution of workers' residences and job locations in a hypothetical linear city.

Equation 2.1 Calculation of the effective size of labor markets

Equation 2.1: Size of labor market calculation
In a less schematic description of a city, the effective size of labor markets can be calculated as follows. Let us assume that the city is divided into polygons identified by their number i. The effective size of its labor market can be expressed as

$$J = \Sigma \; (w_i \, j_i)/\Sigma n_i, \qquad\qquad (2.1)$$

where
J is an indicator of the effective size of the labor market expressed as the average percentage of total jobs accessible in less than 1 hour of commute time per worker;
w_i is the number of workers living in location i;
j_i is the number of jobs accessible in less than 1 hour of commute time of location i; and
n_i is the number of jobs in location i.
This type of calculation would have been prohibitively labor intensive before the availability of GIS technology, but it is now quite feasible to update this indicator regularly. Different transport modes and networks could be tested for their potential impact on the effective size of the labor market.

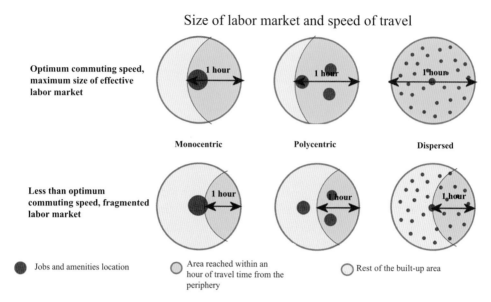

Figure 2.3
Labor market type, speed of travel, and job location.

Figure 2.3 shows a schematic representation of a built-up urban area, represented by a circle. In this circle, smaller red circles represent job locations. Horizontally, I have shown three types of spatial distribution for jobs: monocentric, where all jobs are concentrated in a central business district (CBD); polycentric, where jobs are concentrated in three clusters; and dispersed, where jobs are uniformly distributed in the built-up area. For each pattern of job distribution, an arrow shows the maximum travel distance that a worker can cover in 1 hour from the outer edge of the urban area. The different arrow lengths correspond to different travel speeds.

We will see how different commuting speeds have an impact on the effective size of the labor market, depending on the spatial distribution of jobs.

In the three graphs in the top row of figure 2.3, I have adjusted the speed of travel to allow for accessibility to all jobs in less than 1 hour. On the bottom row, at a lower travel speeds, the workers residing on the periphery can access only a fraction of the jobs in less than 1 hour. The labor market in this case is fragmented and is therefore less efficient than the unified one represented in the top row. In a monocentric or polycentric clustered area, workers who live in a more central area may have access to all jobs in the built-up area, but workers living on the periphery have access to only a fraction of the total jobs available in the city. In this case, the implied productivity of a large labor market is not fully realized. A decrease in commuting travel speed fragments large labor markets into smaller ones and results in a decrease in urban productivity. Increasing travel speed decreases the difference between the effective labor market (the number of jobs accessible in an hour's commute) and the nominal labor market (the total number of jobs in a metropolitan area).

For a given built-up area, the pattern of job distribution is important when defining access to the labor market. When jobs are clustered in a CBD, the distance from all jobs to all residential locations is much shorter than it is when jobs are randomly distributed in the built-up area. This does not necessarily demonstrate that the CBD model is the most efficient pattern or that it will ensure full access to the labor market for everyone. It is true that a centrally located CBD[12] that contains 100 percent of all jobs would decrease the distance from one's residence to one's job for everyone. However, the size of labor markets is limited not only by distance but also by travel time. Therefore, speed of transport (distance/time) is the key parameter that allows access to the maximum number of jobs.

The convergence of all commuting routes[13] toward a CBD usually creates congestion and slows the speed of travel. In contrast, when jobs are dispersed in suburban locations, there is no convergence of routes, and transport speed is usually faster. The average surface transport speed in the center of Paris (within 5 kilometers of City Hall) is about 12 km/h; rush-hour speeds in the suburbs (20 kilometers from City Hall) are about 50 km/h. (Thanks to improvement in GPS technology, we are now able to check variations in rush hour speeds on the Internet in real time for many cities in the world.)

In areas where the major road network was originally designed for a monocentric city, commuting routes from suburb to suburb may be less direct than they should be; this is the case in Paris, Atlanta, and Shanghai. Initially, suburb-to-suburb commuting routes may have to follow minor roads and may include awkward major-road crossings. There is usually a long time lag before a municipality is able to adjust the design of a major-road network from monocentric to a gridlike pattern that will better serve new, emerging routes among suburbs.

In chapter 5, I discuss the influence of different transport modes—cars, public buses, or subways—on transport costs and travel times for various types of urban spatial structure in which population and job densities are distributed differently in the built-up area.

The schematic representation of spatial structure in figure 2.3 is very crude, but it clearly illustrates the impact of speed of travel and job location on the effective size of a labor market. In the next chapter, we will explore more complex and more realistic urban forms and their impact on mobility and land affordability.

In cities where job accessibility has been measured, the number of jobs accessible by commuting time shows large variations. For instance, Prud'homme and Lee (p. 6) noted that in Seoul, "in 1998 the average worker has in 60 minutes access to only 51% of all the jobs offered by the city; and the average enterprise has 56% of all the workers at less than 60 minutes." The additional subway lines built since that date must have increased the effective size of the labor market in Seoul. A comparison of car commuting across US cities in 2010 calculated by David Livingston[14] shows amazing differences in accessibility between US cities (figure 2.4). Within a 30-minute drive, 2.4 million jobs can be accessed in Los Angeles compared with 0.6 million in Atlanta. However, four of the five cities represented in figure 2.4 allow access to all jobs within 60 minutes.

As we have seen in Figure 2.3, a majority of jobs may be concentrated in a central business district, be clustered in several centers, or be completely dispersed across

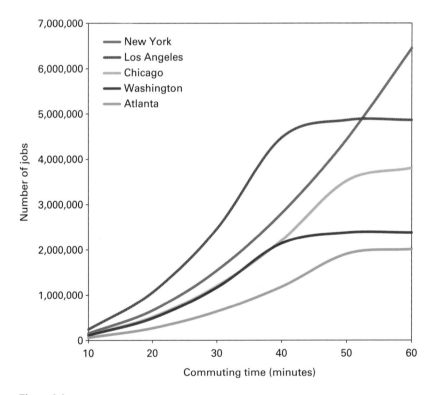

Figure 2.4
Average number of jobs accessible to workers in various US cities, 2010.
The labor market shapes the pattern of commuting trips. *Source*: David Levinson, "Access across America," Center for Transportation Studies, University of Minnesota, Minneapolis, 2013.

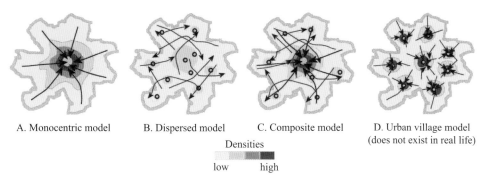

A. Monocentric model   B. Dispersed model   C. Composite model   D. Urban village model
                                                                       (does not exist in real life)

Densities

low   high

Figure 2.5
Model trip patterns in metropolitan areas.

a metropolitan area. I will discuss in more detail in chapters 3 and 4 why jobs are located where they are and how this pattern usually evolves with time. For the moment, let us look only at the possible trip patterns that would allow the labor market to function within each of the following spatial distributions of jobs.

Figure 2.5 illustrates in a schematic manner the most typical trip patterns in metropolitan areas. These trip patterns are based on the structure of the labor market (see figure 2.3). Two labor market structures impact trip patterns—monocentric and dispersed—resulting in three observed models of commuting-route patterns based on labor market structure, labeled from A to C in figure 2.5:

A. **The monocentric model**—most jobs are concentrated in a dense CBD; trip routes follow radial roads and converge on the CBD. Of course, no real city is ever strictly monocentric; a number of jobs are necessarily found inside residential areas, for instance in schools, dispensaries, gas stations, and grocery stores. Mono-centricity is really measured by degree rather than in absolute terms. A city where more than 50 percent of the jobs are located in the CBD is predominantly mono-centric. To my knowledge, no metropolitan area with a population of more than 5 million meets this criterion.

B. **The dispersed model**—most jobs are concentrated in small clusters or com-pletely dispersed among residential areas; trip routes are randomly distributed in the built-up area. If speed of transport allows it, some workers will commute from one edge of the metropolitan area to its opposite edge. As in the monocentric model, workers residing closer to the centroid of the built-up area are closer to all jobs than are workers residing at the edge. Firms located closer to the built-up area centroid are also closer to all workers. However, because commuting speeds are usually not the same near the centroid and at the periphery, firms located close to the periphery might be accessible in shorter time by more workers than firms located close to the centroid. In part, this explains why firms do not cluster close to the centroid, even though doing so would put them at a shorter distance from all their potential workers.

C. **The composite model**—a significant fraction of all jobs are concentrated (say, 30 percent) in a dense CBD, but most jobs are randomly distributed in the rest of the built-up area. Trip routes toward the CBD follow radial roads, while trip routes toward dispersed jobs are randomly distributed but usually avoid the congestion of the CBD. This is the most usual pattern of trips in large cities in Asia and Europe today.

There is also a fourth model of trips that doesn't exist in the real world but is very often presented in master plans as being a desirable alternative to the three trip patterns described above. Because of the prevalence of this conceit in many urban master plans, this utopian alternative trip pattern, labeled D in figure 2.5, needs to be discussed:

D. **The so-called Urban Village Model**—jobs are concentrated in many small clusters. In this model, there are many centers, but commuters travel only to the center that is closest to their residence. The trips toward each job cluster follow radial routes centered on each cluster and behave as if each cluster were an isolated, monocentric city. According to this model, a large city can be made up of many self-sufficient, small monocentric cities.

Unfortunately, the urban village model exists only in the minds of urban planners. Otherwise, it would be a very attractive model, which is why urban planners favor it, as it would not require significant investment in transportation or roads. Furthermore, it would dramatically reduce vehicle kilometers traveled and, as a result, greenhouse gas (GHG) emissions. According to the proponents of this model, everybody could walk or bicycle to work, even in a very large metropolis. To allow a city to grow, it would only be necessary to add more clusters. The assumption behind this model is either that urban planners would be able to perfectly match work places and residences, or that workers and employers would spontaneously organize themselves into the appropriate clusters.

This model does not exist in the real world, because it contradicts the economic justification of large cities: the efficiency of large labor markets. Employers do not select their employees based on their places of residence; neither do specialized workers select their jobs based on proximity from their residences.

The urban village model implies a systematic fragmentation of labor markets in a large metropolis and does not make economic sense in the real world. A firm that would be satisfied to restrict the selection of its employees to the vicinity of its factory or office would not need to locate in a large metropolis where rents and salaries are higher. This firm could locate in a small town where the unspecialized workers it seeks could be recruited for a lower salary. In the same way, a worker living in a large city and looking for a new job would try to maximize job satisfaction measured in part through salary, level of interest in the work and its compatibility with skillset, attractiveness of the work environment, and so forth. The time spent commuting might certainly be a consideration in seeking a job, but if the commuting time were less than 1 hour, it would likely not be a determining factor.

The five satellite towns built around Seoul are an example of an attempt to implement the urban village concept. The government built the new towns under the assumptions that they would be self-contained and that most inhabitants would work and live within their own towns. To achieve this objective, planners carefully balanced the number of projected jobs in each town with the number of projected inhabitants. However, subsequent surveys showed that most people living in the new satellite towns commuted to work in the Seoul metropolitan area, and most of the jobs in the satellite towns were filled by people living outside them.[15] The trip pattern found in satellite towns is consistent with the hypothesis stated at the beginning of this chapter: A large unified labor market is the justification for large cities. It's likely that some households initially decided to move to Seoul's satellite towns because apartments were cheaper than in Seoul's core city or because the environment was better and newer. It is also probable that when these households moved, the heads of household were already employed somewhere in Seoul. After all, had they not been employed, they likely would not have been able to buy a new apartment. Furthermore, after moving to a satellite town, it is unlikely that they would quit their current jobs to find equivalent jobs in the town. The same line of reasoning holds for firms moving to a satellite town. A firm might move from the central city to find cheaper rent or more space, but many of its employees would likely decide to keep their jobs and commute from the core city to the satellite town.

How Common Are Each of the Three Models of Spatial Arrangement?
The spatial distributions of jobs, and as a consequence commuting trip patterns, evolve as cities become larger and more affluent. The monocentric model is a simple, primitive city model that inevitably evolves over time into a more complex form, more closely resembling the composite model. Once jobs have dispersed into a pattern similar to the dispersed model or composite model, it is unlikely that they will eventually concentrate again in a dense, central CBD. This path dependency[16] rule, common to all evolving shapes, is a reality that should seriously limit the freedom of planners to dream up new urban forms. Planners should take into account the path dependency of city shapes when designing new transport systems, as we will see in chapter 5 on mobility.

None of the three models discussed above are immutable. Future urban labor markets, for instance, might not require as many face-to-face interactions among employees, customers, and suppliers as they have in the past. New models of trip patterns might emerge in the future that reflect the new requirements of an evolving labor market. For instance, the recent emergence of telecommuting has put into question not only the pattern of commuting trips but also the very need for commuting. So we should remain agnostic regarding the patterns of commuting trips 20 years from now. However, we can look at the trend in trip patterns over the past decades to inform our understanding going forward. This trend reflects path dependency, as mentioned above.

What effect could a large increase in telecommuting have on current trip patterns? So far, the effect has been modest. In fact, there is a hint that this modest trend may reverse itself among high-tech companies that were the first to initiate it. In 2013, Yahoo's new CEO announced a reversal of its telecommuting policy, which confirmed what we already knew: that serendipitous face-to-face contacts between professionals are necessary for innovation.

However, the question remains: How often should those face-to-face interactions occur? Once a week? Every other day? How large should the groups needing face-to-face interaction be? How much serendipity is required to generate innovation? Whatever the answer, telecommuting will certainly decrease daily commuting flow and change traffic flows, but it will not completely eliminate a worker's need for spatial proximity to his employer or to other workers with complementary skills. It is quite possible that telecommuting will decrease in firms requiring innovation and increase in firms engaged in routine data processing. But one lesson is clear: we cannot plan for it, and we must monitor carefully the spatial implication of this trend and support it with adequate transport infrastructure.

Although the large metropolises of the world show a great variety of histories, cultures, and incomes, the trends (when the data exist to measure them) seem to converge to a greater spatial dispersion of jobs. This trend seems counterintuitive, particularly as the CBDs in an increasing number of cities compete for the distinction of world's tallest skyscraper. But we must realize that a prime office skyscraper contains fewer workers per hectare than the five-story sweatshop that it likely replaced.

Because of the very low built-up densities of US cities, their spatial trend might not be representative of most world cities. However, the US trend has the advantage of being well documented and may still provide some insights into the way changes in labor markets impact urban land use. In 1995 and 2005, Alan Pisarski conducted the most comprehensive nationwide studies of commuting in the United States. The trends he measured over a 10-year interval are clear: the ratio between jobs and resident workers is decreasing in central cities and increasing in suburban areas. Pisarski's studies clearly show that, on average, US metropolitan areas are slowly evolving from a composite model (figure 2.5, pattern C), to a more dispersed model (pattern B). Furthermore, Pisarski's studies indicate that the job concentration in the traditional CBD is constantly decreasing not in absolute terms but as a proportion of the total number of metropolitan jobs.

Pisarski's reports show that in smaller US metropolitan areas, those with fewer than 100,000 people, commuting trips[17] to the CBD represent about 50 percent of all trips—a good approximation of the monocentric model. However, for larger metropolitan areas, those with populations of more than 2 million people, the trips to the CBD drop to about or below 24 percent. This is also observed in very large metropolises with a well-marked, dominant CBD, such as Seoul, New York, or Paris. For instance, in the New York metropolitan area, 24.3 percent of trips are from the suburbs to Manhattan or within Manhattan; 2.1 percent of trips are from Manhattan to the suburbs, and most trips (73.6 percent) are from suburb to suburb. The pattern of trips in metropolitan New York illustrates what I have called the composite model (figure 2.5, pattern C).

Outside the United States, the trends of large metropolitan areas also seem to move toward the composite model, even in cities like Paris, with a historically dominant and prestigious center and a radial/concentric transit system providing excellent access to the center. In the Paris metropolitan area (defined as the Île-de-France region), trips within and to the Paris municipality (historical Paris) represent 30 percent of the total commuting trips, and 70 percent of trips are from suburb to suburb (figure 2.6).

Large metropolitan areas of Asia, although much denser than US or European cities, display the same trends in the suburbanization of jobs and people. Seoul's metropolitan area, with a population of 24.7 million in 2010, is representative of the trend in prosperous East Asian cities that have seen a significant increase in population and household income in the past 30 years (figure 2.7). In Seoul, between 2000 and 2010, the population decreased by 0.5 percent in the central city,[18] and it increased by 92 percent in outer suburbs located more than 20 kilometers from the city center due to the development of transport infrastructure (table 2.1). During the same 10-year period, the spatial distribution of jobs has been more dispersed, with 16 percent of the new jobs being added to the CBD, while 59 percent were added to outer suburbs more than 20 kilometers from the CBD. Seoul, however, still remains more monocentric than Paris or New York, with 31 percent of all metropolitan jobs concentrated in the central city.

As we can see from the historical trend, the monocentric model tends to break down when a city becomes larger. However, empirical evidence does not show an obvious population size threshold beyond which cities cease to thrive as dominantly monocentric. Sometimes topography—rivers or mountains—prevents

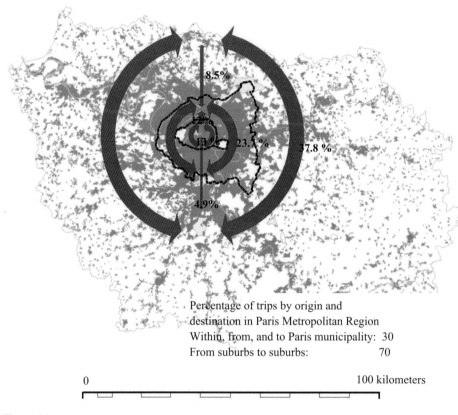

Percentage of trips by origin and
destination in Paris Metropolitan Region
Within, from, and to Paris municipality: 30
From suburbs to suburbs: 70

0   100 kilometers

Figure 2.6
Trip patterns in metropolitan Paris. *Sources*: "Les déplacements des Franciliens en 2001–2002," Direction
regionale de l'equipement d'Île-de-France, 2005, Paris Cedex 15; built-up area, digitization of satellite
imagery by Marie-Agnes Bertaud.

direct communication from suburb to suburb and therefore maintains monocentricity in spite of a large population. An original network of primary radial roads will reinforce a high degree of monocentricity as a city expands by making it easier to go to the CBD than to peripheral locations. This type of radial network can be seen in European cities like Berlin, Copenhagen, and Paris. By contrast, a primary grid network would rapidly encourage the creation of subcenters with good overall accessibility as a city develops. This has been the case for Los Angeles, Houston, and Omaha. The grids in these cities sometimes become irregular, but the availability of wide roads, perpendicular to the radial roads at the fringe of urbanization, stimulates the creation of subcenters and perhaps even encourages job dispersion, because wide roads allow for higher driving speeds and, therefore,

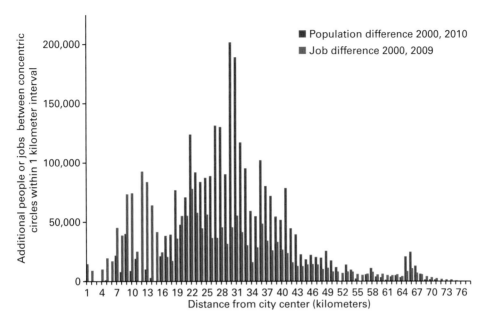

Figure 2.7
Changes in population and job distributions over time, Seoul metropolitan area. *Sources*: Population and job data: Seoul Metropolitan Government Statistical Unit, Census 2000, 2010; built-up areas and densities: GIS analysis by Marie-Agnes Bertaud.

for faster accessibility to areas farther away from the radial roads. Thus a grid network of roads encourages an early shift toward polycentricity.

The Efficient Operation of Labor Markets Requires Mobility and Affordability

Mobility should be understood in two ways, while affordability ensures that mobility is not distorted:

1. Firms and households have the freedom to stay put or migrate at will.

2. Travel within the city remains fast and cheap.

3. Real estate is sufficiently affordable that it does not distort the allocation of labor.

The ability of households and firms to choose where they locate depends on the availability of land and floor space in the areas of the city they deem to have the most favorable benefits—for households, the proximity to jobs and amenities; and for firms, the proximity to clients, employees, and suppliers. Theoretically, the lowest-income household or the least well-capitalized firm should be able to locate

Table 2.1
Seoul: Spatial changes in the distribution of population and jobs, 2000–2010.

	Distance from city center (kilometers)	Census 2010				Increase between 2000 and 2010			
		Census 2010 population	Percent	Jobs	Percent	Population	Percent	Jobs	Percent
Central city	0–10	5,409,428	22	2,676,391	31	(12,593)	-0.5	302,558	16.2
Inner suburbs	10–20	7,644,893	31	2,219,956	26	231,709	8.8	460,789	24.7
Outer suburbs	20–78	11,654,883	47	3,624,400	43	2,423,859	91.7	1,102,002	59.1
Total		24,709,203	100	8,520,747	100	2,642,975	100.0	1,865,349	100.0

anywhere in a city, even where land is the most expensive, if they are allowed to consume as little land as they require. The food carts of Manhattan and the tiny *paanwalas*[19] stalls of Mumbai demonstrate this point. These small businesses sell cheap products but thrive in their expensive locations by consuming only 2 or 3 square meters of land, as opposed to the several hundred square meters occupied by most shops in the same area. Farmers' markets and flea markets are other examples of the trade-off between location and land consumption allowing low-margin businesses to thrive in expensive locations.

Equivalent examples exist for housing; for instance, Paris's *chambres de bonne*[20] are located in the city's most expensive neighborhoods. Typically as small as 9 square meters, they allow students or low-income workers to afford housing in a very favorable location. The residential plots in Indonesia's *kampungs*[21] are another example of the demand for centrally located residences with low land and floor consumption. The availability of these residences allows the poor to consider the trade-offs they want to make regarding location and land consumption. If water, sanitation, and refuse management are adequate, a small, inner city location might be a desirable trade-off compared to a suburban one far from jobs, amenities, and social services. Whether chambres de bonnes or kampungs, the neighborhoods in which such dwellings are located are by no means slums, in spite of the very small size of their dwellings (to be discussed in depth in chapter 6).

Unfortunately, well-intentioned regulations often prevent the poor from making these trade-offs between floor space consumption and location. Urban regulations typically require a "generous" minimum floor space standard for housing. These well-intentioned regulations exclude the poor because the high price of floor area makes it too expensive for them to afford the minimum standard. In Paris, chambres de bonne exist only in housing built before 1930; they are prohibited in apartment buildings that are more recent. These unfortunate regulations reduce the mobility of the poor. As a consequence, their participation in the full labor market is also restricted. In chapter 4, I describe in more detail other urban regulations that reduce the mobility of the poor.

In South Africa, the government housing program for the poor illustrates how well-intentioned planners may limit residents' mobility, reduce their participation in the labor market, and increase their travel time. Starting in 1995, the government embarked on a massive housing program to improve the living conditions of the victims of apartheid. The program aimed to provide subsidized housing to about 80 percent of the poorest South Africans. By 2012, it had already delivered 3.5 million urban dwelling units, a unique quantitative achievement for a government housing program. The standards are generous: 400 square meters per lot, 65 square meters of floor space per house, wide vehicular access roads, and schools equipped with large sports grounds and within walking distance, among other things. The space standards are fixed and similar all over urban South Africa. The subsidy is also fixed, amounting to about 150,000 rand (US$16,000) per dwelling in 2012. The only dependent variable is the price of land. Land for this massive program must be very cheap to allow beneficiaries to enjoy the high space standards prescribed by the program. As a result, the new subsidized housing projects are all located in the far periphery of cities, in settlements that are too dispersed to be easily serviced by public transport. Because of the remote location, the beneficiaries of these projects have a hard time finding employment. Those who are employed pay as much as 50 percent of their income on transport, even when sharing taxis with other commuters. This dramatic example illustrates why planners should not make trade-off decisions involving location and land consumption for households and firms.

In the case of South Africa, the outcome is indeed comfortable housing for poor people, but the large subsidy attached to a house in a distant location prevents the beneficiaries from participating in the labor market. High-standard housing provided to poor people in a remote location becomes a poverty trap. The subsidies are not to blame here. The error is not only tying the subsidy to a specific location but also deciding on the location versus land consumption trade-off without having solicited input from the beneficiaries. A portable subsidy—that is, a lump sum given to poor households to use for shelter anywhere in the metropolitan area—is significantly preferable.

Because planners lack information to make informed decisions about the difficult trade-offs between location and land consumption, they shouldn't have the authority to make these types of decisions. Only a free market allows households and firms to choose the trades-offs that best allow them to maximize their comfort and their participation in the labor market. In the following chapters, I will use the mobility and affordability criteria to assess the efficiency of different urban forms. To benefit fully from a large labor market, households and firms must have ease of mobility. As such, there must be sufficient, affordable options that allow them to make the trade-off decisions between location and land consumption that best suit their needs.

Cities Viewed as Labor Markets: Operational Implications

Looking at cities as unified labor markets should change the generally negative views that urban planners hold regarding mobility. Planners believe that one of their most important tasks is to decrease nuisances created by urbanization, particularly vehicular traffic. They are right—decreasing congestion and pollution is one of the most pressing challenges brought on by urbanization. However, planners, in their enthusiasm to reduce nuisances, often fail to understand the differences between the objective of increasing mobility and the constraint of decreasing the nuisances it creates.

One of the main objectives of urban planning is maintaining mobility—preventing an increase in commuting time as the size of the labor market increases. In other words, the main objective of planning should be to increase the speed of urban transport as a city's size increases. Decreasing the level of nuisances due to transport is a constraint that may increase the cost of achieving the objective. But this cost is fully justified if the marginal cost of reducing nuisances is lower than the marginal increase in productivity due to the expansion of the labor market. For instance, charging vehicles in proportion to the pollution they create or imposing tolls on highways to reduce congestion would increase the cost of transport but at the same time would also increase its efficiency, allow for higher speeds, and improve environmental quality.

However, too often planners substitute the constraint for the objective. For instance, advocates of "smart growth" imply that the reduction of congestion and pollution is the main objective of urban planning. They soon realize that nothing will reduce congestion and pollution more certainly than a decrease in mobility. Reducing mobility is then considered a desirable outcome and is the logical consequence of the confusion between objectives and constraints. For this reason, planners design "urban village" spatial arrangements (see figure 2.5, pattern D), which implicitly reduce mobility.

Matching employment location with residence in large metropolitan areas has become the Holy Grail of urban planners. This recurrent conceit, motivating many master plans and many land use regulations,[22] can only be explained by ignorance of the economic efficiency of large labor markets and the mobility that large labor markets require to function. The choice of spatial location is best left to households and firms themselves.

In the following chapters, the functioning of labor markets will be my guiding principle in evaluating alternative spatial arrangements. I will use "mobility" to designate the ability to reach any area of a metropolitan area in as short a travel time as possible. I will use "affordability" to designate the ability of households and firms to locate in whichever area they deem will maximize their welfare. Increasing mobility and affordability are the two main objectives of urban planning. These two objectives are directly related to the overall goal of maximizing the size of a city's labor markets, and therefore, its economic prosperity.

3 Formation of Urban Spatial Structures: Markets versus Design

The basic economic system should evolve on the decisive role of markets in resource allocation.
—Third Plenary Session of the 18th Central Committee of the Communist Party of China, November 11, 2013

In the previous chapter, we discussed how firms and households relate to each other through the labor market. The labor market obliges firms and households to locate at distances involving commuting times shorter than 1 hour.

Households need land for shelter. Firms need land for workspace. However, for a given population, the larger the area of land consumed per household and per worker, the longer will be the commuting distance between firms and households. It appears, therefore, that there is a trade-off between land consumption and commuting distance.

But commuting distance is only a proxy for commuting time and cost, which are the real constraints limiting the efficiency of a labor market's concentration. Different transport technologies imply different commuting speeds and commuting costs and therefore make distance an imperfect proxy for labor market efficiency. The real trade-off is thus between land consumption and commuting times and costs by different means of transport. This leads to a few logical questions:

• How will the optimum trade-off be achieved between the land consumed and the commuting speed and cost such that the welfare of both firms and households is simultaneously maximized?

• Is it possible to identify an urban spatial structure that would optimize the trade-off between land consumption and commuting speed for all firms and households?

• What is the best way to reach equilibrium between land consumption and commuting distance as population size and household incomes grow and transport technology changes?

To answer these questions, economists tend to favor markets, while urban planners tend to favor design.[1]

In the title of this chapter, I have set markets against design. This chapter will debate the following issues.

- How do markets and design contribute to the development of cities?
- Are markets or is design more likely to shape a city in such a way that an equilibrium is achieved between land consumption and commuting speed?
- Should planners substitute their own designs for market forces to obtain a better spatial outcome or, on the contrary, should planners rely more on markets to guide urban development?
- If the efficiency of spatial urban structures rests on a trade-off between land consumption and commuting speed and cost, what indicators should planers develop to monitor progress in urban structure efficiency?

The Role of Markets and Design in Shaping Cities in Market Economies

In market economies, the combined effect of market forces and deliberate government design generates urban spatial structures. In the last two command economies left in the world, Cuba and North Korea, design is officially the only factor shaping cities. Let us see how markets and design contribute to the shape of most of the cities in the world.

Markets as Urban-Shape Creators

Markets create a blind mechanism that produces and constantly modifies urban shapes, in the same way as evolution creates a blind mechanism that produces and modifies living organisms.

Markets shape cities through land prices. High demand for specific locations creates the large differences in land prices observed in cities. Land prices, in turn, shape cities by creating high concentrations of floor space—tall buildings—where land prices are high and low concentrations—short buildings—where land prices are low. Very high demand for floor space in a limited area explains the concentration of skyscrapers in central business districts (CBD); similarly, low land prices and high incomes explain the spread of low-density suburbs. Very low household incomes explain the high residential density in slums, even in areas where land prices are relatively low. The changing balance between supply and demand, the variations in firms' and households' incomes, and the cost of transport can explain the extreme variety of building shapes and their spatial distribution in a metropolitan area. Urban shapes produced by markets illustrate perfectly what Adam Ferguson, the eighteenth-century Scottish Enlightenment philosopher, called "the result of human action, but not the execution of any human design."

Markets and the Price of Urban Transport

Markets generate different land prices for each location in a city. In most cities, the price of land is usually the highest in the central part, because workers and consumers can travel to it in the shortest time and at the least cost. The price of transport—measured in time consumed and money spent—has traditionally been one of the main "shapers" of urban form. Large industrial cities of the nineteenth century, where walking or riding in a horse-drawn carriage were the most common commuting modes of transport, required very high densities. The high cost of transport in either time or money restricted the extent of the built-up area, as did the absence of mechanized transport. Consequently, the size of the labor market could grow only by accommodating more people and jobs in the area accessible in less than 1 hour, resulting in very high population and job densities. A city's labor market could keep growing, but only if a large proportion of the population accepted consuming less land every year. The high density of the Dickensian slums was the consequence.

At the end of the nineteenth century, the introduction of various mechanized forms of urban transport allowed higher commuting speeds at lower costs. The first underground rail urban transport was built in London in 1862; it was soon imitated in many large cities in Europe and the United States. The introduction of mechanized transport had two main effects on the shape of cities. First, it increased the area accessible within an hour, and therefore increased the size of the labor market even while allowing population densities to decrease. Second, it dramatically increased the accessibility of the city center where the mechanized transport lines converged, increasing the price of land in the central area while decreasing it in the suburbs. Rapid rail transport also suddenly made large areas of rural land accessible from the old city centers. The large increase in land supply made new suburban row houses affordable to the former inner-city slum dweller. This new, emerging transport technology made the concept of Ebenezer Howard's "garden cities" not so utopian after all.[2]

In the mid-1930s, the mass production of cars at a price affordable to the middle class further increased the radius of cities by giving rapid access to areas not yet served by the suburban rail networks. This spatial expansion, made possible by the introduction of a new transport technology, allowed a rapid growth in the size of the labor market while further differentiating the price of land between the city center and distant suburbs and allowing for an increase in the land consumption of suburban dwellers and firms.

The Ratio between Land and Floor Space in Different Locations
The spatial expansion of cities requires land, but the final product of urbanization is floor space, not land. Because land is an indispensable input for the building of floor space, a high demand for floor space in a specific location increases the price of land at this location.

Floor space is the sum of the area built on land, whether public or private. In areas where the price of land is high, developers can decrease the area of land they use to produce a given area of floor space by building taller buildings. As a result, the quantity of land required to build a unit of floor space varies greatly in and across cities, reflecting the large variations in the spatial distribution of land prices set by the market.

For instance, the Shanghai World Financial Center, a spectacular office tower built in Pudong, Shanghai's new financial district, has 101 floors with a total floor space area of 377,000 square meters. This office tower was built on a lot measuring 27,800 square meters. The ratio of floor to land (also called the floor area ratio, or FAR) is therefore about 13.5. In other words, to build the Shanghai World Financial Center tower, the developer used only 1 square meter of land to build 13.5 square meters of floor space.

By contrast, in Huaxinzhou, a suburb of Shanghai located 24 kilometers from the SWFC, a developer building single-family houses used as much as 1,350 square meters of land to build 300 square meters of floor space; this corresponds to a FAR of 0.22. Thus in Shanghai, building 1 square meter of floor space in Huaxinzhou occupies about 61 times more land than in Pudong! The large differences in land consumption to produce 1 meter of floor space in two different locations in the same city reflect the large differences in the price of land set by the land market.

In the New York metropolitan area, we see a similar scenario. Let us compare the FARs of Midtown Manhattan (New York's CBD) with those of Glen Rock, a New York suburb 26 kilometers from Midtown. We see that building 1 square meter of floor space in the suburban location used about 60 times more land than in the CBD, a result very similar to that for Shanghai.

The decision to build tall buildings or short ones is therefore not a design choice left to a planner, an architect, or a developer. It is a financial decision based on the price of land, reflecting the demand for floor space in a particular location. Tall buildings are more expensive to build per unit of floor space than are shorter buildings, but the potential higher sale price by unit of floor space due to high demand compensates for the higher construction cost. The higher FAR values lower the cost of land per unit of floor space sold.

A high or low FAR is therefore not a design parameter. The FAR captures the conversion from land to capital in providing floor space. It is purely an economic decision depending on the price of land in relation to the price of construction. If the price of land is much lower than the price of construction, there is not much reason to construct buildings taller than two or three floors. For instance, in Glen Rock, the New York suburb mentioned above, the cost of land is about $450/m², and the construction cost of a typical wooden frame home is about $1,600/m². Therefore, there is not much incentive to substitute capital for land, and as a result, the FAR of most houses is low, about 0.25. By contrast, in New York's Midtown area, the price of land is about $25,000/m², and the construction cost of a prime office building is roughly $5,000/m², only 20 percent of the price of land. The high cost of land in Midtown significantly increases the incentive to substitute capital for land and thus explains why the FAR of office buildings is about 15. As in Pudong, the existence of tall buildings in Midtown New York does not reflect a design choice but an economic necessity imposed by markets and reflecting high consumers' demand for this location.

Some urban planners may disagree with me and argue that the existence of tall buildings is mainly the result of a design decision imposed by zoning plans, which fix maximum FAR values through regulation. Here is why they may hold this mistaken notion.

In most cities, planners strictly regulate FAR values, because they assume that tall buildings impose large negative externalities on the surrounding neighborhood. Tall buildings indeed cast long shadows and may create congestion in adjacent streets because of the large number of people who are likely to live or work in them. In many cities, because of FAR regulations, the height of buildings is constrained at much lower levels than market demand would suggest. In areas where maximum regulatory FARs are much lower than demand for floor space suggests, most buildings are likely to make full use of the limited FAR permitted by regulations. Eventually, the city's planners may decide to increase the value of the regulatory FAR over the one currently allowed. Developers will then make use of the entire, newly permitted FAR value and will, therefore, build taller buildings. The timing correlation between the increase in regulatory FAR and the construction of taller buildings gives an illusion of causality between regulations and tall buildings. Consequently, some planners think that fixing a FAR regulatory value is a design decision and that new buildings will automatically use the entire FAR value set by regulations.

While this may be true in areas where demand for floor space was previously constrained by regulations, increasing the regulatory FAR value where no demand for taller buildings exists would have no effect on the height of future buildings. In Glen Rock, the New York suburban area mentioned above, the FAR value used in most buildings varies from 0.2 to 0.3, while the maximum permitted FAR is about 0.4. There is not much demand now for the floor space allowed by the current FAR regulations. If planners were to authorize a FAR value of, say, 5, no tall buildings would be constructed following the zoning change.

Markets React to Exogenous Factors That Planners Cannot Anticipate
Changing exogenous forces are constantly modifying the market's equilibrium, and as a result, urban shapes and land uses created by the market constantly evolve as well. These exogenous forces are becoming more numerous and their effects more volatile because of globalization. For instance, some 30 years ago, the skills, salary levels, and availability of clerical workers in India had no impact on the demand for clerical workers in European and American cities. Today, information technology allows clerical workers from India to compete with those from Europe. This outside competition may affect the demand for European clerical workers; consequently, the demand for and location of office buildings in European cities might change. This change in technology as well as the availability and salary levels of Indian workers contribute exogenous forces that may affect European cities' land use. These globally generated exogenous factors likewise impact land use in Indian cities. For example, the recent mushrooming of call centers in Indian cities, a type of land use unknown only a few years ago, is a direct consequence of the availability of new technology and of the higher salaries of European and American clerical workers compared to their Indian counterparts.

Markets react quickly to worldwide changes. Falling demand for some activities translates into lower rents for the buildings where these activities are taking place, triggering demand for rapid land use change. Land use changes caused by markets often occur well before urban planners could possibly be aware of the change in demand, such as global macroeconomic events, shifts in consumer demand and therefore industrial production, or even rapid gentrification.

In cities, markets create new types of land use and make others obsolete. Marx's observation in his *Communist Manifesto* that markets produced "everlasting uncertainty and agitation" and that as a result "all that is solid melts into air" is still true today and could refer to the changes taking place in the most dynamic cities of emerging economies. Economist and Harvard professor Joseph Schumpeter, giving a more optimistic version of Marx's original insight, called this process "creative destruction." Markets thus recycle obsolete land use quasi-automatically through rising and falling prices. This constant land recycling is usually very positive for the long-term welfare of the urban population. In the short term, changes in land use and in the spatial concentration of employment are disorienting and alarming for workers and firms alike.

Responding to the disruptions caused by land use changes, local governments are often tempted to intervene in order to slow down the rate of change and prevent the recycling of obsolete land use by reducing the FAR, mandating commercial versus residential zoning, or freezing particular industrial land uses. However, the long-range effects of maintaining obsolete land use through regulations are disastrous for future employment levels and for the general welfare of urban dwellers. Preventing the transformation of obsolete land use also prevents new jobs from being created in its place. Regulations can prevent land use changes but cannot stop jobs from disappearing from the obsolete areas. A city's labor market then shrinks when the government maintains land under a use for which there is no more demand. Freezing obsolete land use does not prevent Schumpeterian destruction, but it prevents the creation associated with it. "All that is solid melts into air," but the destruction is not followed by any new creation.

Land Use Change: Mumbai

The story of Mumbai's cotton mills best illustrates the tragic consequences of freezing obsolete land uses in the hope of preserving jobs. Indian entrepreneurs built Mumbai's first cotton mills in the middle of the nineteenth century in what was then an industrial suburb of Mumbai. In 1861, the American Civil War contributed to a large price increase for Indian cotton cloth (an external shock already occurring long before the spread of globalization). Consequently, the mills multiplied to employ, at their peak in the 1930s, more than 350,000 workers; they occupied an area of 280 hectares, not including worker housing. However, subsequent competition from other Asian countries and from more modern mills built in smaller Indian cities made the higher price of cotton fabric manufactured in Mumbai increasingly uncompetitive on the world market. Because of outside competition, some mills had to close.

After World War II, more mills started closing, partly because as Mumbai developed, their locations in the middle of a dense and congested metropolis made them too expensive to operate. The productivity of the mills also kept decreasing: Given land expenses, no updates had been made to factories, making the factory layout and technology obsolete. A workers' strike lasting more than a year in 1982 delivered the coup de grâce to Mumbai's cotton mills. The story of the growth and decay of a textile industry is not unique to Mumbai; many European industrial cities, like Manchester and Ghent, went through the same cycles, produced by the same external forces.

However, as the Mumbai mills were closing, the municipality and workers' unions, fought to preserve the high taxes and the well-paying industrial jobs produced by the mills. As a result, they prevented mills' owners from selling the potentially expensive land on which the now-deserted mills had been built. Later, when it became clear that the mills would never open again, the local government imposed such draconian conditions[3] on the redevelopment of the land that it became frozen in court cases. As a consequence, over the course of more than 40 years, an

Figure 3.1
Vacant cotton mills in Mumbai, 1990.

increasing number of mills stood empty in the middle of Mumbai, obliging the city to expand its infrastructure farther north while by-passing the 280 hectares of already well-serviced area occupied by the empty mills (figure 3.1). In 2009, when some of the land formerly occupied by the mills was finally auctioned, the price reached more than US$2,200 per square meter! The total value of the mill land unused for about 30 years would be therefore around US$6 billion in 2009, or more than five times Mumbai's capital budget for 2014.[4]

The failure to realize that urban activities are transient and subject to uncontrollable external market forces led the municipality and workers to try, through regulations, to maintain obsolete activities and land use. They assumed that the problem of the failing mills was local and could be solved through bargaining among local stakeholders. In doing so, they prevented new jobs from being created on the very valuable land occupied by the vacant mills. The misunderstanding caused enormous hardship for the workers and damaged the city's economy. It prevented new jobs from being created to replace the ones that had been lost. It forced an extension of the city's infrastructure into new, more distant areas while already well-serviced land stood empty.

Land Use Change: Hartford, Connecticut

The case of Hartford, Connecticut, referred to as the "insurance capital of the world" in the 1950s, dramatically illustrates how a change in technology can impact local land use and the prosperity of a city that is heavily reliant on one industry. Hartford reached its peak population in 1950, when insurance companies required a high concentration of clerical staff working in close proximity to one another and to management. The digital revolution of the 1980s and 1990s removed the necessity of such concentration. Consequently, many insurance companies decentralized their operations and moved out of Hartford. By 2010, Hartford's population had decreased 30 percent from its 1950 peak, and about 32 percent of the remaining population was living below the poverty line. Hartford's decline was not due to a slump in the insurance sector but to a technology change that in turn had an impact on location requirements. Of course, land use planners had no way to anticipate the changes affecting the insurance companies. However, if they had tried to diversify the type of activities authorized by land use regulations, they may have attracted other industries or services that would have reduced the chances of long-term unemployment for insurance industry workers.

Land Use Change: Hong Kong

Changes in employment location and land requirements are not limited to changes in a particular sector of a city's economy, as was the case for Hartford. The disappearance of some economic sectors and the emergence of new ones may also cause changes in employment location. These rapid changes in economic trends require equally rapid changes in land use if the urban labor market is to keep functioning through the transition and avoid the costly mistakes made in Mumbai's mills.

For example, by the early 1960s, Hong Kong's textile manufacturing industry was the most successful in Asia. In 1980, the percentage of Hong Kong workers still employed in the manufacturing industry represented 46 percent of total employment, and the manufacturing sector represented 24 percent of Hong Kong's nominal gross domestic product (GDP). By 2010, manufacturing had fallen to 1.8 percent of GDP, and employment in manufacturing had been reduced to 3.4 percent of total employment.

This drastic change in the share of the manufacturing sector over 20 years required an equally drastic change in land use and job location. Manufacturing jobs in Hong Kong were largely replaced by new jobs in the service sector. But the location and land requirements of the service sector are completely different from those of the manufacturing sector. The replacement of manufacturing employment by service employment could not be done simply by replacing factories with office buildings. Instead, because Hong Kong planners were often the lessors of office space (and therefore exposed directly to market pricing), they were able to understand market demands to completely reallocate land use and modify urban transport to adapt to a new spatial pattern of job concentration.

These changes in Hong Kong's economy were not the result of deliberate plans made by Hong Kong planners but were imposed from the outside by geopolitical changes, such as the opening of mainland China's economy. The spectacular achievements of Hong Kong urban planners in managing land use changes were not because they had made plans in advance to change land use. Instead, once these economic changes imposed by the world's economy had become clear, they reacted rapidly to adjust the city land use and infrastructure to the new economy.

The Role of Markets in Historical Preservation
Historical preservation is one of the few exceptions for which urban managers might want to prevent the spontaneous land recycling caused by market forces. Historical heritage buildings are fossil buildings produced by ancient market forces. Preserving the highest-quality buildings of the past has many economic and cultural justifications. Conserving historical buildings against market forces seems to contradict the lessons gained from the case studies that I have just discussed. There are important differences, however. The objective of historical preservation is to preserve high-quality buildings rather than a specific type of land use. Indeed, the best way to preserve historical buildings is to allow a new type of utilization that will be compatible with conservation while also providing the new users with a location that is compatible with their businesses' activities.

There are many successful examples of well-preserved historical buildings sheltering successful modern activities: the historical center of Bologna, whose medieval and Renaissance buildings became the prestigious headquarters for banks and retail enterprises; SoHo–Cast Iron Historic District in New York, where the textile sweatshops and printing shops were replaced by artist lofts and high-end retail; Chinatown, next to Singapore's financial district, where traditional restaurants were gradually upgraded to adapt to a business clientele and where small manufacturing workshops were changed into offices for small consultancy firms.

In all these examples, the conservation of existing historical buildings involved a significant change in the use of the floor space inside the buildings. The higher rents charged for the new land use covered the higher maintenance costs required by historical buildings and ensured their preservation.

Design Complements Markets in Shaping Cities

We have seen that market mechanisms are effective in increasing the urban land supply, transforming land use, and setting the quantity of land and floor space consumed and the height of buildings. Markets shape cities through land price variations in space and time. Markets are therefore only effective when land and building transactions are taking place at regular intervals. However, the land occupied by streets and public open space—what economists call public goods—is never subject to market transactions. Consequently, top-down design is the only way to allocate land to streets and to public open space.

Design, as opposed to the blindness of markets, implies the existence of a rational designer, a human control behind the process directing the creation of designed objects. A designer creates objects that meet explicit objectives and functions.[5] In contrast with shapes created by markets, shapes created by design are permanent and are incapable of spontaneous evolution until they are destroyed or modified by a new iteration of rational design. Modifying designed shapes requires the deliberate intervention of a rational designer.

Why Road Networks and Public Open Space Are Not Provided through Market Mechanisms

Why can't street networks be built by the private sector, and therefore, be subject to market forces? There are two reasons for this apparent impossibility. First, major roads need to be aligned and to follow a pre-established path often dictated by topography or by the geometry of a road network. Therefore, there is no possible competition among multiple sellers and multiple buyers to acquire the land required for road rights-of-way; the government must intervene to acquire land through eminent domain, not through a free market transaction. Second, once a road network has been built, it is impractical to allocate and to recover its cost from beneficiaries, since not only roads users but also landowners benefit from better accessibility and hence increased land values.

However, because of improvements in technology, it might soon be possible to generalize the recovery of congestion tolls on most major roads by pricing road usage differently at different times of day. The income from tolls might or might not be able to recover the capital costs incurred in building roads, but at least they should be able to adjust supply and demand in the use of roads. Although the tolls may provide an incentive to create more roads, there will still be no supply and demand mechanism that would automatically increase supply where demand is high in the same way that market forces adjust for consumer goods (e.g., for smartphones).

The same problem occurs with the provision of public open space. On occasion, the private sector can provide and maintain parks and public open spaces, but private provision alone cannot ensure supply in adequate quantity to respond to demand. In addition, a government is more likely than a private developer to provide public access to privileged topographic areas, like sea frontages, lakes, forests, hills, and mountains—only a government can provide the possibility of free public access to these exceptional environmental assets. Because the land market price of such assets is likely to be high, it would normally be impractical for the private sector to provide free access. In addition, there is usually a consensus across cultures that such exceptional assets should belong to an entire nation and not be parceled out to private individuals who could bar access to the public.

Consequently, we cannot rely on market mechanisms to supply major roads and public open space. The quantity, location, and standards of roads and public open space have to be designed by government. There is no possibility of supply elasticity when demand is high (e.g., the quantity of roads cannot be increased when demand for roads in a specific location becomes very high). Government has to substitute design for markets to ensure an adequate supply of all public goods, including roads. An adequate supply of urban roads is particularly important, as roads provide the indispensable mobility that allows labor markets to function and cities to exist.

Eventually, governments have to use the power of eminent domain to purchase land for road alignment to link together local, privately built road segments. While the government may well compensate landowners for their land at an equivalent market price, the acquisition of the land under eminent domain is not a market operation. There is only one buyer: the government, and the seller of the land has no choice but to sell, regardless of whether she is willing to do so.

Increasingly, governments are using contracts with private firms to build major, discrete lengths of road or rail infrastructure. These build-operate-transfer (BOT) or build-operate-own-transfer (BOOT) contracts, however, do not in any way remove the primary responsibility from the government for initiating the design, deciding on the specifications, and imposing the contractual arrangement. In BOT or BOOT arrangements, the government is always the initiator. Therefore, regardless of a BOT contract, the outcome is the same: A major road is always the product of government design, not of market mechanisms, even when a private contractor builds it, maintains it, and collects tolls from its users.

When goods are provided through markets, a high demand for goods will automatically trigger a supply response; eventually, production quantities and prices will reach a supply and demand equilibrium. By contrast, when goods like roads or parks are provided by a government's design, high demand creates congestion, but it does not increase the supply of additional roads or parks.

Urban Road Networks Made of Privately Developed Access Roads Results in Poor Metropolitan Road Networks

So far, cities have yet to find a way to entirely rely on the private sector to design, finance, and operate a metropolitan network of roads without any government intervention.

It is important to distinguish the provision of local access roads from a road network serving an entire metropolitan area. Private developers routinely provide roads in or at the edges of their property lines. Eventually, ownership of these access roads is typically transferred to a local authority and, later, integrated into the public domain to form a network of interconnected streets. An aggregation of originally privately developed roads constitutes the core of many cities, and the two maps shown in figure 3.2 illustrate this process well. The street networks in the Wall Street area in the historical core of New York and in the Marais neighborhood of Paris have many similarities. The street networks followed original property lines with some internal subdivision created by the original developers. They each constitute a nonhierarchical network, providing access to adjacent properties, but not providing road networks or overall mobility across a large metropolitan area. The aggregation of privately built access roads does not constitute a metropolitan network that would allow the labor market to function in the way described in chapter 2.

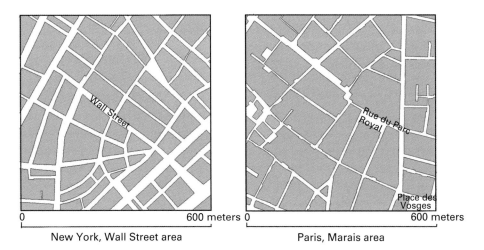

New York, Wall Street area   Paris, Marais area

Figure 3.2
Street patterns in New York (Wall Street area) and in Paris (Marais).

The New York and Paris neighborhood maps also demonstrate how resilient street networks are once they have been designed. The Wall Street area's street pattern dates from the seventeenth century and the Marais street pattern from the thirteenth century. The buildings in the blocks have been demolished and rebuilt many times since the road network was designed. However, the rights-of-way, setting a limit between public good and private good, have barely changed since they were created centuries ago.

To build an effective citywide circulation network, a city needs to connect these privately built local roads with a government-designed network of major roads, linking various neighborhoods and allowing travel speeds consistent with the efficient functioning of the labor market.

Road Network Entirely Designed by Government

In chapter 5, I discuss in more detail the various shapes that a metropolitan road network can take and the impact of network shapes on land values and urban spatial structures. In this chapter, I will only discuss why government intervention is desirable for the design of a street network.

Early in the history of urbanization, local governments recognized the limitations of creating a street network by simply connecting the residual space left between property lines. In the sixth century B.C., the local governments of several Greek trading ports in Asia Minor developed one of the earliest coherently designed plans separating public and private space in advance of settlements. The plan of Miletus, today in Turkey, shows one of the first known examples[6] in the Mediterranean world of a complete street network designed in advance by a local government (figure 3.3).

Hippodamus, one of the earliest known urban planners, designed the plan of Miletus in the sixth century B.C. Incidentally, Miletus was also the birthplace of Thales, the mathematician and philosopher.

The plan by Hippodamus established the boundaries between public space and private lots. In addition to streets' rights-of-way, Hippodamus also planned the location of public buildings and the amenities that contemporary Greeks considered indispensable to the functioning of a city: an agora (where business, justice, and politics were conducted) and an amphitheater (for the staging of dramas and comedies). Hippodamus selected the site for the theater ahead of time because, contrary to a modern theater, a Greek amphitheater had to be built on a favorable slope to improve acoustics, allow for the carving of terraced bleachers, and reduce construction costs.

The plan of Miletus had two advantages. First, it distinguished clearly and in advance the private areas that could be developed by markets from the areas that would remain unsalable (i.e., public goods). Second, it provided a coherent, well-

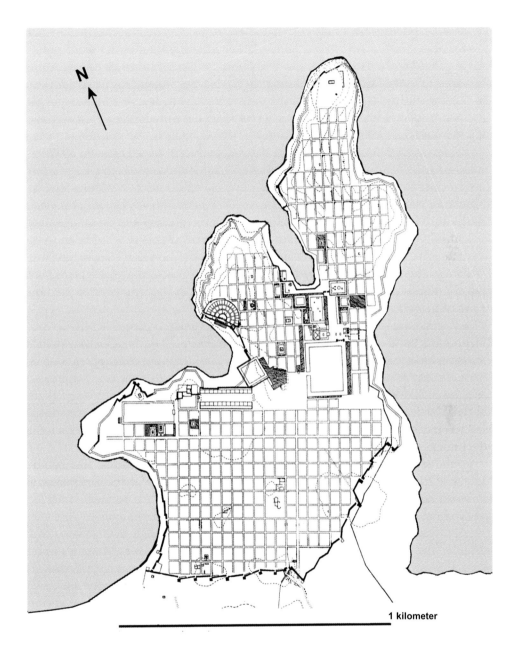

Figure 3.3
Plan of Miletus, sixth century B.C. *Source*: Illustration by A. V. Gerkan and B. F. Weber, 1999, in *The Archaeology of Byzantine Anatolia: From the End of Late Antiquity until the Coming of the Turks*, ed. Philipp Niewöhner (Oxford: Oxford University Press, 2017).

connected, citywide street network that allowed for easy communication among different parts of the city. While Hippodamus identified the locations of public buildings and of the large open space required by the agora, he did not attempt to plan or to control the use of buildings in the private blocks. The excavations of the Miletus site have shown that shops and workshops were built in the areas that anybody familiar with modern land markets could have predicted: along the main axis and near the two ports and the agora.

The design of the street network in Washington, D.C., by L'Enfant in 1792 followed an approach similar to that of Miletus. L'Enfant designed a citywide street pattern and selected the locations of the principal government buildings, but he abstained to exert any explicit control over the use and development of private lots. Indeed, L'Enfant had no way of knowing that K street would be used mainly for lobbyists' offices or that the political and bureaucratic elite would choose to live mainly in Georgetown, a village located outside the perimeter of his plan. L'Enfant's biographies tell us that he was far from modest, but even so, he did not have the hubris of modern planners who attempt to design and control the type of use of every private block in a city.

The advance design of an entire city's street network, as done in Miletus and Washington, D.C., is a rather rare occurrence in the history of cities. Most cities start as unplanned villages with a street network formed by the aggregation of residual space between property lines, similar to the patterns shown in figure 3.2 for Paris and New York. However, when a city's population becomes larger than, say, 100,000 people, this nonhierarchical street pattern hinders the speed of travel between distant locations in the city. Some cities then plan the extension of their street network to new areas for future urban growth, to avoid the replication ad infinitum of the original village's street pattern. In the nineteenth century, the New York commissioner's plan provided a better-designed extension of the existing street network, adding the famous Manhattan grid to the original "village" pattern of streets, which still exists today in the area south of Houston Street. In a similar way, the extension plan designed by Ildefons Cerdà for Barcelona was added to the original Barri Gòtic ("Gothic Quarter") network, which also still exists today. The objective of both extensions was simply to design the streets' rights-of-way in order to preempt developers from defining the street networks from the residual space left between property lines. However, neither design prescribed specific uses or densities for the private plots delimited by the new road network.

Modifying an existing road network—rather than planning a greenfield extension, as was done in New York and Barcelona—is very difficult and consequently, has occurred rarely in the past. The new street network designed by Georges-

Eugène Haussmann in 1865 for Paris is one of the rare examples of extensive modification of an existing street network. Haussmann's design did not aim to provide an extension to the existing street network but to modify the original network itself by opening major streets across the pattern of narrow medieval lanes that covered most of the city at the time. Haussmann's approach is rare, since the necessary use of eminent domain to relocate houses and business makes it very costly and greatly disrupts the social and economic life of the city during its implementation. Haussmann could implement his plan for Paris because he had the strong support of the emperor, Napoleon III. In a democracy, Haussmann's approach would probably never have been possible. In modern times, the muscular and energetic urban management typical in some Chinese cities allows a restructuration of the street network that I would characterize as neo-Haussmannian.

L'Enfant, Cerdà, and Haussmann designed the new city street layouts of Washington, Barcelona, and Paris, respectively, but each design was limited to the layout of streets and to the location of a few civic monuments. The design was limited to marking out the lines separating public goods—streets and parks—from private goods—private plots. Markets remained the main factor shaping the land use in the blocks between streets. Long after the new streets were built, markets remained responsible for the constant modification of the location of commercial activities and for the changes in residential and job densities.

Land readjustment,[7] used at times in several countries (e.g., Japan, India, South Korea, and Germany) is an alternative to eminent domain to acquire street rights-of-way. Land readjustment requires a strong government involvement in allocating land among original landowners, in particular to make sure that the design of local streets is consistent with a metropolitan-wide network. Land readjustment is currently the most common mode of land development in the largest cities in the State of Gujarat in India. While land readjustment does not involve the use of eminent domain, the resulting street network is the result of design based on norms and urban planners' decisions, not on market mechanisms.

Because there is no known market mechanism for creating a network of streets that consistently corresponds to changing demands for accessibility and transport, planners play an important role in designing street layouts in advance of urbanization. L'Enfant, Cerdà, and Haussmann had no knowledge of the future densities in the areas served by the streets they designed. But their choices of street widths and block lengths, however arbitrary, were beneficial in the absence of a market alternative. The designed networks separated, clearly and in advance, public nonsalable land from private land and enabled land markets to work more efficiently by removing uncertainty regarding the location of new streets.

Tracing streets in Yemeni cities in advance of urban development.

From 1970 to 1973, I was an urban planner in Sana'a, Yemen. It is there that I experienced firsthand the urgency of developing a street network in advance of urbanization.

I had been sent by the United Nations Development Programme (UNDP), to work for the Government of Yemen as an "urban planning adviser." There had never been an urban planning department in the history of Yemen before my arrival. My direct bosses were the minister of Public Works and his deputy. To form the embryo of an Urban Planning Department in the ministry, I was asked to hire a staff among high school graduates.

The civil war that gave rise to the Yemen Arab Republic had ended just 2 years before my arrival. During those 2 years, the country had begun to open to the outside world for the first time in its history, triggering a massive urbanization process.

Sana'a, the capital city, was still largely a medieval city, lacking piped water supply or sewage lines. Its population was still small, about 100,000 people. The United Nations estimated that it was growing at a rapid pace of 7 percent per year (a figure later confirmed by formal surveys and census). Forty-seven years later, Sana'a has a population of about 2 million people, and its suburbs expand into the fertile Sana'a valley as well as the slopes of an extinct volcano located on the city's eastern side.

During my time there, the main urbanization problem was not the growth of slums—Yemeni are skilled masons who build sturdy houses out of stones, bricks, or adobe—but the development of far-flung large new settlements. Many of these settlements did not link to any system of roads, a necessary infrastructure component in a city whose population was doubling every 10 years.

My most urgent duty was clearly not to write reports to the minister about how Sana'a should develop, but to create a system to rapidly separate public space from private space in advance of urbanization. In Sana'a I would have to play the exalted role that L'Enfant played in Washington, DC, and Cerdà in Barcelona, but in an extremely modest way, as I had no draftsmen, no surveyors, and no topographical map of the area to be developed. But I did have a set of aerial photographs recently taken by the United Nations, a transit (a simple optical surveying instrument), and a couple of measuring tapes.

It was clear that just designing a plan for the extension of Sana'a and having it approved by the government would not produce any change on the ground. To have an impact, I would have to use the land itself as my drafting board, drawing streets directly on the ground with the agreement of the farmers and tribal chiefs who owned this land.

The challenge was to transfer a simple conceptual plan from a piece of paper to a network of actual streets. Tracing over the aerial photographs, I made a map of the main future arterial roads. To do so, I sought out the layout of existing rural tracks, identified the fastest developing areas, and made a rapid sketch of the network of streets for areas of about a square kilometer at a time.

(continued)

Figure 3.4
The author, with his two assistants, tracing new streets in Yemen, 1970.

The minister and his deputy were extremely supportive of my direct approach. They were practical men with no experience or taste for bureaucracy, and they understood the urgency of creating a major road network. Through the Ministry of Public Works, I managed to contact groups of landowners in the area where new streets were to be traced. Daily I would present to each group of landowners my preliminary sketch for roads pinned to a board. I then explained the principle of the road network for the area and how it would be connected to the city's main arterial network. They were all aware of the advantage of having their lots connected to a designed, surfaced network. They sometime requested modification of my initial sketch when it was designed on the ground, and often argued between themselves about the merits of some street alignments, but they usually agreed on a final layout after a few hours of discussion. They also greatly appreciated my innocence as a foreigner; I clearly had no monetary interest in the outcome, and they readily accepted me as an honest broker in the matter.

Figure 3.4 illustrates the rudimentary surveying exercise preceding the tracing of new urban roads in Yemen in 1970. The Land Rover shown on the photograph was also an essential tool for tracing roads with its wheels in the dry clay of the fields and stone hills.

The first implementation stage was to trace the axes of streets directly onto the ground, using the transit tool to trace straight lines. My assistants then poured lime along the axis line. The landowners would then discuss the width of street. The wider the street, the more land they would lose; alternatively, they also understood that

(continued)

(continued)

---

wide streets would enhance the value of their lots. After some discussion, we agreed on a width, and we drew two parallel lines that became the limits of the new street's right-of-way.

I traced quite a number of streets during the first 2 years of my stay in Yemen. During my third year, the ministry recognized the importance of tracing new streets and hired trained surveyors from other countries of the Middle East, thus amplifying the efforts (and relieving me from drawing streets on the ground).

I wrote several reports on housing, densities, and transport recommendations regarding the development of Sana'a, but I am convinced that tracing streets—the task of separating public space from private space in advance of urban development— was certainly the activity that had the highest rate of return for the urbanization of the city. Looking now at a Google Earth image of Sana'a, I can still see some of these streets, now asphalted and densely lined with buildings.

Planners Attempt to Shape Cities beyond Designing Street Layouts

For some planners, however, limiting planning to the design of a street layout is not ambitious enough. Although the quantity of land allocated to different urban private uses is more appropriately determined by markets, planners believe they can significantly improve it through design. Their lack of information about future users' requirements does not deter them from extending their design activities from road networks to private blocks, thus substituting themselves for markets.

Some land uses have obvious negative impact on neighbors—like allowing a lead smelter to be built next to a school—and planners are legitimately called on to separate these incompatible uses. But such incompatible uses are few in a modern city and easily identifiable. Planners have taken the nuisance issue much further by trying to systematically control not only what activity can take place on private plots but also what height and area of floor space can be built on it. The ways that planners now attempt to reverse past controls and restrictions likely best highlight why this is folly:

• Planners use new regulations to allow mixed land use in many residential areas, where past regulations were aiming precisely at segregating various uses, like commerce and residence.

• Planners use transit-oriented development (TOD) aimed at increasing FAR around transit stations. If FAR had not been regulated around the stations in the first place, they would have long ago reached the level corresponding to demand in these areas. However, TOD could benefit from coordinated urban design to provide better pedestrian access to public transport. TOD is a good example of the arbitrariness that characterizes modern land use planning: a new regulation to correct the effect of an older regulation to obtain the exact outcome that would have been achieved if the first regulation had not existed!

Fortunately, planners' advance designs for entire cities, including every building in the city, are relatively rare and mainly pertain to new capitals. However, the concept of planner design as a substitute for markets is creeping into most urban regulations, implicitly setting land and floor space consumption both through minimum plot and floor area regulations and through maximum FARs. When substituting design for markets, the negative impact on the welfare of inhabitants is not trivial. I show in chapter 6 how planners' detailed designs by regulatory proxy are mostly responsible for the terrible environmental conditions found in the slums of developing countries.

Utopia and Design Substituting for Markets in Distributing Land and Floor Space

I now give two examples of planners' decisions replacing markets in determining the quantity and heights of buildings. In these examples, markets had no influence on the physical outcome. Consumption of both land and floor space was based, in the first case, on an idiosyncratic design and, in the second, on a pseudoscientific norm. The first example, a design proposed by Le Corbusier in 1925, was an attempt at redesigning the center of Paris to be free from the rule of markets. The second example consists of a simple "scientific" housing design norm used in China before the reforms of 1990; these reforms resulted in replacing normative design by market forces in all new urban residential areas in China.

Design Instead of Markets: Le Corbusier's Plan Voisin for the Paris CBD

In 1925, the architect-planner Le Corbusier proposed to replace the old, traditional center of Paris with a "correctly" designed new center called "Plan Voisin" (figure 3.5).[8] Le Corbusier thought that the primary and overwhelming objective in the building of cities was to give each dwelling an optimum amount of sunlight and immediate access to large parks. Being physiologically similar, he concluded that all humans had the same space and sunlight requirements, hence his repetitive tower design. This project, fortunately never implemented, is typical of the design approach to planning. The quantity of floor space produced and of land developed and the number and size of apartments are not driven by supply and demand but by what the designer thinks is the correct design norm based on perceived "needs." Le Corbusier's doctrine consisted of deliberately ignoring

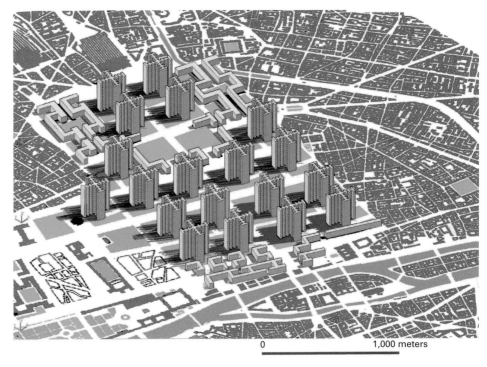

0   1,000 meters

Figure 3.5
Le Corbusier's Plan Voisin for Paris. *Sources*: Paris built-up background map: OpenStreetMap®; Plan Voisin: three-dimensional model by author based on plans and drawings from the "Fondation Le Corbusier" website and from Le Corbusier, *The City of Tomorrow and Its Planning* (New York: Dover Publications, Inc., 1987).

markets and of designing neighborhoods, and even entire cities, based on the norms he selected and on his interpretation of rational human needs.

Counterintuitively, the design approach to urban planning often results in repetitive design, while the market approach results in a variety of designs. This apparent paradox is easy to understand. Design is based on rationality, and rationality has the ambition of being universal. Once the correct, rational design is found, it would be irrational to alter it just for the sake of variety. The Plan Voisin for Paris, shown in figure 3.5, demonstrates this point.

The rational norm argument is useful for designing some manufactured products. For instance, when a rational norm is found for the design of, say, incandescent light bulbs, there is no advantage to endlessly tweaking the norm; repetition of the same design results in a big advantage for all. But incandescent light bulbs have a simple function and a simple objective, about which everyone can agree. By contrast, cities are extremely complex objects inhabited by extremely diverse human beings, whose preferences and circumstances change over time. Consequently, the design of cities cannot be reduced to a simple objective—be that optimum access to sunlight and parks or some other worthy objective. Markets are messy and, indeed, are only muddling toward constantly moving states of equilibrium. However, markets, even when working imperfectly, can easily integrate the complexity of information required to shape cities.

While the Plan Voisin was never implemented, Le Corbusier's ideas had an immense influence on city planning during the second half of the twentieth century. His ideas were given international and universal legitimacy through the periodic meetings of the CIAM[9] and the publication of the "Charte d'Athènes," which promoted his design concept of high residential towers implanted in parks to optimize access to natural light and green areas. The ideological message was that scientific design should replace markets in allocating land and floor space consumption. This message fit well with intellectuals' attraction to totalitarian ideology, which was unfortunately widely shared during most of the twentieth century.

Le Corbusier's influence was felt less through the design of new cities and more through land use regulations and the design of public housing. Practically all housing projects built in the Soviet Union and in China before 1980 were based on norms with foundations in Le Corbusier's concepts. In the liberal democracies of Western Europe and North America, Le Corbusier's influence was limited to the design of large, government-sponsored public housing projects, for instance, Sarcelles in the northern suburbs of Paris and the Pruitt–Igoe housing project in St. Louis, Missouri. The repetitive design of public housing buildings is not due to a lack of architectural skill but to a "design" based on a mythical optimum norm, used as a substitute for markets and pretending to represent universal values. This supposed universal system leads to many negative externalities when confronted with real life. For example, the monotony of the design leads to disaffection for the neighborhood, and lack of access to necessities (like grocery stores and transport) that would have been normally provided through markets creates additional costs for the residents.

Through his books and conferences, Le Corbusier clearly expressed his view that the main objective of urban planning and architecture should be to maximize access to sunlight and to parks and open space. But to my knowledge, he never attempted to optimize his ideas through mathematical formulas. However, his followers in China tried to do just that.

Design Replacing Markets: Chinese Residential Areas, 1960–1985
Having rejected market mechanisms and real estate transactions based on price, countries guided by Marxist ideology had to find a different way to allocate land to various users. Marxists claimed that rationality and science formed the base of

their ideology. It was therefore natural that Chinese urban planners tried to find a universal "scientific" rule to allocate land in residential areas in a country as large and diverse as China.

An urban regulation established in China in the 1950s specified that at least one room per apartment should be able to receive a minimum of 1 hour of sunlight on the day of the winter solstice (December 21), when the sun is at its lowest in the northern hemisphere.[10] This rule was applied to government and enterprise housing built between 1950 and the mid-1980s. While this rule is no longer applied in China, the housing stock built during the 30-year pre-reform period is still largely intact, and it is worth exploring the impact that this design rule has had on the spatial structure of Chinese cities.

At first sight, this single design requirement seems innocuous. Nobody would argue against sunlight. For central planners, substituting scientific rationalism for the messy and unpredictable outcome of markets provides a powerful legitimacy. In addition, a uniform norm for the entire country gives the impression of equality under the law. The norm was used as a rule when designing municipal housing estates or for housing built by state enterprises for their workers. The remnants of these housing estates are trading at the low end of the market and can still be seen in Chinese cities, designated popularly as "danwei housing."

Because the norm had to be used by local governments, every household living at the same latitude would consume the same amount of land, and regardless of that latitude, every household would enjoy a minimum of 1 hour of sunlight every day. The whimsical, idiosyncratic design aspect of Le Corbusier's Plan Voisin disappears and is replaced by a simple mathematical formula (equation 3.1).

A regulation expressed through a mathematical formula linked to the movement of the sun appears to have scientific and universal legitimacy. In reality, it is only pseudoscientific. Even though the height of the sun at noon on the winter solstice at a given latitude is an indisputable, scientific fact, 1 hour of sun exposure per day in one room per apartment is not an established scientific necessity.

Equation 3.1

Equation 3.1 is a mathematical formula for calculating the distance between buildings that allows a minimum of 1 hour of direct sunlight per unit per day for each unit in a building. The distance d between buildings is determined by the height of building h multiplied by the tangent of the angle α of the sun on the winter solstice at 11:30 in the morning using solar time:

$$d = h \tan(\alpha.\pi/180). \tag{3.1}$$

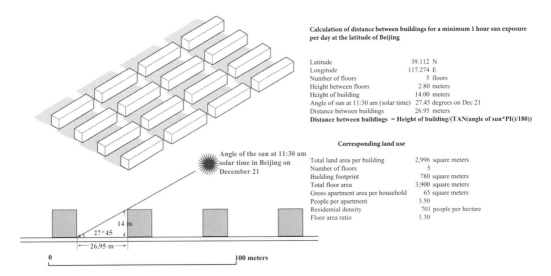

Calculation of distance between buildings for a minimum 1 hour sun exposure
per day at the latitude of Beijing

Latitude	39.112 N
Longitude	117.274 E
Number of floors	5 floors
Height between floors	2.80 meters
Height of building	14.00 meters
Angle of sun at 11:30 am (solar time)	27.45 degrees on Dec 21
Distance between buildings	26.95 meters

Distance between buildings = Height of building/(TAN(angle of sun*PI()/180))

Corresponding land use

Total land area per building	2,996 square meters
Number of floors	5
Building footprint	780 square meters
Total floor area	3,900 square meters
Gross apartment area per household	65 square meters
People per apartment	3.50
Residential density	701 people per hectare
Floor area ratio	1.30

Angle of the sun at 11:30 am
solar time in Beijing on
December 21

14 m
27°45
26.95 m

0   100 meters

Figure 3.6
Distance between buildings in China, determined by the angle of the sun on the winter solstice.

The "1 hour of sun" rule sets the distance between apartment blocks for every city in the country and makes this distance dependent on the city's latitude. Figure 3.7 illustrates the implication of using such a formula for allocating land to housing at the latitude of Beijing. The sun requirement implicitly sets the distance between buildings based on their height. Most housing blocks in China had five stories[11] during the period when this rule was used, the norm therefore inevitably fixed the ratio between floor space and land for every other number of floors. The table in Figure 3.7 shows the required distance between five-story buildings as dictated by the norm at Beijing's latitude. That distance, in turn, fixed the population density that could be housed by estimating an average floor space per apartment. The solar norm, therefore, implicitly mandated for Beijing latitude, for instance, a density of 700 people per hectare, assuming a gross floor space of 65 m^2 per household and 3.5 persons per household.

In addition, figure 3.6 shows the predictable repetitive site plan that such a regulation produces. As we have already observed with Le Corbusier's Paris plan, a scientific design norm inevitably results in uniformity. By contrast, markets are more likely to create variety in individual designs, as each supplier tries to innovate in an effort to capture a larger share of consumer demand.

The implications for urban forms of this alleged rational norm are staggering. First, it implicitly sets the same area of land consumed per area of floor space built for every location at the same latitude, regardless of whether a location is in a

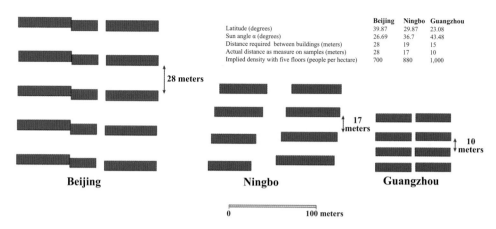

	Beijing	Ningbo	Guangzhou
Latitude (degrees)	39.87	29.87	23.08
Sun angle α (degrees)	26.69	36.7	43.48
Distance required between buildings (meters)	28	19	15
Actual distance as measure on samples (meters)	28	17	10
Implied density with five floors (people per hectare)	700	880	1,000

Figure 3.7
Application of the sun rule—footprint of danwei housing in Beijing, Ningbo, and Guangzhou.

large city or a small one, in the center of a city or in a suburb. Second, it implies that more land should be used to produce one unit of floor space at northern latitudes than at southern latitudes. Or, in other words, it suggests that densities should be lower in Beijing and higher in Hainan! If this rule was applied to the United States, it would prescribe that the densities of Chicago and New York should be much lower than those of Houston and Phoenix.

When I was working on housing reform in China in the 1980s, this norm was constantly cited as a main constraint by my Chinese counterparts when discussing the possibility of looking for an alternative housing design that would make more efficient use of land. But was this design approach really followed in all housing projects in China?

From a limited survey of sample site plans in Chinese cities selected at various latitudes, it appears that indeed this norm was widely applied: in Beijing (latitude 39.9° N), Ningbo (latitude 29.9° N), and Guangzhou (latitude 23.1° N), with greater variation toward higher densities in cities farther away from Beijing (figure 3.7). Indeed, the densities vary with the latitude: higher densities in lower latitudes. The table in figure 3.7 shows the variations between the actual building distances and those prescribed by strict application of the 1-hour rule.

After the market reforms of the 1980s, Chinese municipalities rapidly abandoned the allocation of land through design norms and replaced it with a more pragmatic approach, relying on the market price obtained through auction of land use rights. Post-reform Chinese cities had a strong incentive to abandon the wasteful, normative use of urban land, because they derived a large part of their revenue from the market price sale of land use rights to developers. In spite of having been abandoned, the use of this regulatory norm still had an enormous impact on the structure of Chinese cities. That impact is typical of the unintended consequences of many land use regulations. In chapter 6, I discuss additional examples of regulatory impact on urban forms in greater detail.

Design Extended to the Private Blocks of Entire Cities

Very few cities have been designed in their entirety, including street layouts and buildings, with no provisions made for land use to be modified by market forces in the future. Illustrative attempts to control everything through design—examples like New Delhi, India; Brasília, Brazil; Canberra, Australia; or Chandigarh, India—are very different in concept from Miletus, Washington, or Haussmann's Paris.

In addition to the street networks for these cities, planners imposed detailed regulations specific to each private block. These regulations were so detailed they essentially designed each block's buildings. They specified the use of land, the size of lots, the height of buildings, the area of dwellings, the lot coverage, among other things. These planner-designed regulations completely prevented market forces from contributing to the shape of the city.

Figure 3.8 shows detailed plans of residential areas in Chandigarh and Brasília. Originally, every building—whether a community facility, an apartment block, or a commercial area—was designed in advance through regulations. Nothing was

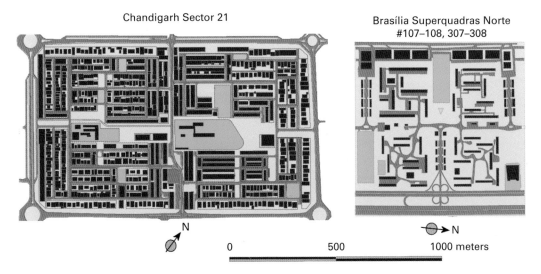

Figure 3.8
The design of buildings in a block in Chandigarh (left) and Brasília (right).
Sources: Topographical maps with built-up areas from Department of Urban Planning Chandigarh Administration, 2005, updated with the help of Google Earth satellite imagery, 2008.

left to markets: prices were ignored, FARs were set for every single block, and land was allocated to residential and commercial use based on arbitrary design norms. However, in Chandigarh, the government originally sold leaseholds for housing units and over the years allowed market forces to transform the original housing design. This did not happen in Brasilia.

In chapter 7, I discuss planners' attempts to shape market-driven cities through complex regulations.

The Growth of Pudong: Markets and Design

Many of the examples that I have used so far to illustrate the role of markets and design in the development of cities were taken from the past—the oldest, Miletus, in the sixth century B.C.; the most recent, Chandigarh and Brasília, dating from 1960. Let us look now at markets and design at work using the example of Pudong, the new financial center of Shanghai, built over the past 25 years.

At first sight, design seems to be entirely responsible for the stunning skyline of Pudong, as seen from the west bank of the Huangpu River (figure 3.9). Architectural firms working for developers have designed the unique shape of each skyscraper. The skyline, formed by the sum of each individual building's design, appears also to be the product of design. Paradoxically, this is not the case.

Figure 3.9
Pudong: Shanghai's new financial center.

Pudong Was Created by Market Forces

The skyline of Pudong, as seen in the picture of figure 3.9, was created by the high demand for floor space in this area, reflecting its high accessibility to Shanghai's labor force. Developers, anticipating a high demand for office space at a price point higher than building costs (including the cost of land), initiated, and financed the building of skyscrapers.

Tall, thin buildings constitute a large part of the skyline's aesthetic attraction. A concentration of tall buildings is always the product of market forces. In Pudong, due to high demand, land is expensive, and as such, developers are obliged to substitute capital for land by building tall buildings. Tall buildings are more expensive to build per square meter of floor space than are squat buildings. However, each additional floor built decreases the cost of land per unit of floor space. Therefore, where land is expensive, the high price of land obliges developers to substitute capital for land by constructing taller buildings. In aggregate, therefore, the skyscrapers of Pudong are not created by design but by market forces. In the absence of market demand for office space, there would be no skyscrapers. If land had been cheap in Pudong, there would have been no skyscrapers, only squat office buildings of 3 or 4 stories as are seen in suburban office parks!

Developers hired architects to design individual buildings on specific plots of land. They told the architects how much floor space they had to accommodate on each land parcel. Variations in the height and shape of a building depend both on the shape of the original lot and on the financial risk a developer is willing to take in projecting demand and sale prices. The first buildings in Pudong were only moderately high. When the demand for office space in Pudong became more firmly established, land prices increased and developers became bolder. Ready to take more financial risk, developers commissioned architects to build taller, more expensive buildings. Thus, the variety of building heights, shapes, and textures, which define Pudong's aesthetic quality, is the product of market forces; however, the design ability of individual architects is still apparent in each building.

Markets produce a great variety of designs because economic conditions change over time and therefore require different designs. In addition, innovative designs in newer developments attract tenants or buyers through more attractive buildings. Markets imply competition; competition stimulates innovation in technology and design. Compare Pudong's skyline to the Le Corbusier Plan Voisin for Paris shown in figure 3.5. The diversity of building shapes and heights in Pudong suggests markets, while the uniformity of building shapes and heights in Paris's Plan Voisin, Chandigarh, and Brasília suggest government design. However, Pudong could not have been built without some initial infrastructure design provided by government.

Design Contribution to the Development of Pudong Financial District

While market forces were responsible for the construction of skyscrapers in Pudong, the design and construction of roads, bridges, tunnels, and underground metro lines were responsible for the changes in land prices that triggered these market forces.

Pudong is located on the east bank of the Huangpu River, about 500 meters across the river from "the Bund," the traditional CBD of Shanghai. Before 1991, ferries provided the only link between Pudong and the rest of Shanghai, and Shanghai had no underground metro before 1993. Because of its poor accessibility and lack of infrastructure, Pudong was only partially developed with a few low-rise industrial buildings and warehouses linked to the port (map on left in figure 3.10). Agricultural land still occupied large areas east of the river, less than 2 kilometers from the Shanghai CBD. In the 1980s, the demand for new office buildings in Shanghai was mostly met along an east-west corridor between the traditional CBD and the old Hongqiao Airport. The poor accessibility of Pudong kept land prices low, which explained the prevalence of low-rise, low-value buildings.

The land in Pudong started to increase in value in 1991, after the municipal government decided to build the first bridge across the Huangpu River, linking "the Bund" and Pudong. Eventually, the construction of two more bridges, four road tunnels, and four underground metro lines put Pudong within a few minutes of Shanghai's traditional CBD (map on right in figure 3.10). The increased accessibility of the new Pudong financial district, combined with the dynamism of

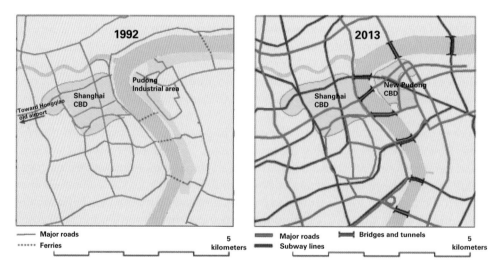

Figure 3.10
The design and construction of roads and subway links to Pudong, 1992 and 2013.

Shanghai's economy, increased demand for office space in the area, further raising land values and triggering the construction of the skyscrapers that gave shape to today's stunning skyline.

By themselves, roads, bridges, and tunnels do not increase land values; they do so only if they provide access to land for which there is a potentially high demand. In the case of Pudong, the designers of the bridges and tunnels correctly anticipated the reaction of markets to the increased accessibility created by the new transport infrastructure.

The infrastructure linking Pudong to the rest of Shanghai was created by design, not by market forces, but the anticipated increases in land market value in Pudong guided the design and justified the government's investment. Markets could not have provided the transport infrastructure linking Pudong to the rest of Shanghai, because the beneficiaries of this infrastructure were dispersed throughout the entire city and because no direct cost recovery was possible except through some form of government taxation. The development of Pudong illustrates perfectly the complementary roles of markets and design in the most successful cities, particularly designs to facilitate expansion. The government let the price of land determine both the building heights and FARs while providing the large infrastructure investment that was required for the price of land to reach its full potential, given the short distance between Pudong and the Bund. Government planners in the case of Pudong understood the mechanism of markets. They designed and built the infrastructure that would maximize the value of land across the river and support the densities created by markets.

Urban Managers Should Understand How Markets and Design Interact to Allow Cities to Adjust to Change

Confusion between Market and Design: The Planning of Densities

Planners who advocate "smart growth" dream of a clever design arrangement that would achieve an optimum trade-off between land consumption and commuting distance. They usually advocate designs with higher population densities[12] to reduce commuting distances. If densities are the object of design, then there must be "good densities" and "bad densities," just as there is "good design" and "bad design."

In the real world, it is only markets that determine land and floor consumption and, therefore, population densities. Indeed, households' decisions concerning their consumption of land and floor space are based on prices and locations, which themselves are based on supply and demand, the variations of which are determined by the market. The area of floor space that a household consumes is dependent on its income (the demand side) and on the price of floor space and the cost of commuting (the supply side). The equilibrium between supply and demand for floor space evolves over time and certainly cannot possibly depend on the design choice of a well-intentioned planner.

For instance, densities in historical parts of New York, Paris, and Shanghai have decreased over time by more than half. These changes in densities are entirely due to market mechanisms, reflecting, in part, improvements in transport and increases in income. These changes in densities could have been foreseen or expected, but they could not have been designed.

This distinction between markets and design has practical, operational implications in the management of cities. Imagine a city in which the mayor considers it a priority to increase the consumption of floor space per household (as was the case in Chinese cities in the 1980s). If we agree that consumption is a market issue, then planners could consider several possible solutions based on market mechanisms that would increase consumption. For instance, planners could increase the supply of developed land by increasing the speed of transport so that more land could be opened for development; they could lower the cost of construction by increasing the productivity of the building industry or by decreasing the transactions costs linked to building permits and land acquisition. Planners could also use a demand side approach, stimulating demand by increasing access to mortgage credit or even by indirectly causing an increase in salaries by opening the city to outside investments in manufacturing or services. All these measures are likely to contribute to an increase in housing consumption per household. Incidentally, the Chinese government took all these steps in the period of reform starting in the late 1990s, resulting in a nine-fold increase in urban housing consumption from 1978 to 2015!!

By contrast, a design solution to increase the average consumption of floor space might establish a minimum regulatory house size to prevent developers from building small houses, or it would require the government to subsidize and build a sufficient number of large apartments for low-income households every year. As the consumption of floor space is a market outcome, design solutions, which aim to increase consumption, never work in the long run. I will discuss this design failure in detail in chapter 7.

Links between Markets, Design, and Urban Indicators

A simple schematic flowchart (figure 3.11), whose inputs and outputs can be calculated in a simple spreadsheet, could help differentiate the role of markets and design in the development of cities. The flowchart should be helpful for understanding the mathematical relationships among people, jobs, floor space, land, and road infrastructure in the framework that I have been using: differentiating between markets and design.

From this flowchart, we will be able to derive the three most important urban indicators that will allow for monitoring spatial changes and comparing different urban spatial structures. The three indicators are the population density, the built-up FAR, and the road area per capita.

• The built-up FAR[13] establishes the numbers of units of floor space that are built on one unit of land area, including land used for streets and utilities.

• The population density measures the spatial concentration of people per unit of land, but it is also a measure the consumption of land per person[14] in cities.

• The road space per capita is calculated by dividing the total road area by the total population of a city. The road space per capita is directly linked to mobility and could be used as an indicator to measure the compatibility of street area per person with different modes of transport.

I will show that a city's average population density is entirely dependent on markets and therefore is not subject to planners' designs. The built-up FAR should be entirely determined by markets; however, its maximum value is often constrained by regulations. Some regulatory constraints on FAR or building heights are of course completely legitimate when they are required for heritage protection or for obvious physical constraints such as the proximity of an airport. However, most of FAR regulations are arbitrary. The road space per capita is dependent on both design and markets: road design norms and regulations set by governments and population density determined by markets.

The Organization of the Flowchart Linking Markets and Design Variables
The flowchart shown in figure 3.11 is divided vertically into two streams—markets and design. Columns a and b correspond to the market stream; column d corresponds to the design stream, and column c contains intermediary results and indicators. The flowchart is divided into nine rows of boxes that contain categories like "households" or such formulas as "Population × Residential floor space per capita = Total residential floor area." Arrows indicate the relationship between input and output variables. To identify specific boxes in the flowchart, note that "box 5b," for instance, relates to the box located on row 5 in column b.

Quantities of Private Goods Are Determined by Markets,
While Quantities of Public Goods Depend on Design
The built space of a city contains two types of goods: private goods and public goods (row 3 in figure 3.11). Residential and commercial buildings are private goods. Private goods are bought and sold on the market. For private goods, the quantity and unit price of the floor space built and the land developed depend

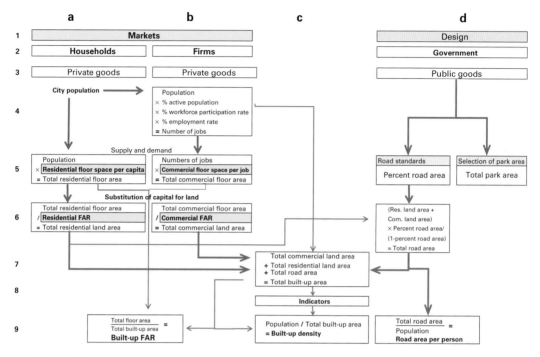

Figure 3.11
Relationship between population, land, and floor space consumption. It is assumed that prices are set by market supply, and demand/supply are constrained by topography and other variables.

on supply and demand (i.e., on markets). By contrast, roads and large public open spaces are usually public goods. Contrary to private goods, the quantity of public goods produced is determined by design, not by markets. Because users do not pay for public goods, it is impossible for markets to determine the quantity that should be produced to reach equilibrium between supply and demand. Instead, governments rely on design standards, projections, and norms to provide the "right quantity" of public goods.

Firms' and Households' Floor and Land Consumption Drive Urbanization, Not Governments or Urban Planners

Firms and households are consumers of private goods. Households consume residential floor space, while firms consume commercial floor space (rows 4, 5, columns a, b in figure 3.11). I have included under the label "firms" all buildings such as offices, shops, warehouses, and factories. Amenities, like museums, theaters, and restaurants function like firms; their employees are part of the labor force, and their patrons are consumers. Less obviously, I have also included under "firms" government-owned and -operated facilities, such as government office buildings, schools, hospitals, jails, and post offices. For the purpose of the labor market, they function exactly as firms. In a school, teachers and staff are the labor; the school is a firm that sells education, a service, to the students, who are the consumers. This is the case even when parents indirectly pay for the service their students consume through their taxes. More generally, I consider all levels of government to be firms; they employ labor that distributes services to their customers, the citizens. For the same reasons, government-owned facilities are under the "market" category, as the real estate they represent should easily be bought, sold, or rented at market price. The fact that only a few governments sell land back to the public or rent buildings from the private sector[15] should not justify putting them in a different category. Nothing should prevent governments from selling or renting land and floor space or from leasing land and floor space from the private sector. It would be quite healthy for governments to routinely assess the capital values of their land holdings and to estimate whether they are using urban land efficiently.[16]

Let us now look at the linkage between variables. We will have two streams of quantitative relationships: the first one concerning the provision of private goods through market forces, the second concerning the provision of public goods through government design.

The Driver of Urbanization: Number of People and Jobs
(Row 4, Columns a and b)
The first input is the city population (row 4), which is exogenous in the flowchart. The size of the population determines both the number of people who will consume residential floor space and the number of workers consuming commercial floor space. The population multiplied by the percentage of active population (people between 16 and 65 years old) times the labor participation rate[17] times the employment rate is equal to the number of jobs. In the flowchart, this would be equal to the number of workers requiring commercial floor space.

Market, Independent Variable: Consumption of Floor Space per capita
(Row 5, Columns a and b)
Firms and households consume floor space. The consumption of floor space per person and per worker depends on supply and demand. This consumption is not fixed but varies constantly, depending on economic conditions. Most regulations set minimum norms for floor consumption based on "optimum" design, but in reality, the floor area actually consumed is entirely defined by that which firms and households can afford, given their incomes and the current land and construction prices. Land and construction prices depend on the supply of land and on

the productivity of the real estate industry. The consumption of floor space per person and per worker is therefore purely determined by markets; it is not a design parameter.

Population multiplied by residential floor space per person provides the total area of residential floor space. The number of jobs times the commercial floor space per worker is equal to the total area of commercial floor space. We can see that the total floor space, residential and commercial, built in a city depends entirely on markets and is not subject to design. This total floor space will change with time, depending on population and market conditions. The prosperity of a city depends on the elasticity of the supply of floor space as economic and demographic conditions change. The quantity of floor space cannot be contingent on a fixed design established in advance by a master plan.

Market, Independent Variable: FAR, the Substitution of Capital for Land (Row 6, Columns a and b)
The area of land required for building the total floor area (calculated in boxes 5a and 5b in figure 3.11) depends on the FARs for residential and commercial areas, as discussed at the beginning of this chapter. The FAR depends on the price of land relative to the price of construction. If a unit of land is more expensive than a unit of construction, then it will be necessary to substitute capital for land (i.e., build taller buildings with higher FARs). The FAR is therefore a parameter best set by markets. However, planners often restrict FARs because of the possible negative externalities generated by tall buildings.

Total residential floor area divided by the residential FAR will be equal to the total area of residential land. We will do the same operation for the commercial floor area to obtain the total area of commercial land. As we have seen, these two areas depend entirely on market conditions. In cities where the FAR is heavily restricted by regulations (i.e., by design), land consumption will be higher per person or per worker than in cities where it is not.

The Flow of Public Goods Is Dependent on Government Design and Investment
The areas occupied by public goods in this model are reduced to two components: total road area and total public open/park area (column d in figure 3.11). Both components are created by design, as there is no known market mechanism that can accurately supply an area of road that corresponds to its demand. The same could be said for large parks and open spaces and for the protection of cultural heritage sites or exceptional environmental assets. The identification of these public goods and the quantities provided can only be done by arbitrary design or norm. Once

the norm has been decided, there will be no market mechanism that can adjust supply or demand. Only a revision of the original design, as arbitrary as the first design decision, can modify the supply of public goods.

Design, Independent Variable: Urban Road Standards (Row 6, Column d)

Governments usually set urban road standards for highways, arterial roads, and secondary and tertiary roads. Master plans, norms, or regulations usually establish the desired distance between each type of road. The result of the various norms can usually be summarized by the percentage of total area developed that must be used for roads. For instance, a norm mandating the creation of a grid system of arterial roads 30 meters wide every 800 meters would implicitly require that 7.6 percent of the total area developed be devoted to arterial roads. In Manhattan's grid, a typical block is 280 meters (920 feet) long with 30-meter- (100-foot)-wide avenues and 18-meter- (60-foot)-wide streets, corresponding to a street area of 33 percent of the total area developed (measured from the four intersections of the axis of streets and avenues). Obviously, the norms for roads are based on rules of thumb and assumptions about the multiple functions of streets: providing light and ventilation for buildings, handling pedestrian and vehicular traffic, providing recreational space and parking, allowing for the planting of trees, and so forth. There is neither a "scientific" nor a market approach for the allocation of land for street space.

In the flowchart in figure 3.11, I assume that the various road regulatory norms are summarized as a single number representing the percentage of the total built-up area (box 5d). This percentage applied to the residential and commercial land area allows for calculating the total road area corresponding to the regulatory norm (box 6d).

Design, Independent Variable: Park and Open Space Standards (Box 6d)

Parks and open spaces are sometimes the object of a regulatory norm in land subdivision regulations, but most of the provisions for parks and open spaces are opportunistic. For instance, a riverbank or sea frontage is often allocated as public space. The quantity of land provided as open space often depends on what I will call topographical or historical opportunities. For instance, in Seoul, most of the public open space has been allocated because of topographical opportunities along the Han River and on the slopes of undevelopable hills. In Paris, by contrast, most of the large open spaces, Bois de Boulogne, Parc de Vincennes, and the Tuileries and Luxembourg gardens, were originally part of the royal domain and were latter transformed into public parks. The area and location of parks in Paris are therefore the results of historical opportunities.

The provision of open space is typically a designed component of urban land use. Because of the idiosyncratic nature of large open spaces, I do not include large parks in the calculation of the built-up areas of cities.

Dependent Variables: Total Consumption of Floor Space and Land and Density Indicators

The demographic, market, and design inputs of the flowchart, as described above, allow us to calculate the dependent variables, which are the total built-up area and the following three indicators:

1. average built-up FAR,
2. average built-up density, and
3. average road area per person.

These indicators are the most important for monitoring the way a city structure evolves over time. Below, I will explain why these indicators are so important and how to use them to monitor the evolution of cities with regard to maintaining affordability and mobility. These indicators measure the impact of the combined effect of markets and design on a city's structure.

Indicator: Built-Up Average FAR (Boxes 9a and 9b)

The average built-up FAR measures the number of units of floor space that can be built per unit of land. It is the average rate of conversion between land and floor space. As floor space is the real end-product of urban development and land is often the most expensive input needed to produce it, this is a very important urban indicator. The demand for urban land depends sensitively on the value of this indicator. For the same population, a doubling of the average FAR decreases the demand for land by half.

Despite its importance, to my knowledge, the average built-up FAR[18] is never part of a city's urban indicators, and master plans never mention it.

Master plans usually constrain the maximum FAR value on individual private lots in different ways, depending on location (New York's zoning plan has more than 20 different values for maximum FARs in various zoning categories). However, for some reason master plans never aggregate the overall impact of these detailed regulations on the overall demand for land. Therefore, they fail to evaluate the maximum area of floor space that users can legally build in a master plan area. The average FAR is important in planning because it allows forecasting of the demand for land based on the projected demand for floor space and on the design norms for roads.

An increase in average FAR does not always increase population density.

Recently the number of "smart growth" advocates has increased. These advocates think that planners can increase urban population densities simply by increasing regulatory FAR values.

Increasing maximum regulatory FAR values will cause densities to increase only in those areas where FAR regulations have been constraining demand for floor space. An increase in the permitted FAR will have no impact in areas where the ratio between land price and construction cost is low, because in these areas, there will be no reasons to substitute capital for land.

In cities like Mumbai, for instance, where FAR values have been heavily regulated, there is no doubt that an increase in regulatory FAR will greatly increase the number of high-rise buildings. However, the cost of construction of high-rise buildings is much greater than it is for low-rise buildings. In cities that have a significant number of households below the poverty line, like Mumbai, new high-rise buildings would be affordable only for the higher income groups, who will consume much more floor space per capita than lower income groups. This explains why in Mumbai very high residential densities about 1,000 people per hectare are found in horizontal slums, while in high-rise buildings, the density barely reaches 400 people per hectare. This paradoxical situation is explained in detail with a specific examples in chapter 6.

In the central areas of affluent cities like New York or Shanghai, it has been observed that the average FAR increases significantly while the density decreases, because households increase their consumption of floor space faster than the growth in FAR. According to Solly Angel,[1] Manhattan density was 575 people per hectare in 1910 but decreased to 350 people per hectare in 2010, in spite of a proliferation of high-rise residential buildings and the conversion of high-rise office buildings into residential use in the Wall Street area.

Population densities, therefore, depend on several economic factors and are not determined by the design of buildings.

---

1. Shlomo (Solly) Angel and Patrick Lamson-Hall, "The Rise and Fall of Manhattan's Densities 1800–2010," Marron Institute, New York University, New York, 2015.

Indicator: Average Built-Up Population Density (Box 9c)

The average built-up population density is an indicator of land consumption per person. It combines the impact of markets and design (in the form of roads) on the overall consumption of land. Although population density is a routinely measured indicator, planners often consider density as a design option rather than a market outcome.

While population density is a useful indicator to project demand for land in the future, there is no reason to consider higher densities or lower densities as a desirable planning objective. However, higher floor space consumption for at least the poorer segment of the urban population might be a legitimate planning objective. Depending on the FAR, it might result in higher or lower densities.

Indicator: Road Area per Person (Box 9d)
The road area per person is a consumption indicator that depends mostly on markets and partly on design. Because the area of roads usually does not change after they have been designed and built, variations in the road area per person depend mostly on the change in densities, which is a market variable.

The measure of the road area per person is an indicator of potential congestion as commuters consume road space at peak hours to travel to jobs. Because the area of roads cannot be adjusted easily after they have been built, the road area per person is a useful guide for transport system designers. Transport systems should be designed to adjust to current spatial structure, not the other way around, as is often advocated. In chapter 5, I discuss the values of road area per person found in various cities and the corresponding implications for urban transport systems. Let us remember that, except in contemporary Chinese cities, the possibility of increasing the street area of large cities seldom exists; the operation conducted in Paris by Haussmann in the middle of the nineteenth century is extremely rare, because of its financial risk and high social cost.

Building a More Complex Flowchart

The objective in developing the land use flowchart described above (see figure 3.11) was to demonstrate that population densities are the result of market forces, themselves reacting to exogenous events. I recommend that planners make density projections to evaluate, for instance, the likely future demand for land to be converted to urban use. However, planners must base their projections on credible markets scenarios based on income and prices and not on their own design preferences for low or high densities.

To be able to make more credible density projections, planners might want to make the flowchart more complex. For instance, disaggregating the population by income group would allow for differentiation between floor and land consumption for several household-income intervals. In the same way, disaggregating commercial land use into various land use types—retail, office, and industrial—would make the projection more realistic.

Planners Should Understand the Role of Markets and Design in Shaping Cities

Most master plans, prepared at great expense to taxpayers, are often ineffective and soon irrelevant; this is particularly true in cities that are developing fastest. The confusion between the impact of market and that of design is mostly responsible for this dismal record.

Projections Should Not Become Regulations

However, this does not mean that planning based on projections is useless. On the contrary, plans able to project urban growth and mobilize the resources to address this growth are indispensable. However, to be effective, plans must rest on credible projected consumption levels based on realistic market assumptions, not on utopian design preferences or populist dogmas.

Planners too often transform their land use projections into regulations. For instance, often projections for industrial land, based on past demand, become zoning laws, fixing the boundaries and the area of future industrial land. Projections are just that—they are always a guess, even if based on past trends. Planners should therefore constantly monitor demand through the evolution of land prices and rent, and adjust their projections accordingly. Zoning plans often misallocate land despite obvious demand change, because erroneous demand projections morphed into zoning laws. The contrast between the attitudes of the planners in Mumbai and Hong Kong (described earlier in the chapter) illustrates the advantages of monitoring demand to allow land use change.

Planners should therefore fully understand market mechanisms. Every planning department should monitor the spatial distribution of changes in real estate prices. Attention should be given to the supply side, including the elasticity of land supply, the productivity of the real estate industries, and the reduction of transaction costs imposed on building permits and property title transfers.

Planners Can Influence Consumption by Using Markets, Not by Imposing Norms

Clearly separating markets from design in the development of cities does not mean that planners should just passively monitor markets. For instance, planners should certainly be concerned by very low housing consumption among lower-income households and should act to increase it. However, they should be aware that the way to increase housing consumption is better achieved through market mechanisms (e.g., increasing supply or lowering transactions costs) rather than through regulatory design (e.g., fixing by law a minimum floor area or lot area or the rent per apartment). If planners want to have more influence over urban development, they should develop a set of indicators, such as land prices, rent, average commuting time under different transport modes. These indicators should be considered as "blinking red" when they pass a certain threshold. Planners should immediately respond to these red-alert levels by removing supply bottle-necks. Supply bottlenecks might include obsolete regulations but also insufficient investment in roads and transport infrastructure. The role of planners in reacting to indicators is discussed in chapter 8.

4   Spatial Distribution of Land Prices and Densities: Models Developed by Economists

The Need to Understand the Functioning of Markets

We have seen that markets are responsible for population densities. High demand for a specific location increases density, while low demand decreases it. Density is an indicator of land consumption, reflecting the equilibrium between supply and demand for land in a specific location. Population density is therefore an indicator dependent on market parameters, mainly household income, land supply elasticity, and transport speed and cost.

In other words, population densities reflect the preferences of consumers when they must make a choice between variously priced options. Large density variations in the same city reflect the diversity of household preferences. This diversity reflects income differences across households, but it also reflects different choices made by households of similar incomes but different urban environments—inner city or suburb, for example.

Planners therefore cannot impose densities through design. However, planners need to be able to project population densities based on their understanding of markets and consumer preferences. Planners' ability to project densities as accurately as possible is important; an accurate projection will greatly facilitate the design of infrastructure and community facilities. However, planners should be aware that markets are subject to external shocks that nobody can anticipate and that their projections are only educated guesses at best. They should abstain from freezing their density projections into land use regulations, and they should be prepared to adjust the capacity of existing infrastructure to the density generated by markets.

To anticipate the likely densities generated by markets, planners should have a good understanding of the way land markets work. Markets do not work in mysterious ways. For instance, increasing households' income or decreasing land supply has consequences on housing prices that economists can easily anticipate.

When markets are submitted to unanticipated external shocks—say, a sudden variation in gasoline prices—the impact on urban spatial structures is not immediate, and planners have time to adjust their projections, providing they understand the implications of the changes.

In this chapter I show that density variations in cities—where the highs and the lows are located—are usually predictable thanks to the contributions of urban economists. The predictability of market forces and the peril of ignoring them is the main message of this chapter.

Economists have contributed greatly to this predictability by enhancing our understanding of the spatial patterns caused by land market mechanisms. Urban economists have developed a family of mathematical models that predict relationships among location, land rent, and quantity of land consumed. The predictive quality of these theoretical models—despite being crude simplifications of a real city—has proved to be largely verified by empirical data, as we will see below.

In the second part of the chapter I show how theoretical models developed by economists can identify potential conflicts between urban development strategies and the predictable functioning of labor and land markets.

Urban strategies that are in obvious conflict with economic reality have little chance of being implemented, and if implemented, are extremely costly to a city's economy. Poorly conceived urban strategies are not just innocent utopias. They misdirect scarce urban investments toward locations where they are the least needed and, in doing so, greatly reduce the welfare of urban households. These failed strategies make housing less affordable and increase the time spent commuting.

Quantitative Models Used by Economists

Planners and urban economists do not have the same objectives. Planners strive to transform existing cities. They like to speak about their plans in terms of "vision."[1] The vision is often expressed with abstract nonquantifiable qualifying terms, such as "livable city," "resilient city," or "sustainable city." An urban planner's vision can be achieved through design, regulations, and capital investments. Economists, by contrast, are content to play a less ambitious but more analytical role. They are mostly interested in understanding the way market forces and government actions interact in shaping cities. Economists attempt to identify the causes that are changing urban prices and shapes by analyzing empirical data. Economists, like other social scientists, specialize; most neglect the spatial dimension of the economy. But urban economists focus specifically on spatial organization.

Economists develop theories and hypotheses that they represent with mathematical models that are usually based on extreme simplifications of the urban reality. However, the purpose of these models is to have both descriptive and predictive powers. Economists test the relevance of their models by comparing the descriptive and predictive values they generate with empirical data collected in real cities.

Simplification is not necessarily a bad thing when we attempt to understand how something works. After all, the maps used by urban planners are also an extreme simplification of the real world. However, despite being a very simplified version of reality, the practical uses of maps are not in doubt. A map at the scale of 1 to 1 would not be very useful. We should not reject a priori a theoretical construct because it rests on a model that is a crude simplification of a real and very complex city. The standard urban model described below is the necessary and appropriate starting point for understanding the way a city's spatial structure is shaped by land prices and how these prices emerge and evolve.

The Monocentric Model or Standard Urban Economics Model

The monocentric city model, or standard urban economics model, that was initially developed and refined over the 1960s and 1970s by William Alonso, Edwin Mills, Richard Muth, and William Wheaton, is exceedingly simple, even simplistic. However, the monocentric model has turned out to be a robust guide or benchmark against which to compare the form of many large and complex cities, and economists therefore usually call it the standard urban model. I will use that term in the rest of this book.

The standard urban model provides the building blocks for more complex models, in which some of the initial simplifying assumptions are relaxed. The more complex models—such as the regional economy, land use, and transportation model (RELU-TRAN),[2] developed by Alex Anas—require many more inputs than the monocentric model. Many of these inputs, in particular the spatial configuration of the main circulation network, are city specific. As a consequence, these models provide more accurate results when some inputs change, as in the case of the RELU-TRAN model's calculations of projected commuting time and nonjob-related trips. However, because these more complex models require many city-specific inputs, using them makes it more difficult to draw general conclusions about the way markets influence shapes and population densities in cities with different spatial configurations.

For this reason, in this chapter I discuss only the use of the standard urban model. Strangely, not only is the simplest version of this model based on an extreme simplification of the spatial structure of real cities, but its assumptions depart significantly from the way real cities are organized. Despite its loose approximation of reality, the standard urban model has strong descriptive and predictive powers concerning the structure of most existing cities, including cities that are not monocentric at all, like Atlanta, Georgia, or Los Angeles.

The standard urban model is not a curious paradox limited to academic debates in specialized journals; planners can use it to solve practical everyday problems, including expected land pricing and population densities. For instance, I will show how a simple form of the model can be used to assess whether a city might be consuming an excessive amount of land at the expense of rural land, what the popular press would call "sprawl." The use of economic models should help clarify many issues concerning densities and land use that are too often approached in a more emotional than quantitative way.

By contrast, cities built without land markets—as cities in the former Soviet Union were—are the only ones for which the standard urban model has no descriptive and predictive power. However, as the model is explicitly built to reflect the effect of land markets on urban structures, this exception should be expected. In addition, when cities that had developed during several decades under a command economy—like the cities of Eastern Europe—resume operating under market conditions, their structures tend to converge again toward the pattern predicted by the model.[3]

The simplest version of the standard urban model is based on the following assumptions:

1. The city is located in a featureless plain where agricultural land has a uniform rent.

2. All jobs are concentrated in a central business district (CBD).

3. People commute to work following an infinite number of straight radial roads.

The reader can see that I was not exaggerating when I spoke about a gross simplification of real cities!

The model aims to predict the variations in land price and density (i.e., land consumption) when land users compete with one another and when their transport costs are proportional to the distance between their residence and the city center. However, planners and economists can also use the standard urban model to analyze a specific city, because it is relatively easy to relax some of the assumptions to reflect reality. For instance, real road distances could be substituted for the "as the crow flies" distances assumed by the model. This is particularly useful when considering cities with unusual topographies, like Abidjan, Rio de Janeiro, or Hong Kong.

The equations predicting land price and population density at a given distance from the CBD constitute the most useful properties of the standard urban model.[4] These equations show that rents, land prices, and population densities will be the highest in the CBD and will fall as the distance from the center increases.

Urban land prices are driven by transport costs paid by users (direct cost of transport, e.g., transit fares, tolls, or gasoline costs, plus the opportunity cost of the time spent traveling). Transport costs increase with distance from the city center. The trade-off made by land users between the cost of transport in different locations and their desire to consume land results in land prices decreasing as transport costs increase. Land users react to differences in land prices by consuming less land where land is expensive and more where it is cheaper. As a result, density decreases when the distance to the center increases. The negatively sloped density curve reflects the way households and firms use land more sparingly when its price increases closer to the city center (figure 4.1). Land users are able to reduce their land consumption by building taller buildings where land is expensive (close to the city center) and less tall ones where land is cheap (on the periphery). The declining price of land from the center to the periphery is responsible for the decrease in density as the distance to the center increases. Put another way, households and firms are compensated for their longer commutes by being able to use more land and floor space.

It is important to realize that high land prices are causing high densities and not the other way around. I will expound on the importance of the relationship of land prices $\rightarrow$ density in the second part of this chapter, which evaluates Hanoi's master plan.

The standard model implies that the land rent function falls with distance and its functional form depends on underlying assumptions. The price of land is therefore expected to decrease as the distance from the center increases, following a profile similar to the one shown in figure 4.1.

The equation that gives the variation of population densities by distance to the center is given by equation 4.1.

The gradient g for density is the most important output of the model, as it provides the rate at which densities change with distance from the city center. The more expensive the transport (in time) and money (relative to households' income) is, the steeper the gradient will be.

In a real city, we can easily calculate the existing density gradient by running a regression analysis on observed price or density points at various distances from the center (figure 4.2).

The graphs in figures 4.1 and 4.2 respectively show the average price and density as a function of distance from the city center. However, in some cities there could be significant variations in price and density gradients, depending on the direction along which the prices and densities are measured. For instance, in cities like Paris—where household incomes are much higher in the western part than in the eastern part of the city—the gradient would be flatter on the west side

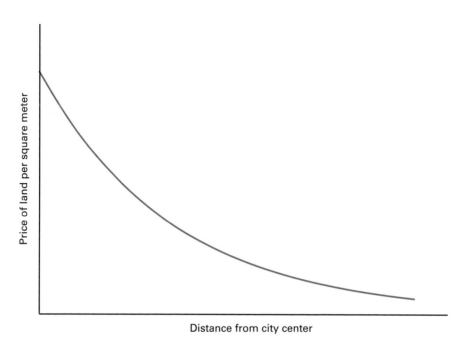

Figure 4.1
Profile of land price versus distance from city center.

Equation 4.1 Relationship between distance and population densities

$$D(x) = D_0 \, e^{-gx} \tag{4.1}$$

where
D is the population density at distance x from the center of a city;
D_0 is the density at the center;
e is the base of natural logarithms; and
g is the density gradient, or the rate at which the population density falls from the city center.

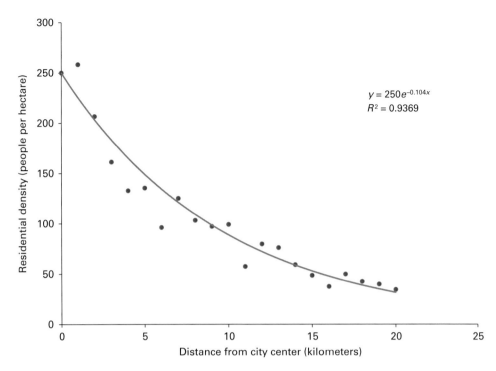

Figure 4.2
Calculation of the density gradient using a regression based on observed densities in a real city.

than on the east side, as the gradient depends on the ratio between household income and transport costs. The same asymmetry would be observed in Chicago for the north side versus the south side of the city.

The profile of densities shown in figure 4.2 will change over time as income and transport technology change. For instance, an increase in household income, a decrease in cost, and an increase in speed of transport would flatten the profile of both prices and densities. Inversely, an increase in population, everything else being equal, would increase both land prices and densities.

In many cities during the past 50 years, household incomes have increased while transport technology has made commuting trips faster and cheaper. As a result, the gradients of land prices and densities have become flatter. The expected flattening in the density profile is such that urban economist Stephen Malpezzi claims that "the monocentric model contains the seeds of its own destruction!" Why? Because as a city grows, as incomes rise, as transport costs fall, paradoxically what starts out as a monocentric city becomes polycentric, and the original "steep" price/rent/density gradients flatten inexorably. These are features and predictions built into the model.

Does the Spatial Distribution of Land Prices Correspond
to an Optimum Spatial Organization?

The economists who developed the standard urban model are not proposing it as an absolute optimum urban structure. They are only saying that, given transport costs, income, and total population, this is the way market forces will distribute prices and densities around a central point, providing the assumptions of the model are met. The objective of the model is to be descriptive and predictive, but not prescriptive. For instance, if transport costs decrease by x percent, with everything else staying constant, the city is likely to expand by y kilometers.

However, economists assume that if the utilities and production functions forming the base of the model are correct, then the welfare of households and firms would be optimized when the land prices and densities reach the equilibrium profile predicted by the model. Households and firms settling farther away from the center are being compensated for their higher transport costs with lower land prices.

The model assumes that if the land market is able to function without too many distortions, the profile of prices and densities will correspond to a distribution of land among users that will reflect the "best and highest use." There is therefore a hint of spatial optimization when subsidies, taxes, or regulations are not distorting land prices and transport costs. While these conditions are probably never met in the real world, the model indicates in which directions the prices and population densities would be moving if the distortions were removed.

For instance, in countries where the price of gasoline is heavily subsidized, like Egypt, Iran, or Mexico, the standard model tells us right away that cities will extend much farther away from the center than in cities where the price of gasoline reflects market prices.[5] In these countries, it is useless for planners to try to devise regulatory barriers against "sprawl"; it is only necessary to remove the subsidies on gasoline to get closer to an optimum equilibrium between distance and quantity of land consumed. The use of an abstract theoretical model can therefore suggest practical solutions in the real world in which planners are working.

The users of urban roads seldom pay market rents for the road area they occupy[6] while commuting; their transport cost is therefore subsidized by the amount of rent they are not paying for using the roads. Users of the standard urban model can then infer that the subsidy for the use of road space increases the built-up area of the city by an area that can eventually be calculated. Pricing the use of roads through tolls could eventually restore land consumption to an optimum level. Using market mechanisms to improve land use efficiency would achieve better results than trying to design regulations to obtain the same results.

Because the model provides the profile of densities and prices under undistorted market conditions, it is possible to compare the current price and density profiles of a city to what the model predicts and calculate the costs of the distortions. For instance, using the standard urban model, the economist Jan Brueckner and I calculated the unnecessary expansion in the city of Bangalore in India created by the poorly designed height regulations restrictions.[7] In another interesting practical application, Jan Brueckner applied the model to calculate the welfare gains obtained by dismantling apartheid policy in the cities of South Africa. He analyzed the changes in prices and land consumption when freedom of residential location is granted to all citizens and demonstrated that there has been a large aggregate welfare gain (i.e., with less spent on transport, it is possible to spend more on goods like housing and food) from eliminating the spatial distortion imposed by the apartheid land use regulations.[8] The results hold for all sorts of segregation imposed by land use regulations or discrimination of various types, income segregations being the most common.

In this chapter I demonstrate that the model is a fairly good predictor of the spatial distribution of prices and densities when a city develops under not-too-distorted market conditions. And, as a corollary, that the model can be used both to test actual market distortions in existing cities and whether a planned spatial strategy contradicts the predictable pattern of land prices and densities set by markets. I will use the Hanoi master plan case study to illustrate this example in the operational use of the standard model.

How Well Does the Standard Urban Model Fit Real Cities?

The standard urban model claims to be both descriptive and predictive. To determine the operational usefulness of the model, it is therefore necessary first to verify how accurately its equations describe the variations in densities and land prices in existing cities, and second, to determine whether changes in density patterns and price follow the predictions of the model when variables like income, transport costs, and population size change.

Testing the Descriptive Quality of the Model

Testing the accuracy of the standard urban model on real cities is relatively easy, though time-consuming. Densities by neighborhood are easier to calculate than prices; the prices of land transactions are not always accurately recorded. With my colleague Stephen Malpezzi and my wife, Marie-Agnes Roy Bertaud, I have calculated population densities in intervals of 1 kilometer from the city center for about 50 metropolitan areas around the world.[9]

Figure 4.3 shows density profiles from a sample of 12 cities in Asia, Europe, and North and South America. The horizontal axis shows distance from the city center from 0 to 30 kilometers, and the vertical axis shows the variations in built-up

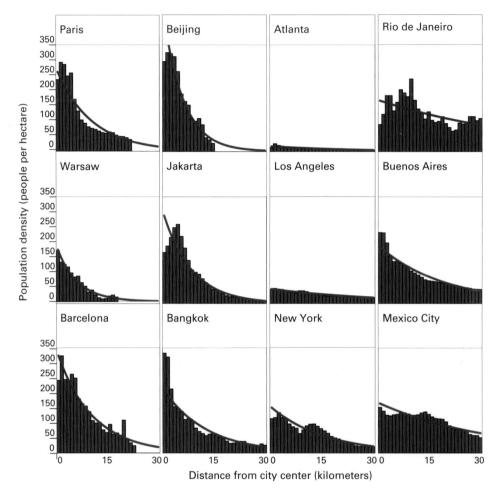

Figure 4.3
Profile of densities in 12 metropolises.

densities from 0 to 350 people per hectare. The bars in the graph show the measured density within each annulus located at 1-kilometer intervals from 1 to 30 kilometers from the city. I obtained the average density by dividing the population of the portion of census tracts in each annulus by the total built-up area in the annulus. The use of GIS software makes this operation not quite as cumbersome as it sounds!

The cities selected have widely different cultures, histories, economies, climates, and topographies. None of these cities meets the strictly monocentric criteria specified by the model. Some have a dense center with a high job concentration,

Table 4.1
Density gradient of 12 cities.

City	Gradient	R^2
Beijing	−0.17	0.92
Warsaw	−0.17	0.86
Jakarta	−0.12	0.97
Barcelona	−0.1	0.89
Paris	−0.1	0.90
Bangkok	−0.08	0.92
New York	−0.07	0.90
Buenos Aires	−0.05	0.95
Atlanta	−0.04	0.84
Mexico City	−0.03	0.81
Los Angeles	−0.03	0.91
Rio de Janeiro	−0.02	0.37

like Paris, New York, and Barcelona. Others have extremely dispersed job locations, like Atlanta and Los Angeles. Most others are in between.

How well do the density profiles of the 12 cities in figure 4.3 fit the predictions of the standard urban model? The model predicts that the population density of a city will decrease from a central point toward the periphery following a negatively sloped exponential curve. The profiles of observed densities for the 12 cities (represented by blue bars in figure 4.3) fit an exponential density curve as predicted by the model. The fit between the actual density profile and the model exponential curve (represented by red lines in the figure) is striking. Table 4.1 shows the R^2 values[10] representing the similarities between the observed density at each kilometer interval and the exponential curve predicted by the model. With the exception of Rio de Janeiro, all R^2 values are above 0.8, and 7 out of 12 are above 0.9!

Why is Rio de Janeiro the only city in my sample of 12 with a significant but mediocre fit, having an R^2 equal to 0.37? Rio has a beautiful but complex topography with numerous ocean inlets and steep rocky hills fragmenting the built-up area. The model assumption that all distances are counted along radial roads converging on the city center is a good enough approximation for cities like Beijing, Buenos Aires, or Paris, which are built on flat plains. However, the approximation is not good enough for cities like Rio de Janeiro, in which topography constitutes a barrier to direct access that lengthens some distances and not others. The model's assumption of radial roads could easily be relaxed for cities with difficult topography by replacing radial distance by real distance measured on the existing road network. The graph in figure 4.3 for the density profile of Rio de Janeiro could then be redrawn to represent real travel distances from the center, following existing roads rather than imaginary radials. If this were done, the fit would probably be better.

Reliable spatial data on land prices or rents is more difficult to collect than it is for densities. There are some difficulties in finding reliable transaction data in cities of developing countries, where many land transactions are informal and even formal transactions are often underreported because of high taxes on title transfers. However, a vast amount of literature covers the changes in land prices by distance from the city center in OECD cities for which reliable data are available. Figure 4.4 shows the land price profile for Paris by distance from the city center (Hotel de Ville). The fit between observed prices and the expected exponential curve predicted by the model ($R^2 = 0.87$) is quite good. Some studies, using historical prices,[11] show that the price gradient moves in directions predicted by the standard urban model when income increases and the cost of transport decreases. One problem is that in very large cities, it is sometimes difficult to agree on what constitutes the center of the city. For instance, the study on historical

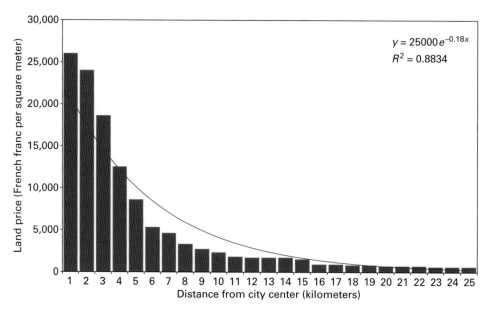

Figure 4.4
Profile of land prices in Paris, 1990.

prices in New York uses City Hall at the central point of reference, while a much more recent study conducted by Andrew Haughwout for the entire New York Metropolitan area in 2008[12] used the Empire State Building as the city center.

We can learn a lesson from the density profiles in figure 4.3 and the price profile for Paris in figure 4.4. Densities and land prices are not produced by design but by market forces. A planner thinking that a city would be improved by having higher densities should therefore advocate higher land prices. More expensive or slower transport would increase the desirability of neighborhoods closer to the city center and therefore increase their land prices, everything else being equal.

The advocates of "compact cities" should realize that a compact city—defined as a city that uses less land for sheltering the same number of people as another city—has a price. This price will not be paid by the urban planner advocating it but by the households and firms who will live in that compact city. Planners advocating a compact city strategy, however, think that it will happen by just assigning densities for different city locations on a master plan.

I am not exaggerating here. Many master plans "design" densities the way an architect may decide on the color of a building. In the last part of this chapter, I give a concrete example of arbitrarily planned densities—Hanoi's master plan—and the problems it causes.

Why Does the Model Seem to Fit Obvious Acentric Cities Like Los Angeles?

Why does the model seem to apply equally well to monocentric cities and to acentric cities like Los Angeles and Atlanta, which have only a weak concentration of employment in their CBD? Figure 4.5 shows the same population density profile of Los Angeles as in figure 4.3, just at a larger scale. The highest density is only 50 people per hectare in the center. At 30 kilometers from the center, it drops by 60 percent to about 20 people per hectare. The decrease in density in Los Angeles is small compared to that in Bangkok, for instance, where densities drop by 93 percent at the same distance from the center. However, with $R^2 = 0.91$, the density profile follows the prediction of the model, even though the city does not meet the initial assumption that all jobs are concentrated in the CBD. Los Angeles's CBD, which is roughly located at the centroid of the metropolitan built-up area, contains only a small percentage of jobs compared to the rest of the metropolitan region (about 11 percent of all jobs in the city, according to O'Sullivan).[13] Let us try to find out why the distribution of densities should be consistent with the one predicted by the standard urban model.

Consider an imaginary circular city with a radius of 12 kilometers where jobs are uniformly distributed in the built-up area (figure 4.6). I will call this type of city "acentric" to distinguish it from the monocentric and polycentric types of spatial

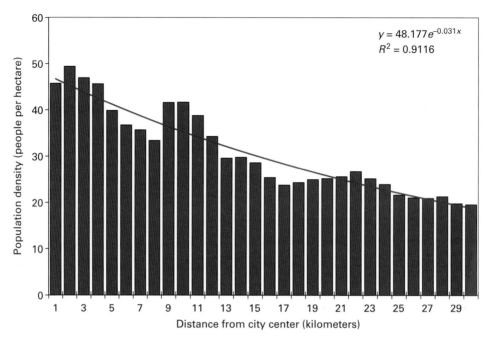

Figure 4.5
Density profile of Los Angeles.
Sources: Population: US Census data, 2000; built-up area: interpretation and vectorization of satellite imagery by Marie-Agnes Bertaud.

organization, where jobs are concentrated in one or several locations. In an acentric city, jobs are evenly distributed in the built-up area. This is roughly similar to the distribution of jobs in Los Angeles. Because, by definition, the acentric city doesn't have any area with a high job concentration, it doesn't have a CBD. But it does have a centroid. The centroid is the point from which the sum of the distances to all other locations within the shape is the smallest.

Consider three workers who are living at different locations, A, B, and C, and let us measure how many jobs they could potentially access in an arbitrarily fixed travel time of 30 minutes at an average travel speed of 20 km/h, which corresponds to a circle with a radius of 10 kilometers. For simplicity, I will assume that the travel time is the same for all three workers in all directions. Below or within 30 minutes' travel time, each of the three workers would be able to reach any job located in an area corresponding to a circle with a 10 kilometer radius. While the area that can be reached in 30 minutes is the same for all three workers, the number of jobs located in the 30 minute travel range would be different, depending on the location of their dwellings in the city.

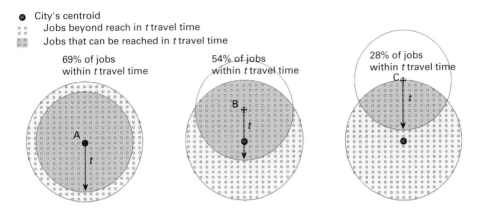

- ● City's centroid
- ○ ○ Jobs beyond reach in *t* travel time
- ○ ○ Jobs that can be reached in *t* travel time

69% of jobs within *t* travel time

54% of jobs within *t* travel time

28% of jobs within *t* travel time

Figure 4.6
Schematic representation of access to the labor market in a city with a uniform distribution of job locations.

Let's examine the worker residing at point A, located at the centroid of the city shape (left graph of figure 4.6). Traveling 30 minutes from A, this worker can reach 69 percent of the built-up area in 30 minutes (the ratio of the 10 kilometer radius circle accessible in 30 minutes and the entire area of the city). This worker can therefore access 69 percent of all job locations in the city, as our hypothesis was that job locations were evenly distributed in the built-up area.

The second worker is located at point B (middle graph in figure 4.6), which is 6 kilometers from the built-up area's centroid or halfway between the city center and the edge of the built-up area. She will have access to only 54 percent of jobs, as the area she can reach by traveling 30 minutes does not completely overlap with the city's built-up area where the jobs are located.

The third worker is located in C, at the edge of the built-up area (right graph in figure 4.6). He will be able to reach only 28 percent of the built-up area and therefore only 28 percent of the jobs in the city. If worker C wants to reach the same number of jobs as, say, worker A, he could do it by traveling for more than 30 minutes.

From this schematic graphic example, we can see that, even in an acentric city where jobs are evenly distributed in a city, the advantage of a central location still exists in terms of access to the labor market and to amenities. Although jobs and amenities are uniformly distributed in the built-up area, a household located close to the center of the urban shape (it does not need to be a CBD) has access to more jobs and amenities than does a household located at the periphery in the same travel time. This locational advantage would generate more demand for more centrally located housing, and it explains the existence of a density gradient with densities decreasing outward from the centroid of the urban shape, as demonstrated by the density profile of Los Angeles (see figure 4.5).

The accessibility advantage of a centrally located household is not as strong in an acentric city as it would be in a monocentric one, but it is still significant. If the hypothesis illustrated by figure 4.6 is correct, we would expect acentric cities with a uniform or quasi-uniform job distribution to have a density gradient that still shows a decrease in densities with distance from the centroid of the built-up area, even in the absence of an identifiable CBD.

Obviously, an acentric city would have a lower density gradient than cities that have retained a dominant CBD, like Beijing, Barcelona, and Paris. The value of the Los Angeles density gradient (table 4.1) is only about 1/6 of Beijing's and about 1/3 of the gradients of Barcelona and Paris, which is consistent with our hypothesis on acentric cities. The small sample presented in table 4.1 does not constitute irrefutable proof that population density gradients decrease when job dispersion increases in a metropolitan area, but it shows that the standard urban model remains relevant for cities that are polycentric or acentric.

Why a Few Cities Do Not Fit the Model at All and Why It Reinforces the Model's Credibility

Empirical evidence shows that the standard urban model's negatively sloped exponential curve can aptly represent population density variations in most monocentric, polycentric, and acentric cities. However, if the use of the standard urban model were limited to a description of existing density patterns in cities, it would be of little use to planners. Existing densities are relatively easy to measure, as seen above, and there would be no need for a model. The model is important because it can predict what will happen to densities and land prices when the values of some market variables change over time. Because I put so much confidence in the predictive power of the model, it is necessary at this point to explain why the density profiles of some cities do not fit the negatively sloped density profile and why cities with completely dispersed job locations fit the predictions of the model very well.

Among the 53 cities for which I collected data, a few do not fit the model at all. For example, the standard urban model does not accurately describe the densities of Moscow in 1990 (figure 4.7), Brasília in 2000, and Johannesburg in 1990.[14] Their densities not only fail to decrease exponentially from their city centers, sometimes they actually increase or follow a U-shaped profile. But these exceptions should not surprise us. After all, the main claim of the model is that it reflects the spatial structure generated by free land markets. Planners and engineers designed these anomalous cities in a political system that allowed them to ignore land prices.

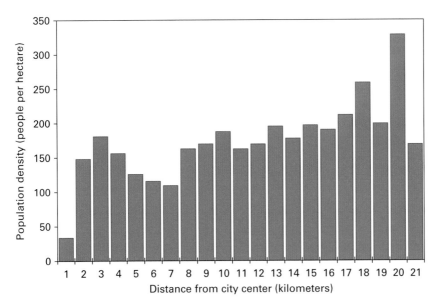

Figure 4.7
Moscow population density profile, 1989. *Sources*: 1989 All-Union Census data, State Committee for Statistics Moscow, 1990; vectorization of satellite imagery by author.

The absence of a market generates alternative forms to the one predicted by the standard urban model. Supply and demand forces, which are absent in a command economy, shape the urban structures predicted by the model.

The Predictive Capability of Economic Models Is Important for Operational Urban Planning

Economic models, in spite of their theoretical simplifications, are most useful for their predictive capabilities. The operational value of economic models rests on their ability to forecast general directions in land and housing price levels and densities when income, land supply, transport cost, and transport speed change. Economic models cannot provide accurate projections of densities in specific areas of the city, but they are useful for anticipating the general direction of relative prices and densities. One of the main lessons to be learned from the use of economic models is that variations in densities and land price are usually predictable and are caused by variations in households' and firms' incomes, transport costs, and by the elasticity of a city's land supply.

Land and housing prices and densities obey the basic demand and supply mechanism. The high land values created at the center of large cities decrease with distance in the same way that the force of gravity of a planet diminishes with distance from this planet. Planning future land use while ignoring the predictable land value based on location makes no more sense than trying to ignore gravity when designing an airplane. The real-world example of Hanoi's master plan, discussed later in the chapter, will illustrate a typical case of planners trying to "design" densities, therefore implicitly designing land values instead of basing their plans on the projection of land values and densities created by predictable variations in income and transport costs.

Fall of Population Densities over Time
The standard urban model predicts that the population density gradient will fall in absolute value as urban incomes rise and transport costs decrease. Shlomo Angel and colleagues observed this flattening of the density curve across a large number of modern cities they surveyed.[15] Angel explores in detail the historical evolution of densities in world cities. He provides historical data for 30 large cities in all five continents, showing the evolution of built-up densities between 1800 and 2000. His data show that, while densities in these cities often peaked around 1900, densities have since significantly declined in all of them, mostly due to increases in income, decreases in transport costs, and progress in transport technology. Another set of data analyzed by Angel shows the density changes in 120 world cities between 1990 and 2000. The data show that densities have increased in only 16 of the 120 cities, all in developing countries. All of the others showed a decline in built-up densities. Angel points out that the decrease in built-up densities was strongly correlated with rising household incomes and decreasing transport costs in proportion to income, which is consistent with the standard urban model predictions. Angel's exhaustive urban density database therefore seems to confirm the predictive quality of the model.

While average overall urban densities tend to fall when incomes and transport costs decrease, how do neighborhood densities change in an urban area under the same conditions? The standard urban model forecasts a decrease in the density gradient. In other words, the profile of densities becomes flatter over time, with densities in the center decreasing and those in the periphery increasing slightly. Figure 4.8 shows the variations in built-up densities in Tianjin between 1988 and 2000 and in Paris between 1990 and 2006. While the history and the economic bases of the two cities have very little in common, the increase in household income and decrease in transport costs relative to income produced the same spatial transformation. Tianjin's density gradient decreased by 1.1 percent per year, while Paris's gradient decreased by a more modest 0.4 percent per year. This difference in density gradient decrease is consistent with the faster increase in household incomes in Tianjin compared to Paris.

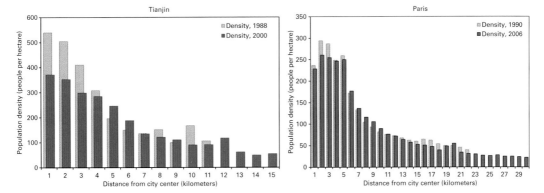

Figure 4.8
Change over time in the density gradients in Tianjin (1988 and 2000) and Paris (1990 and 2006). *Sources*: Tianjin Population Census and Survey data, Tianjin Statistical Yearbook, Tianjin; Paris Population 1990 National Census, population 2006 estimate by Institut National de la Statistique et des Études Économiques, Paris; vectorization of satellite data by Marie-Agnes Roy Bertaud.

The change in density profile is relatively slow in both cities. Even the faster change in Tianjin is still modest in light of the massive economic and construction boom that took place in Tianjin between 1988 and 2000. Urban structures are very resilient and change slowly. The direction of the change in density profiles in both Tianjin and Paris is consistent with the predictions of the standard urban model.

Regulations That Distort Land Prices
Regulations may decrease the total area of floor space that can be built on a given area of land. These types of regulations would of course change the price and density profiles that the standard urban model would project for unconstrained markets. For instance, regulations routinely restrict the heights of buildings or impose a maximum limit on the number of dwelling units that can be built per hectare. If these regulations are binding—that is, if the regulations reduce the number of dwellings that developers would have built to respond to consumers' preferences for these areas—then the regulations will create a shortage of floor space in areas of high demand. As a result of this shortage, the price of floor space will increase compared to what it would have been without the regulations. In turn, the increase in price might result in higher densities, as some consumers might decide to use less floor space to be able to afford an expensive but desirable location.

The limitation on building height imposed by the municipality of Paris illustrates this point. There is a high demand for living in the center of Paris because of its high level of amenities and its high concentration of jobs. Because of the limitation on the supply of floor space imposed by the height limitation, the size

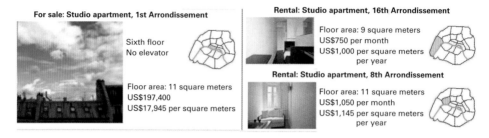

Figure 4.9
Sale price and rents of very small apartments in Paris, 2014.

of apartments decreases and their price increases. The real estate posting in figure 4.9 shows the very high prices of tiny rooms, between 9 and 11 square meters, whether for rent or for sale. The absence of elevators in some historical buildings helps lower the price of apartments, which is the case for the 11-square-meter studio whose advertisement is shown on the left in figure 4.9. The enormous difference between the price of this room (US$17,945 per square meter) and the price of a one bedroom apartment (US$1,944 per square meter) located in the center of Chicago next to City Hall shows that the impact of regulations on real estate prices is not trivial!

I am not suggesting here that the municipality should necessarily amend its building height restrictions in the city central core. The regulation's aesthetic objective is achieved; it perfectly preserves the historical skyline of Paris. However, many in Paris lament the extremely high housing prices and the smallness of apartments. High prices and low housing floor consumption are the direct consequence of preserving historical Paris. If the height restrictions were widely relaxed, it would increase the supply of residential floor space and lower housing prices, but by removing one of the chief attractions of Paris, it might also decrease the demand for a central location that would have a lower aesthetic quality.

In cities other than Paris, most regulatory constraints on floor area ratio aim to control densities and therefore create an artificial shortage of floor space or developed land. Consequently, these regulations usually increase densities—the opposite of the desired result. Mumbai, where planners attempted to reduce densities by limiting the floor area ratio in a draconian fashion, has, as a result, one of the highest average built-up densities in the world.[16]

The same is true for regulations aimed at increasing densities. In the absence of consumer demand, planners cannot increase densities by regulatory fiat. Regulations that limit the number of dwellings per hectare, for instance, are an attempt to design densities through the proxy of regulations.

There is nothing wrong with planners attempting to project the number of dwellings per hectare that the market is likely to supply in a given neighborhood. But to attempt to transform that guess into a regulation is both detrimental and delusional.

Sprawl: The Standard Model and the Expansion of Cities

Models developed by urban economists help explain how land markets shape cities. We have seen that land markets—not planners' designs—generate population densities. Densities are indicators of land consumption.[17] If markets generate densities, then they also define how much total land a city will consume and, by extension, the boundaries between urban and rural land. As I will show below, the standard urban model explains how and why markets, whether distorted or not, establish this limit.

The expansion of cities into the countryside, often called "sprawl" when this expansion is considered wasteful, is probably one the most emotional urban issues discussed by the popular press and by advocacy groups. A Google search for the word "sprawl"[18] returns 5.9 million entries!

The concern about the ever-expanding limits of cities is at the core of the popular advocacy for "smart growth" and for "sustainable cities," which ask for the forceful containment of cities' expansion. Many urban critics and planners argue that unregulated cities expand too far into the countryside, causing increased commuting distances and dangerously decreasing the amount of land devoted to agriculture. These critics call "sprawl" what they judge as excessive urban expansion at what they think are too low densities.

Presumably there is some population density threshold above which a city's development is "non-sprawl" and below which development is sprawl. However, the anti-sprawl advocates clamoring for more compact cities have not yet defined this population density threshold. Opponents of sprawl puzzlingly use the term to describe both American cities like Atlanta and Chinese cities like Tianjin, which have densities of 6 and 170 people per hectare, respectively. At what density would the critics of sprawl say a city is using land reasonably?

Even the World Bank, in 2014, has recently joined the anti-sprawl chorus in its report on urbanization in China by titling a map of the Shanghai-Suzhou-Changzhou conurbation "Sprawl in Shanghai Metropolitan Region between 2000 and 2010."[19] The map just shows the urban expansion that had occurred in this highly economically successful metropolitan region over 10 years. No data presented in the World Bank report constitutes proof that the urban expansion shown on the map is either wasteful or inefficient. Given the large increases in this area's population and household income that occurred during this period, certainly some land expansion would be expected and not troubling. How can we know whether land use is efficient? The standard urban model could provide us with a more rational and less emotional assessment of the matter.

Concern for the Loss of Agricultural Land
Often cities must expand into valuable agricultural land, which might appear to be a zero-sum game between the area devoted to agriculture and the area occupied by cities. Because the reduction of agricultural area is linked in people's mind to a loss in food production, it is understandingly an emotional issue. In reality, increases and decreases in food production have more to do with changes in land productivity and climatic variations than the area under nominal cultivation. But given the historical famines that plagued South and East Asia as recently as the twentieth century,[20] it is quite understandable that a possible decrease in agricultural land raises concern.

The Chinese government, alarmed by the fast pace of urban expansion, has set urban land development quotas that severely restrict the conversion of agricultural land into urban land. The National Plan on New Urbanization (2014–2020), published by the Government of China to guide urbanization until 2020, prescribes a minimum density of 100 people per hectare for every new urban settlement in order to preserve agricultural land. In addition, the use of costly conversion quotas is required for any urban expansion requiring the loss of cultivated land.

Many observers of rapid urbanization in Asia are alarmed by the fact that cities' land coverage expands at a faster pace than the urban population. While I was advising on the development of Tianjin in 2007, the city's managers were alarmed by this phenomenon: Tianjin's developed land area was expanding at a faster pace than its population (table 4.2). Over 12 years, the population of Tianjin had increased by 22 percent, while the built-up area had increased by 63 percent. However, household income in Tianjin increased in real terms by about 55 percent between 1988 and 2000. Residential floor space during the same period increased from 14 square meters per person to 22 square meters, consistent with the increase in household incomes. The increase in land consumption is not alarming when compared with the increase in household income. If income had increased but land and floor consumption had been stagnant, there would be cause for alarm.

The standard urban model has shown that densities will decrease when urban household incomes increase, and urban transportation costs decrease in proportion to income. This change in density is easy to explain without using the model's

Table 4.2
Increase in population and built-up area within the third ring road, Tianjin, 1988–2000.

	Year	
	1988	2000
Population	3,499,718	4,264,577
Built-up area (square kilometers)	153.72	250.74
Density (people per hectare)	228	170
Area of built-up land per person (square meters)	44	59
Increase in population (percent)		22
Increase in built-up area (percent)		63
Increase in land consumption per person (percent)		34

equation. As incomes increase, households wish to consume more floor space. Firms, formerly operating dense sweatshops, acquire more land to provide more working space for their employees and for the more sophisticated machinery they operate; roads become wider to accommodate the increasingly heavy flow of traffic. All these factors imply more land consumption per capita. Therefore, a decreasing density during economic expansion is not necessarily an indicator of wasteful land consumption. It all depends on household and firm incomes, the cost and speed of transport, and the price of agricultural land during the period. Expecting that cities expand at the same densities as their core implies that densities should be uniform from the core to the periphery and that densities had been already optimal since the city's foundation.

The standard urban model tells us that densities will decline as household incomes increase and transport technology improves. This is not a sign of inefficiency but a rational reallocation of inputs. As most of the new land development occurs on the periphery, it is normal that the density of newly developed land will be lower than the city average.

Low density at the edge of urban development is a normal and rational component of development, as it represents a maximization of utility for firms and households when market prices are not distorted. However, it is important to have a yardstick to measure objectively whether land developed at the fringe of cities has an inefficiently low density.

The anti-sprawl movement, while being vocal, does not represent a unanimous opinion. Some planners and many economists, such as Peter Gordon and Harry

Richardson, have argued that an elastic land supply is indispensable to maintaining affordable housing prices as a city's population and income rise. This is also one of the main arguments developed by my colleague Shlomo Angel in his book *Atlas of Urban Expansion*, mentioned earlier. Robert Bruegmann, in his aptly titled book *Sprawl*, puts the question of cities' extension in context and debunks many of the urban legends that are an unfortunate feature of the discourse on cities and that brand them as voracious land consumers.

The work of urban economists demonstrates that there is nothing idiosyncratic about how much land cities occupy, where the limit of urbanization is located, and what the main variables on which this limit depends are. The area occupied by cities and the location of the built-up boundary depend on the relative value of three ratios: rural to urban income, commuting cost to urban income, and agricultural land rent to urban rent. The land area used by cities, whether sprawled or compact, has very little to do with greedy developers, rapacious landowners, or irresponsible car-happy commuters.

My goal is not to review, comment, or paraphrase the work of urban economists but to explain how planners can utilize their work to better understand how cities use land when their population increases and what economic and population variables are responsible for setting densities. I focus on what the standard urban model can teach us about the limits of urbanization and, by extension, what determines the area of cities.

The Standard Urban Model Helps Explain How Far a City Expands and Why

Urban land prices decrease as distance from the city center increases, reflecting the decreasing utility of land to the consumer, whether firm or household, due to increasing transportation costs. The graph in figure 4.10 shows the curve U representing the variations of land price of an imaginary city as distance from the center increases. The line A represents the price of agricultural land at the periphery of this city. It is assumed that that this price does not vary with distance and represents the capitalized rent that farmers obtain from their crops. The more fertile and productive the soil, the higher the price of agricultural land will be.[21] The urban land price curve U intersects the horizontal line A representing the price of agricultural land at a point d at distance x from the city center. The outer limit of built-up area of the city will be located at distance x. At a distance shorter than x, developers will be able to outbid the agricultural price that farmers could otherwise get, enticing them to sell their land. Therefore, at a distance shorter than x, land will be converted from agricultural to urban use. Beyond the distance x,

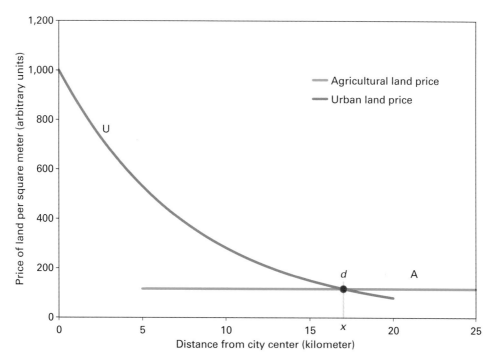

Figure 4.10
Price of urban land and agricultural land define the limit of urbanization.

developers can only offer a price lower than the agricultural price of land. Farmers will therefore be unlikely to sell their land, and the land will remain agricultural. The higher the price of agricultural land, the smaller will be the radius of urbanization x, everything else being equal.

This has an important, interesting implication about the way cities expand. For a given population, a city's land prices and densities will be higher if it expands in highly priced agricultural land.

This dynamic is rather straightforward. Setting the limit of urbanization does not require conspiracy theories involving greedy developers in cahoots with devious car manufacturers, as one of the most persistent urban legends would have it.[22]

We can see, if we accept the firms' and households' utility functions implicit in the model, that the areas and densities of cities (implicit in the location of x), have no normative "good practice" value but depend on the price of urban land at the fringe of urbanization compared to the price of agricultural land. Cities expanding into very productive agricultural land will have a smaller footprint, and therefore a higher density, than cities expanding into a desert, everything else being equal. Imposing a minimum normative density, such as the 100 people per hectare in China, may result in resource misallocation. This density might be too low for cities expanding into valuable agricultural land, while it might be too high for cities expanding into land with little alternative uses, like desert or mud flats.

The Urban–Rural Boundary When the Price of Agricultural Land Is Distorted

The point d on figure 4.10, showing the limit of urbanization, is at the distance x where the price of urban land equals the price of agricultural land. If neither of these prices is distorted, this distance—and by extension the entire built-up area of the city—could be considered optimal. In other words, this distance and built-up area would maximize the utility of urban dwellers and firms as well as the farmers cultivating land at the edge of the city.

However, if one or both prices were distorted, the point d would no longer represent the optimal limit of urbanization. For instance, let us look at the consequence on the urbanization limit, and therefore on a city's land consumption, when the acquisition price of agricultural land is undervalued compared to its real market value when based on agricultural productivity (figure 4.11).

Let us suppose that the acquisition price of agricultural land (line A1) is lower than its real implicit market value (line A2). This distortion in the price of agricultural land could be caused by a government using eminent domain to expropriate land occupied by farmers and paying a lower price than what they would obtain in a free market in which the agricultural land price had been based on the capitalization of the rent produced by the land. This type of expropriation happens often at the fringe of cities in China and in India,[23] where governments use an administrative price that is usually lower than the market price for compensating farmers for expropriated land.

Figure 4.11 illustrates this situation. The price of urban land becomes equal to the undervalued price of agricultural land at point d_1 at a distance x_1 from the center. However, if the market price of agricultural land had been used, then the limit of urbanization will have been in d_2 where the urban land price crosses the line A2 at a distance x_2 from the city center. We can see that x_1, the limit of urbanization with an undervalued agricultural price, is significantly farther away than x_2. Undervaluing the price of agricultural land would therefore contribute to an overconsumption of land by urban users at the expense of agricultural land and is therefore a misallocation of resources.

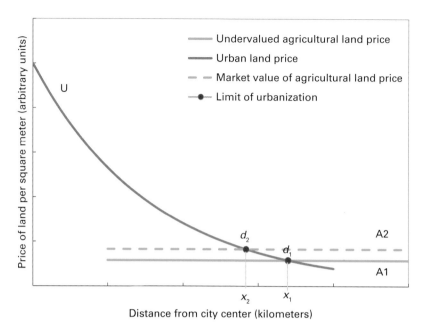

Figure 4.11
Limit of urbanization when agricultural land prices are distorted.

Prices Distortions May Cause an Over- or Underconsumption of Urban Land

The use of the standard urban model is unlikely to allow us to calculate the exact distance corresponding to an undistorted agricultural price. However, it does allow us to be certain that an undervaluation of the price of agricultural land will lead to an overconsumption of land by cities. People concerned about the potential loss of agricultural land caused by urbanization can use the standard urban model to identify distortions that will eventually lead to the overconsumption of urban land. The use of the model points to the obvious solution to reduce land consumption to a more optimal level. The solution is for developers to pay a market price for agricultural land. The alternative solution, drawing a regulatory urban growth boundary (UGB)[24] or a greenbelt at distance x_2 to prevent further urban extension, will not work for two reasons. First, the model is not accurate enough to calculate an accurate x_2 distance. Second, if it was possible to establish x_2 accurately, this distance would not be optimal for long; agricultural productivity, urban incomes, and transport costs are likely to change over time, requiring a displacement of x_2.

Prices can be distorted in other ways. Agricultural prices can be inflated by subsidized irrigation, for instance, resulting in a misallocation of land, this time at the expense of urban land. Urban land prices themselves can also be distorted by large infrastructure subsidies, transport subsidies, or gasoline subsidies. Governments should correct the misallocation of land between urban and agricultural use through the suppression—or at least a decrease—of price distortions, not through design solutions such as zoning regulations.

To remedy perceived excessive urban land consumption, which may or may not exist, planners usually advocate imposing greenbelts or UGBs that use design to limit the city expansion. Economic models allow us to understand which conditions might lead cities to consume an excessive amount of land. When overconsumption occurs, the models tell us what to do to correct it using market mechanisms rather than arbitrarily designed solutions.

Market solutions constantly adjust to changes. Design solutions, such as a UGB à la Portland, Oregon, create rigidities and exacerbate distortions.

What Happens to the Urban Built-Up Boundary When Agricultural Land Price Is Not Uniform?

The most simplified form of the standard urban model assumes that agricultural land prices are uniform around a city. Cities where this assumption approximates reality are expected to develop symmetrically around the traditional city center with a built-up area approximating a circle centered on the traditional CBD. This is roughly the case for Beijing, London, and Paris, for instance.

However, the standard urban model implies that where large differences in agricultural price exist for different directions, a city would logically develop asymmetrically. The city would expand much farther toward the cheap agricultural land than toward the expensive land. Let us test the way the standard model adapts in a real city where the price of agricultural land is not uniform in every direction. The city of Beaune, located in the middle of the Burgundy wine country in France, illustrates what the standard model would predict when agricultural land price is much higher in one direction than in another.

Every year, an international wine auction involving some of the most prestigious and expensive wines in the world takes place in Beaune's medieval city center. Beaune plays the role of Wall Street for Burgundy wine. The vineyards providing the most expensive "grand cru" (Aloxe-Corton and Puligny-Montrachet) and "premier cru" Burgundy wines are exclusively located to the west of the city, along gentle slopes exposed to the southeast morning sun, as shown in figure 4.12.

The land price of vineyards in this area was estimated at about US$500 per square meter in 2013. This is of course an exceptionally high price for agricultural land. By comparison, the average price of agricultural land in Kansas in 2013 was

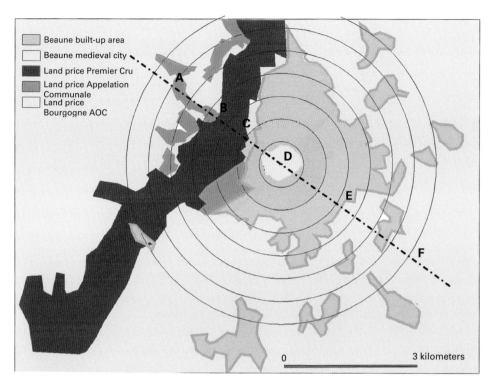

Figure 4.12
Built-up area and premier cru vineyards, Beaune.

about US$0.50 per square meter. To the east of Beaune, the price of vineyards, because of different soil and sun exposure, drops below US$200 per square meter.

We have to adapt the standard model to reflect the asymmetrical agricultural land prices around Beaune. Instead of averaging the price of urban land by distance from the city center, as it was done in the previous figures, let us use the standard model to represent the price of land along an axis AF passing through the city center in a southeast direction (figure 4.12). I represent the profile of the price of urban land prices and the various vineyards' land prices along the axis AF in figure 4.13.

We can see from both the map and the graph that the city expansion is asymmetrical around the city center as predicted by the model. Toward the northwest, the short distance from the medieval city would make land attractive for development, but urban developers cannot outbid the high premier cru (premier vineyard area) vineyard price. The city's built-up boundary toward the northwest is therefore set at a short distance from the city center. By contrast, toward the southeast, the much

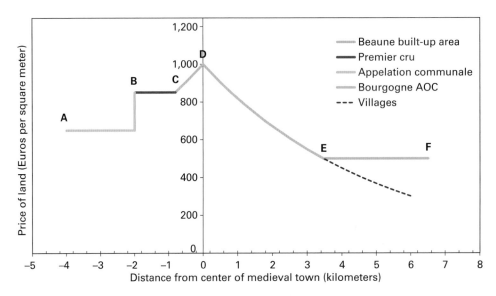

Figure 4.13
Profile of urban and agricultural land prices along the AB axis, Beaune.

cheaper price of vineyards—where "Bourgogne AOC" (second-grade vineyard area) wines are produced—allows the city to expand more freely in this direction. The exceptionally high price of agricultural land surrounding Beaune constrains the expansion of the city and is likely to make urban land exceptionally expensive. Apartments for sale in Beaune near the historical center were advertised at US$4,000 per square meter in 2014.

The Beaune example shows that urban and agricultural prices shape cities. The asymmetry of Beaune's built-up area has nothing to do with design but reflects market price differences. The very valuable land on which premier cru wines are produced does not need to be protected by a green-belt or zoning. It is protected by the high price of Burgundy wine on the world market. This example also shows that, when needed, the assumptions of the standard urban model can be selectively relaxed and adapted to circumstances that differ significantly from the initial assumptions.

Land Development Cost and the Limit of Urbanization

In the previous paragraphs, I have assumed that rural land could be converted, without cost, into urban land. In the real world, this is usually not the case.

In many cities, land subdivision regulations[25] are setting minimum standards that developers have to meet to transform agricultural land into developable urban lots. Complying with these regulations imposes four types of costs:

1. civil work costs for roads, sidewalks, and infrastructure;

2. land costs, as some of the land bought from farmers has to be set aside for roads, social facilities, and open space;

3. overhead costs that include design, supervision, and "paper pushing" to obtain the various permits from different departments; and

4. financial costs represented by interest during construction (interest has to be paid on the amount disbursed between the time land is acquired and the time when the plots are ready to be sold to builders).

The total area of land sold by developers to urban land users is therefore less than the area that developers buy from farmers. The roads and open spaces built by developers are usually transferred free of charge to the local authority. The total cost per square meter of salable developed land that will have to clear the market (i.e., that will be on or below the curve U in figure 4.14) is given by equation 4.2.

The variable k represents the development cost of developing land. The profit of the developer will be the difference between k and the sale price of developed land when it will finally be sold to builders. Because it takes a long time (several years for large projects) between the time agricultural land is acquired and developed plots are ready to be sold to builders, the price of developed land at the time of the sale is often quite uncertain.[26] This sale price could be higher or lower than k. If it is lower than k, the land developer will have to take a loss on the project or wait for the price of developed land to increase in the area until it is higher than k. However, during this period the developer will have to pay interest on k, further increasing the cost of developed land.

Comparing the price of agricultural land to the sale price of developed land and assuming that the difference represents the developer's profit is therefore completely misleading.

Equation 4.2 Cost per square meter of salable developed land that will clear the market

$$k = \frac{a+c+h+f}{1-r} \tag{4.2}$$

, where
k = land development cost per square meter of salable urban land;
a = price of agricultural land per square meter;
c = cost of civil works per square meter;
h = developer overhead;
f = financial cost; and
r = percent of developed land to be devoted to roads and open space.

Let us assume that a developer buys land from farmers at $100 per square meter; that civil works, overhead, and financial costs amount to $50 per square meter; and that regulations require roads and open space to occupy 40 percent of the land developed. Under these conditions, the price of developed land that will clear the market in this location will have to be at least $250 per square meter.[27] The more "generous" the land development standards imposed by the local authority, the higher the price will be that the final land user will have to pay for developed land.

The land development costs itemized in equation 4.2 occur only once, at the time when land use changes from rural to urban.

The large difference between the sale price of agricultural land at the fringe of cities and the sale price of developed land often gives the impression that either landowners or developers are making an extraordinarily high profit in the process. In reality, most of what appears to be a large capital gain often reflects high values for the parameters c, h, f, and k, reflecting a complex and difficult regulatory process rather than some speculative binge by one player or another.

The ratio between k and a, relating the price of undeveloped agricultural land to the price of developed land, is an important urban indicator that has been measured in 53 cities around the world by Shlomo Angel for his work on the Housing Indicators Program, conducted in 1994 for the World Bank. Angel calls this indicator the "land development multiplier." In his book, *Housing Policy Matters*,[28] Angel analyzes the implications of this indicator for housing affordability. He found that in 1990, the median value of the land development multiplier was equal to 4.0 in developing countries and 2.4 in industrialized countries. Thus the expansion of cities in developing countries is even more constrained than in industrialized countries, resulting in higher prices for land and housing. A combination of unrealistically high regulatory development standards and high transaction costs due to poor property registration and bureaucratic red tape are the cause of these higher costs.

Let us now revisit the distance between the limit of urbanization and the city center after taking into account the land development costs set by local regulations (figure 4.14). Line A, which corresponds to the market price of agricultural land (similar to line A on the graph shown on figure 4.10), intercepts the urban land price U at the point d_1 corresponding to a distance x_1. Line B corresponds to the land development cost k (which includes agricultural land price in addition to the other costs of developing land). The intersection d_2 of line B with curve U defines the new limit of urbanization for formal land development. We see that when the cost of land development is taken into account, the limit of urbanization decreases from x_1 to x_2, reducing the total area of land developed. The higher the cost k of formal infrastructure development, the shorter will be the distance x_2

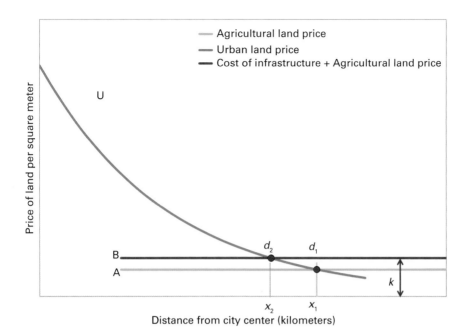

Figure 4.14
Limit of urbanization, taking into account the cost of land development.

compared to x_1 and the smaller the total area of developed land—and consequently, the higher the average built-up density will be, everything else being equal. The value of k, largely defined by planners' design, has a double impact on developed land cost: it increases the cost of developed land at the edge of cities, and it decreases the supply of developable land (by increasing the distance between x_1 and x_2), thus increasing the price of land everywhere else in the city.

Market forces governed by set regulations (such as those dictating road area percentages and overhead costs) impose an urban development limit at x_2. However, an informal building sector that ignores regulations exists in many countries. This informal sector includes individuals as well as developers building houses and commercial buildings that do not meet the minimum standards imposed by regulations, and therefore for whom the x_2 limit is irrelevant. The area between x_1 to x_2 is likely to become an urban fringe area, where the urban labor market will expand by including farmers progressively switching to urban jobs, and where informal settlements will develop in countries with weak law enforcement. In the next section I describe the conditions under which this extension of the urban fringe will occur.

The Labor Market May Expand beyond x_2: Villages at the Fringe of Cities
No new formal urban development will normally occur beyond the distance x_2
shown in figure 4.14. However, farmers already living beyond x_2 might find that
the difference between urban wages and rural wages is worth the expense of
commuting to a city job. These farmers already live in a farm beyond x_2, they do
not have to buy any land to be able to participate in the city's labor market, and
they do not have to pay land development cost k. If the cost of commuting to the
city is lower than the difference between their potential urban salary and their
current rural salary, they are likely to decide to join the urban labor force, even
though they live beyond the urban built-up boundary. The availability of cheap
motorcycles that can move easily on rural roads greatly decreases the cost of
individual commuting without the need to be connected to a major road or transit
network. The use of individual transport, when affordable, greatly increases the
size of labor markets beyond the visible limits of urbanization. We will see the
consequence of the extension of the urban labor markets in rural areas when discussing Hanoi's master plan later in this chapter.

Many Asian cities are located in the middle of dense rural areas. The population
living in rural areas adjacent to big cities often contributes to an increase in the
size of the labor market without requiring migration. This increase might be
important in parts of Asia where the rural population densities are high, as in
Bangladesh, Southeast Asia, and eastern China. For instance, figure 4.15 shows
the large number of villages located 20–30 kilometers to the east of Luoyang,
China. There is no trace of formal urbanization in the area, but a motorcycle would
allow farmers to commute to Luoyang in less than 40 minutes. The populations
of these villages may participate in the urban labor force long before any agricultural land is converted to urban use. These villages are likely to be incorporated
into the built-up area of the city when the price of urban land in their area becomes
higher than the price of agricultural land.

What Type of Development Might Take Place between x_1 and x_2?
The Emergence of the Informal Sector and Parallel Markets
What is likely to happen between x_1 and x_2? Between these two points,[29] at the fringe
of cities, farmers are likely to be willing to sell their land to developers at a price
higher than the agricultural price. However, formal developers cannot bypass a
building permit if they want to apply for construction finance. They will therefore
not buy land between x_1 and x_2, as the cost of development that would meet regulatory standards will not clear the market (between x_1 and x_2, k is above curve U).

Some consumers, however, may be quite satisfied by land development standards that are lower than the ones prescribed by regulations if they result in
cheaper housing. When there is such demand, informal developers, not relying

Villages at about 25 kilometers east of Loyang (Henan), China

Total area shown	54.91	square kilometers
Total area of villages	5.64	square kilometers
Average density in villages	220	people per hectare
Total estimated population	124,000	people
Gross density in area shown	23	people per hectare

Figure 4.15
Existing villages east of the immediate expansion area of Luoyang, China. *Source*: Vectorization of Google Earth Images, 2015; population estimates based on village surveys.

on the formal financial system, will be willing to buy land from farmers and develop it at standards that cost less than k. Between x_1 and x_2, farmers will only receive an offer for their land at a price above the agricultural price from informal developers. Some farmers might prefer to continue farming and wait for urban land prices to increase further to allow them to sell later to formal developers.[30] However, some farmers may decide to sell to informal developers or even informally develop their own land. In cities where urban regulations make land unaffordable to a part of the population, we can expect to see scattered urbanization made up of informal settlements between x_1 and x_2.

Informal developments might be built by developers in a planned fashion or might be created spontaneously by squatters on government land. Developer-driven informal development is, in my experience, much more common than squatter settlements, although there is no hard data on the subject worldwide. I am using the term "informal development" to designate a settlement developed by developers at standards below the regulatory requirements but meeting the demand of one segment of the population, and in general below the cost k as defined in equation 4.2.

Informal developments are likely to develop at the fringe of urbanization in cities where the costs of land development are higher than what a portion of the population can afford (or is willing to pay). When a large part of the urban population cannot afford the cost of the minimum standards imposed by regulation, the enforcement of the planning rules becomes impossible. In many cities of developing and emerging economies, informal settlements typically represent 20–60 percent of the total housing stock. In Mumbai, for instance, the most prosperous city in India, informal settlements represented more than 55 percent of the housing stock in 2010.[31] The growth of informality is not necessarily driven by poverty but by the arbitrariness and high cost of land use regulations.

In advanced economies where new land development is strictly controlled, an informal sector is likely to appear in the built-up area in the form of illegal subdivisions and extensions of existing houses and apartments. A 2008 paper[32] estimates that about 114,000 units of illegal new dwellings were built in New York City between 1990 and 2000. These new units were created by subdividing and expanding legally acquired houses built in existing developments. Therefore, the informal sector created by unaffordable urban regulations exists in both developed and developing countries. In developing countries, the informal sector mostly takes the form of illegal land development; in developed countries, illegal subdivisions and extension of houses or apartments in formal developments are more common. The growth of informal sectors in developed and developing countries has the same cause: poorly conceived land use regulations that do not take into account the income of poor households.

In countries where control over land development is weak, the urban land price curve defined by the standard urban model will reflect two types of development: new formal development that will be located in areas between the city center and x_2, and new informal development that is likely to grow between x_2 and x_1. Eventually, as household income increases and transport costs decrease, urban land prices will increase, pushing the formal development boundary farther to the right of x_2. Formal and informal development will then be found side by side in the same area, while new informal settlements will develop beyond the new x_2 point.

Informal development is a market response to the design rigidity imposed by regulations. Informal land development introduces a form of land supply elastic-

Figure 4.16
Informal subdivision at the fringe of urbanization in Mexico City (left image) and Surabaya, Indonesia (right image; same scale for both images).

ity in cities where the effects of regulations on markets significantly decrease the land supply (x_2 is smaller than x_1). In the absence of new informal developments, the increase in the supply of housing units for low-income households can happen only through the densification of existing low-income neighborhoods, which reduces the amount of land and floor space that low-income households consume. Therefore, the enforcement of urban planning rules frequently contributes to lowering the quality and quantity of housing affordable to the poor (as explained in depth in chapter 6). The two aerial images in figure 4.16 show informal developments at the fringe of Surabaya, Indonesia, and Mexico City's Federal District. In Surabaya, villagers have jointly developed agricultural land below the minimum standards for street width and plot sizes established by their government. However, the Indonesian government rightly tolerates this form of development, provided they form an organized community called a "kampung" which is in many ways similar to a condominium. The local government will later negotiate with the kampung leadership to connect the kampung with the municipal networks of infrastructure.

The informal settlements in Mexico City, shown on the right in figure 4.16, are very different from the Indonesian kampungs because they are and remain illegal. The land development standards—such as street width, plot size, and setbacks—are lower than the ones prescribed by regulations, but the settlement shown is located in an area that is not allowed to urbanize as per the master plan. The settlement is located on a 30 percent slope in the southwestern part of the Federal District in an area where any development is forbidden for environmental reasons. We can see that the area around Mexico City's informal settlements is still farmed. Regardless of whether the area is designated for development by the master plan, the price gradient defined by the standard urban model still defines land prices. Land would probably sell at a discount in an area where regulations forbid any development. But it is the distance to the Mexico City labor market that will ultimately decide the urban land price. If this urban land price is higher than the price of agricultural land, the area will likely urbanize. In an area with a 30 percent slope, agricultural land values might not be very high; therefore, the chance that farmers will sell their land to developers is rather high.

I am not giving these examples as advocacy for disregarding all urban regulations. The environmental regulations that aim to prevent development on the slopes of the volcanoes surrounding Mexico City are certainly sound. However, the price of urban land dictated by distance to the city labor market is still there. The designation of no-construction areas on the master plan does not render the land price irrelevant. Mexican municipalities should acknowledge the strong economic incentives that poor people have to break those regulations. Regulations have a cost. In this case, the cost of the land use regulation is the destruction of the value of the land, owned by the undoubtedly poor farmers toiling on the slopes of the volcanoes. The solution might be to compensate farmers for continuing to farm in the area, providing enough incentive so that the informal development alternative will not be attractive to them. Simultaneously, the government should allow the development of more land that is affordable for low-income households in other areas of Mexico City that are not under such an environmental constraint. Whatever the solution, we can see the link between land development standards and informality, and how the standard urban model can help urban planners anticipate what is likely to happen at the fringe of cities.

A Concrete Application of the Standard Urban Model: An Evaluation of the Hanoi Master Plan

About once every 10 years, many cities prepare a new master plan to guide future development. The master plan preparation usually follows the availability of new decadal census results. Typically, a master plan consists of three components:

- a review of past development trends and an identification of current issues;

- a declaration of development objectives and priorities; and

- a proposal for future development (including a land use map of areas to be developed, a proposal for new zoning regulations, and a list of public investments in civil work and social infrastructure consistent with the implementation of the plan's objectives).

In democratically elected municipalities, public hearings and public participation are expected during the various phases of preparation and before final approval by the municipal government.

The need to review periodically and to adjust a city's development objectives and ongoing infrastructure investments is certainly justified. However, whether this review should be done at set 10-year intervals regardless of other urban dynamics and involving a massive data-gathering exercise is rather dubious. The traditional master plan exercise seems to be a fossil left over from the time when the planning practices of command economies fascinated the world. It would make more sense for cities to monitor data and indicators in real time and to adjust policy and investments according to what works and what does not, rather than waiting 10 years to assess results and eventually changing direction. Some cities, like Singapore and Hong Kong, have adopted a real-time monitoring adjustment approach for managing their development. Their management system has become more similar to that of corporations, which have to adapt rapidly to external shocks.

The master plan concept is based on the false assumption that city development is similar to large civil works projects, requiring the preparation of a detailed blueprint that will be followed by a construction period of 10 years. While I consider the preparation of master plans a waste of money and energy, the reality is that most large cities in developing countries hire large engineering consulting firms to prepare these master plans. It is therefore important to look at their impact on the development of cities. Often, many large international lending institutions, such as the World Bank and bilateral development agencies, finance part of the urban infrastructure in developing countries. For these institutions, master plans, "structural plans," or "city strategies" are a convenient way to provide them with a list of potential investments from which they may select their medium-term lending programs. They therefore tend to support, at times financially, the preparation of such documents, because it simplifies their appraisal process.

Master plans provide a spatial blueprint for the development of cities based on an engineering design approach to city development. Consequently, they usually completely ignore the market forces linking land prices and densities described in the preceding sections of this chapter. They use a top-down design approach and project the spatial distribution of jobs and people across a metropolitan area based on the preferences of the designer, often justified as a "scientific approach" that identifies "needs." The master plan for Hanoi reviewed below is unfortunately quite representative of most of the master plans that I have reviewed during the past 40 years while working for the World Bank and other urban development organizations. We will see that the spatial development blueprint it contains violates most of the theoretical and empirical principles related to the standard urban model.

Hanoi: A Master Plan Based on "Scientific Principles"
In 2010, an international consortium made of reputable international consulting firms prepared a master plan for Hanoi, called the "Hanoi Capital Construction Master Plan to 2030 and Vision to 2050," projecting population, land use, and infrastructure needs for 2030. The plan received the Merit Award for Urban Design in 2011 from the American Institute of Architects of New York.

The authors of Hanoi's master plan say that their design for the spatial distribution of population is based on "scientific design principles."[33] The words "markets" or "land prices" do not appear even once in the entire report, in spite of the declared strategy of the Government of Vietnam to increase the use of market mechanisms to allocate resources. Vietnam joined the World Trade Organization in 2007, a decisive step in moving from a command to a market economy. There is a buoyant real estate market in Vietnam, with many players ranging from small entrepreneurs to large international developers. In her 2008 book, Annette Kim described the functioning and peculiarities of the early stage of Vietnam's real estate markets.[34] Since then, the Vietnamese real estate market has gained in sophistication, and its impressive realizations are seen everywhere, from low-income town houses built by farmers to large urban development that mixes high-end commerce, offices, and residential towers. Walking through the streets of Hanoi, no one could miss the dynamism and creativity of the various entrepreneurs who are busy building this fast-developing city. In contrast with this on-the-ground reality, the absence of a role for those entrepreneurs in Hanoi's master plan projections is astonishing.

The Master Plan's Objectives
I quote the master plan objectives from the plan's introduction:

Among the most important features of the plan is the accepted recommendation that 70% of Hanoi—including its remaining natural areas and most productive agricultural land—be permanently protected from further development as part of a broad sustainability strategy.[35]

Protecting agriculture is explicitly declared to be the main objective that will guide the physical expansion of Hanoi! This is an odd primary objective for the development of a city of 3.5 million in 2012, which grew at 3.5 percent per year between 2000 and 2010. According to the master plan, the projected population for the metropolitan region will increase to 9 million in 2030. Planning the expansion of the city and a transport system that would allow the labor market to function is likely to become a major challenge. Transportation planning is worthy of significant attention in a master plan, but these authors instead focus on preserving agricultural land. Unfortunately, this ignores the reality that tripling the population will require at least a tripling of developed land, which will in the long run lead to poor infrastructure if this expansion is not taken into account. This, in turn, will be detrimental to the goal of sustainability that the authors purport to pursue.

The Master Plan's Spatial Concept: Preserving Agriculture

The schematic projected land use plan is shown on the right in figure 4.17. The existing land use map of the metropolitan area in the year 2010 is shown on the left in the figure. The spatial concept consists of an agricultural belt about 16 kilometers wide splitting the population of Hanoi into two parts: the core city (including the current Hanoi's CBD) and high-density satellite towns. In the agricultural belt, three "Eco-Township/villages" of 60,000 people each will be created, but only agro-industries would be allowed in these villages. Some new expressways, parkways, and rapid rail transits crossing the agricultural belt would link the satellite towns to the main core city (figure 4.17). The land use in 2010 shows that the agricultural belt includes many villages that already occupy about 24 percent of the area. According to the 2009 census, a population of 2 million already lives in the villages in the agricultural belt. The authors of the master plan assume that the population already in the agricultural belt will remain rural and will keep cultivating the area.

The concern for the conservation of fertile agricultural land that surrounds the southwestern part of Hanoi is the justification for fragmenting the city's extension on both sides of the agricultural belt. The authors of the master plan provide three reasons to prevent Hanoi's expansion into the immediately adjacent rice paddies. First, the energy saved on transport in bringing rice to Hanoi will be significant compared to the energy required to transport rice from other parts of Vietnam. Second, the rice fields would provide a greatly needed green area next to the high-density core city. Third, the existing paddy fields surrounding Hanoi are prone to flooding and would have been expensive to develop.

The master plan does not provide numbers to justify these assertions, which are central to the spatial development strategy. We will see below that the costs that the inhabitants of Hanoi will incur by preventing the urbanization of the agricultural belt will be extremely high and will far outweigh any benefits implied by these arguments. My main objection to the creation of an agricultural belt that would split the city into two parts is that it will disrupt residents' ability to interact with one another and to participate efficiently in labor and real estate markets. By ignoring what we know about labor and real estate markets, it will prove to be extremely costly for Hanoi's households and firms.

Let us test the consistency of the master plan spatial concept shown in figure 4.17 with what we know about the workings of labor and land markets. If the spatial extension of the population prescribed by the master plan contradicts the

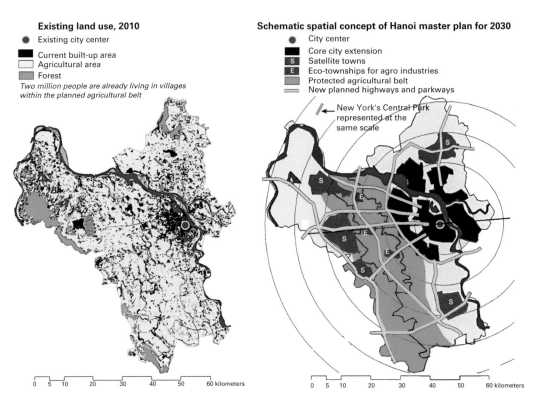

Figure 4.17
Hanoi existing land use in 2010 and Hanoi's capital master plan for 2030.

way labor and land markets work, it is unlikely to be implemented because of the high cost that will be incurred by households and firms. Therefore, it is likely that the city will grow following a different spatial pattern from the one projected by the plan. Unfortunately, it is also likely that the government will build the infrastructure as planned. This will result in further waste, as the infrastructure will not be built where the new population has settled. This is a common outcome of master plans. I have seen it happen in cities as diverse as Karachi and Cairo.

The Master Plan Spatial Concept Is Inconsistent with the Functioning of Labor Markets
The master plan projects that 9 million people will live in the Hanoi metropolitan area in 2030. Among them, 3 million will remain "rural," not because they will live in areas that are too remote to participate in the urban labor market, but because they happen to live within the perimeter of what the planners have zoned as the agricultural belt. The agricultural belt, however, is much closer (from 8 to

24 kilometers) to the center of Hanoi than are the satellite towns. The current land use map on the left in figure 4.17 shows that numerous villages are already located in the projected agricultural belt. According to the 2009 population census, the rural population in the belt is about 2 million people. Many of these villages are already about 40 minutes or less by motorcycle from the center of Hanoi. With the new highways planned, the commuting time to Hanoi will become even shorter in the future.

Workers who are currently cultivating rice in Hanoi's agricultural belt are likely to have wages similar to rice farmers in other parts of Vietnam. If they receive higher wages, then the rice produced in the agricultural belt will have to be sold at a higher price than the rice produced elsewhere, soil productivity being equal. The lower transport cost involved in bringing rice to Hanoi's consumers is unlikely to compensate for the cost of the higher salary of agricultural workers if their wages have to be aligned with those of Hanoi's urban workers. As rice is a commodity good with standard prices set by the market, the price of rice will not rise, so therefore the wages of workers will not rise, resulting in lower incomes for those employed in agriculture than for farmers who decide to seek urban employment. The short distance from the agricultural belt to Hanoi's city center—and increase in the number of roads projected to be built by the master plan, further deceasing travel times—will provide a significant employment advantage to farmers seeking urban jobs over the workers in satellite towns located much farther away. The master plan's assignment of workers to rural or urban jobs is based purely on whether they will live within the arbitrary perimeter of the designated agricultural belt, not on distance from urban jobs.

The arbitrary assignment of workers to rural or urban jobs is solely based on planners' choice and is therefore unlikely to be implemented: no zoning regulations can force people to work in one sector of the economy rather than another! It is very likely that in 2030, owners of rice paddy fields in the agricultural belt will face difficulties finding enough labor to work in their fields, because of the competition with better paying urban jobs. Preventing urban development in the agricultural belt is therefore unlikely to meet its main objective, which was to preserve rice production in this area. Plans that contradict the functioning of labor markets are unlikely to be successful.

The Master Plan Spatial Concept Is Inconsistent with the Functioning of Land Markets

The villages currently in the agricultural belt occupy about 23 percent of the belt area (figure 4.17). As soon as the planned road infrastructure is built, the transport time and cost to commute to Hanoi's main employment areas will likely decrease. Consequently, the price of houses in these villages will increase and will likely follow an urban price gradient centered on Hanoi's city center, as predicted by the standard urban model. The likely high rent generated by floor space located in these villages will be a strong incentive for farmers to increase the number of floors of existing houses or to build new ones in their backyards. The area is likely therefore to densify, sheltering the families of urban farmers and additional urban workers. The density in these villages will increase in the same way that the density in the villages in Hanoi's closer periphery has increased in the past.

The cultivated land around the villages of the agricultural belt will of course be under the same developmental pressure as the land occupied by villages. Initially, the price of land in the agricultural belt will reflect the income generated from cultivating rice. But as urban household incomes increase and transport cost to the center of Hanoi decreases, the demand for urban land from households and firms will increase. Consequently, the price of land in the agricultural belt will increase and become much higher than the price of land under agricultural use. The profile of land prices and population densities will follow the profile predicted by the standard urban model and will be similar to that shown in figure 4.10, with the peak land price and density located in Hanoi's CBD. We may safely assume that most of the agricultural land in the planned agricultural belt will soon have an urban land value much higher than its agricultural value. Already, observations by Google Earth imagery taken in 2014 show that new formal and informal housing developments are appearing in the agricultural belt, consistent with the predictions of the standard urban model.

The Spatial Distribution of Population as Designed by the Master Plan Is Unlikely to Ever Be Implemented

It is unlikely that regulations, even if the government were ready to enforce them, would be enough to prevent urban development in the agricultural belt. In principle, all land in Vietnam belongs to the state. However, farmers have a collective land use right to the land they occupy. And since the reforms of 2005, farmers have been allowed to sell land to developers, though the local government often intervenes as an intermediary, extracting substantial revenue in the process.

Under the spatial concept of the plan, farmers outside the agricultural belt would therefore be allowed to sell their land to developers, raising substantial revenues for themselves and the local government, while farmers inside the agricultural belt limits will have no other option but to keep growing rice on their land. Obviously, this would generate a lot of political resistance, in particular because the limit establishing the agricultural belt is arbitrary. Farmers, local government, and developers will lose a great deal of potential revenue because of the creation of the agricultural belt; they will form a powerful coalition to prevent the belt's implementation. Households seeking low rents or cheap housing in areas with good job accessibility would prefer to settle in the agricultural belt than to be forced to live in satellite towns at a much farther distance from jobs.

The apparent drop in land value caused by the interdiction to build the agricultural belt may also become a large source of inequity and corruption. Local government could expropriate land from farmers, paying agricultural land prices for it—as officially this would be the only use permitted. Later, an unscrupulous intermediary could resell the land to a developer at a much higher price after obtaining an amendment to the master plan by creating enclaves of urban development in the agricultural belt.

What Would Be the Consequences of Constructing the Infrastructure Designed in the Master Plan?

Because the planners who designed the master plan failed to consider how labor and real estate markets work, the spatial distribution of densities in 2030 is likely to be very different from the designed densities shown in the plan. Higher population densities will be concentrated in the eastern part of the agricultural belt, decreasing toward the west. If the government implements the infrastructure investments programmed in the master plan, there will be a mismatch between the infrastructure built and the actual spatial distribution of the population. The new dense developments that will emerge in the green-belt will generate many trips with no matching road and transport network. The large, newly urbanized areas in the agricultural belt will be deprived of a comprehensive sewer and drainage network that could protect the environment and prevent periodic flooding. Indeed, maintaining the rice paddies in the agricultural belt will require preserving the current irrigation network. An urban storm drainage system preventing seasonal flooding is incompatible with irrigation. Eventually, at a much later period when the agricultural belt is fully urbanized, the government will have to build a comprehensive sewer and drainage system, as is being done in Bangkok and Jakarta, but at a far greater cost than if it had been designed before urbanization had taken place. Building a regional storm drainage and sewer system in the monsoon countries where Hanoi is located requires complex hydrological studies of the area, which have not been conducted, because the agricultural belt has been designated to remain rice paddies.

The lack of well-designed recreation areas will be another casualty of the master plan. The plan considers the rice paddies a "green reserve" by themselves and consequently does not identify specific areas in the agricultural belt reserved for recreation. As the rice paddies are progressively replaced by informal urbanization, strategically well-located open spaces may well disappear. Two rivers cross the agricultural belt, feeding ponds and small lakes. In view of the inevitable urbanization of the agricultural belt, it is critical to create a buffer zone around the existing water bodies, which would become formal public parks that should be integrated into the urban storm drainage system.

Would Any Social Benefits Result If the Government Could Enforce the Spatial Distribution of Population Prescribed by the Master Plan?

Most master plans have the same flaws as Hanoi's master plan and consequently are not implemented. Eventually, through derogations of the plan or through the growth of the informal sector, the distribution of densities and land prices will follow a pattern based on the demand for land needed by households and firms, as predicted by the standard urban model. This is predictably the fate of Hanoi's master plan.

Presumably, an authoritarian government, through a draconian enforcement of land use regulations, could prevent the development of the agricultural belt. We can assess the impact of such actions on the welfare of the population through two indicators: the affordability of land and the average commuting distance.

The impact that the plan would have on urban land and housing prices is obvious. The agricultural belt covers 870 square kilometers, an area slightly larger than the 850 square kilometers planned for the total built-up area of Hanoi in 2030! Removing such a large area from the land supply would increase land prices in the residual area where the plan authorizes urban development. It would also further increase densities in the already very dense core city, increasing congestion and decreasing the land and floor consumption of poorer households. The impact of greenbelts on land and housing prices has been well documented by many urban economists, including Jan Brueckner, Edwin Mill, and Kyung-Hwan Kim.

The implementation of the plan would also significantly increase commuting time and energy used by urban transport compared to what it would have been if development prices and densities had followed the standard urban model. The agricultural belt—from 20 to 30 kilometers wide—separates the core city from the satellite towns. This distance will add to the commuting time for those who live in the satellite towns but work in the core city, and for those who live in the core city but work in the satellite towns.

Would the implementation of the master plan create any benefits that could compensate for the higher cost of housing and transport? The master plan mentions three major benefits that would be directly derived from its proposed spatial arrangement. First, the agricultural belt will save on the cost of transport for the rice consumed by Hanoi's urban population. Second, the belt will provide a useful green space for recreation. And third, by avoiding development in rice paddies, the belt will decrease the cost of infrastructure development.

The argument that creating an agricultural belt in the middle of Hanoi's metropolitan area will save on agricultural transport cost is naive at best. It would be much cheaper to transport bags of rice once a year after harvest from any location in Vietnam than to transport millions of people twice a day across Hanoi's metropolitan area.

The second argument—the agricultural belt would constitute a needed recreation area—is no more valid than the first argument. The rice paddies that occupy the agricultural belt in the master plan would be a poor recreational area, considering that they are flooded a large part of the time. The area represented by the agricultural belt is about 10 times the area of Hanoi's core city. It would be large enough to fit more than 300 parks the size of New York's Central Park! If the agricultural areas around Hanoi were urbanized, it certainly would be possible to reserve recreational areas along the two rivers and the several lakes, creating a large and pleasant green space easily accessible from adjacent neighborhoods. Hanoi already has many examples of well-designed and well-used parks along rivers and lakes in the middle of dense neighborhoods.

The third argument, that paddy fields are prone to flooding and are expensive to develop, has somewhat more validity than the first two arguments. However, in 2010, villages inhabited by a population of about 2 million people already occupied 23 percent of the area in the agricultural belt. It therefore seems that the area is not impossible to develop. Anyway, it would be even more expensive to develop a network of highways and rapid transit (see figure 4.17) across the same paddy fields as the ones proposed by the master plan without using the land adjacent to the highways. Many large cities of Southeast Asia, among them Bangkok and Jakarta, have been developed on former paddy fields. Land development in paddy areas requires careful planning of an elaborate drainage system, but it has been done all over South East Asia.

The Final Evaluation of Hanoi's Master Plan

The problem with Hanoi's master plan is not caused by an unfortunate design decision but by a faulty concept. Allocating urban land and activities is not a pure design exercise: It requires an understanding of how labor and land markets work. It is impossible to design the future expansion of a city without taking into account the impact of the labor and land markets on the future distribution of the population. Land prices, rents, and commuting times are not mentioned even once in the master plan's nearly thousand pages of text, maps, and tables. It is a rather typical document that exposes the hubris of planners who think that a city needs only to be designed by a clever engineer, without taking into account market mechanisms that are constantly at play. Trying to obstruct markets always has grave consequences.

The standard urban model has shown us that the price of land in large cities is similar to the gravity field of large planets that decreases with distance at a predictable rate. Ignoring land prices when designing cities is like ignoring gravity when designing an airplane.

The Operational Applications of the Standard Urban Model

An understanding of the standard urban model is indispensable when making informed choices to manage cities. Let us summarize the operational implications of the spatial distribution of prices and densities as derived from the model.

Concerns about the overconsumption of land by cities ("sprawl") are best addressed by identifying possible distortions in the land market, caused by abusing the use of eminent domain, underpricing agricultural land, and subsidizing gasoline. Setting arbitrary spatial barriers to urban expansion, such as green-belts and UGBs, however, results in higher land and housing prices, longer commute times, and other negative outcomes as demonstrated in Hanoi's master plan.

Land prices and population densities are closely related and are produced by market forces. We have also seen that there is no optimum density for urban development, and within the same city, densities may vary by orders of magnitude from the center to the periphery. The population density in a particular neighborhood is determined by trade-offs between households' desire to consume more land and floor space and the commuting cost in time and money. Households with different preferences and incomes make different trade-offs. Some low-income households prefer to reduce drastically their land and floor space consumption in order to reduce commuting costs. Other households with similar incomes may make different trade-offs. Planners cannot possibly know the reasons households may have for selecting a specific housing location and level of land consumption. Therefore, planners should abstain from arbitrarily fixing densities through regulations. Neither should they try to distribute population according to a designed spatial pattern, no matter how clever the geometric arrangement appears to be.

Planners should use the standard urban model to better understand how markets work in the city they are managing. They can use the model to anticipate the effect of regulations and infrastructure on land prices and rents. They can plan, finance, and build the infrastructure that would increase the supply of land and therefore decrease housing costs. They can design transport systems that decrease commuting time and cost, another way of increasing the supply of land and increasing mobility. They should design transport systems that are consistent with the densities set by the land markets rather than design densities that would make a preselected transport system feasible.

The standard urban model is a very crude instrument that provides an understanding of the basic movement of land prices and rent as income, transport costs, and land supply change over time. Planners could design more complex models to anticipate price movements or commuting patterns in cities with specific constraints, in particular topographical constraints like bodies of water or steep mountains. However, no infrastructure or regulatory design decision should be taken without accounting for its impact on the land market.

In general, fixing minimum consumption for land and floor space through regulations on such things as minimum plot size, maximum floor area ratio, and maximum number of dwelling units per hectare introduces rigidities in the market that have negative impacts on poorer households for whom these regulations are binding (discussed in more detail in chapter 6). Planners should therefore abstain from using these regulatory constraints on minimum land and housing consumption, as they hurt the poor the most and trigger the growth of informal markets.

Only after they have a good understanding of how local real estate markets function can planners anticipate future land market values and then plan infrastructure networks that will be consistent with anticipated densities. Constant monitoring of land prices and rent could provide planners with feedback that could help them amend their infrastructure plans if their projection appears to diverge from reality.

Unaffordable housing is a plague affecting many large cities. Monitoring the ratio between median income and median housing price allows us to constantly measure housing affordability. When the price-to-income ratio becomes higher than 4, planners should take immediate action. This action could be to increase land supply through new infrastructure development or to audit land use regulations and building permit practices that may make developed land and housing prices artificially high. Urban planners should be held responsible for unaffordable high price/income ratios in the same way that public health officials are held responsible for infectious disease epidemics, or police are held responsible for high crime.

In the case of Hanoi's master plan, planners should have surveyed house rents and the price of land in new housing developments in the agricultural belt. If they had done so, the very high cost imposed on the 2 million farmers already living there by preventing further development in the agricultural belt would have become evident. A quick survey of agricultural wages compared to urban wages would have also allowed planners to anticipate that most agricultural workers would eventually switch to urban jobs as soon as they had access to them through better transport networks. The lack of understanding of land and labor markets led the planners to design a metropolitan infrastructure that will be at odds with the likely spatial distribution of the population.

5 Mobility: Transport Is a Real Estate Issue—The Design of Urban Roads and Transport Systems

The Need for Mobility

Cities are primarily large labor and consumer markets. These markets work best when the possibility of contact increases between workers and firms, among firms themselves, and between consumers and commercial and cultural amenities. The term "mobility," in the context of this book, defines the ability to multiply these contacts with a minimum of time and friction.

A worker's ability to choose among many jobs and a firm's ability to select the most qualified workers depends on mobility. Mobility is not defined by the ability to get to one's current job quickly, but by the ability to choose among all jobs and amenities offered in a metropolitan area while spending less than 1 hour commuting. Mobility increases when the number of jobs and amenities that can be reached within a specific amount of time increases. Because of the impact of mobility on the welfare of a city, it is important to measure it and monitor its variations—up or down—as a city's population increases, its land use changes, and its transport system improves or deteriorates. I will propose ways to measure and compare mobility in different cities in the section "Mobility and Transport Modes" later in this chapter.

The objective of an urban transport strategy should be to minimize the time required to reach the largest possible number of people, jobs, and amenities. Unfortunately, many strategies, such as "compact cities," only aim to minimize the distance traveled by inhabitants. These strategies reduce the income of the poor, for whom employment opportunities are reduced to jobs located within a narrow radius of their homes.

Cities thrive on changes, possibilities, and innovations. Therefore, an urban transport system that would solely minimize travel time between home and current jobs for all workers would result in poor mobility, as in the future, workers might not be able to reach many alternative jobs that would improve their job satisfaction or salary.

Mobility and Recent Immigrants

During a recent visit to the Tenement Museum in New York, a docent told us that in the 1850s, immigrants who were "fresh off the boat" would typically stay only a few months in a tenement; they would then keep moving as their employment and financial circumstances changed. A typical length of stay in the same tenement would be about 6–8 months. My wife and I then looked at each other, remembering that this was exactly what we did when—in January 1968—we were also "fresh off the boat" in New York. We changed apartments three times in 30 months. We moved from a flophouse on the Upper East Side that was soon going to be demolished, to a studio apartment in an "old law tenement" on the Upper East Side, and then to an entire floor in a townhouse in Brooklyn Heights. I also changed job three times. Each time, I changed for a more interesting job and a higher salary. This is the type of mobility that we will discuss in this chapter: the ability to move from job to job and from dwelling to dwelling made possible by a transport infrastructure that gives access to millions of potential jobs in less than 1 hour of commuting time.

This mobility was made possible by a buoyant housing and job market, ensuring a low transaction cost of changing jobs and location. By contrast, in Paris (where we came from), housing mobility was hampered by 2-year leases that could not be broken without penalties. Additionally, job mobility was frowned on as a sign of instability—changing jobs three times in 30 months would have resulted in a resume that raised a lot of eyebrows.

When—after just 6 months with my first employer in New York—I found a job that was a better fit with my long-term interests, I was terribly embarrassed by the prospect of telling my employer that I was quitting. My colleagues at work reassured me that this was done all the time in New York, and that a higher salary was a very honorable reason to change jobs. Indeed, my employer gave me a good luck party when I quit!

This is mobility. A flexible labor market, an open housing market—the flophouse with its low standards but very low rent was essential to getting us started—and a transport system that is fast, affordable, and extensive enough to allow individuals to look for jobs in an entire metropolitan area rather than just in limited locations.

The benefits of urban mobility are not limited to saving on commuting time. Mobility is also necessary to facilitate random face-to-face encounters between individuals of different cultures and fields of knowledge. These serendipitous encounters increase cities' creativity and productivity. The multiplicity of easily accessible meeting places available outside the work setting increases the possibilities of chance encounters and therefore increases the spillover effects found in large cities. The agora of ancient Greek cities or the forum of Roman cities were precisely fulfilling these needs. Agoras and forums were places where people assembled to conduct business, to meet friends, to attend religious ceremonies and political meetings, to receive justice, and to frequent public baths. Modern cities have many of these functions in separate locations. Unfortunately, rigid zoning regulations often constrain the existence and location of these multi-function places.

When transport systems provide adequate mobility, then the large concentration of people in metropolitan areas increases productivity and stimulates creativity. Empirical data confirm the link between large human concentrations and productivity. Physicists from the Santa Fe Institute have shown that, on average, when the population of a city doubles, its economic productivity per capita increases by 15 percent.[1]

The interesting findings of the Santa Fe Institute's scientists should be qualified, though. Their database included 360 US metropolitan areas with, by world standards, a very good transport infrastructure network that ensures mobility together with spatial concentration. In a way, these scientists' use of the word "cities" assumes the availability of transportation. It would be wrong to interpret their work as demonstrating that human concentration alone increases productivity.

Mobility explains the link between city size and productivity. Human concentration alone does not increase productivity. Some rural areas in Asia have gross densities that are higher than the density of some North American cities like Atlanta or Houston, for instance. However, in these rural areas, mobility is poor to nonexistent between villages. In absence of mobility, there is no increase in productivity despite the high density. The productivity of cities therefore requires both concentration of people and high mobility.

When the time and cost required to move across a city increase, mobility decreases. When this happens, workers have fewer choices among the potential jobs available in a city, and firms have fewer choices when recruiting workers. In these conditions, metropolitan labor markets tend to fragment into smaller, less productive ones; salaries tend to decrease, while consumer prices increase because of lack of competition. In practical terms, labor market fragmentation means that a worker might not find the job for which she is qualified, because she cannot commute in less than 1 hour to the firm who could employ her. Conversely, the firm looking for a worker with specialized knowledge cannot find him because he cannot reach the firm in less than a 1-hour commute. Workers having to commute for more than 1 hour each way are penalized by a social cost that progressively destroys their personal life. Poor mobility may also result in high transport overhead cost for firms having to exchange goods and services in an urban area. Increasing mobility in urban metropolitan areas is therefore indispensable to the welfare of urban households as well as to the creativity and prosperity of firms.

In a city, a worker's mobility often depends on his income. In some large Indian cities, for instance, the poorest workers can only afford to walk to work. Even a very long walk of 90 minutes would give them access to a very small number of possible jobs, decreasing their potential earnings. Planners should measure separately the mobility of different income groups, accounting for the modes of transport that each group can afford.

Mobility generates not only benefits but also costs, including congestion, pollution, noise, and accidents. To reduce those nuisances, many urban planners advocate limiting or at least discouraging mobility. They dream of creating cleverly planned land use arrangements that would require only short trips easily covered by walking or bicycling, even in megacities. These utopian land use arrangements usually rely on complex land use regulations[2] that would enable planners to match employers' locations with employees' residences.

Mobility is an urban necessity that must be encouraged, not curtailed. Poor mobility keeps much of the economic potential of existing large cities from being realized. Unfortunately, in many cities, the lowest-income households suffer the most from poor mobility. They would enormously benefit if their mobility increased, so that they could look for jobs as well as cultural and commercial amenities throughout an entire metropolitan area. Instead, they are limited to the small area around their homes, circumscribed by their limited mobility.

As urban metropolitan areas increase in size and population, their potential large labor markets may fragment into smaller markets because of the lack of mobility. It is therefore necessary to differentiate between the potential and actual size of the labor market. The potential size is equal to the number of workers and jobs in a city. Its real size equals the average number of jobs that a worker can reach in a 1-hour commute.

Commuting Trips and Other Trips

Throughout this chapter, we will examine mobility in the context of commuting trips (trips from home to work and back), even though commuting trips are only a fraction of urban trips. In the United States in 2013, commuting trips represented only 20 percent of weekday urban trips, 28 percent of vehicle kilometers traveled, and 39 percent of public transport passenger-kilometers traveled.[3]

Households and firms generate many types of trips that have different purposes (e.g., trips to work, to school, to visit friends, to shop). Many trips have multiple purposes. Transport engineers call such excursions chained trips or linked trips. On a chained trip, a person might drop a child off at school, go to work, and shop, for instance. Chained trips are both convenient for the commuter and efficient in terms of transportation, as they save time and reduce the distance traveled compared with the same trips done separately. For the United States, the Pisarski and Polzin study indicates that 19 percent of all women's trips are chained trips compared to 14 percent for men. While chained trips are transport efficient, they are nearly incompatible with public transport and carpooling.

Despite commuting trips representing only a fraction of all trips, I will continue to use them to measure mobility. For the economic viability of a city, the most important trips are those to and from work—the commuting trips—as the labor market generates the wealth that makes the other trips possible. In addition, the timing of commuting trips is usually not chosen by the traveler. Instead, they often occur at peak hours, and they are the ones causing most congestion and pollution. Therefore, the transport infrastructure capacity needs to be calibrated on the demand during peak hours, largely determined by commuting trips.

Some elective trips, like holiday shopping or leisure trips on summer weekends, may also cause heavy congestion, but they are seasonal and therefore do not have such high annualized costs as the daily congestion caused by commuting trips.

Improving Mobility Is Not As Simple As Making Cities Denser

Ideally, the closer people and firms are to each other, the shorter the trips required to meet and transact business would be. In an urban area with a given population, people, firms, and amenities are closer to one another when population and job densities are higher. It may seem, therefore, that for a given population, mobility simply increases when density also increases due to the shorter distances between households and firms. Similarly, it would seem that mobility would decrease as the distance between firms and employees increases.

Unfortunately, things are not that simple. Let us consider the average distance d of commuting trips between random points A and B selected in a city built-up area. For a given population, the distance d will indeed be shorter if the city's density is higher. However, mobility increases when the time t needed to cover the trip distance d from A to B decreases, and not necessarily when d alone decreases. Therefore, mobility increases not only when the trip distance d decreases but also when the trip travel speed v increases ($t = d/v$). The trip's speed v depends on the mode of transport and the area devoted to roads. Therefore, increasing densities may decrease the average distance d between people and jobs, but it may also increase congestion and therefore decrease travel speed v.

Let's make this come alive through an example. Nineteen-century London, with its sweatshops and slums, was extremely compact. In 1830, according to Shlomo Angel and colleagues,[4] London's population density had reached a very high density of 325 people per hectare. By 2005, however, the density of London had decreased to only 44 people per hectare. The large decrease in London's density since the Industrial Revolution has not caused a corresponding decrease in mobility. On the contrary, transport modes in London in 1830, largely walking and horse carriages, were much slower than those available in 2015 London with its choice of various motorized transport modes. In 2015, commuters can reach the city center from the suburbs as far as 26 kilometers away in less than 1 hour by public transport. In contrast, in 1830, commutes from the edge of London, about 7 kilometers from its center, would have taken about 1.5 hours. In this case, a seven fold decrease in density did not result in a decrease in mobility; on the contrary, an improvement in transport technology generated an increase in mobility despite the sharp fall in population density.

The goal is to reduce the time spent traveling and the cost of transport, not necessarily to reduce the distance between trip origin and destination. The mode of transport and the design of the transport network will have a much more impact on mobility than distance traveled.

How to Increase Mobility as Cities Expand

The population of successful cities is constantly increasing because of the economic advantages provided by large labor markets. To maintain mobility as city populations increase, urban transport systems must adapt to the new size of cities. In relatively small cities—around 200,000 people, like Oxford or Aix-en-Provence—a combination of transport modes like walking, bicycles, and city buses provide adequate means of transport in the downtown area, while individual cars and motorcycles are used for trips in the periphery. However, when a city's population increases above 1 million, these means of transport become inadequate, and new means of faster transport must be built. Because the land in the center of large cities becomes more expensive, new transport must not only be faster but also should use less of the expensive urban land, hence the necessity to develop underground or elevated transport systems.

Transport systems that may be adequate for a given city size soon become deficient in a larger city. Transport systems cannot just be scaled up but need to be entirely redesigned when cities grow larger. It is futile to use Amsterdam's or Copenhagen's transport system as a model for much larger cities like Mumbai or Shanghai.

As the size of cities increases and traditional land use patterns keep changing, it is imperative to keep monitoring mobility, the direct cost borne by commuters, and the negative impact it creates on the city environment.

Mobility Creates Friction

Urban mobility creates friction. The larger the city, the more severe the frictions caused by mobility will become. These frictions include the time and cost required to go from one part of a city to another and the congestion and pollution created by doing so.

The frictions caused by urban transport are not new. Urban congestion did not begin with the advent of cars. A golden age when cities were congestion free never existed. The Latin poet Juvenal, in his Satire III, mentioned the difficulties of moving around ancient Rome in the first century. Traffic congestion in the Roman Empire is even the subject of a recently published book![5] In the seventeenth century, the poet Boileau wrote a satirical poem about *les embarras de Paris* (the gridlocks of Paris).

At the end of the nineteenth century, pollution due to transport was such a concern that some saw it as a limiting factor in the growth of cities. London was at the time the largest city in the world, with 6 million people. The pollution so reviled then was the enormous quantity of horse manure produced daily by horse-drawn buses and cabs. Indeed, it was a major health concern. Acknowledging London's future increase in population, scientists projected that the quantity of horse manure produced by transport would soon bury the city like a modern Pompeii! With hindsight, we know that the introduction of the automobile saved London from submersion in manure, but congestion and pollution remain a major constraint in urban transport today.

Various frictions caused by urban transport have been a constant concern since the dawn of urbanization. They cannot be eliminated, at least with current technology, but they can be decreased. These frictions will be discussed separately below: they include direct travel cost, time spent traveling, congestion, pollution, and other indirect costs. Any city that can significantly decrease frictions due to transport will see a corresponding increase in productivity and the welfare of its citizens because more time will be left for work and leisure.

A primary task of city managers should be to minimize the frictions caused by urban transport. This job is never done—as a city expands, the distance covered by commuting trips becomes longer. A city structure and its transport system must adapt continuously to its changing scale. As a city expands from 1 million to 10 million (e.g., as Seoul Municipality did between 1950 and 2015), the original transport system cannot simply be expanded; it must change in nature and technology to reflect the new scale of the labor market being served. The goal is to maintain mobility such that the majority of commuting trips stay below 1 hour, in spite of the much longer distances involved.

The unfortunate tendency of many current traffic managers is to restrict trips to avoid congestion. Instead they should better manage the road space available or adopt new technology to allow even more and faster trips.

The Death of Distance Has Been Greatly Exaggerated

In the "Star Trek" television series, the words "beam me up" were all that was needed to transport people and goods anywhere instantly through the teleportation machine. This imaginary technology allowed universal frictionless mobility. Unfortunately, it was fictional.

If frictionless mobility were possible, the dense concentration of people in cities would not be required. I could start the morning in a small town in New Jersey, a few minutes later have coffee and a croissant in a café in Paris, and a few seconds after finishing my coffee, I could start working in an office in Mumbai, or anywhere else in the world. In a world allowing frictionless mobility, location would no longer matter. Most of us have already replaced some physical trips by virtual ones. For instance, I used to visit bookstores on a regular basis; I now buy my books online, and they are delivered to me electronically. The visit to the bookstore was a face-to-face encounter that has been replaced by a "beam me up" operation, except that it is the book that is being beamed up, not a person.

While the teleportation machine from Star Trek is likely to remain fiction, would communication technology—in particular, increasingly realistic teleconferencing—make location obsolete, providing a substitute for frictionless mobility? Or, in simpler terms, could communication technology replace the face-to-face contacts that generate most of our commuting trips? Indeed, it is much cheaper to move data than to move people. This is precisely the main argument developed by Frances Cairncross in her book *The Death of Distance* (2001). Cairncross suggests that the Internet and the global spread of wireless technology are increasingly making distance irrelevant. Communication technology would make face-to-face contact obsolete, and, in this sense, we would be getting closer to a Star Trek–like frictionless mobility, replacing the mobility of individuals by that of data. Virtual reality encounters would replace the necessity of "in the flesh" face-to-face encounters.

Work-at-Home Individuals
The increasing share of people working at home but constantly connected to a front office seems to confirm Cairncross' prediction. Among eight of the ten US cities with the largest number of work-at-home individuals (figure 5.1), the share of people working at home is larger than the share of workers using public transport. In all nine cities, the increase of work-at-home individuals has been larger than the increase in public transport users. However, with the exception of San Francisco, all the cities shown on figure 5.1 have rather low densities by world standards. This may explain the low proportion of growth of urban transport compared to the growth of work at home. In addition, many workers commute only a few days a week and are only working at home part-time. If this trend continues, could the home become the main place of work, rendering commuting obsolete and resulting in trips mostly for leisure or personal reasons?

Working from home is not new, of course. Up to the early twentieth century, artisans and service workers were often working from home, delivering their finished work to their employers weekly. These included washerwomen and lace

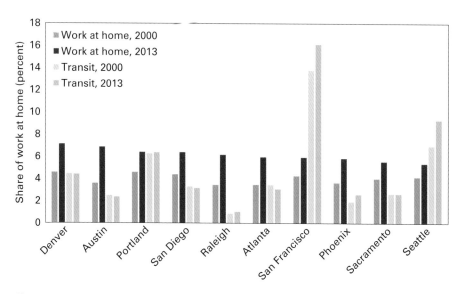

Figure 5.1
Mode share work at home versus public transport in some US cities. *Source*: Wendell Cox, *New-Geography*, May 30, 2015.

makers, but also Swiss farmers making watch mechanical parts. What is new, however, is that clerical and technical workers, who traditionally worked in large office pools, have replaced these manual workers working from home. But is it likely that a very large part of the workforce—say, more than 25 percent—will start working from home full time, significantly reducing peak hour traffic? So far, this possibility seems limited.

A recent Yahoo human resource department's memo requested employees working from home to resume working at the office, arguing, "Some of the best decisions and insights come from hallway and cafeteria discussions, meeting new people and impromptu team meetings. Speed and quality are often sacrificed when we work from home." In Silicon Valley, the most successful firms, like Google and Facebook, are building very large headquarters in addition to the large office buildings they recently acquired in downtown San Francisco. These large and costly real estate acquisitions suggest that they do not anticipate that a large part of their workforce will be working full time from home in the future.

The design of the largest Silicon Valley offices, offering their employees an unusual environment with gourmet food cafeterias, gyms, and kindergarten, demonstrates the intention of management to encourage their employees to work in their office and to interact with one another socially as well as professionally. In a way, it seems that Silicon Valley firms are trying to intensify within their offices the knowledge spillovers that are known to happen in large cities. For these reasons, I believe that the number of work-at-home individuals might soon reach a peak and may not affect commuting flow significantly in the future.

If Cairncross had been right in 2001, by 2015 we should have already seen large changes in the price of urban land across the world. The most environmentally attractive but remote rural areas of the world would have higher prices, while the least environmentally attractive, highest-density areas would have lost value. This is not happening. Real estate prices in New York, London, Delhi, and Shanghai are still climbing, proving that the death of distance might have been greatly exaggerated. High real estate prices demonstrate that even in cities where mobility causes severe friction—as in New York, London, or Shanghai—being physically close to a large concentration of people, jobs, and amenities is still worth a very high price.

Measuring a City's Mobility

A Decrease in Congestion and Pollution Is Not a Measure of Mobility

The objective of urban transport is to increase mobility to maximize the effective size of labor markets. Congestion and pollution are very important constraints on the mobility objective, but they are only constraints. Confusing objectives and constraints when solving problems can lead to false solutions. Urban managers too often try to solve transport problems by focusing exclusively on reducing congestion and pollution without giving much consideration to mobility, as if the objective of urban transport was limited to decreasing the nuisances it causes.

Some policies rely on reducing trip length, others on forcing more commuters into slower transport modes. None of these policies effectively reduces pollution or congestion, but they reduce mobility.

Planners who think that decreasing pollution and congestion is the main objective of urban transport might logically try to fragment a large metropolitan labor market into smaller ones. For instance, some planners suggest that matching the number of jobs with the size of the working population in every neighborhood would significantly decrease trip length to the point where walking and bicycling could provide access to all the jobs in a neighborhood.

Of course, there is nothing wrong with having mixed-use neighborhoods, provided that demand from households and firms drives the land use mix. Even where planners can achieve a perfect match between the number of jobs and housing units, as in satellite towns, experience has shown that workers prefer access to wider labor markets and that there is no decrease in trip length. This has been shown in Seoul's well-planned satellite towns.[6] After an exhaustive survey of land use and trip length in California, the transport economist G. Giuliano concludes that "regulatory policies aimed at improving jobs-housing balance are thus unlikely to have any measurable impact on commuting behavior, and therefore cannot be justified as a traffic mitigation strategy."[7]

Understanding why job-housing balance does not reduce trip length is easy. If it did, it would imply that at least one of the following propositions is true:

• All workers within a household only look for jobs within a short distance from their home.

• When workers change jobs, they also change homes, and moving from one home to another has a negligible transaction cost.

• Proximity to work is the only consideration when selecting a home.

Obviously, common sense shows that none of these propositions is true for the majority of households. If any of these propositions were true, then we would observe a fragmentation of labor markets and a decrease in mobility, and therefore a decrease in urban productivity.

The job-housing balance policy is, of course, not implementable in a market economy. This is because the number of jobs and the number of workers is always fluid, and no government, however authoritarian, can force people to live and work in a specific location. Even in the Soviet Union and in pre-reform China, where large state-owned enterprises provided housing for their workers, who often spent their entire career working for the same enterprise, planners could not achieve a spatial match. As I was working on housing issues in China in the 1980s and in Russia in the 1990s, I was surprised to see that, even in command economies, the utopian dream of matching jobs and housing location could not be achieved. Large enterprises had to expand in locations distant from their workers' housing, and they had to build new workers' residential estates in areas where they could find the land, which was not necessarily close to their factories. As soon as labor markets opened in both countries, the job-housing balance deteriorated further. A fluid labor market (which is what makes large cities so attractive) and a job-housing balance are incompatible.

However, despite these negative experiences, planners still devise land use regulations aimed at matching people with jobs. For instance, a regulation in Stockholm requires developers to match the number of jobs and the number of dwelling units in new suburban locations. Allowing mixed-use development is a good land use policy, as it allows households and firms to select locations that best meet their needs without the rigidity of arbitrary top-down land use zoning. Requiring a perfect match between population and jobs in each neighborhood in order to reduce trip length is an unattainable utopia.

Other policies also eagerly sacrifice mobility to reduce pollution and congestion. For example, several Latin American cities (e.g., Bogotá, Santiago, and Mexico
City) have instituted a vehicle rationing system called "pico y plata" that restricts
the circulation of vehicles on 2 days per week, depending on the last number of
the vehicle's license plate. This policy reduces mobility.[8] It forces drivers either to
switch to public transport or to carpool for 2 days per week. The change of transport mode is likely to require a longer commute time during the days drivers are
obliged to switch. If public transport were faster, they would have used it before
the restriction on driving was put in place.

Studies show that drivers circumvent "pico y plata" regulations by buying a
second car with a different last number on the license plate. Traffic and congestion
initially decreases after this regulation is implemented, but then increases again
when the second cars join the traffic. The result is more pollution, because there
are more cars on the road and because the second car bought is usually an older,
more polluting model. Many studies across cities in different countries and incomes
have confirmed this result. However, the regulation, which restricts mobility in
order to reduce pollution and congestion, is still popular among city managers.
This stance is counterproductive.

In some cities, exceptional climatic events may cause extremely dangerous pollution peaks on some days. In this case, restricting individual car use is, of course,
legitimate as an emergency measure—as it is legitimate to ask factories to stop
operating during the emergency—but it is not efficient to use such restrictions as
permanent policy.

Accessibility and Mobility: What Is the Best Way to Measure Urban Mobility?

Transport policy should aim to increase mobility while decreasing congestion and
pollution. Often, reports that claim to quantify mobility in fact only measure the
cost of car congestion and pollution. For instance, the "mobility report"[9] prepared
by Texas A&M Transportation Institute (2012) argues that a shift from car to public
transport, which indeed obviously reduces road congestion, is considered an
improvement in mobility. For some reason, the reduction in the time spent commuting for the drivers who keep driving is considered a benefit, while the longer
commuting times for the drivers who have shifted to public transport is not considered a cost. Mobility would increase only if the commuting time of the driving
commuters who have changed to public transport becomes shorter because of the
shift. However, if commuting by public transport were faster than commuting by
car, drivers would have switched modes already.

Congestion clearly decreases mobility, but measuring it is not a substitute for
measuring mobility. For instance, imagine a person having to walk 1 hour to work

because of poverty but eventually being able to afford a collective taxi to make the same trip in 30 minutes. The collective taxi will contribute to congestion; walking did not. However, the mobility and welfare of this worker shifting from walking to a collective taxi ride would have increased. We should therefore measure and monitor the variations in mobility for different income groups.

While congestion is usually measured for car traffic only, congestion can occur at bus and Bus Rapid Transit (BRT) stops and in metro stations. While attempting to use the BRT in Mexico City in 2014, I saw three buses pass the station where I was waiting without being able to board, the buses being able to take only a few passengers among the more than 100 individuals waiting on the platform. This is also congestion, which planners should measure. Trying to shift commuters from one congested transport mode to another congested mode doesn't decrease congestion problems. To my knowledge, the Beijing Transport Research Center is the only monitoring institution measuring daily congestion in metro stations. This institution measures the time required to board a train at peak hours.

Consequently, measuring and monitoring mobility for all modes of transport at the metropolitan level is an indispensable step for improving urban transport. A quantitative index measuring mobility improvements or setbacks is necessary to provide substance to urban transport policy. Advocating "mobility" without a way of measuring it will just add a new faddish slogan similar to "sustainability" and "livability." Both slogans are unmeasurable and are too often used by urban planners to justify whatever policies they favor. Measuring mobility is not easy. I will describe some of the methods currently used and some that are emerging thanks to new data-recording technology.

In chapter 2, I explained why large labor markets are the raison d'être of cities. Large labor markets result in higher productivity than smaller ones. However, the size of a labor market is not necessarily equal to the number of jobs in a city. If inadequate or unaffordable transport prohibits workers from accessing all of a city's jobs within an hour's commute, the effective size of the labor market is only a fraction of the total number of jobs in the city. The productivity of a city is proportional to the effective size of its labor market. Mobility allows workers to have access to a measurable number of jobs within a specified travel time and can therefore be measured by the effective size of a city's labor markets given a specific travel time.

A useful measure of urban mobility would calculate the average number of jobs that workers can commute to within, say, an hour one way. We could calculate such a mobility measurement by aggregating the number of jobs accessible in less than 1 hour from every census tract, weighted by their population. A mobility index, therefore, would have to be calculated in two stages: first, by calculating the number of jobs accessible from every census tract within a selected time limit;

second, by calculating the worker-weighted average of the accessibility of all census tracts to form an index reflecting the entire metropolitan area.

Traditionally, transport planners have measured job accessibility from different census tracts in a metropolitan area by measuring the number of jobs accessible from the census tract corrected by coefficients that reflect distance, cost, and elasticity of demand related to distance. The formulas used to measure accessibility of census tracts are usually similar to the ones I highlight in equations 5.1 and 5.2.

A few years ago, such calculations would have been extremely cumbersome and costly and, if performed, unlikely to be repeated for periodic monitoring. Two factors now allow for easy monitoring of an urban mobility index. First, new GIS-based technology enables the development of interactive tools accessible to any user. Second, the standardization of transport data networks (the General Transit Feed Specification, or GTFS)[10] is becoming universal. This allows for the calculation of accessibility based on real transport networks and real travel times—including transfers between stations and walking times to and from stations—instead of crude "as the crow flies" distances between census tracts. In the following paragraphs, I use data extracted from research conducted by Tatiana Quirós and Shomik Mehndiratta[11] for Buenos Aires.

Figure 5.2 shows the area accessible within 60 minutes by car (left) and public transport (right) from an arbitrarily selected suburban census tract (marked by a small red circle) in Buenos Aires. By overlaying the job census data with these maps, one can calculate the total number of jobs accessible in less than 60 minutes from the census tract marked by the circle. The number of jobs that can be reached in less than 60 minutes are 5.1 million jobs (95 percent of the total number of jobs in Buenos Aires) for workers commuting by individual cars and 0.7 million jobs (15 percent of the total number of jobs) for workers using public transport.[12]

The difference in accessibility between the two different modes of transport is striking. However, it is not true that if every worker in Buenos Aires switched to cars, the average mobility would be increased. The commuting speed of the car users depends in large part on the number of cars on the road. An increase in car users would increase congestion and possibly cause gridlock, decreasing the speed and therefore the mobility of car users. I discuss below the necessary complementarity of various transport mode in improving mobility.

Additionally, there are two caveats for car commuting: first, the speed implied in figure 5.2 is an average speed and is not adjusted for different times of day; second, the availability of parking in different locations is not considered. In some areas, the scarcity or cost of parking might significantly decrease the practicality of commuting by car.

My purpose in showing the Buenos Aires accessibility map here is limited to providing a concrete example of the twin concepts of accessibility and mobility.

Equation 5.1 Job accessibility per census tract

The index of accessibility can be calculated using the equation

$$A_i = \sum_{j=1}^{n} K_j e^{-\beta c d_{ij}},\tag{5.1}$$

where A_i is the index of accessibility of census tract i, K_j is the number of jobs in census tract j, e is the base of natural logarithm, β is an elasticity coefficient, c is the unit cost of traveling the distance d_{ij} between census tract i and census tract j. While these formulas provide a way of measuring access to jobs or amenities from a specific location, the measurement they provide is an abstract index dependent on the way distances, costs and speed, and cost elasticity are calculated. Transport planners have a tendency to make accessibility measures more complex by adding more variables reflecting the complexity of commuters' behavior. Unfortunately, this complexity renders accessibility calculations more difficult to interpret. As a result, their "black box" effect prevents their use in formulating transport policies that non specialists like mayors or city councils must approve. It is therefore indispensable to develop a much simpler accessibility index, based solely on the size of the labor market available to residents of a particular census tract based purely on travel time using existing transport modes. The advances in Geographical Information System (GIS) technology allow interactive use of maps where areas accessible within a given travel time can easily be verified, as shown by the Buenos Aires example below.

Equation 5.2 Number of jobs accessible by census tract within a set travel time

---

The first step in developing a mobility measurement that reflects the number of jobs accessed within a set travel time would be to change the traditional accessibility formula into the simpler and more explicit:

$$A_i = \sum_{j=1}^{n} K_j \quad for \ \ v.d_{ij} \leq T,\tag{5.2}$$

where A_i is the number of jobs accessible from census tract i within a commuting time lower or equal to maximum travel time T, and v is the average travel speed to cover the distance d_{ij} between tract A_i and tract K_j using the network of the mode of transport selected.

The values of v and d_{ij} are dependent on the mode of transport: public transport, bicycle, or car. Therefore, we should calculate the different value taken by A_i for each mode of transport. This accessibility index measuring the number of jobs accessed in less than a trip time T would be repeated for all census tracts in the urban area and for the major mode of transport available: public transport, cars, motorcycles, bicycles.

Figure 5.2
Accessibility of a suburban location in Buenos Aires by public transport and by car. *Source*: Wb.BA
.analyst.conveyal.com.

The interactive map found on the website allows any Buenos Aires citizen to test
its accuracy compared to their own experience. This can reduce the black box
effect that habitually decreases the impact of sophisticated transport studies on
urban policies.

Using this method, we could calculate a mobility index for an entire metropolitan area (equation 5.3). This global measure would be an indicator that planners
should monitor regularly as a city develops.

From an operational point of view, it is necessary to be able to measure mobility
by location: how many jobs a worker can reach from a given location within a
given time by different modes of transport. This type of data would show the
most transport-deficient areas of a city. Various combined factors may explain the
high unemployment rate in some urban neighborhoods. Indeed, an adequate transport system that gives easy access to jobs in the metropolitan region is often a
prerequisite to decreasing local unemployment.

Measuring the Cost of Mobility

Mobility is a benefit provided by urban transport, but it has a cost. There is no
point in advocating for increased mobility without also measuring the marginal
cost associated with this increase. However, the economic costs of transport systems

Equation 5.3 City mobility index

After obtaining the job accessibility index of every census tract, we can calculate a city mobility index that represents the average job accessibility of all census tracts weighted by their population. The mobility index M expressed by the formula below shows the number of total jobs reachable within a commuting time T, for a given transport mode, for the average city resident,

$$M = \frac{\sum_{i=1}^{n} A_i P_i}{P}, \tag{5.3}$$

where M is the mobility index, A_i is the number of jobs accessible from census tract i in less than T travel time, n is total number of census tracts, P_i is the active population in tract i, and P is the total active metropolitan population.

are particularly difficult to evaluate. Typically, urban commuters—whether they use public transport or individual vehicles—pay only a small fraction of the real cost of their trips.

Urban transport is different from other consumer products because its users pay only a part of its cost. Car users pay a market price for their car and the gasoline they consume (in most countries), but they are usually not paying for the public road space they use, or for the pollution, congestion, and other costs they have imposed on others. Users of publicly operated transport pay a fare that represents only a small part of the system's operational and maintenance costs and usually pay nothing for the capital cost of the system. Obviously, car owners and public transport users eventually pay collectively all these costs through their taxes, but the cost they pay is not related to the quantity of the service they use. Because of the lack of real pricing, we can expect urban transport to be overused and undersupplied. Because of our inability to recover the cost of trips, mobility is significantly less than it could be. Therefore urban productivity could be greatly increased if we could price urban trips at their real costs.

Evaluating these costs is difficult, as many subsidies are not transparent. In addition, the cost of what economists call "negative externalities" (i.e., the cost imposed on others, like congestion and pollution) is not easy to evaluate. Since the 1980s, it has become clear that we should add the cost of global warming to the other traditional externalities. A worldwide price for carbon emission should reflect the cost of global warming caused by greenhouse gas (GHG) emissions. However, because of the worldwide failure to price carbon, pricing different modes of transport and comparing their price to their performance is even more difficult.

Faced with the difficulty in calculating the real cost of trips, many transport policy advocates renounce any attempt to make even an approximate calculation and just append the word "sustainable" to the mode of transport they favor. When comparing the cost and benefits of different modes of transportation, I will differentiate the transport costs that have a clear cash value (e.g., the cost of a car or of a subway ticket) from those like pollution or GHG emissions, which I will evaluate in units of gas emitted per vehicle/km or passenger/km without attempting to price it. In the same way, I will not attempt to give a cash value to the time spent commuting, but will just provide the average speed or time traveled. Transport economists attribute a dollar value to the time spent commuting based on the opportunity cost of the time of the person traveling. Using this convention, the cost of an hour of travel by a worker earning the minimum wage is lower than the cost of the same hour of travel by an executive paid a multiple of the minimum wage. Although this type of calculation is legitimate to calculate the aggregate economic cost of urban transport, it does not necessarily reflect how individuals select their choice of travel mode. Besides, the social cost of long commutes for low-income workers might be much higher than the one reflected by their hourly salary.

Mobility and Transport Modes

Classification of Urban Transport Modes

Until the middle of the Industrial Revolution—about 1860—walking was the dominant mode of urban transport. The area that workers could reach by walking less than an hour severely limited the expansion of cities. Because of the limitation on the speed of transport, urban labor markets grew primarily through the densification of the existing built-up area. Metropolitan Paris in 1800, before the Industrial Revolution,[13] had a density evaluated by Angel at about 500 people per hectare compared to about 55 today. Since then, many mechanized modes of urban transport have allowed cities to grow geographically, densities to decrease, and labor markets to expand. These larger labor markets, in turn, allowed more labor specialization, which has increased the productivity of cities. Faster and better-performing urban transport modes are therefore a crucial element in the growth and prosperity of cities. In addition to increasing the size of the labor market, faster and more flexible transport modes allow urban land supply to expand and respond quickly to growing demand for new and better housing and new commercial areas.

Since the Industrial Revolution, many mechanical urban transport modes have been added to walking, among them cars, bicycles, motorcycles, buses, subways, tramways, and BRTs. Governments had an important role in allowing or funding the different modes of transport that were becoming available as technology changed.

The modes of urban mechanized transport that were already available at the beginning of the twentieth century have not changed much since then. The efficiency in using energy and the speed of cars, buses, and metros have certainly improved, but no new mode of urban transport has emerged. The invention of the BRT system in Curitiba, Brazil, in 1974 is only the application to buses of a technology applied to tramways at the end of the nineteenth century. However, it is quite possible that during the next 20 years, we will see the emergence of completely new modes of transport. The possibilities presented by the combination of vehicle sharing and autonomous vehicles could completely revolutionize urban transport as we know it today.

While no new mode of urban transport has emerged during the past 100 years, the dominant mode is often changing rapidly in emerging economies. The changes in mode reflect changes in income, city size, and the geographic coverage of public transport systems. Changes in dominant transport modes are instructive, as they reflect users' choices and the way they adapt to the performance—speed, cost, and spatial coverage—of the various modes of transport available.

Individual Modes of Transport versus Public Transport
In a typical medium- or high-income city, commuters choose between a number of transport modes: walking, bicycling, driving, riding in a taxi, or using public transport. They select the mode of transport—or combination of modes—that is the most convenient for their trip, taking into account time of travel, direct cost, comfort, and whether their trip has to be chained with several activities (e.g., working, picking up children at school, shopping). When selecting their means of transport, travelers do not take into account the cost of the negative externalities they create—pollution, global warming, noise, and congestion.

Modes of transport are highly diverse, but they can be conveniently divided into three categories: individual transport, shared individual transport, and collective transport or public transport (figure 5.3). Individual transport and shared individual transport give access to the entire road network, while the various public transport modes are restricted to a network, which by necessity is a fraction of the entire road network. Because individual transport modes use the entire road network, they provide door-to-door travel without the need to change modes of transport on the way. Additionally, individual transport provides continuous 24/7 service, while public transport services are restricted to preset schedules with low frequencies outside peak hours.

Individual motorized modes of urban transport present many advantages over public transport, especially on-demand door-to-door service. Given these

	Individual transport	**Shared individual transport**	**Collective transport transit**
Area served:	*Entire road network*	*Entire road network*	*Limited network*
Schedule:	*On demand*	*On demand*	*Fixed schedule*
From where to where:	*Door to door*	*Door to door*	*Station to station*

Walk
Bicycle
Electric scooter
Motorcycle
Car drive alone

Taxi
Carpool
Uber, Lyft
Uber pool
Self-driving car
i-Road Toyota at stations

Bus
Light rail, tram
Collective taxi
Bus Rapid Transit (BRT)
Subway
Suburban rail

Figure 5.3
Modes of urban transport.

advantages over public transport, why did private firms and then the government provide public transport services?

Complementarity of Various Modes of Transport

In many cities, most modes of transport listed in figure 5.3 coexist. Some modes are heavily dominant, like the motorcycle in Hanoi, which represents 80 percent of commuting trips, or the car in US metropolitan areas (86 percent of all trips). However, in most cities, several transport modes coexist, and their relative share of total commuting trips varies with time. These variations reflect consumers' choices, which respond to changing conditions in household income, urban structure, or transport mode performance.

Dominant Modes of Urban Transport May Change Rapidly

The shift in dominant modes of transport reflects an increase in population and household income. The share of passengers by transport mode reflects commuters' preferences but also government action. This supply and demand tends to change rapidly in cities whose economies are growing fast; less so in cities where population and income are more stable. Figures 5.4 and 5.5 illustrate the rapid evolution of dominant modes of transport in cities like Beijing, Hanoi, and Mexico City compared to the relative stability found in Paris.

Beijing's transport mode underwent a radical change between 1986 and 2014. The bicycle was the main mode of transport in 1986, although the city population was already above 5 million. Many bicycle and public transport users shifted to private cars in the late 1990s. The shift from bicycle and public transport to car trips between 1994 and 2000 corresponds with the rapid increase in household income during this period of about 47 percent. It was certainly not driven by government

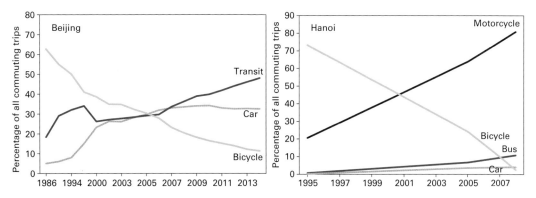

Figure 5.4
Changes in the dominant transport mode, Beijing (left) and Hanoi (right). *Source*: Beijing Transport Research Center, 2015.

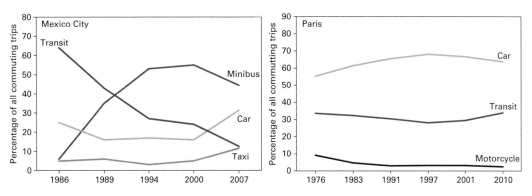

Figure 5.5
Changes in the dominant transport mode, Mexico City (left) and Paris (right). *Sources*: Mexico City: "Gradual Takeover of Public Mass-Transit by Colectivos, 1986–2000," Secretaria de Transito y Viabilidad (SETRAVI) Embarq—World Resources Institute; Paris: Syndicat des Transports d'Île-de-France website, www.stif.info.

policy. The massive investment in public transport—the tenfold increase in the distance covered by subway lines from 53 kilometers in 1990 to 527 kilometers in 2014—reversed the decline in public transport's share of commuting trips. Car traffic congestion combined with a quota system for buying new cars stabilized the growth of car trips. Meanwhile, the share of bicycle users kept decreasing.

Hanoi's transport transformation has been even more dramatic than Beijing's. From 1995 to 2008, the share of bicycle trips dropped from 75 percent to barely 4 percent! But unlike Beijing, the motorcycle became the only dominant mode of transport in Hanoi, accounting for 80 percent of all trips (cars and public transport together account for only about 15 percent). As in Beijing, Hanoi's commuters reacted to changing local conditions. Increased income allowed them to replace bicycles with motorcycles, significantly lowering commuting time—the average commuting time in Hanoi was 18 minutes in 2010. Large areas of Hanoi are accessible through narrow, winding roads that are nearly inaccessible to cars and even less accessible to buses, which were the only means of public transport in 2014. Motorcycles also gave easy access to residents of suburban former villages with only rural unpaved road access, expanding the supply of housing affordable to low-income migrants.

In Mexico City between 1986 and 2007, commuters have dramatically reduced their use of public transport in favor of minibuses and private cars despite strong municipal governmental policies to discourage these private alternatives. The change in dominant mode reflects rising incomes but also a change in the city structure of Mexico. Jobs have dispersed to suburban areas, in part due to government land use restrictions in the Federal District, and traditional public transport networks are less efficient for commuting from suburb to suburb. When jobs are dispersed, minibuses and cars become more convenient. However, the congestion created by cars and minibuses considerably slows down traffic in a city as dense as Mexico City (average density is about 100 people per hectare in the metropolitan area).

In contrast with these three cities, metropolitan Paris between 1976 and 2010 (shown on the right if figure 5.5) does not show any large shift in transport mode. Paris's population and household income have been much more stable than those of Beijing, Hanoi, or Mexico City. The relative share of car and public transport trips reflects the structure of the city: a very dense core of about 2 million people and suburbs of 8 million. Commuters use public transport for most trips within and toward the core, but they use cars for the roughly 70 percent of commuting trips that originate and end in suburbs (reflecting the same share of job distribution). The extension of fast trains in the far suburbs of Paris has somewhat increased the share of public transport since the mid-1990s. However, car travel remains the dominant mode, reflecting the spatial structure of the city with a majority of population and jobs located in suburbs and, as a consequence, trips originating and ending in suburbs.

The change in transport mode in Beijing and Paris shows that increasing the size of the public transport network impacts commuters' transport mode preferences. However, household income and a city's spatial structure are the main determinants of commuter choice. For instance, in Beijing, multiplying the length of subway lines tenfold between 1990 and 2014 has only increased the share of public transport trips by 12 percent. And while Hanoi is building a new subway system that could eventually increase the very low share of public transport, subway trips are unlikely to compete with the speed and spatial coverage provided by the motorcycle.

The existence of various modes of transport reflects the choice of commuters. Commuters choose transport modes based on where they live, where they work, what time they go to work, what time they return home, and what share of their income they are willing to allocate to transport. No transport mode is perfect. Unsurprisingly, residents are often dissatisfied by urban transport. Car commuters complain about congestion and pollution, while public transport users complain about crowding, schedule irregularity, and lack of geographic coverage. In the following sections, I will analyze the pros and cons of the various transport modes accounting for their speed and the various negative externalities they create: congestion, pollution, and GHG emissions. However, we must remember that in the end, the primary objective is to increase mobility while decreasing the negative externalities imposed by that mobility.

Travel Time, Speed, and Travel Mode

The Measure of Travel Time to Work (Commuting)

As already mentioned, average commuting travel time is a common proxy used for measuring mobility. Average travel time becomes a meaningful proxy for mobility if it only includes trips to work and excludes other types of trips when calculating the average. Obviously, an average between travel time to work and travel time to go shopping or to the barbershop would have no meaning as a proxy measure for mobility.

The measurement of commuting travel time should be "door-to-door." Travel time should include the time of travel from the moment the commuter leaves home to the moment she reaches her workplace. In addition, commuting time should be disaggregated by transport mode.

The examples of average public transport commuting time in the municipality of Paris and in Beijing's metropolitan area illustrate the importance of door-to-door time measurement when assessing mobility (figure 5.6). The average door-to-door commuting time for trips using the subway in Paris municipality is 31 minutes, but the actual time spent on the train is only 15 minutes. The time required to go to the station and board the train, and then to walk from the station to the workplace, represents 52 percent of the door-to-door commuting time. For the longer trips in Beijing's metropolitan area, the proportion of "access time" is lower and represents 36 percent of total commuting time.

We should do the same door-to-door calculation for car commuting trips, which typically start from one's driveway in a suburban home but may end in a parking

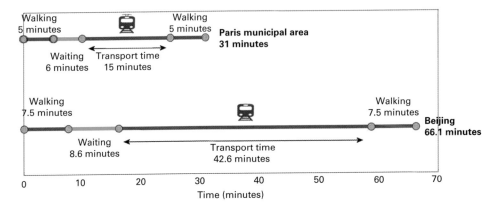

Figure 5.6
Average door-to-door public transport travel time for commuters in the Paris municipality and Beijing metropolitan area. *Sources:* Data for Paris: "Etude sur les deplacements," Regie Autonome des Transports Parisiens, 2014; Beijing: "Beijing, the 4th Comprehensive Transport Survey Summary Report," Beijing Transportation Research Center (BTRC), Beijing Municipal Commission of Transport, Beijing, China, 2012.

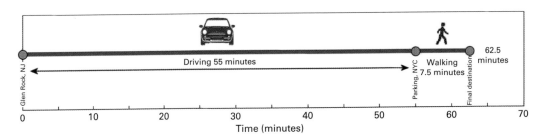

Figure 5.7
Door-to-door commuting time from suburb to downtown New York (case study, no statistical significance).

lot or underground garage, involving a sizable amount of walking time to get to the work place. I could not find statistics disaggregating travel time for car travel that include walking to and from a parking place. My own weekly car commuting from Glen Rock, New Jersey, to New York University in Greenwich Village in Manhattan takes on average 55 minutes of driving time and requires an additional 7.5 minutes walking from an underground parking garage to the university (figure 5.7). Access time is then only 12 percent of total commuting time.

Because the access time to transport is usually high, the speed of various modes of transport is a poor indicator of door-to-door commuting time. When trying to increase mobility, reducing access time to various modes of transport is as important as increasing the speed of the motorized part of transport. Table 5.1 shows

Table 5.1
Ratio between door-to-door speed and transport vehicle speed.

Commuting mode	Paris Subway	Beijing Bus and subway	New York Car
Total average commuting distance (kilometers)	9	19	38
Door-to-door trip time (minutes)	31	66	63
Transport vehicle speed (km/h)[a]	33	25	40
Door-to-door speed (km/h)	17	17	36
Ratio of door-to-door speed to vehicle speed (percent)	53	68	89

a. For Beijing, this is an average speed for bus and subway.

the ratio between door-to-door speed and vehicle speed for Paris, Beijing, and the New York case study. As a city size increases, public transport networks become more complex and less dense, and they often require transfers between modes (e.g., buses to suburban trains). The increasing distance from home to stations and the necessity of transfers tend to increase access time. Car trips are less vulnerable to long access times, if an allocated parking lot exists at the destination. Trips by car from suburb to suburb have very little access time, because usually parking is available very close to the trip origin and destination. The lower value of suburban land explains why this availability is taken for granted.

In the examples above, commuters in Paris and Beijing were walking to access the main motorized transport mode, but, of course, many other means of transport could be combined in a single commuting trip. A commuting case study in Gauteng, South Africa, describes one of the most complex and long commuting trips I have ever heard of.[14] A single mother of four children commutes every weekday from her home in Tembisa, a township in Gauteng's metropolitan area (which includes Johannesburg and Pretoria), to Brummeria, a business district of Pretoria, where she cleans offices. She leaves home at 5:00 A.M. to be at the office at 7:30 A.M. She starts her commute with a 2-kilometer walk to a collective taxi stand, where a taxi takes her to a train station. The train brings her to Pretoria, where she takes another collective taxi to a stop in Brummeria, from which she walks to her workplace (figure 5.8). The entire commute one way takes 2.5 hours, including walking and waiting for taxis and the train. Her commuting distance is 47 kilometers. Her average commuting speed is about 18 km/h, although most of the distance she covers is on a commuter train going at an average speed of 46 km/h. Because of the need to connect to the rail network to avoid the higher cost of the collective taxi, the distance she travels (47 kilometers) is much longer than the shorter road distance of 29 kilometers between her home and her workplace. If

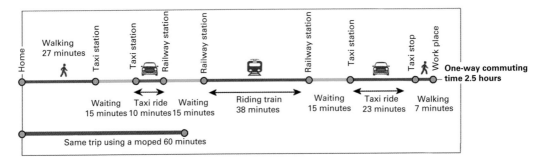

Figure 5.8
Extreme commuting in Gauteng (South Africa) case study. *Source*: "National Development Plan Vision 2030," President's National Planning Commission, South Africa, 2011.

she had access to a motorcycle or even to a moped, she could commute in about 1 hour, instead of 2.5 hours. Access to a moped would allow her to gain 3 hours a day of disposable time!

For a given home and job location, commuting time may show large variations depending on the main mode of transport, the number of transfers, and access time. In the case described here, a moped with a speed of 30 km/h would result in much higher mobility than using a suburban train with an average speed of 46 km/h.

Average Commuting Time by Transport Mode
Commuting by public transport takes longer on average than commuting by individual car. Given the amount of urban congestion plaguing most large cities in the world, this seems surprising. Urban congestion affects public buses as much as it does individual cars, but we would expect that public transport trips would be shorter in cities where many commuters are using underground public transport and dedicated bus lanes. Unfortunately, this is not the case. In a comprehensive and authoritative book,[15] Robert Cervero, a fervent advocate of urban public transport, admits that faster travel time by car, even in public transport-based European and Japanese cities, is the main challenge in increasing the share of public transport over car trips all over the world. Let us try to understand why that is the case by looking at a sample of specific cities.

Commuting time in five large cities—Dallas–Fort Worth, Hong Kong, New York, Paris, and Singapore (figure 5.9)—confirms Cervero's observation: commuting travel time by car is significantly shorter than by public transport in all these cities. The increase in travel time between public transport and car commuting ranges from 53 percent for New York to 100 percent in Singapore.

These differences measure average travel times for trips that have many different origins and destinations. The averages may mask a number of trips where the

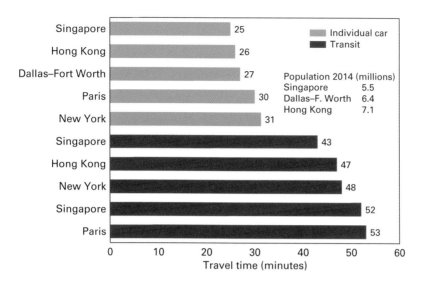

Figure 5.9
Average commuting travel time by transport mode, Singapore, Hong Kong, Dallas–Fort Worth, Paris, and New York. *Sources*: Data for United States: "Commuting in America 2013," US DOT Census Transportation Planning Products Program, Washington, DC, 2013; Paris: "Les deplacements des Franciliens en 2001–2002," Direction régionale de l'équipement d'Île-de-France, Paris, 2004; Hong Kong: "Travel Characteristics Survey-Final Report 2011," Transport Department, Government of Hong Kong Special Administrative Region, Hong Kong, 2011; Singapore: "Singapore Land Transport Statistics in Brief 2010," Land Transport Authority, Singapore Government, Singapore, 2010.

ratio between public transport and car travel time is reversed (i.e., trips that are shorter using public transport than using cars). For instance, some trips in Manhattan or in Paris Municipality are most certainly faster by public transport than by car. Suburban trips for people who live very close to a station and whose workplace is also close to a station might also be shorter using public transport than using a car. We can be confident that when this is the case, commuters choose the faster means of transport. However, average commuting time shows that in all these cities, commuters using cars spend less time commuting than those using public transport. Let us try to find out why it is so.

I did not randomly select the five cities in figure 5.9. Their characteristics are shown in table 5.2. Four of the selected cities have a significant share of public transport use, ranging from 26 percent for New York to 88 percent for Hong Kong. The fifth city, Dallas–Fort Worth, is an outlier with less than 2 percent of commuting trips using public transport. Hong Kong's and Singapore's public transport systems are relatively recent, and they benefit from their modernity and are known for their efficiency. The five cities selected show a large variety of densities. Hong Kong and Singapore have high densities, while New York and Paris have

Table 5.2
Density and share of public transport trips in five sample cities.

City	Population (millions)	Transit share of commuting trips (percent)	Density (people per hectare)	Built-up area (square kilometers)
Dallas–Fort Worth	6.20	2	12	5,167
New York Metropolitan Statistical Area	20.30	26	18	11,278
Paris (Ile De France)	11.80	34	41	2,878
Singapore	5.60	52	109	514
Hong Kong	6.80	88	264	258

Sources: Population: Census 2010. Density and built-up area: author's measurements. Transit: Dallas–Fort Worth and New York, Summary of Travel Trends, 2009, National Household Travel Survey, U.S. Department of Transportation, Federal Highway Administration, Washington, DC; Paris, E 2008 Enquête Nationale Transports et Déplacements, Table 5.1. Commissariat général au Développement durable, Paris 2008; Singapore, Land Transport Authority Singapore Land Transport, Statistics in Brief 2010, Singapore Government, 2010; Hong Kong, "Travel Characteristics Survey-Final Report 2011," Transport Department, Government of Hong Kong Special Administrative Region, Hong Kong, 2011.

medium densities but high job and population densities in their core area, which favors public transport use and makes car use more difficult. Dallas–Fort Worth is the only city in the sample with a very low density (12 people per hectare) but with a population of 6.2 million, about equivalent to Hong Kong's 6.8 million (2011). Given the very low density of Dallas–Fort Worth, car usage is predictably very high at 98 percent of commuting trips.

However, one should not conclude that because current car trips are usually faster than public transport trips, a shift of public transport trip toward cars would decrease the average commuting time and therefore increase mobility. In the four cities with medium and high densities mentioned above, the current speed of cars depends on the proportion of commuters using public transport. Indeed, in Singapore, the government periodically adjusts the cost of using a car to decrease demand for car trips with the explicit goal of maintaining a minimum speed of car travel for those who can afford it. Most cities where public transport is an important mode of transport also try to control demand for car use, although in a manner less explicit and muscular than in Singapore. Reducing demand for car trips takes many forms. For instance, New York increases tolls for cars in bridges and tunnels, Paris reduces the number of car lanes, and Hong Kong increases taxes on car purchases. Beijing establishes yearly quotas for the purchase of new cars and uses a lottery to determine who may purchase a car. Stockholm, London, and

Rome have a special charge to discourage car traffic in the core city. All cities heavily subsidize public transport operation cost to convince commuters to shift from cars to public transport because of the cost difference.

The higher speed of commuting cars in dense and moderately dense cities is due to the high number of trips using public transport. In these cities, the two modes, car and public transport, complement each other. In Dallas, by contrast, the short commuting time is entirely due to low density. As I will show later, low suburban densities provide larger road areas per households than in high-density cities. This large area of road per person allows higher speeds. As I mentioned at the beginning of this chapter, compact dense cities like Hong Kong and Singapore, while decreasing the average commuting distance, are often associated with a much longer commute than very-low-density cities like Dallas–Fort Worth. The potential advantages of shorter commuting trips in high-density cities are entirely offset by the slower speed caused by congestion, including congestion in transit.

Travel Cost
As mentioned above, I drive once a week from Glen Rock in suburban New Jersey to New York University in south Manhattan. The trip length one way is 37 kilometers. The cost of tolls amounts to $14, plus $17 for parking (of which 18.4 percent is a special municipal tax on parking), plus another $5 for about 2 gallons of gasoline, for a total of $36 for a return commuting trip by car (not counting insurance, maintenance, and capital cost). The commuting time door-to-door, one way, is about 63 minutes on average, corresponding to an average speed of 35 km/h.

The same return trip using public transport (bus plus metro) would cost only $14 but would require 102 minutes door-to-door one way, or an average speed of 22 km/h. In addition, outside peak hours, buses to and from Glen Rock leave only every hour. On a two-way commuting trip driving my car, I am spending an additional $22 to gain 78 minutes over public transport travel time, implying an opportunity cost of my time about $17 per hour. This personal case study has no statistical value, but it does explain the way many commuters select their transport mode. The transport costs that I pay for both public transport and car commuting do not reflect the real cost of providing the transport service that I am using—whether car or public transport. The fare of most public transport trips covers only a fraction of operating cost, and usually no capital cost at all. In the same way, tolls and gasoline costs may not reflect all the maintenance cost of the roads and traffic management service I use during my trip, and even less of the negative externalities on the environment and the congestion I impose on others by using my car.

So far, if we look only at the speed and duration of commuting trips, it seems that car trips have an advantage over public transport. Indeed, as jobs tend to disperse into suburbs and household income increases in many large cities of the world, it seems that the ratio of car trips over public transport trips is also increasing, to the alarm of transport planners. The congestion created by cars is a major concern. I alluded to this problem by warning that in denser parts of cities, the shorter commuting time made possible by traveling by car depended on the number of commuters using public transport. The larger the number of commuters using public transport, the higher the speed of commuters using cars will be. This trend explains the popular support for public transport investments in cities like Atlanta, where most commuters are using cars and intend to keep using cars in the future.

Speed, Congestion, and Mode of Transport

Road congestion is a real estate problem. Through regulations, planners or developers allocate portions of urban land to streets when the land is originally developed. Once a neighborhood is fully built, increasing the area allocated to streets is extremely costly financially and socially, as it requires decreasing the land allocated to uses that produce urban rents while increasing the area of street that produces no rents. It also requires the relocation of households and businesses.

In most cases, cars, buses, and trucks do not pay for the street space they consume; they have, therefore, no incentive to reduce their land consumption. The mismatch between the supply of land allocated to streets and the demand for street space creates congestion—too many users for too little street space.

Congestion decreases travel speed and therefore decreases mobility. In our quest to increase mobility, it is important to measure the street area consumed per passenger for each mode of urban transport and eventually to price it so that users who use large road areas would pay a higher price than those who use small road areas. Being able to price congestion in term of real estate rental value would enable us to increase mobility, not so much by increasing supply as by decreasing consumption. The objective remains to increase mobility by pricing congestion, not to select or "encourage" a preferred mode of transport.

In the next sections, I describe how to measure congestion and various attempts to increase road supply to manage demand.

Measuring Congestion
Congestion is the expression of a mismatch between supply and demand for street space. Traffic engineers define a road as congested when the speed of travel is lower than the free flow speed. The free flow speed of vehicles establishes the

noncongestion speed, which traffic engineers use as a benchmark to measure congestion.[16] Any speed below the free flow speed is indicative of congestion and is measured by the travel time index (TTI), which is the ratio of travel time in peak periods to travel time in free flow conditions. For instance, a car driving at 15 km/h on Fifth Avenue in New York at peak hours would indicate a TTI of 2.8, if we assume that the free flow speed in New York is equal to the maximum regulatory speed limit of 40 km/h. The mobility report published by Texas A&M Transportation Institute in 2012 evaluates the urban average TTI in 498 US urban areas at 1.18. Los Angeles, with 1.37, has the highest TTI among US cities. New York's TTI is slightly lower at 1.33. The use of TTI allows us to measure the number of additional hours spent driving compared to what they would have been at free flow speed, and by extrapolation, the additional gasoline spent. From TTI, it is then possible to calculate the direct cost of congestion: the opportunity cost of the driver time plus the additional cost of gasoline compared to what it would have been under free flow conditions.

Using TTI to measure congestion is convenient, but is, of course, arbitrary. Starting November 1, 2014, New York City reduced its speed limit from 30 miles per hour (48 km/h) to 25 (40 km/h). The new regulatory limit is bound to reduce the free flow speed. If we take the new regulatory speed of 40 km/h as the free flow speed, then the TTI for a car running at 15 km/h has consequently decreased from 3.2 to 2.8 between October 31 and November 1. The reduction of the New York speed limit, aimed at reducing fatal car accidents involving pedestrians, obviously did not result in a reduction of average commuting time; it has even probably slightly increased it, in spite of the decrease in TTI implying the opposite. In the case of New York, the decrease in TTI in the fall of 2014 will be a false positive!

Using TTI to measure congestion is useful as a relative measure of mobility in a city (providing the benchmark free flow speed has not changed, of course, as it did in New York in 2014). It is also useful to identify streets where traffic management needs to be improved. However, TTI is not a good proxy for mobility when comparing cities. What is important for mobility is the changes in average travel time.

Passengers using motorbuses are also subjected to road congestion, although they are not the main cause of it, as they consume—at least at peak hours, when the bus is full—very little road space per passenger compared to drivers alone in their car, as we will see later. However, in addition to delays due to congestion, public transport users are also delayed when buses and trains are overcrowded and they are unable to board or when the schedule is unpredictable because of mismanagement or poor maintenance.

Public transport overcrowding is a form of congestion internal to the public transport system, as it does not affect commuters using other modes of transport.

To my knowledge, the municipality of Beijing is the only one to monitor in real time public transport overcrowding, measured as a percentage of train capacity. Figure 5.10 shows that a significant portion of Beijing's metro network is severely congested at peak hours. Trains and buses are assumed to exceed capacity when the density inside the vehicle exceeds 6.5 people per square meter! The discomforts caused by congestion are therefore quite different when alone listening to the radio in a passenger car sitting in traffic versus when sharing a square meter with six other persons in a crowded bus or metro car, or stuck in a subway station unable to board overcrowded cars!

However, public transport congestion does not just result in discomfort for passengers; it also increases travel time and therefore reduces mobility. In Beijing, in spite of the spectacular increase in the length of metro lines built since 2000, reaching 523 kilometers in 2015, the congestion is so extreme during the rush hour that public transport employees have to limit the number of passengers who can

More than 6.5 passengers per square meter
From 5 to 6.5 passengers per square meter

Figure 5.10
Peak hour congestion in the Beijing metro network, 2014. *Source*: "Beijing the 4th Comprehensive Transport Survey Summary Report," Beijing Transportation Research Center (BTRC), Beijing Municipal Commission of Transport, Beijing, China, 2015.

board each train to prevent the train from becoming dangerously overcrowded. In 2015, about 64 Beijing metro stations (about 20 percent of total number of stations) had restrictions on boarding during rush hour. Beijing's metro system had an additional 340 kilometers of lines under construction in 2015. It is hoped that these new lines will decrease public transport congestion.

The Supply Side: Increasing the Area Devoted to Transport

Increasing Road Supply in Already Dense Areas Is Nearly Impossible
Roads are the default transportation system in every city of the world. Roads are indispensable for the construction of a city. The road network is the backbone of any public transport system. Government is usually responsible for the design, construction, and maintenance of the primary road system.

Could the government act like an economic market and supply the road space that would match existing demand? The government or developers are routinely supplying new roads as cities expand into the countryside and in low-density suburban areas. However, attempts to increase the road supply in already dense built-up areas (where demand is highest) have had very limited success in the past.

Haussmann obviously managed to cut into dense existing neighborhoods in the Paris of the nineteenth century (see chapter 3). However, if Haussmann's work is so well known in the history of planning, it is precisely because it has been nearly impossible to replicate it, and it had few precedents. Besides, all the boulevards created by Haussmann are now congested, and it is clearly impossible and even undesirable to widen them further to accommodate current traffic demand.

Demand for more road space usually occurs in areas located in the most attractive and expensive parts of a city. Because of the high value of the real estate bordering Fifth Avenue in New York, Rue de Rivoli in Paris, or Huaihai road in Shanghai, it is unthinkable to widen these streets, although they are extremely congested. The widening of these streets would destroy valuable real estate that makes them attractive, as well as increase the proportion of unpriced land—the roads—at the expense of high-priced land—the shops, offices, and residences bordering the roads. In addition, pedestrians are also major users of street area in central urban districts; increasing traffic flow in downtown areas is usually incompatible with safe and pleasant pedestrian traffic.

As an alternative to road widening, planners have often attempted to increase street area by building elevated highways above existing streets. Elevated highways, while not quite as destructive as widening existing streets, significantly decrease the value and livability of the neighborhoods they cross. In addition, getting in and out of an elevated highway requires the use of ramps, which involves the destruction of additional valuable real estate while obstructing pedestrian flows.

The plan proposed by Robert Moses for the Lower Manhattan Expressway in New York was an attempt to increase street supply in a high-demand area. The popular grassroots movement, led by Jane Jacobs, against the destruction that the expressway would have caused put a stop to the project. Indeed, the negative impact of elevated highways in dense urban areas is not limited to the eventual destruction of existing side buildings; it often extends for several blocks around. Because of the negative impact and high cost of elevated highways, not only has their construction been practically halted around the world, but a reverse movement advocating the demolition of existing ones is spreading.

Supply Side: Using Existing Road Space More Efficiently

Using existing street space more efficiently could increase the area of street available for the circulation of pedestrians, surface public transport, and cars. Many cities that allow extensive on-street parking in their dense core decrease the area available for the movement of pedestrians, bicycles, buses, and cars. On a typical street in Manhattan, parked cars are using 44 percent of the street area available to vehicles (not including sidewalks). Given the scarcity of road space, transferring all on-street parking to privately operated underground garages would greatly increase city mobility, the safety of pedestrians, and the pleasantness of a city in general. The political feasibility of doing so is remote, as many users of free or quasi-free on-street parking consider it as a basic human right. Any mayor attempting to improve mobility for pedestrians, surface public transport, and cars by removing on-street parking would probably not be reelected or might even be impeached.

Clever use of traffic engineering could also improve mobility without the need to increase the area devoted to streets. Samuel Staley and Adrian Moore, in their book aptly named *Mobility First*,[17] devote an entire chapter titled "Seven Steps to Expanding Current Road Capacity" to the various methods that can improve the speed of vehicles in urban areas. These vary from redesigning intersections to introducing "hot lanes." New technology in traffic light management could also improve mobility of the existing road network. Particularly promising is the swarm technology, which consists of real-time updating of traffic light patterns to respond to shifting traffic volume and unexpected events, like accidents or civil events. However, these measures, when taken, would undoubtedly enhance mobility but would not solve the problem of congestion durably without being associated with a demand side solution.

Supply Side: Tunneling to Increase the Street Area

The first underground railway dedicated to urban transport opened in London in 1863. It had a modest length of 6 kilometers and used steam locomotives. The cost was high, but it was an alternative to Haussmann's widening of Paris streets, which had started a few years earlier. The more democratic and liberal nature of London's political system in the middle of the nineteenth century would not have permitted an Haussmann-type operation in London. The decision to create an underground urban transport system in London was justified by the high price of land.

Building a transport system underground is a way of substituting capital for land. While the capital cost might be high, it should be approximately equal to the value of the road area it saves. The economics of building the first subway system in London must have seemed sound, as new subways were soon built in other capitals of Europe and in the main cities of the United States. By 1914, 13 cities[18] worldwide had already built urban underground transport networks.

Building tunnels under the dense downtown area of existing cities is expensive. For example, in January 2017, three stations in a tunnel 2.7 kilometers long, part of the projected Second Avenue Subway, opened in midtown Manhattan at a cost of $4.45 billion (2015) or $1.6 billion per kilometer. It seems an astronomical sum for a relatively short addition to the New York subway network. Is it worth it? The object of the tunnel is to substitute capital for land, or in other words, to create new land by spending capital. To determine whether this cost makes sense, we could compare the cost of the land "created" to the price of land in areas adjacent to the tunnel.

A study of land value conducted by the Federal Reserve Bank of New York[19] in 2008 valued the prime land in midtown Manhattan at about $5,500 per square foot or about $60,000 per square meter. If we calculate the cost of the new area created by the tunnel, assuming a right of way of 25 meters and three underground stations of 6,000 square meters each, we find that the cost per square meter of new land created by the tunnel is around $50,000. This is similar to the prime land price of $60,000 per square meter assessed in the area by the Fed report in 2008. In the context of Manhattan land prices, the $4.45 billion investment in a subway tunnel appears reasonable. In addition, it is likely that the new subway line, when completed, will increase the value of the land along Second Avenue compared to its 2008 value.

We should therefore always associate transport issues to real estate prices. High land prices indicate to planners that there is a high demand for the area, and therefore, a high volume of commuters will try to have access to it. At the same time, high land prices preclude widening streets to accommodate traffic. The justification for an underground network of transport depends on the ratio between the unit price of land and the unit cost of tunneling. If this ratio is about equal to or greater than 1, the underground network may make economic sense. If the ratio is much below 1, then another solution should be found.

Note that the construction cost of $1.6 billion per kilometer of subway is probably a world record. The cost of tunneling and constructing underground tracks and stations varies with many factors, including depth, width, geology, labor costs, and technology used. A brief survey of recent subway construction costs shows very large variations, from $600 million per kilometer for the latest Singapore MRT line, to $43 million per kilometer for Seoul line 9 built in 2009. These variations show that underground transport may make economic sense even in cities where land prices are much lower than in Manhattan.

Supply Side: How Much Land Is Available Anyway?
We may not be able to increase the area of street in already built-up cities, but do we even know how much is available to make better use of such a scarce resource?

Some cities' land use statistics provide a percentage of the built-up area devoted to streets. For instance, the percentage of street area in New York City is 26.6 percent, for London it is 20.8 percent. These numbers are difficult to interpret. It would seem that New York City has about a 28 percent larger street area than London. While the two cities (defined as within municipal boundaries and not as metropolitan area) have about the same population of about 8 million, their population density differs significantly (table 5.3). Because of the difference in density, while the share of road is higher in New York, the area of road per capita is lower in New York than in London. If we assume that the need for street space is proportional to the population, then London offers 9 percent more road space per person than does New York, in spite of a significantly lower percentage of road.

I am using this example to show that any normative approach to fix the area of urban road to an optimum to avoid congestion is a mirage. The population densities in New York and London have varied widely long after the road areas had been fixed forever by property lines. Densities vary with time, and road areas are fixed by history; as a result, the area of road per person, which is clearly correlated with congestion, varies over time. Transport systems have to adjust to what road area is available and not the opposite.

Table 5.3
Street area per person, New York and London.

	New York	London
Census year	2010	2011
Population	8,175,133	8,173,941
Built-up area (square kilometers)	666	941
Population density (people per hectare)	123	87
Percentage of street area	26.6	20.8
Area of street per person (square meters)	22	24

Population and job densities vary enormously from one part of a city to another; so does the percentage of land occupied by streets. The need for street area is related to neighborhood densities. For instance, in midtown Manhattan, the density of jobs reaches an astonishingly high 2,160 jobs per hectare. By contrast, in Glen Rock, a suburb of New York, the residential density is only 19 people per hectare. Clearly, the local demand for road space will be different in these two neighborhoods. If we combine neighborhood densities with percentage of land devoted to streets, we obtain the area of street per person or per job in different neighborhoods, which is already a little more useful than the aggregate at the city level. Figure 5.11 shows the variations of road space per person or per job in a select number of neighborhoods in various large cities of the world. Table 5.4 shows the infinite combination of densities and areas devoted to streets that explains the large variations in road area per person in each neighborhood.

The road space per person can be below 2 square meters in some neighborhoods in Cairo, New York, and Mumbai, and above 50 square meters in some suburbs of Atlanta, Los Angeles, and New York. The road area per person could be an interesting indicator for mode of transport compatibility. In midtown New York, for instance, because of the very low area of street per person, workers would

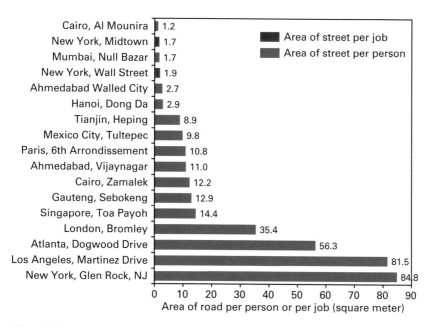

Figure 5.11
Road area per person or per job in various neighborhoods.

Table 5.4
Densities, percentage of road area, and road area per person in various neighborhoods.

City—Neighborhood	Density (people per hectare)	Road area (percent)	Road area per person (square meters)
Cairo—Al Mounira	1,566	19.0	1.2
New York—Midtown, jobs	2,158	36.0	1.7
Mumbai—Null Bazar	1,649	27.9	1.7
New York—Wall Street, jobs	1,208	23.1	1.9
Ahmedabad, India—Walled City	588	16.0	2.7
Hanoi—Dong Da	929	27.3	2.9
Tianjin—Heping	271	24.0	8.9
Mexico City—Tultepec	121	11.9	9.8
Paris—6 arrondissement	266	28.8	10.8
Ahmedabad, India—Vijaynagar	492	54.0	11.0
Cairo—Zamalek	178	21.8	12.2
Gauteng, South Africa—Sebokeng	182	23.5	12.9
Singapore—Toa Payoh	186	26.9	14.4
London—Bromley	49	17.4	35.4
Atlanta—Dogwood Drive, Fulton Co.	22	12.2	56.3
Los Angeles—Martinez Drive	35	28.8	81.5
New York MSA—Glen Rock, NJ	19	15.7	84.8

more than entirely fill the street with vehicles if each of them were using an automobile. At the other extreme, within the suburbs of New York, Atlanta, or Los Angeles, the road area per person is large enough to accommodate a large number of individual vehicles.

The numbers in figure 5.11 and table 5.4 demonstrate that any normative approach applied to densities or road design for an entire city in order to provide better transport is bound to fail. Planners should design transport systems that are adapted to the densities and street design of the neighborhood they are supposed to serve. In the following section, I evaluate the area of street that is consumed per passenger for various mode of transport.

Going beyond Supply

History and the experience of existing cities demonstrate that the possibility of increasing the supply of roads in existing built-up areas is extremely limited. Widening streets or doubling the street area by creating an elevated highway destroys the very quality that attracts traffic in the first place. Tunneling is very costly, and while indispensable in the downtown of large dense cities, it cannot be applied in cities where land is less expensive but where congestion is still very real.

Increasing mobility (i.e., decreasing the time required to go from one part of a metropolitan area to another) therefore requires a concerted action on the demand side. The demand side includes calculating how much street space each commuter consumes and what measures could be taken to decrease not demand for trips but demand for street space.

The Demand Side: Measuring Land Consumption per Commuter per Transport Mode

There are only two ways of decreasing the commuters' demand for street space: reducing the consumption of street space per commuter and reducing the demand for trips at peak hours. Let us first look at the consumption of street space per commuter related to the various modes of transport.

Measuring the Consumption of Street Space per Commuter and Road Capacity in Passengers per Hour

A vehicle moving on a city street uses the area corresponding to the vehicle's dimension plus the area required to prevent a collision with the preceding vehicle. The safe distance between two moving vehicles is set by the time that would be required for the following vehicle to stop if the front vehicle had to stop suddenly. The slow reaction time of drivers, not the size of the vehicles, is responsible for most of the road area required by moving cars. Therefore, the area of street required by vehicle depends on the speed of the vehicle: the higher the speed, the larger the area required will be.

The formal way to calculate the minimum safe distances between moving vehicles involves a number of parameters, including human reaction time, maximum braking deceleration, the adherence of the road surface, among other things. In reality, drivers are told that they should allow a reaction time of 2 seconds[20] between two vehicles.

On congested streets, it is difficult to maintain a 2-second interval, as vehicles change speed continuously and average intervals tend to increase, further reducing the flow capacity of the road. In the rest of this chapter, I assume a standard safe interval of 2 seconds for moving vehicles except for buses moving in exclusive lanes, where the distances between buses will be fixed by the bus schedule.

When a car is moving at 40 km/h, the safety buffer zone required to maintain a 2-second interval represents 82 percent of the total street area consumed by the moving car. This area increases with speed, as shown in figure 5.12. Because cars move in a lane of standard width, and because most of the street area required by a car is dictated by the 2-second interval, smaller cars do not consume significantly less road space, except at very low speeds, as we will see below.

There are only two ways to decrease the street area consumed by moving cars: the first would be to decrease the width of vehicles so that two vehicles fit in the width of one lane (e.g., a motorcycle); the second would be to decrease safely the 2-second reaction time by using technology like self-driving cars. We will explore these possibilities later on.

For vehicles moving on a road, the consumption of street area per passenger is therefore dependent on four parameters: the length of the vehicle, the reaction time to ensure a safe distance between vehicles, the speed of the vehicle, and the number of passengers.

For instance, a commuter driving alone on a New York street at the maximum allowed speed of 25 miles per hour (40 km/h) is de facto required to use 84 square meters of street area per vehicle to stay at a safe distance from the preceding vehicle running at the same speed (figure 5.12). If the car's driver is the only passenger, then the consumption of street space is 84 square meters per commuter. However, in the United States, on average, there are about 1.25 passengers per car in urban areas. An average commuter driving a car in the United States is therefore consuming 67 square meters when in a car running at 40 km/h. The more passengers per vehicle, the less the consumption of street space, as the distance between vehicles stays constant at the same speed.

The number of cars on a segment of road of a given length determines the speed of the vehicles because of the necessity of keeping a safe interval of about 2 seconds between vehicles. For instance, maintaining the maximum speed limit of

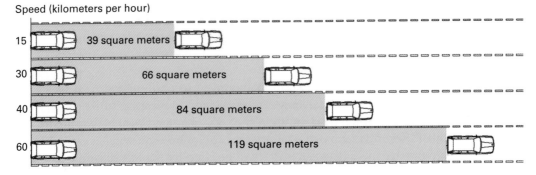

Figure 5.12
Street area requirements for cars running at different speeds with 2-second reaction time.

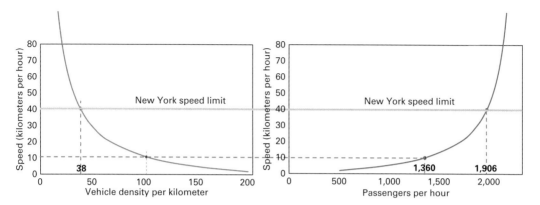

Figure 5.13
Speed versus vehicle density (left) and lane capacity (right) for cars.

40 km/h allowed in New York City would require that there are no more than 38 cars per lane over a distance of 1 kilometer (left graph in Figure 5.13). If more cars enter the lane, the speed of all the cars will have to decrease to maintain the 2-second interval between cars. If the number of cars per kilometer of lane increases to 100, then the speed of all cars in the lane will drop to 11 km/h. This decrease in speed will also reduce the capacity of the lane to carry passengers. At the speed limit of 40 km/h, one lane can carry 1,900 passengers in one direction; at 10 km/h, this capacity is reduced to 1,360 passengers (right graph in figure 5.13). In reality, the capacity will probably be reduced further, because as new cars enter the lane, drivers have trouble adjusting quickly the interval between cars; it then becomes difficult to maintain a constant 2-second interval. Empirical data show that this interval tends to increase as speed adjusts downward, resulting in even lower passenger capacity than the one shown on figure 5.13, which assumes that the 2-second interval between cars remains constant.

Therefore, in New York City for instance, every car added to traffic in a lane with a density of more than 38 cars per kilometer decreases the speed of all the cars in the lane. This additional car reduces travel speed, therefore increases commuting time, and therefore decreases mobility. In addition, it decreases the existing road capacity to bring commuters to their destination.

In spite of these well-documented problems, traffic planners have not yet found any direct way to control the number of cars entering a street in order to maintain a preselected speed. In other areas of the economy, "gatekeepers" are matching demand with existing capacity in the short term. This is what happens, for instance, in cinemas or restaurants where peak demand may often significantly exceed capacity. If more customers than seats available present themselves, gatekeepers will prevent the customers from entering the cinema or the restaurant. In the long run, prices will be adjusted to adjust demand to supply, or eventually extra capacity will be added to match supply to demand. This is unfortunately not possible for roads. If the road users' demand is higher than the road capacity, in the absence of gatekeepers or price adjustments, all users will have to reduce speed until all demand has been satisfied, even if this demand results into total gridlock!

I discuss below the indirect means currently used to decrease the number of cars entering an urban network; except for adjustable congestion pricing as used in Singapore, most methods are often clumsy and ineffective.

So far, we have only looked at the links between vehicle density, speed, and lane capacity for cars, which could be taxis or private cars. Let us now compare these relations for various types of moving vehicles.

Table 5.5 shows the street area required per passenger at different speeds for motorcycles, ordinary cars, short cars ("smart cars"), and urban buses using equation 5.4.

Predictably, people riding bicycles and motorcycles consume less street space than cars (I have assumed that three bicycles and two motorcycles are riding in parallel on a 3.2-meter-wide standard street lane). Smaller cars consume only slightly less than regular cars, and the difference decreases as speed increases. However, the surprising information provided by table 5.5 is how little street area passengers in a full city bus are using compared to any other mode of transport.

Equation 5.4 Street area used per passenger

The street area used per passenger in moving vehicles can be expressed as a function of the vehicle speed S and four parameters: R, L, W, and P:

$$A = \frac{\left(\dfrac{S \times R}{3.6} + L\right)W}{P}, \tag{5.4}$$

where
A is the area of street per passenger in square meters,
S is the speed of vehicle in km/h,
R is the reaction time required from drivers to prevent two vehicles from crashing into each other, expressed in seconds,
L is the length of the vehicle in meters,
W is the width of a lane in meters, and
P is the number of passengers per vehicle.

Table 5.5
Street area consumption per person for various modes of transport operating at various speeds.

	Type of vehicle				
	Bicycle	Motorcycle	Smart car	Regular car	Bus
Reaction time (seconds)	1.5	2	2	2	2
Length of vehicle (meters)	1.8	2.1	2.7	4.0	12.0
Lane width (meters)	1.1	1.6	3.2	3.2	3.2
Passengers per vehicle	1	1	1.25	1.25	86
Speed (km/h)	Street area used per passenger (square meters)				
2.5	3.0	5.6	10.5	13.8	0.5
5	4.1	7.9	14.0	17.4	0.5
10	6.4	12.3	21.1	24.5	0.7
15	8.6	16.8	28.2	31.6	0.8
20	10.8	21.2	35.3	38.7	0.9
25		25.6	42.5	45.8	1.0
30		30.1	49.6	52.9	1.1
35		34.5	56.7	60.0	1.2
40		39.0	63.8	67.1	1.3
45		43.4	70.9	74.2	1.4
50		47.9	78.0	81.4	1.5

At 40 km/h, a passenger in a car consumes more than 50 times the street area used by his counterparts riding at the same speed in an admittedly crowded bus![21]

This is an argument often used by people who advocate eliminating cars from city streets. It is also the subject of a poster produced by the city of Munster, Germany, in 2001, which went viral on the Internet.[22] The poster shows three side-by-side views of the same street with the area of street used by cars, bicycles, and buses to carry the same number of passengers. The goal of the poster is to dramatize the difference of road consumption per person between cars, bicycles, and motorbuses. The street area consumption figures in table 5.5 seem to support the poster's claim that cars as a mean of transport are extremely wasteful compared to buses.

If it were possible to transport passengers in a bus at 40 km/h across a city using only 1.3 square meters of street per passenger, as implied by the numbers in table 5.5, it would probably justify banning all cars from cities. Unfortunately, both bus consumption numbers in the table and the claims of the Munster poster are grossly misleading.

Speed and Road Capacity
All types of vehicles listed in table 5.5 follow each other at a distance required by safety. However, buses cannot follow each other the way cars can. Buses have to keep a larger distance between each other than cars do, as we will see below. This is why the very low street area consumption shown on table 5.5 is theoretically correct but irrelevant for practical purposes.

Bus departures from bus stops have to be spaced at regular time intervals, called headways, which are much longer than the few seconds that are required between two successive cars. Typical headways in city centers range from 1 to 10 minutes, not the 2- to 3-second headways required for car safety. It is not possible to fill a city street entirely with buses running at 2-second intervals. For this reason, the very small street area that buses use per passenger is irrelevant, as buses using the same bus stop have to run at several hundred meters from each other, and the space between successive buses have to be filled with cars or be left empty.

Why do city buses have to be spaced at headways of often several minutes? The buses must stop at regular intervals to let passengers board and alight, which usually takes between 10 seconds to a minute for each stop. The time buses spend at bus stops is called the dwell time. The dwell time depends on the time required by passengers who are boarding and alighting. The more numerous the passengers boarding and alighting at a bus stop, the longer the dwell time will be. Therefore, dwell time is longer at rush hour, and it has an element of unpredictability, as it depends on the passengers' agility when boarding and on the number of passengers. Bus headways must take into account the possible accidental variations of dwell time.

Imagine a column of buses following each other in a lane between two stops at a 2-second safety interval. The entire column will have to stop, say, 20 seconds to allow the first bus at the head of the column to let its passengers board and alight. The process will repeat itself for every bus in the column. Therefore, the speed of this imaginary column of buses will be, at best, the length of a bus every 20 seconds or about 2.2 km/h, about less than half of a pedestrian walking speed.

The departure of each bus must be timed in such a manner that there will be a sufficient time interval between buses to prevent following buses from bunching up at bus stops if the preceding bus is detained at the stop. To avoid this problem, the timing between buses is tightly scheduled. Setting headways is a major constraint in the operation of city buses in dense areas where bus stops are close to each other.

In New York, for instance, a typical city bus stops every 160 meters; express buses, operating only at rush hour, stop about every 550 meters and alternate with regular buses. The bus route M1 going from Harlem to Greenwich Village (running nearly the full length of Manhattan) has an average headway of 5 minutes during rush hour (between 7:00 and 9:30 A.M.), including both regular and express buses. The M1 route schedule indicates that the average rush hour speed varies between 9 and 12 km/h over the length of the line for both express and regular buses, express bus average speeds being closer to 12 km/h while regular bus speeds are about 9 km/h. The main advantage of running express buses is to be able to decrease headway. As these buses alternate with regular buses but bypass many stops and have longer runs between stops, the risk of their bunching at bus stops decreases.

Let us compare the speed and lane capacity for buses and cars on a segment of Fifth Avenue between 110th Street and 8th Street, at rush hour between 7:00 and 8:30 A.M. I will use the speed and lane capacity of the M1 route alone and that of the three other bus routes that use the same segment of Fifth Avenue as the M1 route. These other bus routes use different bus stops, which allows compressing headways without bunching. While the average headway of M1 is 5 minute at rush hour, the combined headway of the four bus routes using the same road segment is 1 minute and 48 seconds. Using different bus stops for different routes on the same street allows operators to increase headways and therefore the road capacity for public transport passengers.

Let us now look at the performance of buses and cars as shown in table 5.5 in terms of speed and capacity expressed as passengers per hour per lane (figure 5.14). The lane capacity for cars varies with speed, while the capacity for buses is independent of speed (horizontal lines on the graph) but depends only on headway. Obviously, lane capacity for cars also depends on distances between cars that vary with speed, while public transport headways are independent of speed.

The speed and therefore the lane capacity of ordinary cars depends on the density of cars per kilometer, as we have seen in figure 5.13. If the cars' density allows a speed of between 20 and 40 km/h, the lane capacity will vary from about 1,650 to 1,900 passengers per hour per lane. If the density is such that the speed drops below 5 km/h, then the capacity will drop rapidly to close to 0, when congestion creates gridlock.

By contrast, the number of passengers per hour carried by buses is independent of bus speed; it depends only on headway, which is designed to be constant (equation 5.5).

In New York, the M1 buses that depart at 5-minute average headways are therefore able to carry only 1,032 passengers per hour $((60/5) \times 86)$, less than cars when they are running at speeds above 6 km/h (figure 5.14). However, when the four bus routes that are using this segment of Fifth Avenue are taken into account, the combined capacity of the buses reaches 2,800 passengers per hour.

In practice, the buses are practically using the right lane exclusively and the second lane partially to allow express buses to overtake regular buses. The other

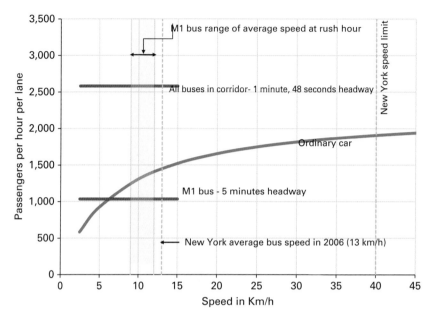

Figure 5.14
Speed versus lane capacity for buses and cars along M1 corridor in Manhattan.

lanes cannot be used by buses and are therefore used by cars. The total capacity of the three usable lanes on Fifth Avenue when buses are combined with cars reaches about 5,000 passengers per hour per direction. This is more than the capacity that would be obtained if this segment of Fifth Avenue was used exclusively by cars or exclusively by buses. Therefore, as currently designed, cars might be clumsy and inefficient, but they are an indispensable component of urban transport systems. In addition, if the density of cars could be kept below, say, 50 cars per lane-kilometers, then they will provide a faster way of moving around the city than does public transport. However, the complementarity of the two means of transport is important. In dense urban areas like New York, London, or Shanghai, the large number of public transport passengers contributes to keeping the car density low, and therefore allows their passengers a higher mobility.

Let us now look at the comparative performance of all the various transport modes shown on table 5.4. We will look at speed and road capacity expressed as passengers per hour per lane (equation 5.5). The parameters used to draw the curves in figure 5.15, like reaction time, length of vehicle, lane width, and number of passenger per vehicles, are the same as those used in table 5.5.

We see that bicycles provide a much higher road capacity at speeds below 15 km/h than any other mode of transport. This result is based on the assumption

Equation 5.5 Lane carrying capacity

$$C = \frac{60}{H}P$$ (5.5)

where
C is the lane capacity in passenger per hour per direction,
H is the headway expressed in minutes, and
P is the number of passengers per vehicle.

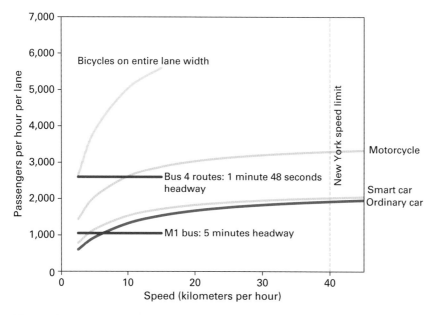

Figure 5.15
Speed versus lane capacity for various transport modes along M1 corridor in Manhattan.

that bicycles are running on an entire lane dedicated to them, as is often still the case in Chinese cities but is not common in European and American cities. However, this performance in most cases remains theoretical, as demand for 5,000 bicyclists an hour along one road is unlikely in most large, dense cities. The more modest narrow bicycle lanes provided in many cities like New York or Paris have very low bicycle densities. However, figure 5.15 shows that in cities where traveling by bicycle is culturally well accepted (i.e., where there is a high demand for bicycle trips), bicycle lanes could contribute significantly to mobility. The low speed of the bicycle, however, prevents it from becoming a significant mode of commuting in cities of more than 1 million people. Because of their higher speed and increased comfort, electric bicycles, where they are authorized (as in Chengdu, China), could meaningfully compete with buses or cars as a means of commuting in larger cities.

Motorcycles also prove to be an interesting alternative to buses in terms of both speed and road capacity (figure 5.15). In countries where they are culturally well accepted, as in the countries of Southeast Asia, motorcycles could become a very efficient means of mass transportation on a metropolitan scale. Motorcycles use both energy and street space more efficiently than cars do. The noise and pollution associated with traditional motorcycles are soon becoming a problem of the past with the proliferation of electric motorcycles. The increased risk of accident associated with two-wheelers is real, but it is compounded by the neglect shown by urban managers in adapting traffic engineering and design to motorcycles in cities like Hanoi, where they are the major mode of transport. The emergence of more stable, fully enclosed tilting electric three-wheelers like the Toyota i-Road[23] suggests that the mobility advantage enjoyed by the citizens of Hanoi could be provided in the future without the nuisance, risks, and discomfort caused by the traditional motorcycle.

By contrast, compared to the motorcycle, compact Smart car performance (except for energy use) in terms of road capacity is not much better than that of an ordinary car (figure 5.15). The width of the vehicle, not its length, is the important parameter to consider when trying to reduce street area consumption. A compact Smart car is 166 cm wide, while a Toyota i-Road vehicle is only 87 cm wide, allowing two vehicles to run in parallel on a standard 320-cm wide lane.

Figures 5.14 and 5.15 show us that speed and road capacity are equally important when assessing the performance of different transport modes. We will see below that the exclusive focus on road capacity, while disregarding speed, may lead to decreased mobility while apparently reducing congestion.

Demand Side: Allocating Street Area to a Preferred Mode of Transport

We have seen that the consumption of street area per commuter varies with transport mode. A passenger riding a bus filled at capacity running at a speed of 30 km/h consumes about 1 square meter of street space, while a passenger in a car running at the same speed with an average occupancy of 1.25 passengers per car consumes 55 square meters.

Given that congestion is a major problem in most large cities of the world, it is understandable that urban managers try to prioritize allocation of road space to transport modes that use less street space per passenger in order to increase street capacity. For instance, many municipalities reserve lanes for the exclusive use of buses and taxis. Many suburban highways have special lanes reserved for high-occupancy vehicles (HOVs) in an attempt to decrease the area of road used per commuter by encouraging carpooling. Commuters will use the HOV lanes when these are not congested and, therefore, they will be rewarded by higher speed. However, carpooling has been decreasing in the United States from 19.7 percent of all commuting trips in 1980 to only 9.7 percent in 2010.[24] This trend can be explained by the higher commuting times involved in carpooling. In the United States, apparently, the potential reduction of travel time offered by HOV lanes is not a sufficient incentive to compensate for the additional time required to pick up carpooling passengers. Carpoolers will gain time by using HOV lanes only if they can maintain a speed close to free flow, say, 60 km/h. That supposes a distance between vehicles of about 33 meters or a density of about 30 cars per kilometer of lane. If there are more than 30 cars per kilometer of HOV lane, the speed of vehicles will decrease and possibly become equal to non-HOV lanes. If the car density is less than 30 cars per kilometer, then the speed in HOV lanes will be free flow and carpooling would become an attractive alternative to driving alone. However, if the density falls much below 30 cars per kilometer, then the highway capacity will be reduced and the HOV lane would increase congestion for the majority rather than reduce it.

High-occupancy toll (HOT) lanes are likely to replace HOV lanes in the future. HOT lanes are reserved for HOVs and cars that are willing to pay a toll to go faster. The definition of a HOV is more restrictive than in traditional HOV lanes, which ensures that the traffic in HOT lanes is fluid while the number of vehicles per hour is sufficient to ensure full use of the lane capacity.

HOV and HOT lanes are attempts by local governments to allocate scarce road area to the vehicles that use it more efficiently. We will see below how the use of congestion pricing and technology might one day be generalized to ensure an even more efficient use of urban roads.

The recent multiplication of BRT systems constitutes another way of allocating street area to the exclusive use of one mode of transport. Let us explore how successful this new mode of transport had been in increasing mobility.

Allocation of Roads for BRT Systems

The invention of Bus Rapid Transit in Curitiba, Brazil, in 1974 provides a more radical example of road allocation among transport modes. The first BRT was created in Curitiba as an affordable substitute to a subway. The challenge was to show that it was possible to increase the carrying capacity of a street lane to approach the capacity of a subway at a fraction of the cost. An ordinary bus line with a full load of 86 passengers per vehicle and a 3-minute headway is able to transport about 1,720 passengers per hour per direction (PPHPD). Curitiba BRT is able to carry about 10,800 passengers per hour per direction per lane. More recent BRTs, like Bogota TransMilenio, are able to carry up to 33,000 PPHPD by adding additional express lanes and wider rights-of-way than the one used in Curitiba. A typical subway carries from 22,000 (London Victoria line) to 80,000 PPHPD (Hong Kong Metro).

Since Curitiba's success, many cities around the world have adopted similar BRT systems with some variations in design and performance. Mayors and urban planners have often celebrated the invention of BRT as a silver bullet that could solve the problem of mass transport in large cities without the heavy capital investment required for the construction of underground metro systems. BRT's objective is not to add road area, as the BRT is usually created on existing roads, but to increase the capacity of existing roads by allocating existing road space to the most efficient users.

A BRT has two main features: an existing road area reserved to the exclusive use of buses and a system of specially designed bus stations where passengers pay their fares before entering the bus and where they can board and alight quickly, reducing dwell time to 20 seconds or less. The BRT vehicles are usually specially designed with many large doors to reduce dwell time and large passenger capacity: often up to 270 passengers in articulated buses. The high PPHPD capacity is made possible by running very large buses at very short intervals with headways of about 90 seconds.

Does BRT use street area more efficiently than ordinary buses?

In Curitiba, an elevated curb physically separates the BRT lanes from the lanes used by cars. Stations from which passengers board and alight are located about every 500 meters. Figure 5.16 shows the layout of a two-block portion of Curitiba's BRT Eixo Sul line on Avenida Sete Setembre. The BRT lanes and station use 44 percent of the total road space exclusively for the use of BRT vehicles. In addi-

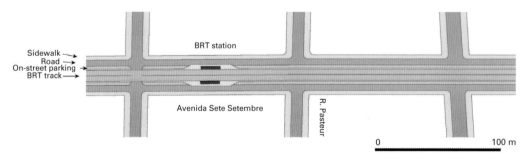

Figure 5.16
Map of a typical station and right-of-way for the Curitiba BRT (Eixo Sul line).

Equation 5.6 Area of street used per passenger for a BRT

$$A = \frac{100\,H \times S \times W}{6\,P}, \tag{5.6}$$

where
A is the area of street per passenger in square meters,
H is the headway in seconds,
S is the speed of the bus in km/h,
W is the average width of the BRT's right-of-way, and
P is the number of passengers per bus.

tion, to maintain speed and avoid traffic lights, crossings are minimized by interrupting about three cross-streets out of five.

A bus sharing a lane with cars uses only the street area that it needs to keep a safe distance from the vehicle in front of it. At 30 km/h, the passengers of ordinary buses use only about 1 square meter of road per person (see table 5.4). However, for a BRT, the street area used per commuter is different from that of an ordinary bus. A BRT uses its own road space, which is not available to other vehicles. Equation 5.6 defines the area of street used per passenger for a BRT.

The area of street consumed per BRT passenger varies with headway (figure 5.17). The larger the headway, the more street area a passenger consumes. To increase capacity, BRT operators have a strong incentive to reduce headway and to increase the number of passengers per bus. Increasing the number of passengers per bus has the added incentive of reducing operating costs, as the salary of drivers usually represents more than 60 percent of bus operating cost. This is why Curitiba's BRT uses very large articulated buses, each with a capacity of 270 passengers.

Headways, however, have a lower limit. When the headway gets too short, say, below 1 minute, buses run the risk of catching up with preceding buses, resulting in bunching at bus stations. Some Curitiba reports are mentioning headways of 90 seconds. This is extremely tight for articulated buses containing 270 passengers. Most common headways for BRT at rush hour seem to be about 2 minutes.[25] The use of road space per passenger is dependent on headways and bus occupancies. I show in figure 5.17 how the road area used by passenger varies with headway and vehicle occupancy.

For a headway of 90 seconds and full bus occupancy, the street consumption per passenger is an impressively low 8 square meters (figure 5.17), about seven times less than the road space used by a commuter in a car running at 30 km/h. However, BRT street consumption per passenger increases rapidly as the headway

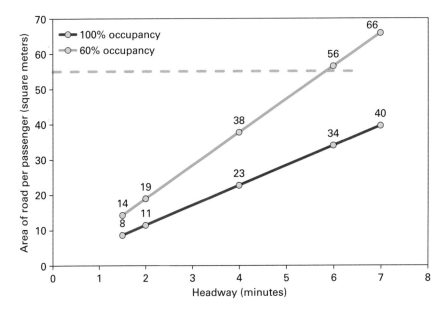

Figure 5.17
BRT use of road space per passenger when headways vary. Dashed horizontal line indicates the road area per passenger for a car moving at 30 km/h with a headway of 2 seconds.

increases and the occupancy decreases, as can be seen in figure 5.17. With a 6-minute headway and 60 percent occupancy, the road consumption of a passenger riding a BRT is similar to that of a commuter in a car. A 2004 report[26] on Curitiba's BRT analyzing data from various sources shows that headway on the north-south axis varies from 3 to 7 minutes. Checking the schedule of bus 507 at 7 P.M. in 2015 confirms a headway of 7 minutes. If these are the range of operational headways for BRT, the resulting street area consumption per passenger for the highest headway is 40 square meters at full occupancy and 66 square meters at 60 percent occupancy. This consumption is not any more impressive when compared to the 55 square meters consumed by a passenger in a car running at 30 km/h.

By contrast, at any speed and even at less than 10 percent occupancy, the road consumption per passenger of an ordinary bus remains a small fraction of the consumption of passengers in a car. To be efficient, BRT lines have to be built along an axis where the demand for capacity at peak hours ensures full occupancy and justifies the very short headways. It is often the case that after initial operation, headways are increased. Based on the basic statistics of bus movement, it appears that the actual headway at peak hours on the main BRT axes varies from 3 to 10 minutes.

BRT requires an existing rather wide right-of-way of at least 36 meters and preferably 42 meters for higher performance. However, because of the more efficient use of road space and their relatively low cost, BRT systems have spread rapidly all over the world in the past 20 years and, in particular, in cities that already had a subway system. Do they constitute an alternative breakthrough to the traditional bus and subway systems by providing mobility while avoiding congestion? BRT is an innovative way of using scarce road space, but its application will be limited in the future by three factors: first, the wide right-of-way it requires; second, the monocentric or linear city structure it implies; and third, its limited speed, which makes it inadequate for large cities.

BRT's ability to reduce significantly the demand for street space is very much dependent on a continuous high operating performance: maintaining very short headways and high occupancy. Because of the typical distance between stations of about 500 meters in a BRT, maintaining headways as short as 90 seconds requires a faultless system. The dwell time spent by a bus at a station for letting passengers board and alight should not be above 20 seconds. Any delay occurring during boarding or alighting will cause buses to queue at the same station, as the distance between stations is too short to make up the dwelling time delay by increasing bus speed.

It is important to realize that the road capacity expressed in PPHPD, whether high or low, does not imply anything about speed. Figure 5.18 shows the PPHPD corresponding to eight BRT systems and eight different cities' subway lines currently in operation and their respective speeds. These speeds are the average speed of buses and trains from beginning to end of the line; the vehicular speeds are much higher than the actual speeds of passengers when traveling from their origins to their destinations.

While the capacity of the best-performing BRT may overlap with that of the worst-performing subway line, no BRT can match the speed of a subway line. Hong Kong's subway has a capacity seven times larger than Curitiba's BRT and a speed about 75 percent higher.

The limited speed of BRT systems (figure 5.18) suggests that there is a city size beyond which BRT is too slow to provide the mobility required in very large cities. For instance, Seoul's metropolitan area extends across a circle of more than 100 kilometers in diameter. It is obvious that at a speed of 25 km/h, even the fastest BRT would not be able to provide access to the full job market of a large metropolitan area like Seoul. BRT, however, might be useful for providing high-capacity mobility in a restricted area (like a CBD) or for joining two dense job clusters. However, trips in large metropolitan areas would have to be provided by faster means of transport. The argument that high-capacity public transport reduces

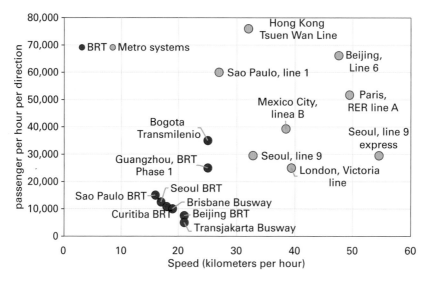

Figure 5.18
Transport system speed and capacity versus speed, BRT and Metro. *Sources*: BRT data are from Walter Hook, "Bus Rapid Transit: An International View," Institute for Development & Transport Policy, New York, 2008; "Mass Transit Railway: Business Overview, Operations and Services," www.MTR.com.HK, Hong Kong, 2014.

congestion is not convincing if the resulting trip duration is longer than what it would have been in a vehicle subject to congestion.

In addition, BRTs and subways are usually designed to serve radio-concentric trips, from periphery to CBD with high job concentration. However, in large metropolitan areas, employment is dispersing into suburbs. The high capacity at relatively slow speeds provided by BRT lines are not well adapted to the newly emerged spatial pattern of dispersed employment. The increase in the number of motorcycles and collective taxis in cities as diverse as Mexico and Johannesburg suggests that commuters are selecting the modes of transport that are more adapted to their trip patterns: low capacity on many diverse routes at higher speed. Unfortunately, most city managers do not accept motorcycles and collective taxis as legitimate means of transport and consequently do not provide road design and lane marking that would increase these vehicles' efficiency and safety.

Decreasing Congestion by Managing Demand through Pricing

We have seen that, through design and regulations, local government may decide to allocate scarce street space to a preferred mode of transport. The allocation of street space to HOV lanes, exclusive bus lanes, and BRT corridors is motivated by a desire to use street area more efficiently. An administrative allocation of land may be justified in some cases, but it might often result in an inefficient use of street area when demand for road space shifts. For instance, HOV lanes are often either not used enough or are congested. The same problem may plague BRT lines that are justified only when the demand for capacity is high, when headways are below 2 minutes, and when vehicle occupancy or load factor is close to 100 percent design capacity. Administrative allocation of street space to a specific mode of transport may result in some positive outcomes in some circumstances, but it also introduces a rigidity when demand fluctuates at different hours of the day or over time. The rigidity introduced by an administrative allocation of street area to a preferred mode of transport may result in a loss of mobility.

In market economies, supply and demand is matched through pricing mechanisms. Would it be possible to have a pricing system that determines the optimum mix of different modes of transport through a pricing mechanism without relying on administrative allocation of street space to an exclusive mode of transport?

As I have suggested earlier, we should approach urban transport as a real estate problem. A municipality is the owner of the streets. The rent charged for using the street should be based on how large an area, how long, when, and where a commuter is using it. A commuter using an urban street should be submitted to the same type of pricing system as a traveler renting a room in a hotel or on an airline flight. The price to pay for a hotel room depends on its location, its size, the date of rental, and how long it is rented. Ideally, matching supply and demand perfectly would require that a similar rental system be applied to vehicles using urban roads. The charge, as it is practiced for hotel rooms, should be adjusted to maintain as close to full road occupancy as possible. In the case of urban roads, the objective of the congestion charge is not to maximize a city's income but to prevent congestion above a set level. A car should therefore be charged for the increased travel time imposed on all other drivers due to its presence on the road.

Congestion pricing adjusts demand for roads in two ways: it discourages driving during peak hours for trips that could be done at other hours, and it encourages using vehicles more efficiently, either by increasing occupancy, sharing vehicles, or using less road-intensive means of transport (e.g., motorcycles or public transport).

Singapore is probably the only city in the world so far that is progressively getting toward this theoretical pricing ideal, although the practicality of converting this ideal into reality has not been fully achieved yet.

Singapore was the first city to implement congestion pricing, which it did in 1975. Initially, it was just a toll collected to enter the business district. Eventually, as new technology became available, electronic road pricing was introduced in 1998. The objective of road pricing in Singapore is to guarantee a minimum peak-hour speed for cars in the CBD, main arterial roads, and expressways. The toll is adjusted during the day for time and location. The monitoring of vehicle speed is done continuously, and toll rates are adjusted quarterly to maintain the minimum speed. In addition, measures have been taken to limit the number of cars on the island by auctioning periodically the right to buy new cars.

The effectiveness of Singapore's congestion pricing policy is demonstrated by figure 5.19. Between 2005 and 2014, the average speed at peak hours has only varied between 61 and 64 km/h for expressways and between 27 and 29 km/h in the business district and arterial roads. During the same period, Singapore's population increased by 31 percent!

The Singapore congestion pricing system is the closest in the world to the theoretical model I suggested above: charging a rent for roads the way one is charged for a hotel room (ideally, for a room rented by the hour of use). The toll is charged through gantry when entering different zones. However, the charge is not adjusted for the time passed in the area of high demand, although the rate is adjusted depending on the time of entry and the type of vehicle. I have no doubt that the Government of Singapore will keep improving its pricing system as new technology becomes available that allows charging by time of road use without high transaction costs.

Some cities like London and Stockholm are charging a fee for entering the downtown area, but this is a fee and not a rent, as it does not reflect the area consumed or the length of time it is consumed.

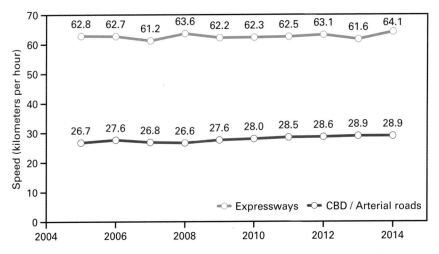

Figure 5.19
Evolution of vehicular speeds at peak hours, Singapore. *Source*: Data are from "Singapore Land Transport Statistics, 2005–2014," Land Transport Authority, Singapore, 2015.

Charging for Road Maintenance and Capital Cost

The objective of the congestion fee is to prevent congestion, or rather to maintain commuters' travel at a set speed during peak hours. However, there is another issue facing urban travel: users are not charged for all the costs involved in building and maintaining roads. This implicit subsidy given to road users may result in an overuse of roads and, therefore, an increase in congestion.

Typically, governments recover the cost of maintaining roads, if not building them, through a tax levied on gasoline price. However, many governments impose a gasoline tax that is much too low to cover the maintenance of urban roads. For instance, in the United States, the Federal gasoline tax is only 18.4 cents per gallon. The tax was last raised in 1993 and is not indexed to inflation. Each state adds its own tax to the Federal tax, but the amount varies widely even in adjacent states and is clearly more influenced by local political considerations than by a desire to rationalize transport economics.

In any case, the imposition of a tax on gasoline to recover from users the cost of roads is rather clumsy, even when the tax is indexed to inflation. Cars built more recently—including hybrid cars—consume much less gasoline per kilometer than older ones, paying even less tax per kilometer of road and further distorting the real cost of using roads. In addition, cars that are entirely electric will soon replace a large part of the current gasoline car fleet, making the cost of driving even more remote from its real cost. In addition, energy and, in particular, gasoline is often subsidized in many countries, further distorting the real cost of using roads.

Pricing urban transport closer to its real cost, including energy used, negative externalities generated (pollution, global warming, and accidents), and real estate utilized, would greatly increase the economic efficiency of urban transport. New GPS technology and transponders should allow users to pay the real cost of trips by distance traveled, including fixed costs like insurance. With a more transparent cost per kilometer traveled, trip decisions and transport mode choices might be different. This would include the choice between owning or sharing a car, or using public transport. The pricing of trips closer to their real economic cost may also alter urban land use in the long run. With a transparent real price for transport, it is urban users, in all their diversity, that will decide the proper mix of transport mode and the proper densities, rather than being submitted to clumsy top-down urban planning decisions. "Getting the prices right" is not just an economist's theoretical dream. It could result in a more grassroots-driven urban environment, improved mobility with less congestion and pollution, and a better supply of affordable housing.

Street Space Allocated to Parking

In every city, a large part of the street area is not allocated to moving traffic but to on-street parking. The possibility of stopping curbside for loading or unloading people and goods is indispensable to the operation and maintenance of cities. Unloading goods to be sold in a store, food to be prepared in a restaurant, and materials to build or repair a building are necessary activities that keep a city functioning. However, it is absurd to use scarce street area to permanently park idle cars on congested streets.

On most Manhattan streets, 53 percent of the street area is allocated to vehicle use, of which 44 percent (usually two lanes) is reserved for on-street parking. Only a small portion of this area is subject to metered parking fees. In Washington, DC, residents of many neighborhoods have to pay only $25 annually to park their cars permanently on the street. A parking space in a private parking garage costs from $200 to $350 per month. Because cars parked permanently occupy most of the street curb space, the indispensable loading and unloading function requires double parking and reduces further the area devoted to traffic, causing more congestion.

Why should a municipality allocate so much scarce street space to permanent parking and subsidize its use? Originally, the high transaction cost of recovering parking fees discouraged pricing parking. However, new technology makes it much easier.

The difficulty has always been to differentiate loading/unloading from permanent parking. The solution, as for traffic congestion, is pricing. The parking fee for each neighborhood could be set so that 20 percent or even 75 percent of the curb space is always vacant. It is the same principle as congestion pricing.

New York implements metered pay parking reserved for commercial vehicles to load and unload in a few streets in Manhattan CBD. The parking time is limited to 3 hours per vehicle with a slightly increasing rate starting at $4 an hour for the first hour, increasing to $5 an hour for the third hour. While the rate progressivity is a step in the right direction, the rate is far too low to maintain enough empty space during the day. The high cost of enforcement—a municipal employee having to check time of parking printed on a ticket deposited on the vehicle dashboard—is unlikely to deter delinquency and abuse. High transaction costs to enforce payments based on parking meters prevent the policy from being effective. The free or underpriced use of public street space for parking will really disappear when technology can automatically identify the vehicle parked (as well as how long and at what time it was parked) and automatically debit the vehicle's owner for the rent accrued—a system similar to the transponders already used on toll roads.

Concluding Thoughts on Pricing as Affected by Supply and Demand

Congestion is due to a mismatch between road space supply and demand.

Because increasing the supply of urban roads is expensive and difficult, the most efficient way to reduce congestion is to address the demand side. Charging commuters for the use of roads is the best way to adjust demand to supply and to reduce congestion. Tolls are increasingly used to reduce demand for urban road space. However, urban tolls are usually a fixed amount irrespective of how long street space is used. Tolls are therefore a clumsy way to charge for the temporary use of a good in short supply. Considering that urban roads are not a public good but are part of the real estate market, municipalities should charge a rent for their use. The rent charged should vary with the time of day, the location, the area, and length of time the road is used. The rent charged for roads should be similar to the fares charged by airlines to passengers or the room rates charged by hotels, except that the rate would not be for a fixed 24 hours but for the number of minutes the roads are actually used.

Up to now, the transaction cost of charging vehicles for this type of road rent would have been prohibitive. However, current technology could easily be used to charge road users a "road rent" that would reflect all the characteristics of real estate rents for short-term users. The effect of road rents on congestion would be immediate. Commuting trip departure would be spread more efficiently throughout the day or night. For instance, truck delivery would be strongly incentivized to be done at night. Smaller-footprint vehicles would be rewarded, thus decreasing congestion without decreasing the mobility of individual commuters. Charging road rents would have also a beneficial effect on land use. Many activities that generate a lot of vehicular traffic would have an immediate strong incentive to locate in areas where demand for road is low compared to their supply (i.e., suburban areas). Carpooling achieved by electronically matching similar itineraries would also reduce demand for road space while not reducing the mobility of commuters.

Mobility, Pollution, and GHG Emissions Due to Transport

Mobility, Pollution, and GHG Emissions
Mobility consumes energy. Since the Industrial Revolution, energy has been cheap, and its source has come mostly from fossil fuels. Consequently, urban mobility has been a major source of pollution and GHGs. Urban planners, alarmed by pollution caused by transport, are advocating for a reduction of the footprint of cities (increasing the price of housing) instead of concentrating on transport technology

that would reduce the pollution created by transport. Constraining land use is the wrong strategy; promoting pollution free transport is the right strategy, and it is now achievable. Because of technology changes, increasing mobility by allowing longer and faster trips is not necessarily the equivalent of more pollution and GHG emissions. It is possible to increase mobility by increasing a trip's speed and length while both reducing the energy used per passenger and reducing pollution and GHGs per unit of energy used, as I show below.

Pollution and GHG Emissions Are Two Different Problems

Concerns for pollution and GHG emissions are often lumped together under the "sustainability" agenda. In reality, pollution and GHG emissions are two very different issues that require different approaches. Pollution due to transport causes more harm when it is concentrated in central urban areas. The same quantity of pollutant creates very little damage when dispersed over a large area, but it can be lethal when concentrated in a densely populated urban area. In addition, some tailpipe pollutants, like carbon monoxide, are not stable in the long run and are soon changed into innocuous gases. By contrast, GHGs—mainly carbon dioxide— are not dangerous at the location of emission, even if concentrated; however, carbon dioxide is extremely stable and accumulates in the atmosphere. The dangers and associated costs posed by transport pollutants and GHGs are therefore completely different and should be addressed separately.

Urban Mobility and Pollution

Urban transport is responsible for a large part of urban pollution emissions. However, the effect of these pollutants on human health varies widely depending on concentration. Concentration is dependent on three factors: the concentration of vehicles in one location, the rate of emissions of individual vehicles, and a city's topography and climate. Cities like Los Angeles, Delhi, Beijing, and Paris could have surges of very dangerous levels of pollution when wind and temperature combine to prevent pollutant dispersion. Therefore, the impact of urban pollution on health could be very different among cities whose vehicles are meeting the same emission standards. Measures to curb pollution should therefore be adjusted for each city depending on its climate and topography.

Trends in Pollution Due to Gasoline Vehicles over the Past 20 Years

There is a clear consensus on the necessity of curbing pollution emissions from urban transport vehicles. Ideally, charging for pollution measured at the tailpipe would eventually reduce pollution to an acceptable level or even to zero. So far, the technology to do so is not yet available. The heterogeneity of urban transport vehicles using different types of engines and different fuel qualities makes direct as-you-go measurement difficult.

Governments in North America, Europe, and Japan have established mandatory maximum pollution standards that they impose on new cars. In the fall of 2015, the scandal caused by Volkswagen's deliberate evasion of new car emission testing shows that government standards are not foolproof, and more progress must be made not only in setting standards but in enforcing them. However, the trend in pollution reduction over the past 30 years has been conclusive in the more affluent countries that maintain maximum pollution standards, in spite of the enforcement shortcomings.

In the United States, the Environmental Protection Agency (EPA) describes the evolution of pollution due to cars between 1970 and 2004 as follows:

The Clean Air Act required EPA to issue a series of rules to reduce pollution from vehicle exhaust, refueling emissions and evaporating gasoline. As a result, emissions from a new car purchased today are well over 90 percent cleaner than a new vehicle purchased in 1970. This applies to SUVs and pickup trucks, as well. Beginning in 2004, all new passenger vehicles—including SUVs, minivans, vans and pick-up trucks—must meet more stringent tailpipe emission standards.[27]

Figure 5.20 shows the changes in pollution in Germany from new gasoline non-diesel cars over several decades. The changes show that government mandates, while imperfect tools, are still effective at triggering the technological changes necessary to reduce pollution that markets, in the absence of pricing mechanisms, have been unable to provide.

The decrease in pollution emissions shown in figure 5.20 is due to a combination of technological change allowing a decrease in gasoline used per kilometer and changes in engine and exhaust treatment that reduce tailpipe pollutants.

The data presented in the figure concerns only gasoline vehicles. In the past few years, hybrid cars and electric cars have been manufactured commercially, although they still represent a very small portion of the overall urban transport vehicle fleet. In addition, hydrogen fuel cell vehicles have moved beyond their experimental phase and are slowly appearing in selected cities.[28]

Electric cars and hydrogen fuel cell vehicles, when they eventually become a sizable part of the urban transport fleet, will completely change the environmental quality of cities. The pollution emission will not occur at the multiple tailpipes of vehicles but at the electricity source. This would not necessarily mean an absence of pollution, but at least it would avoid the pollution concentration in urban areas and will liberate cities in unfavorable climates and topographies from the peak of pollution that currently affects them. The enforcement of pollution standards at electricity sources would be much easier than the current system obliging

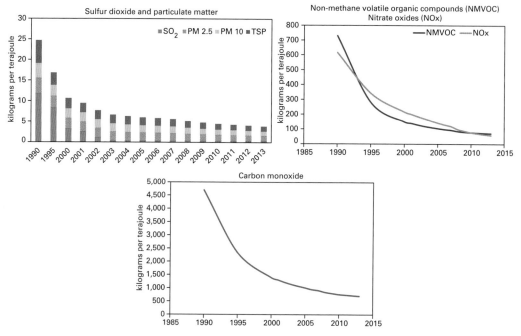

Figure 5.20
Changes in gasoline-car pollutant emissions in Germany, 1990–2013. *Sources*: Table 2: Fuel-specific IEF for passenger cars, in Fkg/TJ, Ministry of the Environment, Federal Environment Agency (Umweltbundesamt, UBA), Dessau-Roßlau, Germany.

environmental agencies to test periodically millions of vehicles. This would also greatly improve the possibility of emission control in less-affluent cities that cannot afford periodic pollution control of urban vehicles. Finally, the pricing of pollution at the source of electricity generation would have a better chance of being implemented without large transaction costs or political resistance.

Urban Mobility and GHG Emissions

Gas-Powered Vehicles
As we have seen, pollution due to transport is difficult to measure and price at its real cost. The measurement of GHG emissions poses an even greater challenge.

The simplest measure consists of measuring tailpipe carbon emissions, also called tank-to-wheel emissions. This is rather simple, as every liter of gasoline burned in an engine releases about 2.3 kg of CO_2. Therefore, the lower the gasoline consumption, the lower the CO_2 contribution will be to global warming. The

GHG measurement appears to be simpler than for pollution, which depends not only on gasoline consumption but also on the design of the engine and of the exhaust system. However, this simplicity is only apparent. Many argue, with reason, that what we should measure is the well-to-wheel carbon emission: the carbon emitted when extracting, refining, and transporting 1 liter of gasoline to the tank of a car. This well-to-wheel measurement adds about 10 percent more CO_2 to the tank-to-wheel emission, increasing GHGs emissions to about 2.73 kilograms per liter of gasoline. Finally, to be more accurate when measuring the GHG emissions due to transport, it might be legitimate to include the GHG emissions produced when manufacturing the vehicle, maintaining and recycling it, building and maintaining roads, and so forth. This "life span" emission calculation might be tempting to tackle, but it is probably counterproductive, because the complexity of the calculation and its many attendant assumptions might require the development of an entire academic field. Should the GHG emitted by the workers commuting from home to the factory manufacturing the vehicle be included in the final calculation of the CO_2 emitted by a liter of gasoline burned in an internal combustion engine? I can imagine every country's department of transportation becoming a gigantic accounting office, similar to the Soviet Union's Gosplan, preparing gigantic input-output tables to calculate ever more accurate GHG numbers emitted by a single liter of gasoline. In the following paragraphs, I will use the well-to-wheel emission figure for gasoline-powered vehicles.

We should not forget that a market economy avoids the Kafkaesque complexity of the Soviet Union's Gosplan by simply using prices to transmit information through the entire economy. If our governments could agree to put a price on carbon, there would be no need to calculate a vehicle life cycle emissions of GHGs. Emissions would decrease in all industries in proportion to the cost of reducing them. The carbon price would stimulate the creation of new technology that would reduce emission across industries.

In the absence of carbon pricing, the second-best solution is for the government to impose industrywide standards. In the United States, the National Highway Traffic Safety Administration and the EPA issued jointly a new national program to regulate fuel economy and GHG emissions for cars built between 2012 and 2016. The European Union, Japan, and Korea are also issuing their own annual mandatory CO_2-equivalent (CO_2-e)[29] maximum emission standards for new cars. The changes in emission standards for new cars since 2000 are shown in figure 5.21.

The emission standards reflect only new cars, not the entire fleet. However, they anticipate the average emissions of the entire national fleet in the near future. The actual GHG emissions from 2000 to 2014 in the EU have decreased by 23 percent,

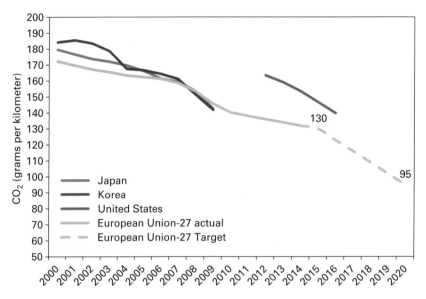

Figure 5.21
Average mandatory CO_2-e emission standards in various countries, 2000–2020. *Sources*: Data for Europe, Korea, and Japan: "Monitoring CO_2 Emissions from New Passenger Cars and Vans in 2015," EEA Report No 27/2016, European Environment Agency, Copenhagen, Publications Office of the European Union, Luxemburg, 2016; United States: "Light-Duty Vehicle Greenhouse Gas Emission Standards and Corporate Average Fuel Economy Standards; Final Rule," U.S. Environmental Protection Agency (EPA) and the Department of Transportation's National Highway Traffic Safety Administration (NHTSA), Federal Register, Vol. 75, No. 88, May 7, 2010, Rules and Regulations.

and if the target is met in 2020, it would represent a decrease of 44 percent. It shows that in the absence of more efficient price signals, mandatory standards are effective in decreasing GHGs.

Hybrid, Electric, and Fuel Cell Vehicles

The standards shown in figure 5.21 concern only gasoline, hybrids, and diesel cars. Increasingly, electricity or hydrogen fuel cells are likely to power an increasing share of the vehicles used for commuting in urban areas. Currently, the market share of electric cars is very small. In 2014, San Francisco, with 5.5 percent of all vehicles, had the largest market share of electric and hybrid cars among major US cities. However, given the R&D investment being poured into electric cars and batteries, it is likely that the market share of electric vehicles will eventually dominate the urban fleet.

The drop in the price of oil in 2016, reflecting an oversupply, might be a damper on the development of electric cars. However, electric technology presents many advantages for urban transport, in particular the absence of noise and pollution. This superior technology will eventually prevail on its own in the future. As a Saudi oil minister once remarked at an OPEC meeting, "The end of the Stone Age was not caused by a shortage of stones!"

For electric vehicles, the power plant generators alimenting the electrical grid will then produce the GHGs, not the car engine itself. Concerns for GHG emissions would then shift to the source of electric power generation and away from car manufacturers.

Currently, there is a wide difference in GHGs emission in various electrical grids, depending on the source of energy fueling the generators (figure 5.22). The low emissions from Swedish and French grids are explained by a combination of nuclear and hydroelectric generation, while the high emissions of the Polish and US grids stem from the use of coal as a fuel in some generators. However, the emissions from the California grid are nearly half those of the US average! The regional differences in emissions in the US grid are also explained by the differences in fuels used for electricity generation: California has a high proportion of

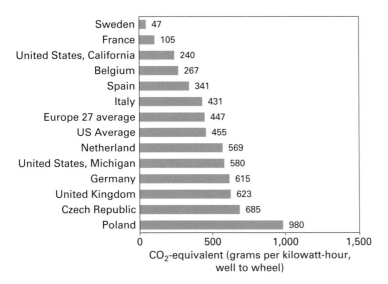

Figure 5.22
Emissions of CO_2-e per kilowatt-hour for the electrical grids of selected countries. *Sources*: United States: United States Environmental Protection Agency, 2018, eGRID Summary Tables 2016, https://www.epa.gov/sites/production/files/2018-02/documents/egrid2016_summarytables.pdf; Europe: Alberto Moro and Laura Lonza, "Electricity Carbon Intensity in European Member States: Impacts on GHG Emissions of Electric Vehicles," Transportation Research Part D: Transport and Environment, Elsevier, July 2017, https://ac.els-cdn.com/S1361920916307933/1-s2.0-S1361920916307933-main.pdf?_tid=60efef4a-0c3a-4e20-a91b-04dfdd346516&acdnat=1523304207_75045ee3d86fb842b4de3ff23f425ce0.

hydroelectricity and nuclear plants, while in Michigan generation plants the dominant production fuels are coal and crude oil.

Anybody concerned with GHG emissions should certainly switch to electric cars in Sweden, France, and California, but should use gasoline when driving in Michigan or Poland!

CO_2 Emissions by Various Modes of Transport

Let us now compare the GHG emissions from urban transport vehicles in grams per passenger-kilometer (g/pkm), depending on the brand and the technology used (figure 5.23). For gasoline and hybrid cars, the amount of CO_2 equivalent is calculated at the exhaust pipe. The real amount of GHG emission per vehicle is in reality higher than the tailpipe emission, as additional GHG-emitting energy is required to produce and transport the volume of gasoline consumed by the vehicle engine itself. For electric cars that get their energy solely from the electric grid, I have used the average GHG emissions in grams by kilowatt-hour of the electric grid available in the country where the car operates. However, the GHG emissions of the electric grid in various countries is calculated from well-to-wheel (i.e., the emission figures are taking into account the GHG emitted during extraction and transport of the source of energy of each national or regional grid). I have selected the Nissan Leaf as a typical example of electric car among the several models currently available on the market. This GHG emission per kilowatt-hour is then multiplied by the average number of kilowatt-hours required to transport one passenger for 1 kilometer. The large variations in GHG emissions shown in figure 5.23 for electric cars with the same kilowatt-hour consumption reflects the different sources of energy used to produce electricity in their respective countries, as was shown in figure 5.22.

Figure 5.23 includes data on the emissions in New York, the most widely used public transport system in the United States. Measured in grams of CO_2-e by passenger-kilometer, city buses emit about three times more GHGs than do subways. The explanation is simple: subway lines follow the routes with the highest demand. Many buses are feeders to subway stations and often serve suburban areas with less demand. To maintain patronage for public transport, buses have to run nearly empty outside peak hours. In addition, because drivers' salaries are one of the major operating costs for a bus service, the size of buses has been increased to carry the maximum number of passengers per driver. This is financially efficient during peak hours but is energy inefficient when the demand is low (i.e., when very large buses carry few passengers outside peak hours). Bus stops are typically located every 150 meters, obliging buses to accelerate and brake at full load very often. This contributes to more energy use, and therefore more emissions. By contrast, New York subways are connected to the New York grid,

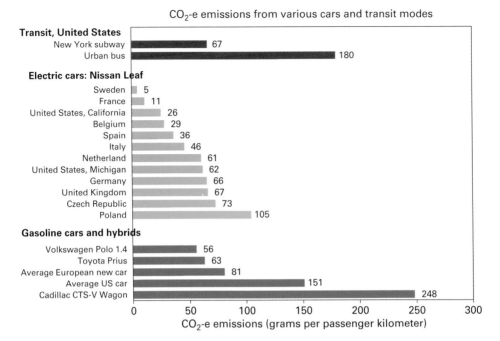

Figure 5.23

Tailpipe emissions of CO_2 per passenger-kilometer for various cars and public transport modes, 2015. *Sources*: United States: United States Environmental Protection Agency, 2018, eGRID Summary Tables 2016, https://www.epa.gov/sites/production/files/2018-02/documents/egrid2016_summary tables.pdf; Europe: Alberto Moro and Laura Lonza, "Electricity Carbon Intensity in European Member States: Impacts on GHG Emissions of Electric Vehicles," Transportation Research Part D: Transport and Environment, Elsevier, July 2017, https://ac.els-cdn.com/S1361920916307933/1-s2.0-S136192 0916307933-main.pdf?_tid=60efef4a-0c3a-4e20-a91b-04dfdd346516&acdnat=1523304207_75045ee3d86f b842b4de3ff23f425ce0; and various car manufacturers, 2016.

which according to EPA, emits 411 grams of CO_2-e per kilowatt-hour—a rather low emission rate compared to the average US grid.

The bottom of figure 5.23 shows the CO_2-e in g/pkm emissions for the most common cars in the US fleet. The trip of a commuter riding in an average US car is responsible for more than twice the CO_2-e g/pkm emitted by a trip of the same length by a commuter riding a subway. However, this car trip produces significantly less CO_2-e than the same trip by a commuter using a city bus. Commuting trips using hybrid cars, still a very small part of the total number of urban trips, produce about the same CO_2-e as the same trip riding a subway. Finally, trips from commuters in electric cars in some Western Europe countries and in California emit about half the CO_2-e of a passenger in a New York subway, while the CO_2-e emissions from electric cars in Sweden are practically insignificant. Actually, the

5 g/pkm CO_2 emission of a Nissan Leaf being driven in Sweden will be less than the 6 grams per kilometer exhaled by a person weighing 70 kilograms and walking at 4.7 km/h![30]

The point of figure 5.23 is not to advocate that commuters shift from city buses to Nissan Leaf cars but to show that we should not exclude individual vehicles as a potential transport mode in modern cities because of a concern about global warming. As we have seen, mobility in cities would increase if some trips were made by individual vehicles, possibly shared. Because of the rapidly changing technology, the inclusion of redesigned, possibly shared, individual vehicles as a major transport mode might decrease GHG emissions compared to current modes of transport, whether public transport or individual traditional gasoline cars.

Trends in energy use per passenger-kilometer by mode of transport (figure 5.24) in the past few years confirm the results of figure 5.23. The energy used by commuter rail (including subway and suburban rail) has remained roughly constant and is the most energy efficient compared to traditional gasoline cars and buses. The energy efficiency of public transport (buses and rail) depends in great part on the load factor (the number of passenger per vehicle), which can vary a lot as a city's spatial structure changes and as incomes increase. By contrast, the load factor of cars used for commuting remains roughly constant (about 1.3 passengers per car in urban areas). Technological improvements stimulated by government fuel economy mandates are responsible for the decrease in the energy per passenger-kilometer in individual cars over time. The large increase in energy per passenger

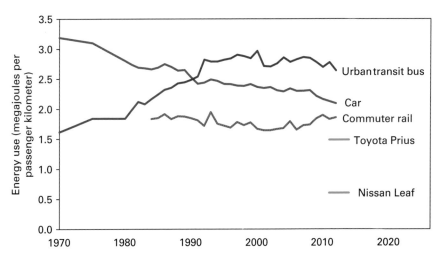

Figure 5.24
Changes in energy use per passenger-kilometer for different modes of transport, 1970–2012. *Source*: US Department of Energy, *Transportation Energy Data Book*, 33rd ed., Washington, DC, 2014.

used by city buses is probably due to the two factors discussed earlier in this subsection: the extension of bus services into low-density suburbs and the increase in the size of city buses.

Finally, the newest cars like the Toyota Prius hybrid and the "plug in" all-electric Nissan Leaf are far more energy efficient than all prior modes of transport, whether public transport or gasoline cars. However, these cars are still using scarce road space inefficiently. While they could be a better solution for low-density suburb-to-suburb trips, they would cause as much congestion in dense city core areas as do traditional cars. In addition, at the moment, these cars represent an insignificant part of the urban car fleet.

Mobility in Evolving Metropolitan Urban Structures

The Three Plagues of Current Transport Modes
Current urban transport systems inflict three major plagues on the cities they serve: congestion, heavy pollution concentration, and high GHG emissions. I have discussed these different aspects in the preceding sections of this chapter. Here I briefly summarize the contribution of each transport mode to the "three plagues."

• Individual cars. Their major problem is congestion. The valuable real estate that a car, whether running or parked, occupies in the densest part of a city is extremely costly and is usually unpriced. The concentration of pollution is still a serious problem but could be solved in the long run by a change in technology that is clearly emerging. Cars still contribute a sizable part of GHG emissions. In spite of their shortcomings, they are the fastest mode of transport for suburb-to-suburb trips and therefore are likely to remain an important mode of urban transport in spite of their shortcomings.

• Motorcycles. Their use of street real estate is efficient, but they are noisy, polluting, and dangerous. Municipalities do not take them seriously as a means of transport, and consequently these vehicles do not benefit from elementary traffic management measures like special lane marking. They are fast and efficient for providing access to suburbs where the municipality has not yet provided proper roads. They are likely to become a major mode of transport in lower-middle-income cities. The shift from gasoline to electricity or fuel cells would eventually solve the noise, pollution, and global warming problems that these vehicles contribute to.

• Collective taxis and rickshaws. They usually are a major source of pollution and congestion. They provide route flexibility and are often the only means of transport affordable to lower income workers, but they are difficult to manage, their drivers often compete violently for the same routes, and the municipalities are usually more interested in suppressing these vehicles than in managing them efficiently.

They have the advantage of adapting rapidly to changing demand in newly developed areas.

• City buses. They use scarce road space efficiently, have flexible routes, and are efficient for short distances. However, they are too slow for long distances in large cities, because they have to stop too often, and they are energy inefficient because of the low load factors outside peak hours. They are inefficient for suburb-to-suburb routes.

• Bus rapid transit (BRT). These systems are higher capacity than buses, but too slow for large cities and long commuting distances. They are not easily adaptable to changing routes, because they require the use of already existing wide right-of-ways. They use too much real estate per passenger outside peak hours. BRTs considerably slow down freight and other traffic because of the dedicated lanes they occupy. And they are not useful for low-volume suburb-to-suburb trips.

• Subways and suburban rail. These systems do not contribute to the pollution of cities. Their contribution to GHG emissions depends on the electrical grid efficiency. They are space efficient in the core of dense cities like New York, London, and Seoul. They are efficient modes of transport for trips from suburb to core city but are subject to heavy congestion in very dense cities like Beijing or Shanghai. They are inefficient for suburb-to-suburb commuter trips. High capital costs limit their extension in low-income cities.

Expanding Current Urban Transport Modes into Ever-Larger Cities Will Not Work

Currently, commuters choose between some mode of public transport and individual vehicles. Many public transport users use two modes, rail and feeder buses, resulting in long commutes because of the long transfer times between modes. Few commuters combine cars and public transport because of the high cost or unavailability of parking around stations. Most metropolitan transport policies consist of trying to increase the number of public transport commuters and decrease the number of car commuters, even in cities where public transport is heavily congested, as in Mumbai. However, in most cities, public transport users' travel times are always longer than that of car users. It seems that the purpose of many public-transport-focused policies is not to decrease overall travel time but to decrease car travel time for those who can still afford it, as observed by David Levinson in his article aptly titled "Who Benefits from Other People's Transit Use?"[31]

The objective of an urban transport policy should be to increase for everybody the number of jobs and amenities accessible in less than 1 hour, not to decrease travel time for those who already have the shortest travel times (car users). The new technologies that have emerged in the past 20 years should allow radical changes in urban transport modes, which have not changed in the previous 100 years! Tentatively, let us now explore (1) the changing special structure of large cities, (2) how transport must adapt, and (3) the role of new demand-driven technologies in driving change.

The Spatial Structures of Large Metropolitan Areas Are Changing

The spatial structures of cities are changing in most of the world. Large lower-density suburbs are developing around the traditional urban core and CBDs. In Asia, where urbanization is still low compared to the rest of the world (except Africa), we are seeing the emergence of large urban clusters like Delhi, Mumbai, Beijing-Tianjin, Shanghai-Suzhou, the Pearl River Delta, and Seoul-Incheon.

These cities of more than 20 million people are evolving into much larger clusters with populations expected to exceed 30 million people by 2020. The spatial structures of these cities are demand driven and reflect the modernization of their economies, wherein large supply chains of services and manufacturing have different spatial requirements than the ones encountered in the traditional monocentric city of the past.

As these cities develop different spatial forms, current transport systems—consisting of mass public transport, collective taxis, and individual transport—are becoming inefficient. Transport inefficiency results in the fragmentation of potentially large productive labor markets into smaller, less efficient ones. In addition, transport inefficiency results in increased congestion, pollution, and high GHG emissions.

Transport Systems Have to Adapt to Constantly Evolving City Structures

Alarmed by the poor performance of current urban transport modes, municipalities and planners often try to contain urban expansion in a more compact form that they feel would be easier to serve with traditional public transport modes: public mass transport and city buses. Policies constraining the emerging demand for land required by the new economy result in extremely high land prices and, in many cases, informal developments not served by adequate infrastructure expansion—as is the case in Mexico City, for instance. Advocates of compact cities often ignore the fact that the compact part of their city is already extremely congested and that governments are unable to provide the public transport line intensity that would prevent congestion for commuters using public transport as well as individual cars. The example of the congestion in Beijing's new subway lines (see figure 5.10) discussed above is a good illustration of this issue.

Municipalities and planners should face the reality of changing urban land use required by the new economy. Instead of fighting the expansion of cities, which

Typical trips pattern in
a metropolitan area

Expected trips pattern
in an urban cluster

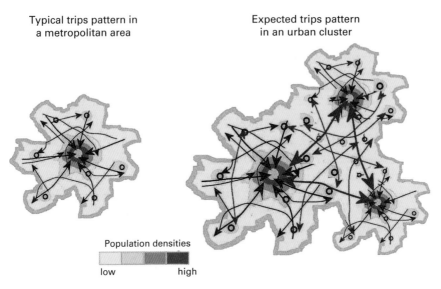

Population densities

low   high

Figure 5.25
Urban trip patterns in a typical metropolitan area compared to that of an urban cluster.

is largely demand driven, to preserve an obsolete and congested type of land use, planners should try to create new transport systems that could serve both the traditional high-density CBDs and the more recent dispersed forms of urban clusters. The schematic representation shown in figure 5.25 illustrates the changes in spatial structures occurring in many large cities and the trip patterns that they generate. The left schematic in figure 5.25 is representative of cities like New York or London, where already more than 70 percent of commuting trips are from suburbs to suburbs. The right schematic in the figure represents the emerging structures of megacities like Delhi, Beijing, or Shanghai, where commuting and freight trips suburb-to-suburb are becoming more numerous and are evolving into even more complex routes. The current urban transport systems in these cities, consisting largely of radio-concentric public transport lines fed by city buses and complemented by cars and collective taxis or rickshaws, are ill adapted to serve the complex urban shapes shown on the right in figure 5.25.

Emerging Demand-Driven Technology Could Allow Labor Markets to Function in Large Clusters

How should transport systems adapt to new urban forms? The emergence of large urban clusters expanding to distances of about 100 kilometers across and including high-density cores surrounded by low-density suburbs where jobs are mixed with residential areas suggests that we will see major changes in urban transport modes. Emerging technological changes would facilitate this transition.

First, cars will have to become more compact to use less road space and less energy, making them look more like a hybrid between cars and motorcycles. Examples of such vehicles already exist and are being manufactured, for instance, the Toyota i-Road.

Second, individual compact vehicles should become available at subway or suburban rail stations on a rental or share basis. This is already happening—the Toyota i-Road is available at some Tokyo suburban stations and at the Grenoble (France) main railway station. Such vehicles will allow commuters to combine the convenience of individual vehicles with the speed of suburban rails on longer distances for large intra-metropolitan trips.

Third, subway and suburban rails should have fewer stations and run at higher speeds to allow commuters to cross an entire urban cluster in less than 1 hour. That would require rail speed of about 150 km/h. The catchment area of stations would be increased to more than 200 square kilometers because of the availability of individual vehicles at stations (compared to the current 2 square kilometers limited by the 800 meter walking distance from stations). Figure 5.26 and table 5.6 compare the catchment area of a traditional subway with stations spaced 1 kilometer apart to that of a suburban rail system with stations spaced every 10 kilometers but accessible by small individual vehicles (ranging from bicycles to the Toyota

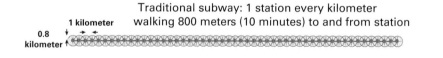

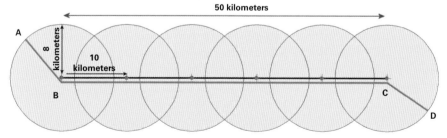

Figure 5.26
Comparison of the catchment area of traditional subways and that of high-speed suburban rail associated with individual urban vehicles.

Table 5.6
Comparison of distances between stations, speeds, and catchment areas for traditional subways and high-speed suburban rail.

		Traditional subway and walking		Fast suburban train and individual vehicle
Suburban rail line length (kilometers)		50		50
Average train speed (km/h)		32		110
Distance between stations (km)		1		10
Number of stations		50		5
Radius distance to station (km)	walk	0.8	vehicle	8
Speed from trip origin to station (km/h)		5		35
Catchment area of one station (square kilometers)		.01		201.06
Total catchment area of the line (square kilometers)		**53.79**		**623.76**
Train riding time for 50 kilometers (minutes)		94		**27**
Walking or individual vehicle riding time (minutes)		19.2		27
Total trip time (minutes)		113		55
Total trip length (kilometers)		51.6		66.0
Total trip time (minutes)		113		55
Average speed (km/h)		**27**		**72**

i-Road) with a range of 8 kilometers. Using the speed assumptions shown in the table, a commuter could travel a distance of up to 66 kilometers in less than 1 hour and have access to a destination area of more than 600 square kilometers.

Fourth, self-driving minibuses should be able to pick a few passengers running on the same route and drive them to individual final destinations without having to stop on the way to pick up and drop off other passengers.

Local governments should not favor a specific mode of transport but should favor and facilitate a large mix of transport modes, including combining fast heavy rail with individual vehicles for the same trip. Subway and fast suburban train stations should be designed with large areas for loading and unloading passengers for self-driving vehicles (figure 5.27).

Calls to Action for the Future of Mobility

1. Maintaining mobility is an essential task for municipalities and urban planners. This is best done by allowing multimode transport systems to reflect consumer demand. Commuters should be able to choose among the various transport modes available those that best fit their commuting needs.

2. Planners should not select densities and urban spatial structures in order to best fit an existing preselected transport system. Instead, new transport systems should adapt to evolving spatial structures.

3. Because pricing of pollution and GHG emissions are currently difficult to apply without large transactions costs, governments should set pollution and GHG emission targets as a substitute for price (until technology is available to directly charge for pollution emitted and GHGs released).

4. The pricing of road space is also an important metropolitan authority task. Flat tolls on roads should be progressively replaced by congestion pricing that constantly adjusts depending on time and location to maintain a set speed on specific road segments. As currently practiced in Singapore, the target set speed is different in the CBD and in the suburban arterial roads. The technology to do this is currently available.

5. Eventually, individual commuter cars will have to be redesigned to reduce their road footprint and their weight. Emerging new personal mobility vehicles, such as the Toyota i-Road, are examples of a possible replacement for the traditional car that would provide more mobility for less road space and less energy, pollution, and GHG emissions per kilometer.

6. Finally, the possibility of sharing small self-driving vehicles on demand could provide a very efficient alternative in the future for many suburb-to-suburb trips. Self-driving cars would have three important advantages over traditional cars. First, they would save street space by being able to run closer to one another without requiring the 2-second reaction time that human drivers require; that would save about 65 percent of road space at speeds of about 60 km/h. Second, they would dramatically reduce accidents and, therefore, the unpredictability of road commuting times. Third, they would not require large parking spaces in the center of cities where real estate is the most expensive.

Figure 5.27
The Toyota i-Road personal mobility vehicle (left) and the Beijing three-wheeler (right) already provide on-demand trips from station to door and from door to station.

Many new technologies are emerging that will have a large impact on urban transport. These technologies could reduce pollution to near zero, greatly reduce urban transportation's contribution to global warming, prevent most transportation accidents, and increase the capacity of existing urban roads without creating congestion.

A little more than 100 years ago, the horse as the only nonpedestrian means of urban transport was replaced by mechanical vehicles. These vehicles completely changed cities by allowing them to expand without densifying into Dickensian slums, while enlarging the potential labor markets that greatly increased the productivity and welfare of urban dwellers. Since that time, the automobile, buses, and subways as major modes of urban transport have not changed much. We might now be on the verge of an urban transport revolution that could be comparable to the replacement of animal traction by mechanical traction and could also greatly enhance the welfare of the very large part of humanity that is likely to live in cities toward the end of the twenty-first century.

The emergence of small footprint, on-demand, shared vehicles (very different from large buses running on fixed schedules and routes) will change the way urban transport is organized. The pattern of roads and arterials may also change to adapt to these new modes of urban transport. Instead of concentric traffic on a few high-capacity highways or arterials, numerous smaller low-capacity roads would allow the flexibility required by trips from dispersed origins to dispersed destinations.

New types of specialized urban vehicles—collective or individual, shared or not shared, self-driving or with drivers—are likely to multiply in the future. The speed, street footprint, and size of these vehicles will be adapted to the types of trips and commuters that they serve. The types of urban vehicles will therefore be different in very large, dense cities like New York and Mumbai from much smaller cities like Amsterdam and Key West.

6   Affordability: Household Incomes, Regulations, and Land Supply

"The Need to Do Something" Affordable Housing

A major impediment to a more efficient spatial allocation of labor is housing supply constraints. These constraints limit the number of US workers who have access to the most productive of American cities. In general equilibrium, this lowers income and welfare of all US workers.

—Chang-Tai Hsieh and Enrico Moretti[1]

We have seen that prosperous cities depend on well-functioning labor markets. Hsieh and Moretti, two economists, found that the high price of housing in some otherwise extremely successful US cities has a ripple effect, distorting the spatial allocation of labor nationwide. They calculate the cost of this misallocation to about 9.4 percent of US GDP. Housing affordability is therefore not a trivial issue. Hsieh and Moretti argue that regulatory housing supply constraints contribute significantly to the high price of housing, a position with which I concur and support in this chapter. Some affordability problems are due to poverty, but in most cases, they are created or exacerbated by human-made constraints on the supply of land and floor space.

Household Dilemma

For labor markets to work, households and firms must find an affordable space in which to locate. When selecting this affordable space, they must make trade-offs between rent, floor area, and location. Their final location choice will reflect the trade-off that maximizes their welfare. Location is of course extremely important, as the location provides access to the rest of the city and its labor market. The well-worn real estate developers' cliché "location, location, location" reflects a reality and a wisdom that many government housing affordability experts tend to forget. The floor area, location, and price per square meter of a household's housing unit constitute its current level of "affordability" for each potential occupant. This currently occupied "affordable housing unit" represents each household's best possible choice among all other housing choices offered by the market.

However, even in a free market, lower-income households' optimal housing options often do not meet socially acceptable standards (e.g., access to water and sanitation, floor space standards per person, or distance to labor markets). In low- and moderate-income countries, these homes are often poorly constructed and are considered unacceptable by standard metrics. In high-income countries, the housing quality is usually socially acceptable; however, other metrics may be unacceptable, such as floor space per person relative to their neighbors, paying more than 30 percent of income in rent, or driving more than an hour to work. Some households therefore may consume deficient housing (e.g., in quality, price, or distance to labor markets) when they cannot afford the high cost of land and construction in a large city.

Government Response

The low housing standards and the high rent that affect the lower-income population will legitimately soon attract public attention. Social pressure will eventually force governments to "do something about housing."

This need to "do something" pushes governments to formulate new housing policies that will provide socially acceptable housing standards at an affordable price for all. Angus Deaton, in his book, *The Great Escape*, writes "the need to do something tends to trump the need to understand what needs to be done. And without data, anyone who does anything is free to claim success."[2] This perfectly characterizes the design of many housing policies.

Unfortunately, governments often exacerbate the high cost of housing in a city by limiting the supply of housing through regulations and underinvesting in urban expansion.

In their search for solutions, urban managers often ignore that households' housing choices are driven by a combination of three attributes: floor area, location, and price per square meter. Because floor area and construction quality are the most visible of the three attributes, planners tend to concentrate on improving the design and increasing the area of dwellings when drafting a housing policy. They tend to ignore housing location and its corollary access to a city's labor market.

For example, government affordable housing programs are never designed to entice households who live in a different city or rural area to move to the city providing the housing. On the contrary, social housing programs usually specify that potential beneficiaries must have resided in the city several years to qualify for government help. This resident-only policy is meant to prevent an immigration stampede to the city, but it misses an important point: unacceptably long commutes to labor markets by workers.

When low housing standards are largely due to poverty, ignoring location to provide larger homes might devastate the very population the policy is supposed to help. Some examples in this chapter illustrate this point.

In this chapter, I show how improving low-income households' housing standards requires identifying the relative role of both factors—poverty and inflated housing prices—caused by supply constraints. I discuss housing affordability policies in several cities and show how these policies have impacted four key attributes: floor area, land area, price of land, and price of construction per square meter (equation 6.1).

As we will see, the homes that families end up occupying are starkly different from those they would have chosen if their incomes had simply increased by the implicit subsidy they receive. I will judge the merits of various housing policies by comparing the homes they end up with to those they would have chosen with an income subsidy.

For developers, the cost components of producing housing units are much more complex. In addition to the physical cost described above, developers' cost will include financial costs, overhead, management, and design costs. The ratio between the land and floor area will be usually constrained by regulations. The cost of construction will also depend in part on regulations. However, for households, the price of land and the price of construction aggregate all these cost components.

Equation 6.1 Price of housing (P) for households

$$P = (\text{Land area}) \times (\text{Price of land}) + (\text{Floor area}) \times (\text{Cost of construction}), \qquad (6.1)$$

where P is the price of housing.

The rent paid will also be related to the four variables on the right side of equation 6.1.

The price of land depends on location; a location with high job accessibility or close to high-quality amenities will correspond to a high price of land. In general, a highly desirable location has a high land price.

The cost of construction depends on the quality of construction. It is possible to build an informal shelter made of lumber, plastic, and corrugated iron roof for as little as US$25 per square meter; while the price of construction for an apartment fully equipped with kitchen and bathrooms may cost several thousand US dollars per square meter (about US$2,500 per square meter in New York in 2013 for residential buildings three to seven stories tall).

Therefore, households searching for housing at a given price have to make a trade-off between location, land and floor area, and quality of construction. At times, I will use location as a proxy for the price of land, and quality of construction as a proxy for price of construction.

Defining and Measuring Housing Affordability

Housing Affordability Is Different from the Affordability of Any Other Consumer Product

"Affordable" means something different when it is used for housing instead of for other objects, say, a cell phone or a car. A person who cannot afford a cell phone or a car does not have one. However, when housing is said to be unaffordable for households below an income of X, it does not mean that all households with incomes less than X are homeless. It only means that these households are living in housing units that are unacceptable in quality or floor area, or that these households are spending an unacceptably high proportion of their incomes on rent or mortgage payments.

Housing affordability therefore determines whether housing is "socially accept-able," not whether a household occupies a housing unit. When we read that housing is unaffordable to households with incomes below X, it means that the trade-offs necessary for these households to rent their current dwelling units are inadequate in terms of rent paid as a portion of income, floor area, quality of con-struction, or location.

The socially accepted minimum housing standards in each city do not corre-spond to a scientifically accepted universal norm. In this it differs from many other norms. For instance, minimum nutritional daily intake is a universal norm defined for all human beings. Most air pollution norms are established by the World Health Organization and are accepted as universal. By contrast, minimum accept-able housing standards are related to the prevailing standards in the city where they are applied. The socially acceptable minimum housing standards in Stock-holm are very different from the standards in Dhaka. This is due to differences in climate and culture in addition to differences in household incomes between the two cities.

While many households in Dhaka might happily live in homes meeting the minimum norms prevalent in Stockholm, there is no evidence that Dhaka's households suffer irreparable damage by living in houses of significantly lower standards. Minimum housing standards are thus always arbitrary and contextual. These standards might be useful as a benchmark, but when they become enshrined in laws and regulations, they can do great harm to the very population they are supposed to help, as we will see below.

In many countries, such as South Africa, the government identifies a set of minimum housing standards that define a national norm for minimum housing. Setting minimum housing standards is a political act. Governments tend to select high standards as an optimistic signal for the future of the city, the sort of opti-mistic projection that politicians are all obliged to make. Statisticians then compare the standards of the existing urban housing stock (obtained through surveys and the census) with the national minimum housing norm established by the government. The number of existing dwelling units below the national housing norm is said to constitute a housing "backlog." To eliminate this backlog, the government commits itself to building enough housing units each year to clear the backlog. For example, South Africa created new housing stock for 38 percent of its citizens over a period of 17 years—a feat that we will investigate as a case study later in the chapter. Note that the housing program was defined only through two attributes: price and a physical housing standard. Location is absent from the policy, leading the South African government to build some homes as far as 30 kilometers from a city center. In any case, it would be difficult to define a location standard at the national scale. South Africa's housing program provides a warning of the adverse consequences of ignoring location when defining housing affordability.

How governments define housing affordability is therefore very important when developing housing programs to help the poor. Government bureaucrats tend to make different trade-offs than the households would make for themselves when choosing between price, location, area, and quality. If the trade-offs made by government differ a lot from those that households would make, then the housing program will fail despite the money invested and the good intentions of the expert designers. Urban planners do not have enough information to enable them to select an optimum combination of rent, floor area, and location for each household and firm. The choice of the quantity of land and floor area consumed in a specific location is therefore better left to the end user when possible.

I have seen many governments implement "slum relocation" programs that send households from slums to high-quality and subsidized formal housing units in a remote location. To the dismay of government officials, the former slum dwellers often abandon their formal housing to return to a slum, where building quality is lower but access to the job market is better. This return is often attributed to slum dwellers' lack of judgment. This is not the case. The residents return because they prefer a well-located home of lower quality than a poorly located home of higher quality. Policymakers had failed to choose the best trade-off between rent, location, and housing standards.

This is not meant to imply that deficiencies in housing quality are a government invention. Many low-income households aspire to much higher quality housing than what they can currently afford. In many cases, the insalubrity or bad location of their dwelling slows low-income households' integration into the more productive part of the urban economy.

"Affordable housing" policy aims to increase low-income households' housing consumption until they have reached a socially acceptable level. To design this policy, we need to establish and quantify a fact base: first, the minimum socially acceptable housing consumption level, and second, the number of households who consume less housing than this level. Once these two numbers are identified, municipal governments can have an informed discussion about what they can do to address the affordability issue. Should they build affordable housing at or above the minimum standard and then sell or rent this housing below market prices? Open up new areas for urban development to increase housing supply and lower market prices? Revise regulations that restrict developers from providing housing that meets the minimally acceptable standard? Expand the financial sector to provide mortgages to lower-income households? Or directly subsidize households' incomes so that these households can afford a higher-quality dwelling in a location of their choice?

Almost always, affordability issues require several simultaneous actions involving investment programs and regulatory reforms. No silver bullet can easily solve housing affordability. However, governments cannot design a credible policy without first establishing a clear fact base. Therefore, before discussing specific policies in detail, let us first discuss the various methods of measuring the affordability threshold and the number of households that fall below it. Fuzzy data on household incomes and current housing standards is a significant impediment to creating sensible affordable housing policies.

A Simple Affordability Index: The Price/Income Ratio

The price/income ratio (PIR) measures housing affordability in a city by comparing the median price of a dwelling with the median household income. This simple definition makes it is easy to compare the price of housing in different cities that have different income levels. However, this index does not say anything about how much housing a household gets for the median price or where this dwelling is located. The PIR also applies only to sales and not to rentals, although a rent/income ratio could be developed using the median income.

The Demographia International Housing Affordability Survey,[3] issued every year since 2004, compares the PIRs for some 367 metropolitan markets in nine developed countries. Among these cities, 87 metropolitan areas have a population larger than 1 million. Because the index consistently uses the same methodology, it provides a valuable tool for comparing PIRs between cities as well for watching how these ratios evolve over time.

Let us look at the PIR for 30 cities in the year 2015 (figure 6.1). The cities selected are representative of the variations of PIR shown in the entire Demographia survey. Among the selected cities, Atlanta has the lowest PIR (3.1), while Sydney has the highest (12.2). Why are there such large variations in affordability? We notice that many of the cities—San Francisco, Auckland, Vancouver, and Sydney—with high

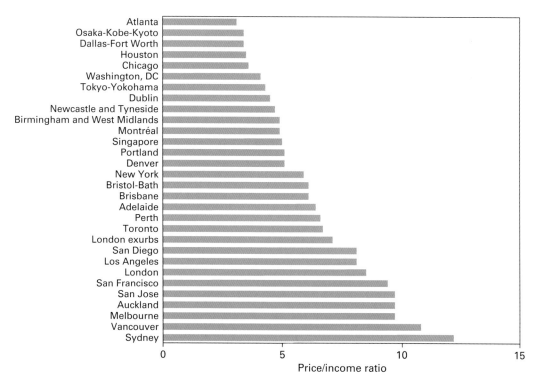

Figure 6.1
Price/income ratios for a selection of world cities, 2015. *Source*: Wendell Cox and Hugh Pavletich, *12th Annual Housing Affordability Survey* (Belleville, IL: Demographia, 2016).

PIRs have a difficult (though beautiful) topography. The mix of water and land makes for attractive cities but restricts the land available for development. This topographical constraint on the land supply is likely to have an impact on land prices and therefore on housing prices. But while topography certainly explains some of the variations in PIR, it is not the entire story. Cities like Chicago, Washington, DC, and Tokyo-Yokohama also have important water areas close to their CBDs but have successfully managed these issues. Those cities have PIRs that are less than Sydney's. We will see below that land use policy and regulations constraining city expansion are often largely to blame for high PIRs.

What Does It Mean for a City to Have a PIR above 8?
Intuitively, we feel that households' welfare should be higher in a city with a low PIR than in a city with a higher one. If a smaller proportion of income is spent on housing, more can be spent on other items. However, a very low PIR might indicate economic stress. In the Demographia survey for 2015, Detroit's PIR is a low

2.8. Some Russian cities with heavy population losses have home prices close to zero in the absence of demand. Obviously, the PIR needs interpretation. While low housing cost compared to income is generally a good thing, it might also indicate other problems. Given the city's economic woes, it would be absurd to use Detroit's PIR to justify using that city as a model of good housing policy and affordable housing.

What PIR value would indicate an affordable housing stock? Demographia suggests that housing is affordable in cities where the PIR is equal to or below 3. None of the cities shown in figure 6.1 qualifies, although Atlanta, with a PIR of 3.1, comes close. Demographia's complete degree of affordability categories are as follows:

Category	PIR value
Affordable	≤ 3
Moderately unaffordable	3.1–4.0
Seriously unaffordable	4.1–5.0
Severely unaffordable	≥ 5.1

Households usually borrow money to buy their first dwelling, so let us calculate the mortgage payments associated with various PIR values. Figure 6.2 relates the cost of housing as a percentage of yearly income for different values of PIR under three possible borrowing interest rates: 5, 7, and 9 percent (for 25 years with a down payment of 20 percent). Mortgage lenders usually provide loans to households only when their monthly payment does not exceed 30 percent of their income; the horizontal dashed line in figure 6.2 represents this affordability threshold. When the interest rate is 5 percent, only in Atlanta, Houston, Tokyo, and Singapore will the median household be able to obtain a mortgage for the median priced home. With a higher interest rate of 9 percent, only in Atlanta and Houston will households with median incomes be able to obtain a mortgage for the median priced home. What would happen to households in the other cities, where the high PIR implies that households at the median income would not be able to afford a mortgage to buy a median priced dwelling?

Some households might have bought a dwelling some years before when the PIR was still in the affordable range. These households then live in a house that they could not afford to buy now with their income alone, but the increase in PIR means that their capital assets have increased. They could, however, afford to buy a new house by selling their current house, even though the PIR shows that a new house would be unaffordable. These households are therefore probably quite satisfied by the increasing PIR value, even if it shows that housing is unaffordable

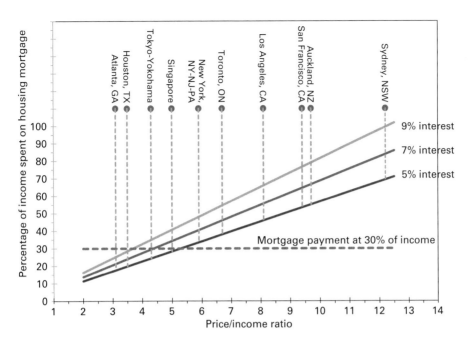

Figure 6.2
Price/income ratios and affordability for 10 selected cities. *Source*: Wendell Cox and Hugh Pavletich, *12th Annual Housing Affordability Survey* (Belleville, IL: Demographia, 2016).

to them. This fact may explain the regulatory policy of some cities that seems intended to constantly increase housing prices by restricting new supply.

However, households that have not benefited from previous PIR increases but live in a high-PIR city cannot afford to buy a new dwelling. Some might decide to move to a different city with a lower PIR, but changing cities has social and financial costs and risks. More likely, the new household will try to find an alternative to buying a home. For instance, newly formed households might rent rather than buy a dwelling. Often, in high-PIR cities, monthly rents are lower than mortgage payments for equivalent dwellings. I have compared the PIR of new owners to the percentage of income spent on rent in a sample of 10 US cities (figure 6.3). This allows us to understand the relationship between buyers' and renters' incomes devoted to housing—both data sources are reported by the government and remain constant even as interest rates change. While the percentage of income spent on rent tends to increase in cities with higher PIRs, renting tends to be more affordable than buying dwellings. San Francisco is an outlier with a very high PIR of 9.4 but rents at a rather affordable 32 percent of renter income.[4]

Figure 6.3
Percentage of renting households' income spent on rent and the price/income ratios of homeowners for 10 selected cities, 2015. *Sources*: Price/income ratio data: Wendell Cox and Hugh Pavletich, *12th Annual Housing Affordability Survey* (Belleville, IL: Demographia, 2016); Rental household income data: American Community Survey, Furman Center, New York University, New York.

However, given market equilibrium, the number of dwelling units available for rent might decrease when the PIR is high, as landlords would have an incentive to sell due to high home prices and low rents.

Some households might choose to leave the city and look for a city with a lower PIR, even if this means having a lower income. But the majority of households will have two options. Either adjust their living standards and opt for a lower standard of housing, or spend a much higher part of their incomes on housing. When households opt for lower-quality housing to continue living in a city, this choice has a cascade effect, where people are consuming lower-quality housing and outbidding those at lower-income tiers than themselves. This leaves the lowest-income households unable to afford existing units, with options to leave the city or accept much smaller units (e.g., by subdividing and sharing existing spaces). In Auckland, New Zealand, for example with a PIR of 9.7 in 2015, it is reported that some households are living in garages, trailers, or their parents' homes. These are households near the bottom of the income scale that cannot outbid any lower-income group. In Mumbai, some median-income households, while their incomes have been rising, have been forced to move into slums as the PIR has increased faster than their incomes have.

The PIR Is a Useful Index for Identifying an Affordability Problem, but It Is Too Crude to Identify a Policy Solution

The PIR is a useful and easily understood index to identify an affordability problem in high-income cities. However, it only relates the median income to the median home price. It has nothing to say about the quality or location of the house at the median price. While the PIR is simple and uncontroversial, collecting income and home price data can be difficult in countries that do not have a systematic sale-registration system and in cities that have a large informal sector. This is why Demographia does not yet cover developing countries. Finding the median housing price implies that all transactions are equally well known. In many developing countries, it is easier to find prices at the high end of the housing market than at the low end. It is also easier to find prices of new housing than that of existing houses. In many cities, the data required to calculate a credible PIR do not exist.

How Do Households Adjust to Unaffordable PIRs?

In cities with a high PIR, housing is assumed to be unaffordable not only to the poor but to the middle class. However, we do not see people leaving high-PIR cities en masse for more affordable cities. It seems that in cities like Sydney, Vancouver, or San Francisco, life goes on as usual despite a very high PIR. The same could be said of cities for which no PIR can be calculated but that have notoriously high real estate prices, such as Mumbai, Lagos, and Jakarta. Obviously, the vast majority of households adapt to "unaffordable" prices by choosing not to leave their current city. We even see that the population keeps growing in cities with unaffordable prices because of migration and the formation of new households.

But high real estate prices are anything but benign. This apparent business-as-usual response to rapidly increasing housing prices might hide a deteriorating quality of urban life for all but the most affluent residents. Households adapt to housing prices that rise faster than their incomes by consuming less floor space and spending a higher share of their incomes on rent or by commuting longer distances.

High prices or absolute poverty force poorer households to consume less housing than the minimum socially acceptable level set by regulations, as mentioned above. Falling below this minimum will further decrease the housing standards of the poor. Consuming less housing than what is prescribed as socially acceptable often prevents their housing from attaining legal status and permanence. This will compound their misery through a vicious cycle as poverty that causes low housing consumption which causes more poverty.

In middle- and high-income countries, many less-affluent people can respond to high prices by subdividing existing dwellings into smaller units, formally or informally. In other cases, new households cohabit with their parents or other relatives much longer than either party might wish. In either case, high housing costs result in lower housing consumption. Two case studies discussed below illustrate these forced adjustments: the subdivision of apartments in Beijing suburbs and the cohabitation of adult children with their parents in Europe.

Finally, sometimes cities revise their socially acceptable minimum housing consumption to reflect the demand from a changing socioeconomic group. This occurred in 2016 in New York, where the existence of many single-person households convinced city regulators to lower the minimum housing standard. This case is also discussed more in detail below, as it illustrates the futility of setting minimum socially acceptable standards in the first place.

Informal Subdivision of Apartments in China

Chinese cities have very few identifiable informal settlements. However, the housing consumption of low-income households is often difficult to measure. Many of the new apartments built on the periphery of Chinese cities are too large to be affordable for low-income households. As a result, low-income residents afford housing by renting a room in a subdivided apartment. The street poster appearing in 2013 in a northern suburb of Beijing (figure 6.4) advertises an 18 square meter room to be rented in a larger apartment with a kitchen and bathroom to be shared by other tenants. Fortunately, Beijing's government tolerates this practice, although

[*Translation*]
Large guest bedroom at low price

High-quality finish, full appliance package

Could cook, connect to Internet, bath

Close to transit and shopping, full set of furniture and appliances

Bedroom (18 m²) 800 yuan/month

No miscellaneous fees

(Condo fee and heating charges included, no brokerage fee)

Please contact me if interested at

133 -----------------------------

Figure 6.4
Poster advertising a room to rent in a subdivided apartment in a suburb of Beijing, 2013.

some apartment owners in the same condominium complex protest the practice and routinely try to convince the municipality to ban it. From a housing supply point of view, this adjustment is desirable, because it transforms the built housing stock into housing that is affordable. Once a block of apartments has been built, it is very difficult to reduce the size of units to meet the demand for smaller units. Informally subdividing existing apartments is the fastest way to match supply and demand. This situation need not be permanent. Over time, the supply of newly built housing can better match demand, and the practice of subdividing apartments will disappear by itself.

Governments should monitor but not ban the practice of subdividing apartments. If the practice of subdividing apartments persists over time, regulations may be to blame. For example, an arbitrary minimum apartment size, or a maximum number of dwellings per block, might be responsible for the mismatch between supply and demand. Removing these regulations, which have no discernable benefits, would allow the housing market to respond to changing consumer demand.

Young People Living with Their Parents
In affluent countries, assessing the impact of high price-to-income ratios on the housing consumption of specific income groups can be difficult. A 2013 Pew Research Center survey shows the proportion of people aged 25–35 who live with their parents in European countries and the United States (figure 6.5). This percentage varies from 1.8 percent for Denmark to 56.6 percent for the Czech Republic. Cultural factors may explain some of the differences among countries. However, economic factors, like employment rates and housing supply issues, also affect the rate. Whatever the reasons for the international differences, my point is that housing consumption adjusts when there is a discrepancy between supply and demand for housing.

Lowering "Minimum Socially Acceptable" Housing Standards:
Mini- and Micro-Apartments in New York
In New York, a 1987 city zoning regulation specified that the area of apartments should be at least 37.2 square meters. But the supply of apartments of this size is constrained by another zoning regulation that puts a maximum limit on the number of dwelling units per area, thus implicitly reducing the number of small apartments that could be built in a block, regardless of whether there is a demand for such apartments.

However, the demand for small apartments has been increasing as the number of people per household has decreased over the past 50 years. In 2015, the number of nonfamily households (i.e., households formed by a single person or unrelated individuals) represented 38 percent of all households. Recognizing this

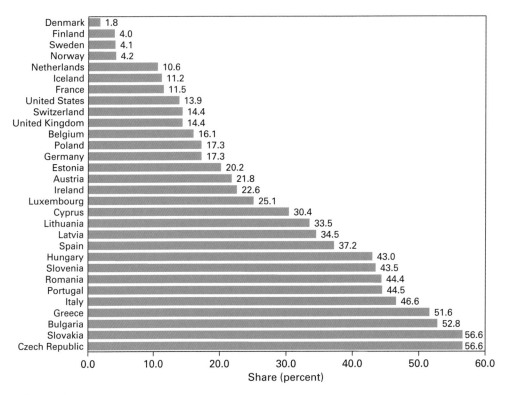

Figure 6.5
Share of young people aged 25–34 living with their parents in Europe and in the United States, 2010.
Source: Pew Research Center, Washington, DC.

problem, in 2015, the zoning board allowed the construction of 55 mini-apartments ranging from 24 to 33 square meters, in a single nine-story building on the East Side of Manhattan. This was a timid step toward using a commonsense approach to repeal minimum socially acceptable standards.

When the 55 mini-apartments appeared on the market, there were 4,300 applicants for each apartment! This demonstrated the large demand for small units, which is arbitrarily constrained by the regulation on minimum apartment size. The apartment building is centrally located with excellent access to New York's labor market. Relaxing the minimum apartment size gave individuals the freedom to make their own choice in the trade-off between larger apartments in less central locations and centrally located smaller apartments.

However, if the municipality removed the apartment minimum-size constraint for the entire city, developers would still not build more mini-apartments. Another regulation limiting the number of dwelling units per block would prevent that.

Housing type	Year	Floor area of apartment (square meters)	Floor area of smaller room (square meters)	Assumed number of persons per unit	Floor area per person (square meters)
A. Tenement	1860	27.5	6.0	6	4.6
B. Old Law Tenement	1880	26.7	6.0	6	4.4
C. Old Law Tenement remodeled	2016	26.7	na	2	13.3
D. Studio minimum size	2016	38.0	na	2	19.0
E. Micro-apartment	2016	27.8	na	1	27.8

Figure 6.6
New York City minimum acceptable housing standards since 1860.

Limiting the number of dwelling units per block was meant to limit residential density. But since the regulation was put in place, residential density has fallen as the average household size has fallen. Layers of regulations, whose original objective has often been forgotten, prevent housing supply from matching demand. These multiple layers of regulations must be repealed for housing supply to become responsive to housing demand.

In New York, minimum housing regulations have evolved over centuries. Figure 6.6 shows examples of floor plans of apartments of the smallest acceptable size at different dates. In 1860, housing construction standards were practically unregulated. Developers responded to housing demand from all socioeconomic groups. The typical floor plan of a tenement (plan A in figure 6.6), built in 1860, shows each floor has four apartments of 27.2 square meters each. Each apartment has three rooms. Only one room in each apartment has windows. Bathrooms were shared among all building tenants and provided on the ground floor in the back yard. The apartments are designed such that households could occupy only one room or several connected rooms. At the time, households were very large, often six or seven persons per household. The population density in tenement neighborhoods was about 660 people per hectare in 1860.[5] The density peaked at 1,530 persons per hectare in 1910 and fell to 390 persons per hectare in 2010.

The minimum socially acceptable housing standard evolved over time, and a reform movement resulted in the Tenement House Act in 1879 (plan B in figure 6.6), which required rooms to have access to ventilation shafts. In addition, regulations required a bathroom and toilet on every floor shared by the tenants. The smallest apartment was 26.7 square meters.

In more recent times, these "Old Law Tenements" were renovated by moving the interior walls and introducing a kitchen and a bathroom, creating a studio apartment with a total area of 26.7 square meters (plan C in figure 6.6). My wife and I lived in such a tenement with our toddler for a year after our arrival in New York. The floor space per person for our family was 8.9 square meters. As kitchens and bathrooms are not considered rooms, we were occupying a dwelling with three persons per room. We were just at the limit of the socially acceptable minimum standard set by the state of New York,[6] which is 50 square feet per person per livable room, as our only room had an area of 14 square meters (or 150.7 square feet)! The UN Habitat defined overcrowding as more than three persons per room, so we barely qualified for not transforming our tenement into a UN-designated slum! In reality, the individual bathroom, a gas stove, and air conditioning made our life significantly more comfortable than that of the original tenement occupants must have been. We thoroughly enjoyed our stay in this tenement because of its great location.

In 1987, the minimum apartment size allowed by regulations was 37.2 square meters. The plan of a studio of this size, built in 2016, is shown in plan D in figure 6.6. Finally, the plan of one of the 55 micro-apartments of 28 square meters to be built in the middle of Manhattan mentioned above is shown in plan E. The micro-apartments are still slightly larger than the renovated Old Law Tenements that still form a significant part of Manhattan and Brooklyn housing stock (I could not find the exact number of Old Law Tenements still being used in New York City, but they are easily identifiable on Google Earth imagery).

These examples illustrate the futility of controlling maximum densities or minimum floor area per person by regulations. The very high densities of the tenements in the 1860s were not generated by design or regulations but by the market. The tenements' excellent locations and the tenants' very low incomes created the high density.

Many of these Old Law Tenements survive to this day in Manhattan. A study by Stephen Smith and Sandip Trivedi, published in the *New York Times* in 2016,[7] shows that about 40 percent of the existing buildings in Manhattan could not be built today because of the compound effect of overlapping regulations! It is difficult to understand the rationale for such regulations, although practically every city in the world has similar rules.

Informal Subdivisions in New York Can Create Affordable Housing below the Minimum Socially Acceptable Standard

Subdividing large apartments into rooms individually rented to people who share a kitchen and bathroom is usually legal in many cities (with some restrictions, e.g., New York limits this right to no more than three unrelated individuals per apartment). However, subdividing apartments or houses into individual independent units with their own kitchen and bathroom is illegal in most cities.

In New York, a 2008 study[8] showed that between 1990 and 2000, about 114,000 new housing units were illegally created by subdividing existing houses and transforming basements and garages into new units. These unauthorized dwellings accounted for half of the housing stock added in New York in the 1990s. The dwellings represented about 4 percent of the total housing stock, and provided shelter to about 300,000 to 400,000 people.

Subdividing homes like this is illegal, but the action creates affordable new units without any government subsidies. Another study describes the plight of new emigrants from Bangladesh who settle in New York. Most of these households have very low incomes and would be unable to afford any legally built dwelling. Several families pool their resources to buy a detached house in a low-income part of Queens. They then subdivide it into several independent units where they live. These illegal units enter the market and are subsequently either sold or rented.

The city sends inspectors to prevent this from happening. The argument against these informal subdivisions is that they overload the utility system, urban transport, and schools because of the higher population density they create. However, it is unlikely that the utility system is really affected, because of the decrease in most household sizes over the past 30 years. School might indeed become overcrowded, because immigrants tend to have more children than native-born households. However, a primary function of a municipality is to provide school space to all the city's children. It does not make sense to prevent families from settling in a neighborhood under the pretext that the existing number of classrooms is insufficient. The interdiction against subdividing is usually a pretext to hide the municipality's inability to provide adequate numbers of classroom to its residents. Many zoning regulations are established to prevent changes of any nature, including preventing lower-income families from living in middle-income neighborhoods. In the case of the Bangladeshi migrants, they outbid their more affluent neighbors by consuming less floor space than the existing residents. It is the opposite of gentrification. While the city planning department claims social inclusion (i.e., neighborhoods with mixed household incomes) as its objective, it prevents the emergence of mixed-income neighborhoods by creating zoning laws that block lower-income households from being able to afford to live in higher-income neighborhoods.

The above examples show how households adjust to high prices by consuming less housing. Ideally, there would be a match between housing supply and demand. Because of the inevitable lag between changes in demand and supply—for instance when households size decreases—regulations should allow these informal adjustments to occur legally.

When the Poor Are Unable to Substitute Capital for Land

As cities expand, centrally located land becomes more expensive. Households and firms respond to this by moving into multistory buildings—apartments and office towers—which reduce their land consumption. By this action, they substitute capital for land. By building multistory structures, they can increase their consumption of floor space while decreasing their consumption of land. By substituting capital for land and therefore consuming less land per dwelling unit, lower-income households can compete with higher-income households for the same land.

This is possible in cities where lower-income households can afford the increased cost of multistory construction, a structure of at least about 18 square meters[9] in reinforced concrete, which would be structurally strong enough to support stacking up apartments one above another. In the lowest-income countries, where construction is the cheapest, households would need to be able to afford at least US$6,000 for a studio of 12 square meters; US$6,000 is the global market commodity price for the basic construction materials of concrete and steel required to build 12 square meters. In other words, substituting capital for land requires a minimum of capital. In some cities, the poorest households cannot afford this minimum cost threshold. Because they are unable to substitute capital for land (i.e., build higher), the floor space they consume is even smaller than the land they occupy. They can afford a shelter by consuming very little land and even less floor space. For example, in figure 6.7 (column A), informal settlements consume a 1.16 ratio of area of land to floor space. Additionally, the extremely narrow passageways found in slums in many cities is not due to "poor design" but is a rational choice for households who desperately need more floor space and are ready to trade off street space for additional floor space, as they are too poor to build higher houses. This results in a more than 30 percent difference in land allotted for roads and open space in informal versus formal settlements (figure 6.7).

Let's investigate this further—the following example, taken from Bhayandar West, a northern suburb of Mumbai, illustrates the consequence of being unable to substitute capital for land. Figure 6.7 shows two settlements built side by side. On the left, settlement A is a very-low-income community living in an informal settlement, where houses are built of scavenged wood and corrugated iron, structures too weak to be extended vertically. On the right (settlement B) is a middle-class community made up of apartments in seven-story buildings. Community A is too poor to substitute capital for land; community B can afford do so. Let us compare the way their consumption of land and floor space differs, shown on the table in figure 6.7.

The middle-class community B consumes an average of 23 square meters of floor space per person, while the poor community A consumes only 3.5 square meters. However, the land consumption of both communities is relatively close: 4 square meters for the poor versus 6 square meters for the middle class. The poor households who cannot afford the minimum building cost of US$6,000 for one room in an apartment block are obliged to use more valuable land per unit of floor space than the wealthier households in the formal settlement B. The poor households in settlement A must use 1.16 square meters of land per square meter of floor space, while households in B use only 0.27 square meters of land per square meter of floor space. Households in B, because they can afford apartments in multistory buildings, can also afford to allow 46 percent of the land to remain as open space compared to 13.5 percent in the horizontal settlement A.

Despite consisting of only ground-floor structures, the residential density of the horizontal settlement A is much higher than that of the vertical settlement B.

The housing units in the informal settlement A have been built mostly by the households themselves, often by recycling scavenged materials. However, as soon as a dwelling is erected, its sell price or rent is established through the informal market. The main constraint for very poor households is therefore access to land. Although settlements A and B consume about the same area of land per dwelling, the layout of settlement A is not tolerated by regulations but the one of settlement B is.

It seems that about US$6,000 (in 2016) is the cost threshold below which poor households who cannot afford this sum are condemned to live in informal horizontal developments. In large cities where land is expensive, the poorest households are often obliged to consume more land per unit of floor space than

Comparative land use between formal and informal settlements

	A Informal	B Formal
Average number of floors	1	7
Average floor area per dwelling[1] (square meters)	17.5	81.3
Area of floor space per person (square meters)	3.50	23.21
Area of land per person (square meters)	4.04	6.16
Area of land per square meter of floor space	**1.16**	**0.27**
Area of land per dwelling (square meters)	20.22	21.55
Percentage of roads and open space	13.5	46
Gross floor area ratio (FAR)	0.87	3.77
Net residential density (people per hectare)	2,473	1,624

Figure 6.7
Informal and formal settlements, northern suburbs, Mumbai.
[1]Including common corridors and staircases.

are higher-income households. This results in extremely low housing consumption for low-income households.

By contrast, in cities where poor households can afford to spend more than US$6,000 per house, the horizontal slums shown in figure 6.7 tend to disappear and be replaced by multistory apartments that allow a much higher consumption of floor space. The urban village housing in Shenzhen discussed below will illustrate this case.

The development and diffusion of building technology, like prestressed small prefabricated beams, could substantially lower the US$6,000 cost for an apartment in a multistory building. Such technology would therefore increase the housing consumption of the poor far beyond the savings in construction costs, because it would allow a much larger number of households to substitute capital for land, as higher-income groups are routinely doing.

In addition, constructing multistory apartment buildings typically requires financing. It is nearly impossible for households to self-finance such a structure, the way they can for horizontal housing, which can be improved in stages. A city's financial sector must therefore be able to provide mortgages as well as construction finance for developers to improve land efficiency.

Measuring Income Distribution in Relation to Housing Consumption Is Indispensable for Sound Policy Formulation

Using Household Income Distributions for Cities

Using a median income to measure affordability is a justified simplification when comparing different cities or when looking for a trend in a time series. It is also an acceptable simplification for cities with a large middle class for which most household incomes are closely clustered around the median income. However, when trying to improve housing affordability in a specific city, it is necessary to look at income distributions in which households with median incomes may represent only a very small socioeconomic group. This is particularly true in large cities in developing countries, where incomes are more widely dispersed than in more affluent cities.

Figure 6.8 shows the distribution of household income in Shanghai in 1998. The income is displayed in equal intervals along the horizontal axis. The bars show the number of households in each interval (using the scale on the left axis). The dashed red curve superimposed on the bar chart shows the cumulative percentage of households within each income interval (using the scale on the right axis). The graph displays the number of households in different socioeconomic groups that compete for land and housing. This graphic representation of all income groups in a city conveys much more information than using median income or the imprecise terms "low income," "medium income," and so on. For instance, using figure 6.8, it is clear that the 180,000 households with annual incomes below 6,000 yuan have a very different affordability problem than the 260,000 households with annual incomes around 14,000 yuan. However, both groups have incomes well below Shanghai's median income of about 21,000 yuan (horizontal dash-dot line in figure 6.8). A city's income distribution curve is an indispensable tool for analyzing and quantifying housing affordability issues.

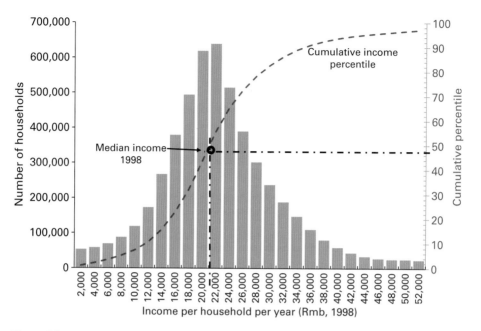

Figure 6.8
Shanghai household income distribution, 1998. *Source*: Jie Chen, Qianjin Hao, and Mark Stephens, *Assessing Housing Affordability in Post-Reform China: A Case Study of Shanghai* (London: Routledge, 2010).

Housing Stock and Flow, and the Trickle-Down Theory

The shape of the income distribution curve may also help anticipate the policy impact of affordability. The graph enables testing of whether the "trickle-down" affordability theory[10] is likely to be relevant. For instance, imagine that developers increase by 10 percent the number of new housing units affordable to households with an income of about 14,000 yuan (or about 24,000 new units). This would improve affordability for households with incomes lower than 14,000 yuan, as the number of dwellings vacated by the beneficiaries will likely trickle down to lower-income groups and have a significant impact, as these groups have fewer members than the original beneficiaries. However, if the same 10 percent increase in new housing units is built for households with incomes around 36,000 yuan (or about 10,000 new units), the increase in number of housing units will also trickle down toward lower-income groups but will soon have an insignificant impact because of the much larger number of households among the lower-income group. The trickle-down effect does occur in every case, but its effect will be completely diluted if the increase in dwelling units is targeted to households whose income is much to the right of the distribution mode (in the case of Shanghai shown in figure 6.8, the mode corresponds to households with incomes of about 22,000 yuan). If the number of households in each income interval were equal (if the bars were all of the same height), then the trickle down would work perfectly.

Of course, the trickle-down effect could also become a trickle up. Imagine that a government constrains the housing supply of higher-income groups and favors exclusively the building of lower-cost housing units (say, for incomes of about 12,000 yuan in figure 6.8). In the absence of new supply, higher-income groups will outbid the lower-income group to occupy the only new units on the markets. The trickle down will then become a trickle up. Trickle up means that housing units previously affordable to lower-income households are being bought by upper-income groups (gentrification). This happens quite often in government-subsidized housing when the overall housing market is heavily constrained by land use regulations or the lack of infrastructure expansion, which constrains land supply. Higher-income groups then "invade" the housing stock of the lower-income groups. The effect is particularly severe when higher-income groups acquire existing dwellings only to reassemble them into larger ones, thus decreasing the number of housing units in the entire stock.

In Chennai, India, in the 1970s, the municipal government had a vigorous program to build subsidized public housing while constraining the development of land for all other income categories through regulations and inadequate infrastructure development. However, low-income households, who had been carefully selected based on income to benefit from public housing, often sublet or informally sold their apartments to higher-income households. The government did not react by adjusting its housing policy to release more land for housing. Instead, it concentrated on preventing trickle-up sales or subletting. It required all members of households in public housing to have identity cards with photographs that could be presented to inspectors who conducted random visits. This was an example of a trickle-up effect that is quite common when land development policy and regulations are at odds with housing policy. I will discuss this topic in more detail below when looking at housing policy options. The reaction of the Chennai government is also typical of governments in many countries. When data show that a policy is not working—as when beneficiaries sell their subsidized dwellings to higher-income groups—governments try to force the policy's success by imposing more regulations.

Household income distribution curves show the complexity of any housing policy aimed at ensuring a supply of affordable housing to all households, especially when incomes vary widely. I will use the income distribution curve as a major tool to test housing policy options.

What Happens When Incomes Increase Rapidly?
Figure 6.8 shows Shanghai's 1998 income distribution. The shape of the curve will likely be quite different after only a few years. New unskilled migrants might increase the number of very low-income households on the left side of the graph, while the income of other households, who have been urbanized for a longer time, might increase rapidly because of increased productivity and skills. The increase in income will add households to the middle and right side of the graph. The change in household income distribution will change the demand for housing and require an adjustment in the supply of new housing units. The price and standards of new housing should adjust to the new demand.

Let us compare the income distribution profile of Shanghai of 1998 with that of 2003 (figure 6.9). During this period, Shanghai's median income increased from 21,000 yuan to 32,000 yuan in real terms, a 58 percent increase for an average annual rate of 8.8 percent.[11] This very high growth rate of incomes is exceptional. In Shanghai, it was a period when bold economic reforms and large infrastructure investments implemented in the previous decade dramatically increased urban productivity. During the same period, the number of households increased by 17 percent, or an average of 3.3 percent a year, also an exceptional growth rate for a city with a population of 15.5 million in 1998. The natural demographic growth rate of Shanghai during this period was slightly negative, at –0.08 percent. The population growth rate was therefore entirely due to migration.

While the population and income growth rate of Shanghai are exceptional, they provide insight into housing affordability issues that emerge when urban income distributions are changing. The changes in Shanghai are compressed over a short period of 5 years. In other cities, comparable changes may be spread over a longer period, say, 10 years, but they are nevertheless daunting and need to be addressed. In managing a city, nothing is more damaging than assuming a static situation.

The 58 percent increase in the median income does not reflect a uniform increase among all income classes. The way household incomes are distributed has important implications for housing affordability. In spite of the large increase in median income, the number of households in the very-low-income group, below 6,000 yuan per year, increased by 53 percent, representing 70,600 additional households. This increase is consistent with the high rate of migration. A large number of immigrants are coming from the countryside and have not yet acquired the skills needed to obtain productive urban jobs.

In the next category, low middle-income from 6,001 to 24,000 yuan, the number of households decreases by 1.9 million or –58 percent compared to the number of households in this category in 1998! By contrast, the income group above 24,000 yuan increased by 2.09 million households (an increase of 124 percent over the number of households in 1998).

According to the Shanghai Municipal Statistics Bureau, 153.8 million square meters of residential floor area were built during this period, or about 165 square meters per additional household. In aggregate, it seems that the supply of housing has more than kept pace with the growth of population—a remarkable achievement given Shanghai's fast demographic growth. However, the aggregate amount of floor space does not tell us the total number of units built, how large they were, their price or location or what category of households were able to afford them.

Housing affordability should not be calculated in aggregate but by income group. Square meters of floor space are not sold individually but in lumps as apartments in specific locations that determine their price. Low-income households therefore may not have access to all the floor space built. Affordability assessment also cannot be done in aggregate by comparing new household formation to new housing units built. The flow of new supply, measured in housing units rather than aggregate floor space, should be disaggregated by the number of new units

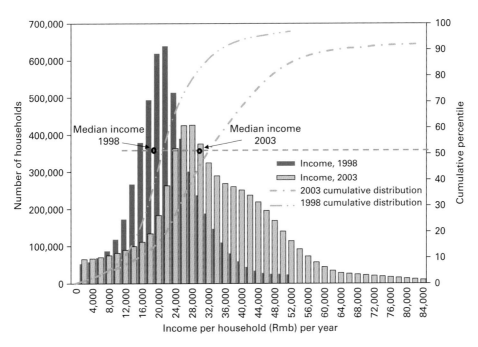

Figure 6.9
Shanghai changes in household income distribution between 1998 and 2003. *Source*: Jie Chen, Qianjin Hao, and Mark Stephens, *Assessing Housing Affordability in Post-Reform China: A Case Study of Shanghai* (London: Routledge, 2010).

put on the market that are affordable to specific income groups. When conducting affordability evaluations to test the effectiveness of a policy, it is necessary to disaggregate the number of units produced with respect to price and incomes, floor consumption, and location.

Income Distribution Related to Housing Typology

I have shown the wide variation of income that exists in a city. Every household whose income is represented on an income distribution curve lives in some kind of shelter that it can afford under current conditions. However, the quality of this shelter may range from 2 square meters of cardboard on a sidewalk to a luxury villa with an indoor swimming pool. To identify the real affordability issue, we will have to match income distribution with shelter consumption and to decide at what point the shelter consumption has fallen below the socially acceptable minimum. In looking for a policy solution, we will have to know how many households currently live in a shelter below the minimum acceptable home quality. The policy options will be different, depending on the number of households that fall under this minimum. Imagine that in a city of 1 million people, only 500 people are living in shelters made of cardboard and plastic. The solution is probably a welfare budget allocation to move these 500 households to adequate shelters in a central location, while providing them with education and training so that they eventually integrate into the city's labor force. However, if in the same city, 30 percent of the population lives in cardboard and plastic houses, the policy solution will require a very different approach that involves looking carefully at demand and supply for land and housing. The solution to the housing problem will require a market intervention, even if some demand subsidies are also used. Developing a housing policy therefore necessarily relates housing affordability deficiencies to the number of households who suffer these deficiencies. This is what I propose in the following section. Whether looking at housing affordability issues in Mumbai or in New York, the household income distribution curve will be the first building block in developing a solution. It is necessary to quantify the problem in terms of the proportion of households that fall below the socially acceptable minimum standard.

Household income distribution should then be related to housing consumption by income range; an important dimension that is missing from the PIR index. It is important to link housing payments with what households get for their money. The objective of a housing policy is to increase the housing consumption of households who consume an unacceptably low standard of housing due to their low incomes. Therefore, a housing policy should never aim just to supply a certain number of housing units per year to fill a "backlog" of substandard housing. This approach would only be valid if the old units needed to be demolished. The example of the renovated Old Law Tenements in New York, described earlier in the chapter, shows that there is often no need to destroy every old unit.

All the households shown in the left-hand graph of figure 6.10 live in dwellings that can be observed on the ground or from above through satellite imagery or aerial photography. High-resolution satellite imagery can be analyzed to identify housing types that can be ranked by their cost and physical characteristics. The area occupied by each housing type can be measured. The entire residential housing supply of a city can then be divided into housing types. Census data and field surveys can complement the information obtained by satellite image interpretation. The entire population of a city can then be distributed among different housing types. Each housing type corresponds to a housing price or rent range that can be related to a household income. It is then possible to merge the type of income distribution graph shown in figure 6.8 with the housing typology data to obtain a representation of the distribution of the entire set of households by income group and housing type. Figure 6.10 illustrates the results of this method. It shows Hanoi's household income distribution on the right and the housing typology superposed on the income distribution on the left. The graphs show what type of housing is currently affordable to each income group—as they are currently living in it—and the number of households in each housing type.

Hanoi's population has been distributed among eight housing types. These housing types are specific to Hanoi and can easily be identified in satellite imagery. There is no standard housing typology that can be used across cities; for each city, a new typology has to be defined, reflecting the local history and culture. In the

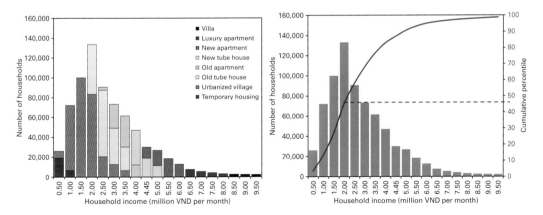

Figure 6.10
Hanoi's income distribution related to housing typology, 2005. *Source*: Data are from Hanoi Integrated Development and Environmental Programme (HAIDEP) Hanoi Institute of Statistics, 2005, and author's estimations from field surveys and satellite images.

case of Hanoi, two housing types are specific to Vietnam—urbanized village housing and "tube houses." Urbanized village housing corresponds to housing units that were originally located in villages that were on Hanoi's periphery but have been absorbed by the city's expanding urban footprint. These villages retain their original street layout and plot sizes. "Tube houses" are traditional row houses with a frontage of about 3.5 meters and a depth of 22 meters. They can sometimes have up to six or seven stories. They may be used by one extended family or subdivided into apartments or may even be rented room by room. The income groups that can afford tube houses can therefore vary greatly from neighborhood to neighborhood and over time.

The choice of a typology is important when analyzing housing policy. The number of units of certain house types can increase over time, while other types are bound to decrease. For instance, the housing stock constituted by old tube houses and old apartments located in the historical core of Hanoi cannot expand and can only slowly disappear through demolition and transformation into other types of housing, for instance, "new apartments," which would be affordable to a different, usually higher-income group.

Figure 6.10 shows only a snapshot of the housing situation in Hanoi at the time of the survey. The income distribution will change, and the housing stock will be transformed by demolition, reconstruction, and extension into new greenfield development. Neighborhoods rarely remain static; they are subject to gentrification or its opposite: degentrification. In general, when incomes are increasing rapidly, as in Shanghai in the 2000s, higher-income groups tend to move toward newly built units, while lower-income groups replace them in the older units they previously occupied. However, higher-income groups may also move back into renovated housing units in older neighborhoods when these neighborhoods are either well located or have historical cachet.

For instance, in Beijing the hutong neighborhoods were often inhabited by high- and middle-income households before the revolution. They were subdivided when the Communist government took over in 1947, resulting in densification and subsequent degentrification. In the 1980s, the municipal government considered the dense hutongs to be slums and bulldozed them to replace them with high-rise apartments. In the early 2000s, some hutong areas became popular and were subsequently regentrified into low-density one-family compounds or into pricey hotels. The cycle between degentrification and regentrification lasted about 50 years. Most cities' ancient neighborhoods have similar stories with longer or shorter cycles between gentrification, degentrification, and regentrification—for instance, the West Village in New York, the Marais in Paris, and Soho in London.

The main lesson to draw from the constant transformation of historical cities is that the entire housing stock might transform. An affordable housing policy should therefore project the likely housing stock and flows. The stock and flow approach is more useful when applied to a housing typology. For instance, in the case of Hanoi, we know that the "old apartment" flow will be by necessity negative, while the villas and new apartments are likely to have positive flows.

It is a common mistake to look at only a slice of the housing market, such as low-income neighborhoods, and concentrate on new supply through greenfield development, while the entire housing stock is subject to transformation. In particular, low-income households are usually better-off moving into existing centrally located neighborhoods newly affordable to them than moving into newly developed low-income housing on the periphery with long and expensive commutes.

Relating Income Distribution with Housing Consumption

After relating household incomes to a housing type, it is necessary to relate household incomes to actual measured housing consumption. Many consumption indicators could be used: floor space per household, land area per household, residential utility consumption (e.g., water and electricity), access to transport, and community facilities. We could also use a composite index that reflects the weighted aggregate housing consumption of households, including all of these components.

Whatever consumption measures we select, all housing units are distributed among households according to their price rank. This price will theoretically be directly related to household income. By relating household housing consumption to income distribution, we can identify the groups that are particularly deprived and develop a housing policy to address this deprivation.

Hanoi's income distribution is related to consumption of floor space in figure 6.11.

Figure 6.11 reproduces the household distribution in figure 6.10 at the bottom of the figure, and I have added a new graph above with the same horizontal axis corresponding to household income but with a vertical axis representing floor area per household as it varies with income. The solid line in each graph is an average per income; different households may consume different quantities of floor areas depending on their circumstances, preferences, and home location. However, these variations between people in the same income group average out across income groups. This is why consumption can be conveniently represented by a curve showing the average consumption per income interval rather than by a scatterplot including all the surveyed cases.

The two graphs in figure 6.11 show how many households consume how much housing. The initial step for most housing policies consists of defining the socially

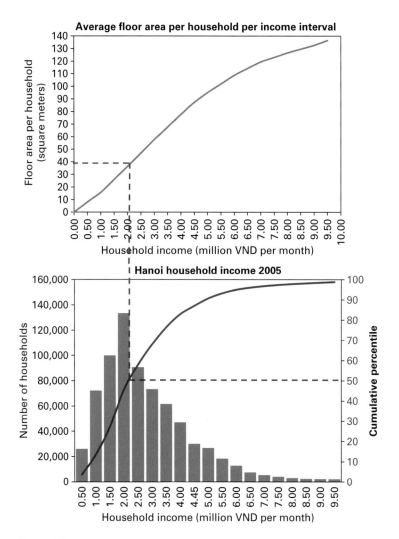

Figure 6.11
Hanoi's household income distribution (bottom) and floor consumption (top). *Source*: Data are from
Hanoi Integrated Development and Environmental Programme (HAIDEP) Hanoi Institute of Statistics,
2005.

acceptable minimum housing consumption, usually in term of floor area. The use of an income distribution curve linked to average housing consumption per income interval would allow one to evaluate the number of households that are below a set consumption threshold. The policy and possibly the threshold could be adjusted accordingly. For example, in Hanoi, 50 percent of households consume less than 40 square meters of housing (figure 6.11). Should the government set a standard that more than 50 percent of its population currently does not meet? Obviously not! The average floor area consumption per income interval could also be replaced by other consumption indicators linked to income, for instance, water consumption or any other indicator.

The representation of the two graphs in figure 6.11 is a simplification of reality, as many households with the same income might show different housing consumption levels, but it is a useful one for understanding and discussing policy options, as we will see in the following sections.

Using the Income–Consumption Relation to Test Policy Options

We can use the graphs relating income, number of households, and housing consumption to test alternative housing policies. To test alternative policies, I will use a hypothetical case not related to a specific city, to avoid describing the idiosyncratic circumstances that may affect outcome or policies. Later in this chapter, I will use the income–consumption graph to discuss the efficiency of various housing policies in specific case study cities.

Housing Policy Options

Governments often declare that the poor housing quality affecting a large part of their urban population is due to a market failure. In reality, the very poor quality of some of the housing stock is due to poverty. As we know, the market is a blind and cold mechanism that is not subject to compassion. The market will predictably provide very-low-quality housing to households with very low incomes, and no housing at all to households who must spend their low incomes almost entirely on food. In a city that includes a significant number of very-low-income households, the market is unlikely to provide them with anything looking like a dwelling. Should the government then provide housing to households with the lowest incomes?

There is nothing wrong with governments substituting themselves for markets to provide socially acceptable housing units to the very poor. In fact, it is precisely one of the roles of government. If these housing units are also associated with decent schools and health facilities, their provision is not only a compassionate effort but also an investment in the future welfare of all urban citizens. For instance, the government should obviously provide a shelter to homeless people. There are no market solutions for people with no income.

However, as soon as the government decides to build housing for low-income households, five questions have to be answered:

1. How many households should be included? Expressed another way: How far along the income scale should the government become a substitute for the market?

2. What standards should be provided?

3. How many housing units should the government subsidize every year?

4. How many years would be required to provide a subsidized housing unit to all potential beneficiaries?

5. What budget allocation would be required yearly?

The government should provide clear answers to these questions at the very start of formulating its housing policy. The final policy formulation would require some iterations until the number of beneficiaries and the standards selected correspond to an annual cost that the government can afford. Too often, public housing programs include only numbers responding to only one or two of the five questions. The numbers usually reflect perceived needs rather than what can credibly be done. As a result, many housing programs lose credibility in a very short time due to the low standards provided and less volume supplied than promised due to budget problems, administration constraints, and the like.

A credible public housing program should include a quantitative evaluation relating standards, beneficiaries' incomes, and total number of beneficiaries. There is often a temptation to overreach and to include a large number of beneficiaries whose housing cost will be beyond the means of the government.

Income Distribution, Housing Consumption, and Market Outcome

Linking Income Distribution to Housing Consumption as a Diagnostic Tool

I show a typical income–consumption curve in figure 6.12. The bottom panel shows the demand side—the relationship between income and number of households. The top panel shows the supply side—the relationship between income and consumption. The vertical axis displays an index reflecting housing quality that includes floor area but also characteristics like connection to safe water. Alternatively, the housing quality index could be replaced by only one parameter contributing to housing quality, such as floor area per dwelling or water consumption per person.

The curve *ab* in the upper panel shows the variations of housing quality under market conditions in the absence of subsidies. The curve passes through the origin

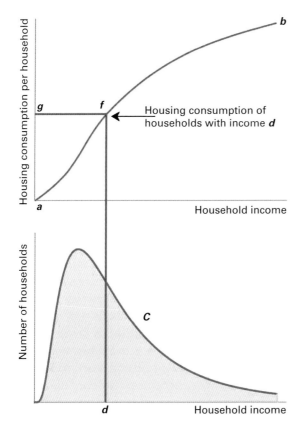

Figure 6.12
Income and housing consumption—market outcome.

(0, 0), because with zero income the market allows only zero consumption. Usually, as income increases above zero, housing consumption initially increases only very slowly. It then increases faster when household incomes reach the middle-class level.

The consumption curve **ab** relating housing consumption to household income reflects market conditions. The market is only a mechanism. It does not have feelings or respect moral values. The slums and the very low housing consumption found in many cities of low- or middle-income countries do not indicate market failures; they only show the market outcome under the specific equilibrium between supply and demand. For instance, in figure 6.12, a household with income **d** will consume a quantity of housing **g**.

The Objective of a Housing Policy Is to Modify Current Housing Consumption

The objective of a housing policy is to modify the profile of the housing consumption curve *ab* so that the housing consumption of households with the lowest incomes increases to socially acceptable levels. Government policy in some social sectors (e.g., health and education) should aim toward an egalitarian distribution across incomes—although this ideal distribution is rarely achieved in the real world. A horizontal line crossing the vertical axis at *g*, for instance, would show an equalitarian distribution of housing.

Housing policy, however, rarely aims at an equalitarian distribution—all households living in identical houses, whatever their income. In the former Soviet Union and in pre-reform Communist China, housing was considered a factor of production, not an object of consumption that could be bought and sold and would reflect consumer preferences. There was indeed an effort to produce identical dwelling units differing only slightly by the number of rooms adjusted by household size. My experience of working in Russia in the early 1990s and in China in the 1980s convinced me that even in a regime driven by ideological equalitarianism, the housing equality objective had been impossible to achieve; even if "equal" sized units are provided, one unit may be in the city center while 30 more are kilometers away, signifying a very unequal access to the place of work and a resulting unequal desirability value of the actual housing stock. Housing policy objectives usually ensure that the lower-income groups do not fall below some minimum housing consumption, but the policy is indifferent to the consumption of higher-income groups.

In the following paragraphs, I will assume that the majority of urban citizens want the lowest-income households to be able to afford a minimum housing consumption that is determined by a number of physical standards. These physical standards could be such things as minimum floor area, minimum water consumption, access to sanitation, refuse disposal, storm drainage, or community services.

Impact of an Increase in Urban Land Supply   Figure 6.12 shows the relationship between housing consumption and income under current market conditions in a specific city at time *t*. Household income distribution and housing consumption are usually changing over time, as we have seen above in the case of Shanghai.

Without any changes in household incomes, the government could increase housing consumption by removing supply side constraints. Some supply side constraints are simply administrative, for instance, the prescribed process for obtaining building permits. Other measures are regulatory, such as mandating the height of a building; density of the surrounding area; floor space of the unit; barriers to urban expansion (greenbelts); or even limits on construction design, inno-

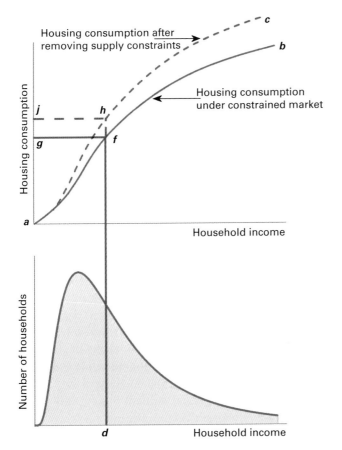

Figure 6.13
Impact on housing consumption of removing supply side constraints.

vation, or technology. Other types of supply side measures would require investments; for instance, increasing the supply of developable land by expanding the primary road and infrastructure network. The dashed line *ac* in figure 6.13 shows the potential increase in housing consumption for all households when supply side constraints are removed. The positive impact of removing supply side constraints varies with income groups. For instance, households with income *d* would see their consumption increase from *g* to *j* after the government has removed some of the constraints on housing supply.

While in the long run every household benefits from removing supply side constraints, the size of the benefits is not the same for all income groups. We can see in figure 6.13 that the benefits of very-low-income households (to the left of the income distribution curve) are much lower than the benefits accruing to middle-income groups. Even with better-functioning markets, very-low-income groups may still have very low housing consumption; new units are purchased by middle- to high-income groups and do not directly benefit low-income groups. It is therefore often necessary for governments to take additional actions to increase the housing consumption of the very poor, even after supply side reforms have been successfully implemented.

The increase in housing consumption after removing supply side constraints could be quite large, and it is usually not very costly to governments (and actually could increase the tax revenue base, assuming more people are able to live in more units). Why don't governments systematically audit their administrative rules and regulatory system to provide the benefit of increased housing consumption to all its citizens? One possible reason is that supply side reforms typically take several years to show results. It is therefore difficult for the reforms initiators to take credit for the improvement of the housing stock, so the incentive to enact change is lower. There is also a lack of clarity on how regulations affect private sector decisions, which are incentivized by profit calculations. Therefore, very few predictive math-based models are created by cities to project how regulations affect private developer profits and incentives to build new housing stock at different income levels. And, as we have seen earlier, the desire "to do something" about housing, and to do it fast, trumps the necessity of taking the time to understand the problem through surveys and regulatory audits.

Access to Mortgages May Increase the Housing Consumption of a Large Number of Households

Access to housing finance in the form of mortgages tends to increase the housing consumption of those who can qualify for them. Instead of relying entirely on their own savings to purchase a dwelling, households may borrow a part of the necessary sum from a bank. That allows them to buy a larger or better located house than if they were relying solely on their own savings. Households having access to mortgages may also buy additional dwelling units that they could rent out, thus significantly increasing the housing stock. The availability of mortgage finance therefore tends to increase the consumption of housing for those who qualify for it, as shown in figure 6.14. I assume that banks will provide mortgages to households with income higher than d. The housing consumption of households with an income of d increases from g to $g1$, and all households with incomes higher than d will increase their consumption in a proportional way. I assume here that the supply of housing is elastic (i.e., that when demand increases for better houses, developers are able to respond quickly to demand). In this case the new consump-

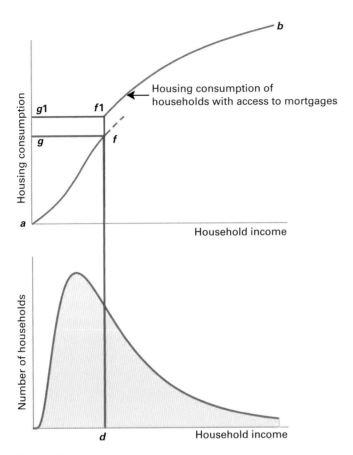

Figure 6.14
Housing consumption with mortgage for some.

tion curve is no longer continuous and instead consists of two segments *a–f* and *f*1*–b*.

However, imagine that because of regulations, or because of lack of developable land, developers are not able to respond to the increased demand generated by the availability of mortgages. The increased resources of households who have access to mortgages are then concentrated on the few houses that are produced, and the result is likely to be a general increase in housing prices rather than in an increase in consumption. Any demand stimulus, whether it comes from increased income or increased purchasing power, while very desirable in an urban economy, would result in higher housing prices if the supply of housing is constrained by poor regulations and a shortage of developable land.

In figure 6.14, I have assumed that only households with an income higher than *d* would have access to a mortgage. That represents roughly about the wealthiest third of the total population. This situation would be typical of a low- to medium-income economy in which capital is scarce and the financial sector is still rather shallow and undeveloped.

Why are mortgages provided only to households with incomes higher than *d*? The financial sector may not have been able to mobilize much savings, and because capital is scarce, banks lend to the most affluent first as they are perceived to represent lower risk. As the financial sector develops, the lower lending limit will move toward the left, including increasingly more middle-income households. Eventually it could reach possibly up to 70 percent of urban households. Countries like Malaysia and Thailand have achieved this penetration, but that was the result of continuous, consistent policy aimed at developing the financial sector. The results are spectacular, but they appear over the long term.

However, a large number of households with informal employment and uncertainty over land titles may also combine to limit the number of households having access to mortgage financing. Governments could therefore increase housing consumption by setting the rules that would allow the financial sector to develop.

Fixing Minimum Housing Consumption Increases the Size of the Informal Housing Sector

Why Would Governments Fix Minimum Housing Consumption?

Under normal housing market operations, the relationship between household incomes and housing consumption becomes similar to the curves in figure 6.12: the poorer households consume much less housing than middle-class households. In cities with a high annual migration rate, the number of poor households is larger, and their housing consumption is even lower. Newly arrived migrants with low urban skills are crowded into dense slums. Slums are characterized by not only very low consumption of land and floor space but also by very low consumption of urban utilities (e.g., water and sanitation) and a low level of community facilities (e.g., schools and health clinics). When the number of slum dwellers becomes large, and therefore visible to higher-income groups, political pressure forces the local government to "do something."

The first reaction of government is usually to set minimum housing standards, below which it will be illegal to build new housing. All the countries I worked in had minimum housing standards. New regulations then specify minimum housing consumption, usually expressed as a combination of minimum plot sizes, minimum floor areas, maximum densities and floor area ratio (FAR), in addition to minimum standards for road width and open space. Regulators pretend that preventing by law the construction of housing units deemed socially unacceptable will also prevent the crowding and unsanitary conditions in which low-income households are living.

By regulating minimum housing consumption, governments are de facto trying to regulate their cities out of poverty. Regulating minimum housing consumption has the opposite effect. The minimum housing standards defined by regulations correspond to a minimum cost. When this cost is above what a certain number of households can possibly pay, the only effect of minimum housing consumption regulations is to render illegal those settlements that have been built below the new standards. In addition, the regulations expand into the future the extent of illegal settlements that are the only ones affordable to the poor.

The inhabitants of illegal settlements become by association illegal and may not be able to receive services and the normal protection of the laws against evictions. The settlements whose houses do not meet the minimum standards are usually called "the informal sector" or even slums.

The regulations fixing minimum housing consumption are therefore not benign, even when they are not enforced—and usually they are largely unenforceable. Their only effect is to make more difficult the life of poor households living in settlements below the minimum standards. The people living in informal settlements are usually poor, and their poverty is further exacerbated by the very regulations that make their settlements informal.

For the poor, the costs of informality are high. First, informality implies an enhanced degree of tenure uncertainty, and therefore the possibility of demolition and expropriation without compensation. Second, many municipal services like water supply, storm drainage, and refuse disposal are often denied to informal settlements. Third, social services like health and education, if provided at all, are often substandard, because the informality of settlements implies an impermanency, and no government would invest in building schools or dispensaries in impermanent settlements.

Let us look at the impact of minimum-standard regulations on the housing consumption of households at the bottom of the income distribution in figure 6.15. Government sets the minimum housing consumption at level m on the vertical axis of the top graph. This consumption level m intersects at point h the market housing consumption curve C. From h we draw a vertical line that intersects at n the horizontal axis of the bottom graph showing household income. The number of households living in settlements below the minimum standards is shown in the area under the curve c to the left of the line hn shown in dark blue in the bottom graph. The neighborhoods containing the households to the left of hn become illegal because of the regulations.

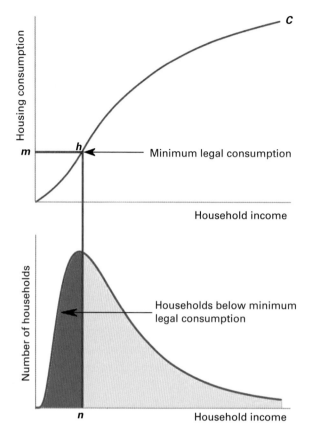

Figure 6.15
Government set minimum consumption.

If the government increases the standards *m*, the number of households in illegal settlements will increase. When *m* is lower, the number of households in illegal settlement decreases.

The choice of a minimum housing standard is arbitrary. There is no such thing as an optimal housing standard. I would suggest that access to safe water and sanitation is indispensable, but there are many ways of providing this minimum service without imposing a minimum area for floor space, land, and access road. And when specifying a minimum access to water and sanitation, what quantity of water per person and per day should be included in the standard? The 30 liters per capita per day (lpcpd) corresponding to the consumption provided through a public tap shared by five households? Or 150 lpcpd as in Europe? Or 863 lpcpd as in California? The same reasoning could be used for minimum plot size or minimum size of floor area. We will see the positive impact of avoiding setting minimum standards in the case study below describing the kampung policy in Indonesia.

Regulating minimum housing standards is not a technical task but a political act. In many cities in developing countries, but also in cities like New York and Paris, the minimum standards are unreasonably high. It seems that there is a minimum political cutoff value for housing standards. No local politician would approve a minimum standard value below this cutoff. Politicians feel that by accepting very low consumption standards, which may be the only one affordable to a part of the population, they somehow accept poverty as a permanent state, and that by setting high standards they are being progressive.

Another even less benign explanation for the existence of unreasonably high housing standards is the desire to keep poor migrants out of cities and poor households out of specific neighborhoods. Many of the residential zoning laws in developed countries are designed to ensure a "homogenous" community—that is, to prevent people with lower incomes from moving into the neighborhood.

What are the consequences of regulating minimum housing consumption values? People consume very little housing because they are too poor to afford more. The regulations will not lift the poor out of poverty.

However, the regulations will prevent the construction of the only type of housing poor households can afford. If some developers are ready to continue building housing below the minimum standard, these houses will become illegal, exposing poor households to expulsion or to demolition of the only type of house they can afford. Regulations fixing minimum housing consumption thus deprive poor households of property rights.

The households who cannot afford housing standards meeting the minimum regulatory value are therefore confronted with two choices; live in an illegal settlement in the city of their choice or return to a rural area where housing is cheaper or where housing is not regulated. Obviously, the great majority makes the former choice. The ubiquity of slums in many cities in developing countries demonstrates that often a large number of households can only afford a primitive form of housing without much of the infrastructure that makes an urban high density environmentally tolerable. Slums are due to poverty, but government imposition of minimum housing standards makes poverty worse. It denies such basic services as water supply, sanitation, and refuse disposal to households who live in settlements that are illegal only because the people living in them cannot afford the arbitrary standards imposed by minimum consumption regulations.

Infrastructure providing a minimum of safe water supply and sanitation and removing solid waste is relatively cheap to provide compared to housing. The lack of safe water and sanitation has a much more devastating effect on the health of the poor than does the size or construction quality of their dwellings.

It is of course legitimate for a government to wish that every citizen should enjoy at least a certain amount of floor space, infrastructure, and social amenities. However, this government should be ready to complement through a subsidy the difference in rent that households would have to pay to afford these minimum standards. The debate on the minimum housing consumption level is therefore one of affordability. What households cannot afford should be affordable to the government. Too often governments set high housing consumption standards together with the promise of subsidizing housing but without having the resources to do so. The outcome for poor households is then similar to the one shown in figure 6.15. Because the government has set the minimum standards so high that neither households nor government can afford them, poor households end up living in illegal settlements that cannot be connected to urban services, as the municipality assumes that a government program would soon provide a "decent" housing unit to every household living in illegal settlements.

Contrary to popular belief, governments setting housing standards too high are not just guilty of benign economic optimism but are making decisions that have disastrous effects on the poor.

If minimum housing standards have such an obvious disastrous consequences for the poor, why do most urban planners continue to include them in their master plans? The only answer I can think of is planners' propensity for utopia and their dislike for reality. A quotation from Albert Hirschman, "an oppression of the weak by the incompetent,"[12] best illustrates this point.

Let us now look at housing policy options open to responsible governments that are interested in improving the housing consumption of the lowest-income groups and are ready to make the reforms and invest the taxpayers' money that would be required to do so.

Demand Side Subsidy: Impact of a Demand Side Subsidy Program

Imagine that a local government decides that all households should at least enjoy a level of housing consumption corresponding to m in the top graph of figure 6.16. To achieve this objective, the government decides to allocate a voucher to every household whose income is insufficient to afford the housing standard corresponding to m. The amount of the voucher will be equal to the difference between the market rent of a housing unit of standard m and the rent that a household can afford, expressed as a set percentage of the household's income (say, 30 percent).

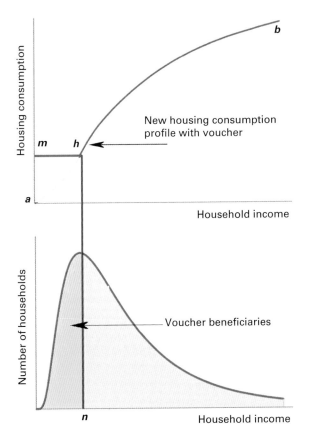

Figure 6.16
Theoretical effects of housing vouchers (partial equilibrium).

Or the government could decide that any household whose income is below *n* (bottom graph in figure 6.16) would receive a voucher to allow consumption of at least *m* on the current housing market.

The voucher system is currently used in a number of countries—in the United States[13] and Chile,[14] for instance. It appears to be the most sensible way to ensure a minimum housing consumption to all and to make the financing of the subsidy transparent. In addition, the voucher system allows households to select both their housing standards and location, which supply side subsidies do not allow. Let us look in more in detail at some of the issues raised by housing voucher programs.

The new housing consumption profile when vouchers are distributed to all beneficiaries is the curve *mhb* in figure 6.16. The cost per household for each income interval is the difference between the line *mh* and the curve *ah*. The subsidy from government decreases as the income of the beneficiaries increases. The number of beneficiaries is represented graphically by the area shaded in yellow on the income distribution curve. It is easy to calculate the total cost to the government by multiplying the number of beneficiary households in each income category by the subsidy to which they are entitled. For households with incomes close to zero, the voucher pays the entire rent. When the income increases, the voucher adjusts to a smaller portion of the rent.

Depending on the government resources, it might be necessary to adjust the consumption standards m by increasing or decreasing it. It might also be possible to have h slightly higher than m, so that all beneficiary households have an incentive to increase their income to have a better house. When the number of beneficiaries is known, the government should make the voucher available over a relatively short time. In addition, based on demographic and economic projections, the government should calculate how many new households every year will require a voucher and what yearly budgetary allocation will be required in the future to support the program.

Governments are often tempted to select a standard m or a qualified income n without looking into the budgetary implications caused by the number of beneficiaries who would qualify for vouchers. We can see in figure 6.16 that a higher qualifying income n or a higher housing standard m would increase the total number of households who should be able to benefit from the voucher. This number is represented by the yellow area in the figure.

The government has only a limited budget to allocate to vouchers; therefore, when selecting either m or n, it should make sure that all current households who qualify should get their voucher after getting on a waiting list no more than, say, 3 years. If the average time on a waiting list is much longer than 3 years, there is not much point in designing the program for such a large number of beneficiaries if they cannot obtain a voucher anyway. Housing policy based on a low-odds lottery (as New York has resorted to) is a little cruel for those who are deemed as deserving a subsidy but might never win it.

In September 2016, an NGO website assisting applicants for vouchers through the Section 8 program in New York City had this ominous warning: "There are nowhere near enough vouchers to meet the need of everyone who qualifies for and applies for them. Once waiting lists are open, agencies are flooded with applications. You only have a few days to apply."[15]

In fact, in January 2016, 86,610 households in New York were currently receiving vouchers, but 143,033 qualified households were on a waiting list. The government does not tell prospective voucher beneficiaries how long the wait will be before obtaining vouchers. It might well be infinite.

A voucher program should be able to disburse rapidly to the qualified households. However, a fast disbursement would create a large demand increase for new dwellings. The housing supply should be able to respond rapidly to the new demand. If the vouchers are distributed within a few years and if the number of beneficiaries is large, it is not certain that developers will be able to provide immediately a large number of houses of standard m. If there is a supply constraint—if land is difficult to buy or takes a long time to acquire, if building permits are slow to process—the additional capital suddenly injected into the building sector may create an increase in prices, and reaching the housing standard m might require higher cost than envisaged at the time the program was designed. This inflation created by the voucher program might result in higher prices for all low-income households. So in reality the program could cause a decline in standards compared to the initial situation represented by the original consumption curve ab.

This occurred in Malaysia in the 1980s, resulting in an increase in housing prices of about 19 percent per year over a period of 10 years, while nominal income increased by 10.5 percent per year. A World Bank study that I coauthored indicated that regulatory supply constraints combined with a financial stimulus in the form of subsidized mortgage interest rates were largely to blame for higher housing prices.[16]

This problem is extremely common. Housing supply bottlenecks occur in many cities. They might be caused by a lack of infrastructure that prevents new land from being developed, by greenbelts or other urban growth boundaries, or by regulatory constraints on land development or on construction itself. Less frequent are constraints in the building industry itself, such as a shortage of labor or materials. A voucher system can be successful only when the government has been able to remove all supply bottlenecks. Removing supply bottlenecks would have the opposite effect of inflation; it would push the consumption curve ab upward, as shown by the dashed line in figure 6.13.

Demand side subsidies like vouchers (or other types of subsidies directly given to households) address the main cause of low housing consumption: the very low income of part of the urban population. It allows households to make their own trade-offs between dwelling size and location. It allows a variety of housing designs and technical innovations. The subsidy involved is transparent and allows governments to include it in its budgets. It allows financing a large number of dwellings without creating a vast bureaucracy. However, it requires that the government be able to afford the cost of the vouchers, so that low-income households are not given the false hope of a low-odds lottery. It also requires that supply constraints on land and construction be removed in advance of the distribution of vouchers.

Supply Side Subsidies: Public Housing, Inclusive Zoning, and Rent Control

In spite of the advantages of demand side subsidies, many governments prefer supply side subsidies. Supply side subsidies do not give the subsidies directly to households but to developers to build a predetermined type of housing in a specific location for a specific price.

To benefit from supply side subsidies, households have to move to the dwelling that receives the subsidy, whose location, size, and design have been selected by planners, not by the end user. To keep the subsidy, beneficiaries have to remain in the subsidized dwelling. They therefore lose mobility; they cannot change dwelling type or location when their circumstances change without losing the subsidy (getting on a new waiting list). Let us look at the impact of supply side subsidies on the housing stock by using a graph linking income distribution and consumption (figure 6.17).

Let us assume that a government decides to address the problem of low housing consumption of slum dwellers by establishing a public housing program. The government makes all decisions concerning the location, size, and design of all housing units to be rented to a selected target group. The beneficiaries are usually identified by their incomes. In the graph the income of beneficiaries is between q and n, and the number of qualified beneficiaries is represented in blue on the income distribution curve (graph 1 in figure 6.17). The current housing consumption of this income group varies from p to h on the consumption curve ab. The government builds a number of flats to move the beneficiaries represented by the red area between q and n. The standards of the newly built public housing are between $p1$ and $h1$, significantly higher than the original standards p to h of the target beneficiary group, which is precisely the objective of the public housing program. The rent paid by the beneficiaries is set by the government and represents an affordable fixed percentage of their income not directly related to the cost of providing housing of standard $p1$–$h1$.

The government could renew the operation until the entire target beneficiary group, represented by the blue area on the graph, has been housed in public housing units. This is unlikely to happen, as it would require an enormous annual financial commitment, plus the need to expropriate large tracts of urban land, not an easy process in a democracy. Still, at the end, a number of low-income households would have seen their housing standards increase significantly compared to what they could afford on the open market. So, what is wrong with the public housing approach? Many things, which I will now describe!

The major problem with this approach is that the households that benefit end up with higher housing standards than households that have higher incomes,

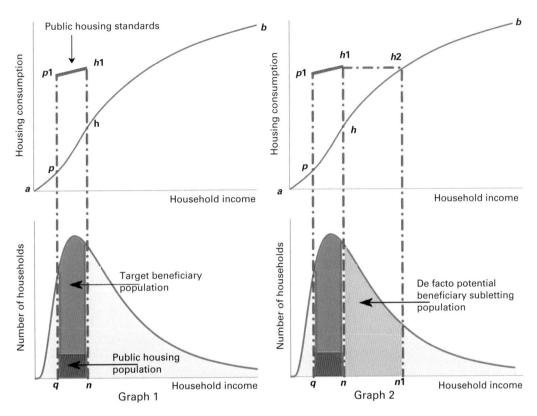

Figure 6.17
Impact of public housing supply side subsidies on housing consumption.

because of the way the income brackets of beneficiaries are selected. The housing standards of households in public housing at incomes below or equal *n* are much higher than the standards of households with higher income shown to the right of *n* in figure 6.17. Some households benefiting from public housing are likely to cash the potential rent by subletting their public housing apartment to higher-income groups, who under current market conditions can only afford housing standards that are below the level shown as *h*2 in graph 2 of figure 6.17. The number of households who are then potential beneficiaries of the public housing program becomes much larger. The informal extension of the group of beneficiaries reaches the income *n*1, and the additional number of potential beneficiaries is represented as the shaded area below the income curve included between the line *n–h*1 and *n*1–*h*2.

Why should a household receiving a subsidized housing from government be tempted to sublet it to a higher-income household? Subletting obliges the household to move into a substitute housing unit, for which it will have to pay a market rent. The subletting makes sense providing the market rent of the subsidized housing, minus the market rent of the substitute housing, minus the rent of the subsidized housing, is positive and therefore produces a flow of additional income to the original beneficiary of the subsidized housing unit. A household receiving a subsidized housing unit would have a strong incentive to sublet if the household placed a higher value on the extra income resulting from subletting than on the higher standard of the subsidized housing.

Subletting will likely occur when the standard of the subsidized unit is sufficiently high to be attractive to households with much higher incomes compared to that of the original beneficiary. This is what is represented graphically in figure 6.17 where housing standard *h1* is high enough to be attractive to households with an income *n1*, much higher than the income *n* of the beneficiary household. The subsidized housing units generated by New York's inclusive zoning schemes, described below, meet these conditions. Subletting of subsidized housing units, when it occurs, shows that the beneficiary household would prefer the cash value of the subsidy rather than the value in kind represented by the higher housing standard.

The subletting or the informal sale of public housing by their beneficiaries is relatively common. Nearly all public housing regulations strictly forbid subletting and spend significant resources trying to control it—demonstrating that subletting is an endemic issue in public housing. I have already mentioned that to avoid the subletting of public housing units by its intended beneficiaries, the Tamil Nadu Housing Board in Chennai, India, issued identity cards to all its public housing tenants to allow periodic checking by inspectors that the original beneficiaries were indeed occupying the apartments. Although enforcement is usually not as cumbersome as what I observed in Tamil Nadu, forbidding the subletting of public housing units is not unique to Chennai; it is also forbidden in New York, Paris, Bangkok, and most other large cities. The only difference between cities is the way the law is enforced.

Subletting by itself should not be a problem, in spite of being usually forbidden. After all, the beneficiaries, while not the intended ones, have housing standards below what the housing board considered minimum. The real problem is that it expands the number of beneficiaries to a much larger proportion of the population, and it discourages the private production of housing in this income range.

But the increase in the number of beneficiaries is not the only problem created by public housing. As I mentioned earlier, planners, not the beneficiaries themselves, have selected the location, size, and design of the public housing dwelling units. Consequently, public housing projects create ghettos by segregating households with similar low incomes in a housing project design selected by members of a board, who, while usually meaning well, do not have a clue about the priorities of low-income households. The absence of commercial sites (like stores and service-oriented shops), which is typical in public housing projects, is symptomatic of the artificiality of the design.

Furthermore, households in public housing units cannot change dwellings without losing the subsidy that they are receiving, or if they are permitted to do so, they have to move to another public housing project subject to availability. Households whose income increases beyond the income limit n either have to move and lose their subsidies or stay while disguising their increased income.

Finally, because of the lengthy bureaucratic process involved in all government contracts, the government is usually unable to deliver the number of apartments to all the potential beneficiaries of public housing. The number of households obtaining apartments remains a small fraction of the number of households in the target group, as shown in figure 6.17. Many applicants typically remain for more than 10 years on a waiting list to benefit from public housing. For example, in Paris, the current wait is 19 years if one divides the number of qualified applications (234,000) by the number of yearly assignments (12,000).

Other housing programs are relying on supply side subsidies. In the United States, the Low-Income Housing Tax Credit provides a tax credit to developers who provide rental units affordable to households who have incomes below 60 percent of the area's median gross income. Inclusive zoning programs, like the New York project discussed below, rely on a mix of tax incentives and zoning bonuses. Rent-control programs make the private sector pay entirely for the subsidy, although the municipality loses property tax income because of the low value of rent-controlled properties. Many of these supply side subsidy programs suffer from the same problem as public housing. They prevent beneficiary mobility, because the subsidy is linked to a specific housing unit, which will be lost if the household moves to another apartment.

If the shortcomings of supply side subsidies are so evident and well documented, why do so many municipal governments seem to prefer them to demand side subsidies? I suggest that politicians like to cut ribbons in front of tangible brick and mortar projects; they do not have this opportunity for demand side subsidies like vouchers. In addition, in many countries the large bureaucracy in charge of building public housing is a reliable source of patronage jobs and contracts. The assignment of subsidized units to beneficiaries also becomes a source of patronage that politicians find difficult to resist.

Four "Affordable" Housing Approaches; Four Outcomes

In this section, I describe four different approaches to the provision of affordable housing that I had the opportunity to observe on the ground and to talk with their local advocates and detractors. The first one, in Gauteng, South Africa, is a traditional supply side public housing strategy. The second, New York Inclusionary

Zoning, is also a supply side subsidy strategy, but the cost is supposed to be borne by developers receiving tax and regulatory incentives, which are not costless. The third, the Kampung Improvement Program (KIP), in Surabaya, Indonesia, consists of setting aside formal urban perimeters where land use regulations are waived, but where government subsidizes infrastructure. The fourth example, in Shenzhen, China, is similar to the Indonesian KIP waiver of land use regulations in well-delimited enclaves, except that the enclaves operate as a condominium, where all local infrastructure costs are borne by the beneficiaries; the government provides only bulk connection to the city infrastructure. We will see how these four different strategies to provide affordable housing perform in terms of supply and meeting the needs of the target income group.

Example 1: Supply Side Housing Subsidies in Gauteng, South Africa

Most public housing programs in the world consist of building rental apartments in multistory buildings. Public housing programs usually fail to deliver the number of units planned because of the high cost to the treasury and the difficulty of acquiring land in a timely manner. Consequently, the number of actual beneficiaries is small compared to the announced target, and the waiting list for subsidized housing gets longer every year.

South African Supply Side Housing Subsidies Are Different in Nature and Performance

By contrast, South Africa's subsidized housing performance, in terms of number of units delivered, is spectacularly better than public housing programs in most other countries. However, as we will see, in spite of its success in delivering large numbers of affordable housing units, it shows some of the unavoidable shortcomings associated with supply side subsidies.

The South African Constitution includes a citizen's right to "adequate housing." One of the main priorities of the post-apartheid government, which came to power in 1994, was to embark on an ambitious housing program to fulfill its constitutional obligations.

Given the complexity of the housing delivery problem, the South African government wisely created several housing subsidy instruments—many addressing the supply side, some directed to the demand side. These included eight instruments encompassing demand side subsidies like personal subsidized loans to buy in the existing stock, or even loans to repair and expand existing houses for low-income households.

However, the political necessity to provide rapidly a large number of new housing units pushed the government to devote most government resources to supply-driven initiatives, including an instrument called the "project linked subsidy," later named "Reconstruction and Development Program" (RDP). The RDP consisted of providing subsidies directly to suppliers, often private, provided they would build units following the adequate-housing norms mentioned in the constitution. The qualified beneficiaries of RDP, contrary to most public housing programs, immediately become the owners of their dwellings. The subsidy was therefore transmitted immediately from the government to the developer and passed on to the beneficiary. Indeed, project-linked subsidy programs are faster to implement on a large scale, as appraisal of housing units to qualify for the subsidy can be done in bulk for thousands of identical housing units at the project level. The government provides the subsidy to the supplier, who passes it on to the beneficiary. Supply side subsidies are simpler to administer, because the beneficiaries do not have to be consulted about housing design or location. There is also a clear economy of scale that reduces building costs by implementing very large contiguous projects.

The Definition of "Adequate Housing" in South Africa

The first step in implementing RDP required defining what constituted the "adequate housing" stipulated in the constitution. The government recruited a group of technical experts and politicians that established a set of standards covering housing, roads, public services, schools, and health facilities. The standards of adequate housing set by a group of experts included a house of 40 square meters on a lot of 250 square meters. The land use in the new communities was also fixed at about 50 percent of the land to be used for residential lots, 30 percent for roads, and 20 percent for open spaces and community facilities. This uniform normative definition of adequate housing greatly facilitated project appraisal and contractual relations between the government's housing agency and private developers building the units, thus improving the chance of a speedy delivery for a large number of units. However, it constituted an enormous built-in rigidity when selecting potential sites, privileging the choice of very large empty building sites, where land was cheap, and therefore far away from urban centers.

The same standards were to be applied to all urban housing under RDP, irrespective of location or local land prices. This uniformity was politically logical, in the sense that it gave an apparent sense of equality in housing consumption among citizens. When market principles are abandoned in allocating resources, there is no reason to use market benchmarks to price what has been allocated administratively. A 250 square meter lot will have a very different market value depending on whether it is located at a distance of 5 or 20 kilometers from the center of Johannesburg. The large difference in the values of similar lots depending on their location would in reality result in economic inequality among beneficiaries.

But the appearance of equality is often more important than its reality as soon as housing program administrators decide to ignore markets.

This argument about inequality in market values of different lots became moot anyway, as most RDP projects were located in such distant locations that the value of the land on which they were built did not differ much and was mostly uniformly very low. The setting of generous land use standards and the high land consumption involved (see the land use table in figure 6.18) ensured that RDP projects could be built only on very cheap land at great distances from city centers.

Estimating the Number of Beneficiaries

The second step required estimating the potential number of beneficiaries. To do so, the government conducted a complete survey of existing housing standards across cities. The results of the survey were used to compare the existing housing stock to the adequate-housing standard. The government then calculated the housing backlog that represented the difference between the number of housing units meeting the adequate-housing standard and the existing stock. Adjusting for population increase, the government found that about 8.5 million households, or about 84 percent of the population in 2000, would have to receive a subsidy in order to get rid of the housing backlog, thus allowing the South African government to fulfill its constitutional obligations to supply adequate housing.

The staggering number of potential beneficiaries raises the question of whether the RDP was really an asset redistribution program from the rich to the poor as intended, or a way of mobilizing fiscal resources from the entire population (via the corporate and individual tax base) and redistributing it in kind in the form of housing.

South Africa Reconstruction and Development Program (RDP) Program for Gauteng

Number of subsidized housing units built in Gauteng from 1995 to 2014	925,202
Average per year	51,400
Subsidy per unit in 2012	US$ 16,194
Total number of households in Gauteng in 2014	2.45 million
Percentage of beneficiaries in 2014	38

Land requirements

For 1,000 plots	1,000	lots		Average household size	3.60 people
Individual lot area	250	square meters		Population density	72 people per hectare
Total residential lot area	25	hectare	50%	Land area per beneficiary	139 square meters per person
Roads	15.00	hectare	30%	Land area per year	7 square kilometers
Community facilities	10	hectare	20%	Land area over 17 years	121 square kilometers
Total area	50	hectare	100%		

Figure 6.18
Number of units supplied under the RDP housing subsidy program and land use requirements.

The strategy worked extraordinary well when it came to delivering a large number of housing units at a set price. For instance, in Gauteng alone,[17] an average of about 50,000 subsidized units were delivered every year from 1995 to 2014 (figure 6.18). The 925,000 households who benefited from the program represented about 38 percent of all households living in Gauteng in 2014. This percentage is short of the "backlog," but it is an extraordinary logistical achievement nevertheless, compared to similar supply side subsidy programs in other countries.

Housing Supply and Labor Markets Where the South African Program Failed

However, building a large number of housing units rapidly does not ensure the success of a public housing program. A large metropolis like Gauteng exists because of the efficiency of large labor markets. The low-income households who should benefit from the subsidy program would have a chance to escape poverty only if they are able to be part of the urban labor force. Therefore, a good access to the job markets is the most important characteristic that new housing for the poor should provide.

The spatial structure of South African cities still shows the mark of pre-1994 apartheid. Low-density, high-income neighborhoods—not very different from those found in US suburbs—still occupy the central areas of cities. Jobs are dispersed in many subcenters across metropolitan areas surrounded by low-density affluent communities. Under apartheid, black African workers were located in distant denser "townships" separated from white suburbs by wide buffer zones. The structure of South African apartheid cities was the reverse of urban spatial structures generated by markets, where high densities of jobs and people are concentrated in central areas. Unfortunately, the supply mechanism of the RDP housing program unintentionally contributed to reinforcing the deficient spatial structure inherited from apartheid, continuing to concentrate the poor in high densities in areas far away from the city center. The map of population densities in 2001 already shows the spatial impact of the program and the dispersion of population (figure 6.19). The spatial distribution of households in 2001 still reflects the characteristics of apartheid urban structure, not markets.

While the new communities built under RDP were all well connected by major roads and sometimes suburban trains to the rest of the metropolitan area, the distances to employment centers are extremely large, sometimes more than 30 kilometers. In addition, jobs in Gauteng are dispersed over a large area, making mass transit uneconomical.

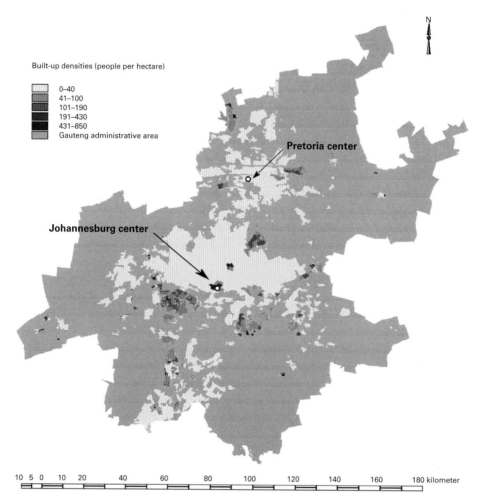

Figure 6.19
Gauteng's spatial distribution of population density, 2001. *Sources*: Census 2001 Municipal report Gauteng, Statistics South Africa, Pretoria, 2003; vectorization of built-up area using satellite imagery by Marie-Agnes Bertaud.

The type of suburban housing where the white minority lived at the time of apartheid inspired the layout of RDP projects, although at somewhat lower standards. Removing glaring racial differences in housing types was indeed the point. However, individual transport is the only viable means of commuting for this type of suburban settlement. Most of the low-income households in the subsidized projects cannot afford individual motorized vehicles. The collective taxis that low-income households are obliged to use in Gauteng to access jobs are slow, expensive, and require long waits for transfers. They have also proved very difficult to regulate, often resulting in violent turf wars between drivers.

The massive subsidized housing projects may have further fragmented the labor market of South African cities, contributing significantly to lowering their productivity. Unemployment rates in South Africa have been hovering around 22–26 percent between 2006 and 2016.[18] This high unemployment rate cannot be entirely attributed to the poor location of the subsidized housing scheme, but certainly, this massive program of building individual housing units in widely dispersed communities with no economic and speedy means of transport did not help.

The lack of access to jobs from the newly created communities is not merely a regrettable design oversight. It is engrained in the system of uniform building norms in which the price of land is the only variable in a housing project. This is the characteristic of most public housing projects. Let us look at the mechanism that created these inaccessible large communities.

Developers had to use the same spatial norms (e.g., plot size, house area, area for community facilities, and width of streets) whatever the location of the project. To achieve the maximum economy of scale and deliver rapidly the maximum number of units at the agreed-on price, developers had to look for large vacant areas of land at a low price. A developer will find large vacant land parcels only in the far periphery of cities. Any developer would normally adjust land use variables—height and size of building, open spaces, and street width—to the land prices in the area where her project is located. In the case of RDP projects, all the land use variables were fixed to fit the adequate-housing norms. The developer is then limited to finding a location where the low price of land would make the project financially viable when using fixed spatial norms. This location is bound to be a faraway suburb where land is cheap because the area is not very desirable for any other uses.

Although the RDP projects are land intensive, their density—about 70 people per hectare—is still higher than the higher-income suburbs that are closer to one of the several urban centers of Gauteng, such as Johannesburg, Pretoria, or Sandton. The projects contributed to a reverse density gradient—densities higher in the periphery than in the center—and therefore in longer commuting trips and an increase in the dispersion of the population.

Was a Better Alternative Possible?

Given the extraordinary political circumstances that preceded the adoption of RDP as a housing policy, could the South African government have possibly designed a different strategy? Theoretically, yes. It should have removed immediately all zoning regulations that preserved large single-house residential lots in centrally located areas. It could have adjusted its minimum standards concerning plot size and house size to make housing affordable to low-income groups in centrally located areas. It could have chosen a demand side approach involving vouchers that low-income households would have been free to use anywhere in the metropolitan area.

But these are only theoretical recommendation. In reality, given the time it takes in a democracy to adjust existing land use regulations, it is unlikely that the regulatory constraints on the supply side would have been removed until much later, probably more than a decade later. In the absence of supply side reform, any large demand side program, like vouchers, would have only generated higher prices, not more housing. The expectations at the fall of apartheid were extremely high. Sadly, I have to admit that the RDP program, however defective, was probably the only politically feasible one at the time it was implemented. After all, the South African government had already designed many alternative housing subsidy schemes. If the RDP received the bulk of the resources, it is because it was the only one that could deliver rapidly a large number of dwelling units.

How Can the Households Living in RDP Projects Be Integrated into the Metropolitan Labor Market?

What are the options now that millions of individual low-income houses have been built in distant suburbs of South African cities? This is a much more relevant question than what should have been done in the past. The government should now focus on getting housing beneficiaries into the labor market as the only way to escape poverty. How to connect low-income people living in distant suburbs to jobs in an urban structure similar to the one shown in figure 6.20?

Right now, collective taxis represent the most common mode of transport available to low-income households (72 percent of all public transport trips). In an urban structure like that of Gauteng, this means of transport is expensive and slow, but it is the only one serving the low-income population.

Traditional mass transit (like buses, BRTs, or suburban trains) is unlikely to be very useful in a dispersed urban structure like Gauteng. Recently built BRT lines between the center of Johannesburg and the Orlando stadium and Gautrain, and

Figure 6.20
Typical subsidized RDA housing project in Gauteng.

a modern rapid train linking Tambo International Airport with the centers of Johannesburg and Pretoria are certainly useful additions to Gauteng's transport network, but they will not be of much use for low-income households having to commute from dispersed suburbs.

In most cases, using light electric motorcycles that run at a maximum speed of 35 km/h and can take a more direct route between origin and destination would be the best way to improve the mobility of workers living in RDP projects. These motorcycles could also link residences with suburban railways and Gautrain stations. Petty crime and the possibility of motorcycles being stolen when parked might well prevent the spread of this mode of transport. The government could ensure the safety of these vehicles on the road by creating specially marked lanes and, at destinations, by creating safe guarded parking garages. What is clear is that the many housing units built by RDP in South African cities are here to stay. The challenge is now to link workers with their places of work by commuting trips of less than 1 hour. Two lessons are to be learned from the South African experience: Housing policy should not be designed without understanding labor markets; and new urban transport systems have to be designed to serve existing urban structures, no matter how flawed these structures may be.

Example 2: Inclusionary Zoning in New York

The South African RDP experiment has delivered a large number of low-income housing units at a high cost to the central government budget. However, the total housing program cost has been transparent and the annual number of units delivered regularly published. While many governments want to appear "to do something" about housing affordability, they may not be politically ready to allocate a large part of their budgets to low-income housing the way the South African government did.

Inclusionary Zoning Is the Latest Stage of the Long Quest for a Costless Solution to Affordable Housing

Finding a costless solution to providing affordable housing for the poor has been the Holy Grail of many governments. The goal is to appear to do something about an obvious social problem while not spending too much taxpayer money on it. Creative new housing regulations had been the approach most commonly used to find costless solutions to housing affordability.

Having developers pay housing subsidies to poor households is the main objective of these creative regulations. These types of policies are politically attractive, as they appear generous to the poor without involving any apparent disbursement of taxpayer money. Developers are usually not a particularly popular social class and have the reputation of being rich. This is the ultimate Robin Hood approach: take from the rich to give to the poor. Here I briefly survey the various types of "costless" approaches to housing affordability, and I will illustrate the inclusionary zoning strategy with a recent example (2016) from New York.

The oldest and rather primitive regulatory approach simply tried to outlaw poverty by establishing minimum standards that should oblige developers to provide "decent housing" for the poor. Formal developers have to build houses at standards above the legal minimum. The minimum standards have a minimum cost, which is usually higher than what the poor can pay. Consequently, poor households cannot find a house they can afford in the formal market. The poor who cannot find affordable formal housing do not leave the city; they find housing in the informal sector, which by definition supplies housing at prices the poor can afford but at standards below the minimum legal ones.

The minimum-standard rules, as we have seen earlier, contribute to the deterioration of housing conditions of low-income households by creating an informal sector—either slums in poor countries or overcrowding and informal subdivision of formal housing in rich countries.

A more recent and more sophisticated regulatory approach, usually named "inclusive zoning" or "inclusionary zoning," consists of enacting municipal zoning ordinances that request developers of housing projects above a certain size (usually above about 200 units) to provide from 20 to 30 percent of units at a price or rent fixed by the municipal government below market price and defined as affordable. For the rest of the units, the developer is free to use market prices or rents. Usually, as an incentive the municipal government gives the developer a development bonus in the form on an increase in FAR above the current one imposed by the zoning. In some cities, the bonus may include property tax reductions for a number of years. The current value of the FAR increase and of the tax reduction is seldom calculated and is anyway off budget.

This strategy, seemingly providing affordable housing at no apparent cost to the municipal government, has spread all over the world and is practiced in many municipalities in various forms, from New York City to Mumbai! Is there anything wrong with this method? Could it resolve the low housing consumption problem common to many poor as well as economically prosperous cities?

The inclusive zoning strategy is typical of what Angus Deaton, previously quoted, calls the "need to do something" that trumps any real analysis of the problem. Inclusive zoning belongs to the category of "free-lunch" strategies, and as with any promise of a free lunch, it has some major hidden flaws that I describe below using a specific example.

The Supply Mechanism of Inclusionary Zoning

It is obvious that private developers are not going to decrease the market price of a percentage of the housing units they build out of charity. The households who pay market price for their dwellings will eventually have to pay for the subsidy provided to the below-market units. While the price of the numbers of so-called affordable units produced is going to be lower than market price, the prices of the majority of units sold at market prices are going to become higher, in particular in cities where inclusionary zoning becomes generalized. As a consequence, if the process is implemented over a long period, the number of potential beneficiaries is going to increase, because market housing prices will increase and the number of households that can afford to generate the subsidy will decrease.

Let us look at a specific recent inclusionary zoning project in New York as implemented in 2016. The building, called VIA 57, located on the West Side of midtown Manhattan, has a total of 709 units, of which 142 (20 percent) are being offered as affordable housing to selected beneficiaries. The annual income of potential beneficiary households is set by the city. To qualify, potential beneficiaries must have an annual income between a minimum of US$19,000 to a maximum of $50,000. In New York in 2016, about 888,000 households were in this income bracket, and they represent about 29 percent of all households, shown by red bars in the city's income distribution graph (figure 6.21). The households who rent at market price in the same building have an annual income varying from US$160,000 to $470,000. Their income group, representing about 9 percent of all New York households (about 240,000 households), is shown by blue bars in figure 6.21.

The above numbers demonstrate that a limited number of households can be a source of the cross-subsidy, one of the main flaws of inclusionary zoning policy.

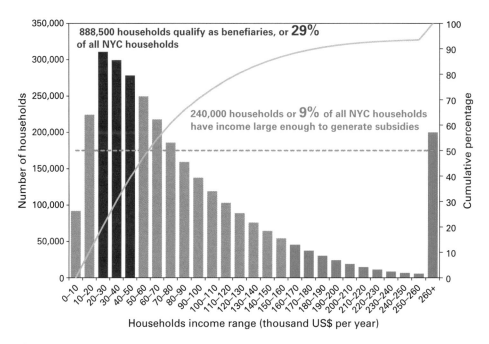

Figure 6.21
Household income distribution in New York, 2012, showing income ranges that benefit from inclusionary zoning (red bars) and those that generate subsidies (blue bars). *Source*: Derived from US Census American Community Survey, Integrated Public Use Microdata Series, Furman Center, New York University.

In New York, the annual flow of affordable housing intended to benefit 29 percent of the population depends on the number of housing units being built each year for the 9 percent of the wealthier households. Every eight newly built market units generate only two units of affordable housing. The mismatch between the limited supply and the large potential demand from eligible households is embedded in the concept itself of inclusionary zoning.

Recent data confirm the mismatch. There were 91,000 applicants for the 254 affordable units available in a recently built apartment under inclusionary zoning located on 42nd Street, in the same area of Manhattan as the VIA 57 project. Final beneficiaries must be selected through lottery. Indeed, the program is likely to have the same distributional impact as a lottery, rather than that of a social program aiming to provide affordable housing to low- to middle-income populations.

The mismatch between supply and demand is not the only problem faced by inclusionary zoning. The very large difference between the market rent and the subsidized rent of units in the same building with the same very high standards is raising several issues over potential misattribution and equity.

Luxury Apartments for the Happy Few Poor

One of the stated objectives of the inclusionary zoning in New York is to provide a mix of incomes and social interactions in each neighborhood. It is certainly a desirable objective. However, the objective of income mix in a neighborhood has been extended to income mix in a building. The new rules in New York stipulate that all subsidized apartments have to be mixed randomly in the building: all subsidized apartments must have the same design and standards as market ones. As inclusionary zoning can be provided only in areas of very high demand and high prices, it means that subsidized apartments have to have the same area, design, and standards as luxury apartments. For instance, three-bedroom apartments have to have three bathrooms as expected in luxury apartments.

These new rules were applied as a reaction to the "poor door" incident.[19] In 2015, in a new apartment building that had subsidized units under inclusionary zoning, the developer provided a separate entrance to give access to subsidized apartments, which were all located in a segregated part of the building. This created a popular outcry against the "poor door." As a result, it was decided that henceforth subsidized apartments had to be mixed with markets units and to be of identical design. This new rule resulted in a de facto objective shift.

The original objective of the inclusionary zoning was to provide as many affordable housing units as possible to a specific low-income group. After the identical-unit rule, the policy objective shifted to providing similar housing units for rich and poor. From redistribution to equality. While an equalitarian objective is desirable in the delivery of health, justice, and education, it might not be feasible for housing without lowering substantially the housing standards of everybody else. This was the policy used in the Soviet Union and in pre-reform Communist China. A standard design for housing was applied throughout the country and was made available to all (with the exception of a few high-level party cadre).

Let us look at the equity consequences of the current New York inclusionary policy. Figure 6.22 shows both the subsidized and the market rents paid by tenants in the same building. The subsidized rent varies from US$565 to $1,067 per month depending on apartment size, household size, and household income. The market rents, as advertised by the developer on its website, range from US$3,400 to $8,700 per month. These are the lowest rents, advertised as "starting at. …" The subsidies consisting of the difference between the market rent and the subsidized rent are increasing with income and apartment size. The highest subsidy of US$8,957 per month goes to households with yearly incomes of US$29,000–40,000 for a three-bedroom apartment. The yearly rent subsidy of US$107,000 represents 3.7 times the beneficiary's income!

Is the enormous rent subsidy per household an efficient way to use the large tax collected from market tenants—about US$1,000 per month per market apartment?

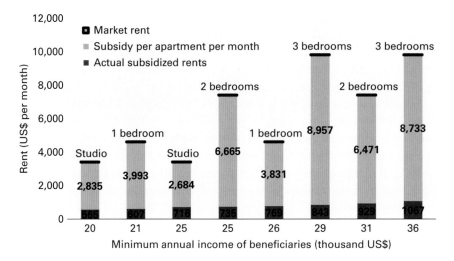

Figure 6.22
Market rents and subsidized rent at the VIA 57 building, New York. *Sources*: Data is from application from for subsidized apartment at VIA 57 and developer advertisement for market rate rental in same building.

(See figure 6.23 for details on aggregated subsidies.) If a household qualifying for the subsidy was given the choice between receiving an additional income of US$107,000 a year or the possibility of living in a three-bedroom apartment in the VIA 57 building for a monthly rent of US$857, would the household prefer the apartment to the additional income? My guess is that the additional income would be likely to be preferred. With this additional income, the household would rent a more modest apartment with one bathroom and three bedrooms and would use the difference between the market rent and the subsidy for other needs. The value of the subsidized apartment to the beneficiary tenant is less than the cost of subsidy that the taxpayer is paying for it. Urban economists call this the consumer surplus. For instance, Richard Green and Stephen Malpezzi have written convincingly on the issue of consumer surplus in subsidized apartments.[20] In many cases the consumer surplus is lower than the taxpayer cost representing the subsidy and therefore results in a net loss to general welfare. Green and Malpezzi demonstrate that forcing a large subsidy on poor households, when this subsidy can be obtained only by living in an apartment that the household would not have selected, is a very inefficient way of allocating tax dollars.

The large subsidies also raise a serious equity issue. The income distribution curve in figure 6.21 shows that the subsidy is restricted to households with incomes ranging from US$19,000 to $50,000 per year. The limit is obviously arbitrary. Under the inclusionary zoning, households earning US$49,000 a year might get a subsidy

Inclusionary zoning at 625 West 57th Street , New York City   25%

Category	Number of apartments receiving subsidies	Yearly income range of beneficiaries		Household size allowed	Monthly rent charged to beneficiaries (US$)	% of income of beneficiaries		Monthly market rent of equivalent apartment in same building (US$)	Subsidy per month per apartment (US$)	Total subsidy per month (US$)	Yearly income of households generating subsidy (US$)	Rent subsidy as multiple of beneficiaries income
		Low	High			max.	min.					
studio	14	19,622	24,200	1	565	35%	28%	3,400	2,835	39,690	163,000	1.7
1 bedroom	47	21,016	27,640	1 to 2	607	35%	26%	4,600	3,993	187,671	221,000	2.3
studio	14	24,519	30,250	1	716	35%	28%	3,400	2,684	37,576	163,000	1.3
2 bedroom	8	25,200	34,520	2 to 4	735	35%	26%	7,400	6,665	53,320	355,000	3.2
1 bedroom	47	26,270	34,550	1 to 2	769	35%	27%	4,600	3,831	180,057	221,000	1.7
3 bedroom	2	29,124	40,080	3 to 6	843	35%	25%	9,800	8,957	17,914	470,000	3.7
2 bedroom	7	31,492	43,150	2 to 4	929	35%	26%	7,400	6,471	45,297	355,000	2.5
3 bedroom	3	36,389	50,100	3 to 6	1,067	35%	26%	9,800	8,733	26,199	470,000	2.9
	142									587,724		

Total number of apartments in building =   709

1,037 Av. US$ per apartment generating the subsidy

4,139 Av. US$ per apartment receiving the subsidy

Figure 6.23
Rents and subsidies received by inclusionary zoning beneficiaries residing in the VIA 57 building, New York. *Source*: Application form for subsidized apartment at VIA57 and developer advertisement for market rate rental in same building. http://www.via57west.com/#neighborhood-gallery; http://www.57and11lottery.com/assets/VIA_Ad_and_ApplicationUpdated-d02a4451c02942f28cc0fb5af0b9b5f4312dab4999438b7c85c4f01a3071151d.pdf.

that amounts to US$100,000 every year, but those earning US$51,000 a year will get nothing. The inequity is even worse for poorer households earning less than US$19,000 a year who will not qualify for any rent subsidies under the program.

The housing consumption profile shown in figure 6.12 is suddenly broken in segments with a small group of low earners consuming much more than households that earn just a little more than the group members. This is not equitable. Equity could ensure that every household below a set income is guaranteed a minimum level of housing consumption, not that some consume a lot and others very little.

The benefits of being in the required income brackets are so high that there are large incentives to try to game the system, for instance, by underreporting income or for one member of a household to abstain from working during the application period so that the household's income remains within the beneficiary bracket.

A Frozen Pool of Affordable Housing
Do the newly built subsidized units under inclusionary zoning constitute a pool of affordable housing that will be available in the future to households with a qualifying income? To constitute a permanent pool of affordable housing, the households living in them should be able to move when the units no longer fit their needs, as happens for those households in the market part of the housing stock. It would mean that the subsidized units should have a constant vacancy rate of about 4 or 5 percent, so that new tenants can progressively replace the original tenants. This is unlikely to happen, as the subsidy, obtained through a lottery system, is linked

to the apartment and not to the household. The subsidy is not transportable, and it is so large that the original tenant is unlikely to enjoy an increase in income that would be large enough to convince them to give up the subsidy.

Imagine a young household, for instance, a schoolteacher having just obtained a job at a school in the neighborhood. The household's income would most probably qualify them for inclusionary zoning. Would they ever find a vacancy in the VIA 57 building or any other similar building in the neighborhood? This would be very unlikely, as no subsidized original tenant is likely to ever abandon her subsidy. By contrast, in market rentals, households with increasing income are likely to move out of their current housing units and look for an alternative corresponding better to their new income or to a new job location. However, with such a large subsidy, no original tenant in subsidized inclusionary zoning apartment is likely to ever move out, even if their income increases twofold, as moving out would represent an immediate large drop in housing consumption. In New York, the subsidy is granted in perpetuity. It is therefore likely that descendants of original tenants will succeed their parents when they retire, as currently happens for rent-controlled apartments. The inclusionary zoning apartments are, therefore, unlikely to constitute a pool of affordable housing in the future. In addition, the large subsidy attached to a specific apartment tends to decrease the mobility of tenants who benefit from it.

Incentive to Sublet

If presented with a possibility to receive the monthly subsidy as income, tenants would probably prefer this option rather than remaining in the luxury apartment allocated to them. But this possibility is not legally open to them. However, the large difference between the subsidized rent and the market price constitutes a strong incentive to cash the subsidy informally, if there is such a possibility. A tenant with a monthly income of US$2,500, paying a subsidized monthly rent of US$843 for a three-bedroom apartment with a monthly market rent of US$9,800, must have a powerful incentive to sublet it informally to a more affluent household for, say, US$8,000. The total monthly income of the original tenant becomes $8,000 + 2,500 − 843 =$ US$9,657 per month. With this income, the tenant can easily find an apartment in a less desirable location and with more modest amenities for a monthly rent of, say, US$1,500, which is equal to the median rent in Manhattan in 2014.[21] The new disposable income of the tenant (income minus rent) becomes $9,657 − 1,500 =$ US$8,157 per month, instead of $2,500 − 843 =$ US$1,657 per month if the tenant remains in the subsidized unit. This is a very powerful incentive. Whether the tenant takes the risk of subletting illegally or not, it is clear that she will be better-off with a monthly disposable income of US$9,657 compared to

US$1,657. Anybody interested in the welfare of this tenant should advocate for her right to sublet at market price. After all, she won the lottery!

The Real Cost to Government to Provide Incentives to Developers
So far, I have discussed the impact of inclusionary zoning on tenants benefiting from such zoning regulations. Let us now look at inclusionary zoning from the perspective of developers and governments. Developers cannot provide 20 percent of the apartments they produce at below-market rents without going bankrupt if other developers are allowed to rent 100 percent of their apartments at the full market rate. A government wanting to use inclusionary zoning to provide housing units below market price therefore has only two choices: make inclusionary zoning voluntary but provide fiscal and regulatory incentives to compensate developers' cost, or make inclusionary zoning compulsory for all developers in some designated area, thus leveling up the playing field for all developers who are competing in the same neighborhood.

The incentive approach has a high cost to government and to the public, as we will see, but at least it can be tested and monitored to adjust incentives. The compulsory approach can be applied to a smaller number of neighborhoods where the demand for high-priced apartments is known to be high. This approach greatly reduces the number of subsidized units that can be produced. The compulsory approach acts as a direct tax on market units and therefore increases their price and reduces demand. In a city like New York—and specially in Manhattan, where vacancies are scarce—reducing the supply of housing units in general might not be a good idea.

Whether the voluntary or compulsory approach is used to produce affordable housing, inclusionary zoning does not look like a free lunch anymore.

When inclusionary zoning is voluntary, the government must provide developers with incentives, either a regulatory change allowing more apartments to be built on the same parcel, or a tax abatement (or both). The regulatory change offered as an incentive is usually a bonus in FAR (i.e., permission to build more floor space than the current zoning allows) in exchange for building a set number units priced below market rents. In New York, the inclusionary zoning program, in addition to a zoning bonus of about 20 percent, used to include a tax incentive called 421-a that exempted the developer from an increase in property tax due to development for up to 20 years. The 421-a exemption expired in June 2015, but some new buildings are still receiving it because they applied for it before the termination of the program. It is uncertain whether the New York state legislature will ever renew it because of its cost. New inclusionary zoning projects will have to rely entirely on the FAR bonus as an incentive. That might be the reason the city has just established new areas in which inclusionary zoning is now compulsory.

The Cost of a Free Lunch: Tax Incentives and FAR Bonuses

According to a June 2015 report from the New York City Independent Budget Office, the current 421-a tax incentive program costs the city US$905,000 per apartment rented below market for the duration of the tax incentive (amounting to an annual tax cost of US$45,000 per housing unit). The yearly tax incentive per apartment is slightly less than the average subsidy per year per apartment (shown in figure 6.23) calculated for the VIA 57 project. So much for the Robin Hood policy of taking from the rich to give to the poor!

The annual cost to government is equivalent to the annual incomes of beneficiaries at the high end of the target income bracket. The tax incentive is obviously very costly, and its impact on New York's budget increases every time new below-market units are created. For obvious reasons, it is politically more expedient to approve tax incentives than to dedicate a part of the municipal budget to subsidize below-market housing. The cost to government is the same, but the calculation of tax incentives (such as the 421-a program) that extend far into the future is complex and therefore not very transparent. A tax incentive sounds much more innocent than a taxpayer-paid subsidy, but of course the amount paid by the taxpayer is the same. The lack of transparency and the fact that the incentive is paid by installment into the future make it easier to allocate subsidies in the form of tax incentives to developers than to provide an equivalent direct subsidy to households to buy or rent an apartment of the quality and location of their choice.

The 421-a tax incentive program was initiated in 1971 as a stimulus for the construction of residential buildings in Manhattan, and even luxury hotels qualified. For instance, the Grand Hyatt Hotel in mid-Manhattan, completed in 1980, received a tax subsidy that was evaluated at US$359 million by the *New York Times*.[22] Initially, to receive the tax incentive, developers were not required to construct some affordable housing units. This requirement was added only recently.

In addition to the tax incentive, the developer who agrees to provide 20 percent of below-market-rent units receives a FAR bonus of about 20 percent on average. This means that if the current zoning allows a developer to build an area of floor space equivalent to 10 times the lot area (FAR = 10), under the incentive zoning, the developer will be able to build a floor area equal to 12 times the lot area (FAR = 12).

This bonus FAR increase raises an interesting question. FARs are supposed to be limited by regulations because of the negative externalities that they might produce, for instance, casting shadows on other buildings, sidewalk overcrowding, or other problems. But the government practice of increasing FAR at will as an incentive for developers to do something that is deemed socially desirable demonstrates that the negative externality does not really exist, or at least is so low that it can be overlooked easily by urban planners when convenient. A government using regulatory constraints limiting FAR to negotiate with developers has a strong incentive to increase these constraints to the point of making development financially infeasible, so that developers are forced to negotiate with the city. By keeping FAR relatively low in areas where demand for floor space is high, the city creates an artificial shortage of floor space and contributes to the high price of housing. In areas where demand for floor space is much higher than the floor space allowed by the regulatory FAR, the city can then demand that developers provide for "free" something that the city wants. It might be a plaza, a park, or any amenity the city would like to have built. Under this system, the city acts like a monopolist on the supply of new floor space. It has an incentive to keep the supply of floor space low in order to keep the price of floor space high. Thus, it is ironic that the city feels obliged to increase regulatory pressure and thus makes housing more expensive for everybody in order to be able to produce a limited number of housing units below market price!

The welfare cost to citizens of keeping the FAR below demand is difficult to calculate. As for tax incentive, the difficulty of calculating the cost of the FAR incentive is one of the main political advantages for adopting such a system. This is probably why FAR incentives are increasingly used around the world, under the pretext of extracting a few affordable units from developers of luxury apartments. The restrictions on FAR have devastating effects in cities like Mumbai.

Inclusionary Zoning Is an Expensive Way of Creating a Few "Affordable" Apartments

Inclusionary zoning is obviously not the miracle solution that planners and politicians would like us to believe it is. Inclusionary zoning shows the shortcomings common to all housing supply side subsidies. It prevents mobility for households benefiting from it, because the subsidy is attached to a specific housing unit; its cost is not transparent and usually increases with time. It fails to adjust the subsidy to changing income. It makes beneficiary households overconsume housing at a high cost to the community. And finally, it fails to respond to demand for housing at a specific rent in sufficient quantities. According to the New York City Department of Housing Preservation and Development, an average of only 172 units per year have been produced through inclusionary zoning between the start of the program in 1988 and 2013!

In many ways, New York is a very successful city. It remains one of the world leaders in art, culture, fashion, finance, engineering, and technology. However, its housing policy, which in the past has been mainly based on supply side subsidies, remains a failure. In 2015, 42 percent of all dwelling units in New York (or 1.3 million housing units) were subsidized and rented below market price. In addition, a total of 405,000 households are currently on various waiting lists for rent assistance. There is nothing wrong with subsidizing the housing of the poorest households, but when the number of households being subsidized is coming close to half the city's households, it might be time to look for different solutions. Subsidies imply the transfer from the majority to the poorest. But when the recipients of subsidies are close to becoming the majority, it is evident that in the end their city taxes are paying largely for their own subsidies.

Tinkering with more supply side subsidy schemes to add more subsidized units to the current ones might not help anymore. It is time to look for radically different solutions. One of them, already partially in use, has been demand side rent subsidies or what is called in the United States "Section 8 housing." It consists of complementing qualifying households' income with a housing subsidy that allows them to search for housing units produced by the market, in the location and standards that households select themselves. When the household's income increases, the subsidy is progressively decreased. Households whose income rises above the maximum cease to qualify for the subsidy, but they may stay in the same apartment and pay the market rent. Because their subsidy is portable, households may change location and keep the same rent subsidy. Section 8 housing thus removes the more serious downsides of supply side subsidies.

Up to March 2016, in New York, 90,150 households have benefited from Section 8 rental subsidies, and an additional 147,000 are on a waiting list for the program. However, demand side subsidies increase the demand for housing by adding the subsidies to the income of beneficiaries. If the supply of new housing is constrained by arbitrary regulations like low FARs, for instance, or by a poor urban transport system, the demand subsidies may result in higher housing prices, not in more housing units.

A change in housing policy would require a general audit of all zoning regulations and construction practices that currently are responsible for high housing prices. Many neighborhoods in the New York metropolitan area are zoned for detached individual housing. There is a strong case to progressively amend these zoning regulations to allow the construction of townhouses in the locations where demand is high and where access to transit is adequate. The informal and illegal subdivision of detached houses in some suburbs of New York indicates a demand for more housing units on smaller lots. Finally, the limits on FAR should not be imposed to obtain a strong bargaining position when the city is negotiating with developers. FAR and height limitations should be set purely as a response to real quantifiable constraints, such as historical preservation or, say, air-traffic flight paths.

Finally, housing supply could be greatly increased by improving the urban transport system. Areas with low demand because of poor accessibility to jobs have necessarily a low density. Improving accessibility to jobs by increasing transport speed or introducing new transport technology should increase the de facto land supply of cities. Unless the regulatory and infrastructure housing supply constraints are removed, adding new subsidies to housing, whether supply side or demand side, would have very little effect on the welfare of the city's lowest-income households.

The above example of inclusionary zoning is not just an anecdotal illustration of a poorly designed housing policy. It represents a trend in many of the most economically successful cities in the world. The increasing regulatory frenzy that characterizes some cities like New York imposes large economic costs on the entire country. In a paper published in 2015, the economists Chang-Tai Hsieh and Enrico Moretti found that, between 1964 and 2009, the high cost of housing in some US cities relative to wages had lowered aggregate US GDP by 13.5 percent:

Most of the loss was likely caused by increased constraints to housing supply in high productivity cities like New York, San Francisco and San Jose. Lowering regulatory constraints in these cities to the level of the median city would expand their work force and increase U.S. GDP by 9.5%.[23]

Many of the regulations recently introduced in cities around the world that aim to improve the housing consumption of low-income households, not only do not deliver the number of housing units promised, but also contribute to lowering the economic opportunity of the very people they are supposed to help. It is time to audit these regulations and policies, taking into account the increasingly valuable economic literature on the subject.

Cities Are Reluctant to Accept Housing Standards That Are Affordable for the Poor: The Exceptions

Cities in low-income countries, where urban migration annually adds a large number of unskilled people, cannot afford to subsidize the housing of the large number of poor. However, cities in Indonesia, using an "integration" approach to low-income settlements, have been successful in absorbing new migrants into the urban labor force while maintaining an acceptable level of environmental health in the poorest neighborhoods.

In many Asian countries, large numbers of people migrating to cities have been creating dense urban villages in an urban setting but without any urban infrastructure. These small, simple structures provided the shelter these people needed at a price they could afford. It also allowed them to participate in the urban economy. However, the lack of connection to the city infrastructure soon created unacceptable sanitary conditions when these urban villages aggregated in large contiguous neighborhoods of several hundred thousand people. In addition, the lack of schools and health facilities contributed to slowing down or even preventing the integration of younger generations into urban society.

The predictable first reaction of governments has usually been to set minimum urbanization standards to prevent the legal construction of these unsanitary urban villages. The regulations made the situation worse, as they prevented these informal settlements from obtaining normal urban services from the municipality. They also created a risk of future demolition, which discouraged housing improvement that the households would have naturally done themselves. Eventually, many governments slowly regularized the older informal settlements in a piecemeal fashion, as is the practice in India, for instance. But the regularization of informal settlements usually had been conducted with a provision that after a set date, no more informal settlements would be regularized.

The outcome of these successive policies—first ostracism, then benign neglect followed by reluctant integration—has been disastrous. A significant share of the urban labor force, otherwise gainfully employed, live in large "informal" settlements often with unsafe water supplies, deficient sanitation, and sporadic solid waste collection. In Mumbai, one of the economic powerhouses of Asia, 60 percent of the population lives in slums.

I discuss below two case studies in Indonesia and China. These countries, for different reasons and in different ways, took a different approach to integrating affordable low housing standards into the city infrastructure. The outcome for the poor migrant households was significantly better than in the countries where a strict regulatory approach had been followed. In these two countries, the government allowed low-income households to use the standards they could afford and to make their own trade-offs between location, road space, lot space, and floor space. The government role was limited to providing connections from these settlements to the trunk city networks for transport, water, sewer, and storm drainage.

Example 3: Indonesia's Urban Enclaves with No Minimum Standards

In the densely populated island of Java, expanding cities absorb large existing villages, called "kampungs," whose population then integrates rapidly into the urban labor force. The former agricultural fields are soon built on by formal developers, while new informal constructions are added in the kampungs that have been absorbed into the city. So far, this is not too different from what happens in the rest of Asia, where countries are urbanizing rapidly.

There is one important difference. Indonesian kampungs always had a formal robust administrative structure based on traditional laws, and that administrative structure has been able to survive their absorption into a larger urban municipality. Confronted with urbanization, the kampung traditional leadership organized themselves to absorb newcomers. Lots were subdivided, but always on the initiative of the original owner, and within the kampung traditional regulatory constraints and social norms. To use modern terminology, we could compare kampungs to a form of condominium association: They have their own internal regulations and norms, forming a sort of local authority at the lower level than a municipality or a ward. One difference from a condominium is that the kampung local microgovernment also has jurisdiction over land use. Therefore, adjustments can be made to plot size, width of access to individual lots, and drainage of waste water by using traditional norms developed over centuries of practice of good-neighbor rules while overruling the development standards imposed by the municipality that surrounds the kampung. Formal developers building on adjacent greenfield land, however, had to follow the municipal land use standards rules concerning land development and subdivisions.

Because the income and preferences of new settlers were well known to the original kampung inhabitants, land use standards evolved to adjust to the new economic reality facing kampungs; standards were adjusted to increasing land values, so that plots would remain affordable to newcomers, who were usually poor migrants. Because the local traditional norms were respected, it did not result in an anarchic aggregation of houses that would be wasteful of land, as often happens in spontaneous squatter settlements where migrants aggregate without forming an organized community. A network of small roads, footpaths, and passages was maintained, reflecting the former village structure.

As Indonesian cities developed, the kampungs located closer to city centers densified more rapidly, as expected by their favorable locations closer to employment. The low income of their inhabitants, the lack of access to finance, the fragmentation of properties into small lots, and the lack of access to infrastructure prevented the construction of multistory buildings. However, the subdivision of existing village lots and the narrowness of internal access streets reflected the opportunity cost of land and soon resulted in much higher densities than that of the original villages, often resulting in densities of more than 500 people per hectare.

However, this increased density has a downside. The traditional source of water and means of sanitation—consisting of shallow wells and seepage pits— became grossly inadequate to serve the new higher densities. The low absorption capacity of the traditional sanitary system transformed the kampungs into dense unsanitary slums. The traditional storm drainage network, built around former irrigation canals, was insufficient to prevent flooding during the monsoon because of enhanced impermeability of the area caused by urbanization.[24]

Innovative Housing Policy Concentrating Subsidies on Infrastructure,
Not on Housing Structure

So far the history of the Indonesian kampungs does not appear to be very different from that of informal settlements in many other developing countries. What made a difference was a decision taken in 1969 by the government of Indonesia to concentrate its resources on the improvement of the kampungs' infrastructure without trying to remove or restructure the existing housing, however small or inadequate it was. The provision of urban infrastructure and services to kampungs was called the Kampung Improvement Program (KIP). Compared to the prevailing housing policies of developing countries in the 1960s, which consisted mostly of bulldozing informal settlements to relocate their inhabitants in public housing flats, this approach was revolutionary.

And, even more exceptional, since 1969 to this day, the Indonesian government's support for KIP has been unwavering, in spite of political upheaval and constitutional changes. The government housing policy objective consists of allowing the poor to settle in and around existing villages at the standards of their choice, while the government concentrates its efforts not on housing construction but on gradually improving residential infrastructure and services to all residential settlements. The policy has proved largely successful. The living and sanitary standards in most kampungs of Indonesia are far above what is found in informal settlements in countries with similar GDPs.

No kampung was ever bulldozed. No large groups of households were promised free housing. No large central government institution has tried to replace the many small KIP contracts for civil work on infrastructure in kampungs with larger contracts involving the construction of a massive program of public housing.

Operationally, the KIP continues to provide financial and technical assistance to the existing kampungs' traditional administrative structure to build connections to the municipal water supply network, to pave foot paths, to build drains using existing rights-of-way, to establish a system of solid waste collection that feeds into main collection bins that are part of the municipal solid waste collection system. The maintenance of the internal network and waste collection was and to this day is managed by the kampung community itself, with some financial assistance from the municipal government. The decentralization of decision making and the participation of the communities were embedded in the KIP from the beginning.

The KIP has been complemented with citywide investments in transport and, most importantly for Southeast Asia, in storm drainage networks to prevent periodic flooding of residential areas.

Indonesia, with a GDP per capita of US$10,500 in 2015, remains a lower-middle-income country, according to the World Bank. The overall standards of living reflect this income category. However, because the government concentrated its scarce resources on providing urban infrastructure to all urban residents, instead of increasing the housing consumption of a few poor households selected by lottery for public housing, every poor Indonesian received benefits. And these benefits increase over time. The government focus on infrastructure assistance allowed households to use their own resources to invest in their own housing, either as self-occupied dwellings or as investment in rental housing. The housing standards, defined as the size and quality of the structure, may therefore vary from very low to good in the same neighborhood, but access to safe water, sanitation, education, and health is ensured for all.

The demand-driven land use standards allowed by regulations in Indonesia are illustrated by the site plans of two neighborhoods in Surabaya, Indonesia, as surveyed in 2010 (figure 6.24). On the left in the figure, a kampung site plan shows the variety of plot and housing sizes that are possible in the same neighborhood. Some structures located in the back of lots facing the main passageways are very small and of poor quality, but they have access to safe water and sanitation. They have also access to the same schools and health facilities as their more affluent neighbors.

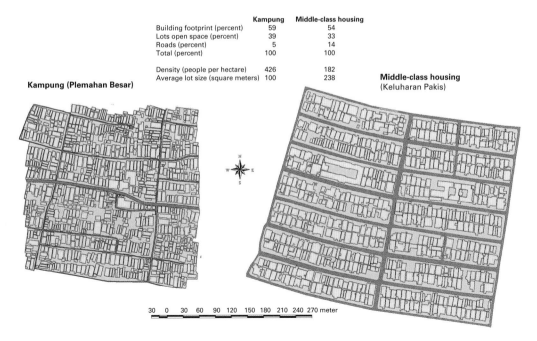

	Kampung	Middle-class housing
Building footprint (percent)	59	54
Lots open space (percent)	39	33
Roads (percent)	5	14
Total (percent)	100	100
Density (people per hectare)	426	182
Average lot size (square meters)	100	238

Kampung (Plemahan Besar)

Middle-class housing (Keluharan Pakis)

30 0 30 60 90 120 150 180 210 240 270 meter

Figure 6.24
Kampung and middle-class housing site plans in Surabaya, Indonesia. *Source*: GIS analysis of Surabaya topographical map by Marie-Agnes Bertaud.

The road system allows only emergency and construction vehicles but is adequate for local motorcycle and pedestrian traffic. On the right in the figure, a site plan designed by a formal developer, which shows a different, more standard type of residential layout with much less variety in lot size and more homogeneity in house area, reflecting middle-class standards.

Kampung Integration Policy Has Successfully Provided a Flow of Low-Income Housing

Because the kampung boundaries have always been protected since Indonesia started its rapid urbanization, kampungs are found in every neighborhood of Indonesian cities. Consequently, kampungs are always located side by side with commercial areas and higher-income areas, providing a socially desirable income mix at the neighborhood level. Because kampungs and middle-class areas share the same trunk infrastructure for water and sanitation, little discrimination is possible in public investment.

I have observed kampungs' evolution and improvement on a regular basis, since my first work trip to Indonesia in 1977. Many housing units in kampung areas look more middle class than low income. This reflects the increase in household incomes in Indonesia over this period. The inability to use a car as a means of transport in kampungs (because of the narrowness of the streets) prevents any large displacement of the poor from the best-located kampungs. The low road standards are the best guarantee against massive gentrification.

Some households that have reached sufficiently high incomes are likely to leave the kampung and move into formal development neighborhoods. This movement creates vacancies in the kampungs that are immediately filled with poorer households who rent or buy a dwelling. Low-income households do not need to be on a waiting list and do not have to submit a proof of their income to buy or rent in a kampung. Expansion zoning plans are reserving land around existing kampungs located in the periphery to ensure a flow of new low-income housing in the future.

The Indonesia kampungs and the KIP program demonstrate that it is possible for a government to provide large benefits to its large low-income population without creating long waiting lists. It shows that allowing standards to adjust and, consequently, population densities to float, not only provides affordable housing but also improves the city structure by allowing higher densities in areas accessible to jobs.

Example 4: China's Urban Villages

Legal Status of Land in Chinese Villages

As in Indonesia, many cities in China are absorbing large numbers of villages as they expand. I will use the term "urban villages" to indicate the villages surrounded by an urban area administered by a municipality. The land occupied by these villages has a special status by law. The use of village land is controlled by a village collective, not by the municipality, although according to the constitution of China, all land belongs "to the people" (i.e., the central government). But there is a difference between full ownership, which involves the ability to sell property, and ownership of land use rights only, which is limited to the right to develop land and to rent floor space or land to a third party. Villagers in China are free to set their own building standards and land use; they can rent land and whatever structure they build to a third party, but they cannot sell either the structure or the land. Only the government can acquire land from farmers by expropriation with compensation.

For Chinese farmers living in urban villages, therefore, the value of their land parcel is represented by the present value of the flow of rents generated by whatever structure they can build on this parcel. Contrary to farmers living in traditional market economies, they do not have any incentive to sell their land to a developer, as the compensation price they would receive from the government is likely to be less than the capitalized value of the flow of rents. This explains why villagers in China resist selling land to the government whenever they can, and many protest forcible acquisition.

When the built-up area of an expanding city reaches a village, the municipal government expropriates the fields around it but usually abstains from expropriating the village itself, as the compensation paid to villagers is based on a "replacement value" of the floor space demolished, while the fields are compensated based on the value of crops. Expropriating the village and providing alternative housing units is therefore much more expensive for government than expropriating open fields. As a result, villages are often initially spared demolition and become an enclaved urban village with a special status over the control of land use. As a city expands, the land value increases in the villages that were initially at the fringe of urbanization, to the point of becoming higher than the compensation to be paid to farmers for whatever structures they have built. The municipal government then tends to evict farmers after compensation or relocation and sell the land to developers. However, the process is long and cumbersome, and many urban villages survive a long time before redevelopment occurs.

Redevelopment of Villages Driven by Demand for Housing

While the village survives, the outcome is roughly similar to that in the Indonesian kampungs. That is, the villages form legal enclaves where the use of land is controlled by a small community—the village collective—that is independent of the municipality surrounding it. As in Indonesia, the land use within the village boundaries is driven by demand rather than by urban regulations designed by distant urban planners. As a result, land use standards—heights of buildings, areas of apartments, widths of streets—are the object of trade-offs reflecting the priority of the inhabitants as rents keep increasing as the cities expand.

Why Are Villages Major Suppliers of Low-Cost Housing?

Most of the residential land in formally developed areas over greenfields is auctioned to developers, who build and sell apartments as condominiums. Chinese developers usually do not build apartments for rental, as is done in US and European cities. The demand for apartments for sale comes from the newly affluent and well-educated city dwellers whose family have been living and working in cities for one or more generations. Recent migrants do not have the accumulated capital and regular income that would allow them to buy an apartment with a mortgage and a substantial down payment. Rental opportunities are few in the formal market.

In Chinese cities, therefore, the supply of housing units affordable to new migrants is mainly provided by rental units in urban villages. The standards and the rents of newly developed housing units constantly adjust to demand. As in Indonesia, some housing units might be overcrowded, they may have to share a bathroom with other units, but all of them have access to a safe water supply and sanitation, solid waste is removed regularly, and all housing units in urban villages are close to urban transport. Because urban incomes in China are much higher than in Indonesia, urban villagers can afford to build several-story buildings, if the projected flow of market rent is sufficient to ensure an attractive financial return.

Land use in a village collective is therefore entirely market driven, without any hindrances from regulations. Therefore, it evolves rapidly to reflect economic changes and the priorities of the prospective tenants. Chinese urban villages located in cities where incomes have risen rapidly are therefore a unique laboratory to observe what happens when urban land use standards are continuously being reevaluated as a function of changing rents. This is in contrast to the majority of cities in market economies, where land use is deliberately constrained by regulations to prevent changes, even when these changes would make economic sense and increase the welfare of the city.

Rapid Adaptation to Economic Changes in Shenzhen

In no other city in the world has economic change has been more rapid than in Shenzhen—a city with special economic status, created by Deng Xiaoping, China's leader from 1978 to 1989. The territory surrounding the fishing town of Shenzhen was declared a special economic zone in May 1980. This special status allowed markets to drive prices, rents, and salaries within the perimeter of the zone. This was truly revolutionary for China. Outside Shenzhen, at the time, salaries and prices were still largely fixed by governments, and housing was provided for a token rent by employers or municipalities. In Shenzhen, salaries were much higher than in the rest of China, but workers had to find housing on the market. Some employers provided dormitories for their workers, but a market rent was deducted from their salaries.[25]

In 1980, the town of Shenzhen itself had a population of only 30,000 people. However, it was surrounded by villages whose aggregate population numbered around 300,000 that were soon integrated into Shenzhen's labor market. By 2015, Shenzhen's population had reached 14 million people, having grown at an astonishing average yearly growth rate of 11 percent! The high productivity level of the Shenzhen labor force and the consequent higher salaries compared to the rest of China explain the rapid demographic growth rate. In 2014, Shenzhen per capita GDP reached US$25,000, the highest GDP per capita in China. The combination of free markets, a libertarian approach to housing standards in urban villages, and a very high population and household income growth rates produced Shenzhen's unusual low-income housing design that I describe below.

In the 1980s, the initial pattern of Shenzhen village streets was irregular and the lots uneven, with the majority of houses having two floors covered by a traditional tile roof. The original occupants of the village were farmers or fishermen. They were soon deprived of their farming land and of their fishing boat landings as the land was acquired by the government to develop the infrastructure, factories, administrative buildings, and formal housing that formed the backbone of Shenzhen economic development. The individual plots of land on which their houses were built were the only assets remaining to the former farmers and fishermen. By building additional rooms that could be rented at market prices to migrants, villagers could produce a flow of revenue that would more than compensate their former agricultural or fishing incomes. In less than 10 years, the job of Shenzhen's farmers changed from collective rural laborer to real estate investors, managers, and builders!

Many villages were located close to the new Shenzhen city center. They became soon close to newly built metro stations that provided access to many more jobs in a shorter commuting time. The demand for housing in the villages' favorable locations increased as more jobs were created within commuting distance. The demand for floor space from migrant workers became so high that it became difficult to increase the number of floors around the irregular street pattern of the original villages.

The Startling Physical Layout of Shenzhen Villages

To increase the potential return on the land they controlled, Shenzhen former farmers formed associations to pool their resources in land and capital, then redesigned and redeveloped their original irregular street layout to optimize the use of land. In the new design, the villagers were not constrained by regulations; instead they were guided only by their knowledge of the requirement of prospective residential or business renters and their own priorities, as most of the original villagers still live within the redesigned villages.

To obtain a higher ratio of floor space to land, villagers designed a grid pattern with square blocks of about 14 meters along the street axis. Street widths varied from a very low 2.6 to 6 meters. The footprint of buildings covered 100 percent of the lots. A staircase gave access to a central hall, with access to four apartments of about 22 square meters each, including a small kitchen and toilet. Lower floors located on the wider streets are often rented for retail shops, businesses, or even small manufacturing.

These types of new development were nicknamed "handshake" buildings because of the short distance between the windows of apartments on opposite sides of a street. On average apartment buildings were about seven floors high (figure 6.25). Within the village perimeter, the population density is about 3,000 people per hectare. By contrast, densities in most new urban residential developments in China are about 700 people per hectare.

The contiguous area of individual urban villages redeveloped as handshake buildings are limited to a few hectares per village. Apartment buildings are seldom more than five buildings removed from a main road with access to public transport. While the streets giving access to apartment blocks are extremely narrow and can give access only to construction and emergency vehicles, no block is farther away than about 80 meters from a main road.

The first Shenzhen urban villages redeveloped in this dense and unusual pattern were eventually copied by other villages in the metropolitan area, but to my knowledge, never outside Shenzhen. This suggests that this unusual residential design received wide acceptance from renters and owners in Shenzhen but also that the trade-offs that generate the design are also unique to Shenzhen.

There are regional cultural precedents for the high densities of handshake buildings. The old walled city of Kowloon was located in the Hong Kong Special Administrative Region, just 27 kilometers from Shenzhen. It was demolished in 1993. The old walled city had a similar structure and gave shelter to about 33,000

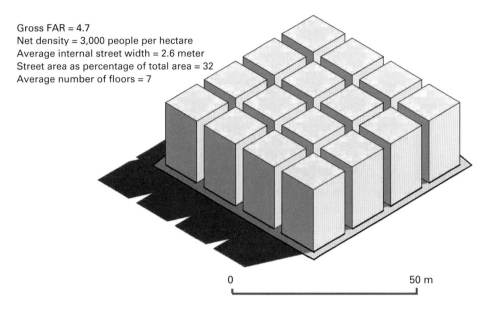

Gross FAR = 4.7
Net density = 3,000 people per hectare
Average internal street width = 2.6 meter
Street area as percentage of total area = 32
Average number of floors = 7

0   50 m

Figure 6.25
Three-dimensional view and typical land use of a Shenzhen handshake village.

people with a density of about 12,000 people per hectare on a total area of about 2.6 hectares, or about four times the density of Shenzhen handshake villages. The acceptance of high population densities depends more on cultural factors than on a normative rationale.

Design Evaluation
The physical layout of handshake housing is so unusual that it deserves some comments. I do not know of a city in any part of the world where this type of building could pass local land use regulations. However, the original design has been replicated with some variants across the Shenzhen area, demonstrating its appeal and acceptability. Walking through the alleys and streets of a handshake village is a unique experience of thriving intense urban life usually absent from "affordable housing" built to government norms. While the geometry of the hand-shake buildings offers few variations, except for an occasional wider commercial street, the inside of the identical buildings with their central hall on each floor allows for a maximum of flexibility. The rooms can be assembled in larger apartments or fragmented into individual smaller units of one room only.

The handshake buildings contradict everything we expect from a modern residential area in terms of abundant fresh air and green walking areas. Their design makes a deliberate extreme trade-off between maximum floor space on a minimum amount of land, in the best possible location to access a maximum number of jobs in a minimum commuting time. Is there any justification for the complete abandonment of public open spaces in a residential area? For reducing street dimensions and distance between buildings to the width of an emergency vehicle? To have windows through which the sun will never shine? The most radical architect-planner, including myself, would never dare propose such types of standards. Only the users themselves could generate such a radical residential design and justify these extreme trade-offs between open space and access to jobs and amenities.

From Ebenezer Howard to Le Corbusier, we have been taught to value fresh air, trees, and open space as the indispensable design attributes of residential areas. But Howard and Le Corbusier were themselves reacting to the nineteenth-century hovels produced by the Industrial Revolution in the dismal cold and humid climates of London and Paris. Their revolutionary proposals were linked to a historic moment and to a specific geographical location.

A review of the design of public housing around the world may suggest that Ebenezer Howard and Le Corbusier may have set residential norms that are permanent in time and universal across cultures, climates, and incomes. However, user-generated design, typified by Shenzhen handshake buildings, demonstrates that communities living in a completely different cultural, climatic, and technological contexts may select different values expressed as a set of new standards for what would constitute desirable housing. Indeed, the trade-offs that generated the handshake buildings make a lot of sense when seen in their urban and climatic context. It is quite understandable why the original Shenzhen farmers adopted this design and why many migrant workers compete to rent them.

Let us look at light, ventilation, and the absence of open space in the Shenzhen context. The climate of Shenzhen is tropical, usually hot and humid for about 8 months of the year. The average winter temperature in January doesn't fall below 13° C and hovers around 33° C in the summer months. This is not the climate of Dickens's London! Most of the urban villages are located close to the abundant well-landscaped public parks provided by the city. While the residents of urban villages are often workers with relatively low incomes, the rooms rented have a steady supply of electricity, all have fans, and increasingly they have air conditioning. The ubiquitous access to a steady electricity supply in a tropical country where direct sunlight into rooms is seldom desirable makes the Shenzhen handshake building design much more viable. Social gatherings take place in shared public spaces or in the numerous lively restaurants and tea houses found at street level. The function of apartments is reduced to places for sleeping and storing personal property. The apartment concept of handshake buildings is like cabins on a cruise ship—by the way, a model advocated by Le Corbusier himself after crossing the Atlantic on a trip to New York!

When residents of handshake buildings want fresh air and exercise, they can easily obtain it in parks within a walking distance from their houses. This is not the case in most areas of other large cities of Asia, where electricity is sporadic in low-income areas and public parks are nonexistent.

The design of handshake buildings allows many low-income households to have rapid access to a large number of jobs and to be close to numerous urban amenities, like shops, restaurants, and entertainment. In addition, the possibility of using the ground floor for small businesses increases the economic advantages of the area.

Let us compare the low-cost housing neighborhoods provided by the South African government's RDP with Shenzhen's handshake villages. In South Africa, experts designed comfortable houses surrounded by a small garden, but with poor access to jobs and amenities. The poor living there have plenty of fresh air, their children can play soccer in the streets or even in formal soccer fields, but they cannot access jobs without spending a large part of their incomes on transport. Streets are devoid of basic shopping amenities. The poor households living in these isolated neighborhoods are likely to stay poor, although in relative comfort. The workers in Shenzhen handshake buildings now have much higher incomes than their South African counterparts, but when they initially migrated to the city, most of them were as poor as the South African typical migrants. It is the access to multiple jobs and urban amenities that lifted them out of poverty. When designing a housing policy, we should remember that a city is above all a labor market. Ignoring the functioning of a labor market in providing housing creates poverty traps for the beneficiaries of housing projects.

While recognizing urban villages' contribution to the supply of affordable housing, Chinese municipal authorities are usually not thrilled by their existence. They mostly argue that urban villages are out of control. Indeed, they are. This is precisely the reason for their success. Some of the handshake buildings in Shenzhen no doubt shelter some illicit activities, like gambling, bootlegging, and prostitution. Because of the fluidity of the rental market, authorities have difficulties keeping track of people living in them. But these administrative problems have nothing to do with the narrowness of streets and the lack of sunlight. When Shenzhen's migrant workers' incomes increase to the point of allowing them to find a more desirable affordable alternative, they will certainly abandon handshake buildings. Meanwhile, it is premature to envisage eradicating an imperfect but popular housing model that gives shelter to millions. Governments eager to get rid of handshake buildings should first allow the building of alternative models, then wait to see whether they are successful before suppressing the only part of the housing stock currently affordable to new migrant workers. If attractive alternatives to handshake buildings existed in Shenzhen, their tenants would rapidly move out to the better-quality housing. The handshake building sites, empty of tenants, will then be ready for redevelopment. But before this happens, demolishing the only source of low-income rental housing would only harm the city and the welfare of its inhabitants.

Lessons from These Four Urban Examples

I have discussed above the performance of four types of low-income housing projects in Gauteng, New York, Surabaya, and Shenzhen. In the first two cities, the government substitutes itself for the market: in Gauteng, by building subsidized housing sold at a nominal price to low-income households; in New York, by obliging private developers to set aside some apartments at a rent set by the government as a function of the income of the beneficiary household. By contrast, in Surabaya and Shenzhen, the private sector builds housing for a price or a rent that households can afford. And since the trade-off between prices and standards are set by user preferences, the government's role is reduced to connecting these settlements to the city infrastructure and providing social facilities.

Let us summarize the outcome of the four policies. In Gauteng, the housing design standards are comfortable, but the location of the housing projects is such that the very long commuting times and high costs result in beneficiaries having a good chance of remaining unemployed. In New York, the location and housing design are both excellent, but there is no hope for the large number of potential beneficiaries ever having access to these attractive apartments except as winners of a lottery with very low odds.

In Surabaya, the housing designs range from poor to excellent, and the location allows residents to participate in the city labor market; the number of kampung housing units expands with demand as the city grows. In Shenzhen, the housing constitutes an adequate shelter: the location is excellent for participating in the labor market and having access to city amenities. The space standards adjust to what households can pay. Both Surabaya and Shenzhen have a wide range of incomes within the same housing project, thus avoiding income segregation.

These are only four case studies illustrating different approaches to the provision of "affordable" housing. Next let us review the different approaches that are possible for maintaining a housing stock that is affordable for the wide range of incomes found in successful cities.

Maintaining Housing Affordability: Quantifying, Monitoring, and Considering Alternative Policies

Here I summarize the various operational steps that a local government can take to improve the housing consumption of the lowest-income groups. The objective of a housing policy should be to increase housing consumption, understood as the optimum trade-off between location and floor space made by the end user. I may, however, use the term "affordable housing" as a short cut because of its wide use in the press and in the housing literature.

I have defined housing as "unaffordable" when housing absorbs an abnormally large part of households' income (say, when rent represents more than 35 percent of income) or when the housing standards that are affordable fall in quality or quantity below a socially acceptable standard. It is understood that this minimum socially acceptable housing standard may vary across cities and may vary in time within the same city. I will use this definition of affordability in the rest of this section.

Housing Markets and Government Interventions

Most cities of the world are now operating in a market economy. Housing is a consumer product. Well-functioning markets are supposed to respond to consumer demand and to supply housing in quantities and quality corresponding to demand. When there is evidence that the housing market does not do that, the government has to intervene, first to improve the functioning of markets, and eventually to supplement the income of the households that fall below an agreed-on housing consumption threshold.

The first government task is to find the cause of high housing costs. The second is to quantify the number of households affected by it (i.e., the number of households occupying unaffordable housing units). The third task is to develop a housing policy. Finally, the fourth task consists of constantly monitoring the impact of the selected policy on households' housing consumption.

The above appears rather obvious. However, most housing policy takes for self-evident that the poor housing conditions of lower-income households are due to market failure. Therefore, the first two tasks are ignored, and a housing policy is developed, consisting of ignoring markets and providing housing units at below market rents, whether these units are newly built or existing. We have seen that this approach has two drawbacks: It usually falls short in delivering the number of subsidized housing units needed, and it prevents households from exerting their choice among different options (including prices, housing standards, and location).

A recurring myth consists of declaring that the real estate industry would never provide low-income housing and is only interested by developing high-income housing. For the believers, it logically follows that the government has to be the monopolist provider of housing for a segment of the population. While this is true for the temporarily homeless, the observable evidence shows otherwise for the rest of the population. When regulations do not allow the formal market to provide affordable housing, the informal market takes over.

Before we discuss the interaction of government and markets in providing affordable housing, I want to make clear that I am not implying here that all housing issues can be solved through market solutions. Many cases of homelessness, for instance, particularly in affluent cities, stem from social welfare policies and require an immediate government action. It is important from the beginning to clearly separate emergency social welfare from housing policy. Too often, housing policy is conceived as an extension of social welfare applied to the middle class.

The Need for Emergency Shelter and Social Housing

In every large city, a small number of households—some may be one-person households—are unable to pay for their housing. They end up in the streets. These households may be permanently or temporarily disabled—physically or mentally—or may have experienced bad luck that results in long unemployment periods. It is certainly the duty of the government to provide a shelter for them as an emergency service. Once in an emergency shelter, social workers can identify those who are likely to be permanently unable to earn an income and then direct them toward a social housing shelter, where specialized staff will follow up on their case. Other homeless households may need only temporary help to find a job and a house they can afford before they rejoin the city's active population. The provision of homeless shelters is not part of a housing policy, as it has little to do with supply and demand.

In Large Cities, a Temporary Mismatch between Housing Supply and Demand Is Unavoidable

Urban housing prices are constantly adjusting to changes in supply and demand. An increase in housing demand is usually due to demographic changes—increases in population or decreases in household size—or to an economic change. An increase in household incomes will increase the demand for larger or more modern housing units. An increase in job creation will also increase demand for housing. There is not much a planner should do about increasing housing demand, except rejoice and monitor it carefully. Fortunately, the time is largely past when planners were trying actively to prevent urbanization by decreasing deliberately the housing supply.

Increases in housing demand—by itself a good thing—will have the effect of increasing housing prices, unless supply (the number of new houses built) increases immediately by the same quantity as demand. This is unlikely to happen because of the complexity of the supply chain that produces new housing units. Usually, the larger the city is, the longer it takes to acquire land, obtain financing, get development approval, and secure all the permits and inspections required to complete construction. Therefore, planners can expect to see housing prices rise when demand for housing unexpectedly increases. The actions or inaction of planners to these movements in housing demand will have a large impact on housing supply and therefore on housing prices.

Unfortunately, many planner initiatives, described below, often contribute to a decrease in or stagnation of the housing supply. Let us look at the housing supply chain, and where the more common bottlenecks are that prevent housing supply from responding to housing demand—and most importantly, what a planner can do about it.

Reforming the Supply Side Should Precede Demand Side Housing Subsidies

High housing prices are often due to constraints on the development of land and on the construction of floor space. In consumption sectors other than housing, the market usually responds adequately to demand coming from the wide range of income groups found in a city. This market response can be observed for the supply of clothing or food. Expensive designer clothing stores coexist with cheap or even second-hand clothing stores. In every city, shops supply designer shoes as well as cheap plastic sandals. The same can be observed for food: expensive and fast food restaurants are found side by side, while even cheaper meals can be bought from food carts. Fast food restaurants, catering to a wide range of incomes are even more likely to succeed than very expensive specialized restaurants.

Why should housing be different from other consumption products? I believe that land development and the construction sectors are uniquely constrained by the regulations that restrict the availability of developable land and the construction of floor space. I am here talking only about regulations that prescribe a minimum consumption of land (like FAR, building height, or building footprint) and a minimum consumption of floor space (like minimum dwelling area). Sometimes these regulations are not binding. A regulation is not binding when the demand is lower than the maximum imposed by the regulation. For instance, if a regulation requires all buildings to be lower than five floors in an area where there is no demand for tall buildings, the regulation is not binding.

All binding urban regulations increase the cost of housing—I insist: all binding regulations. Indeed, regulations always require builders to use more land than the market would require by fixing maximum FARs, maximum heights, and minimum lot sizes; and similarly to use more floor space by fixing minimum dwelling areas. Incredibly, regulations impose higher land consumption for consumers of housing, while at the same time they reduce the supply of developable land by putting arbitrary limits on city expansion (such as green-belts or urban growth boundaries). The result is predictably higher prices.

Removing regulatory barriers to city expansion is essential but it is not enough. As discussed in chapter 3, government has a de facto monopoly on the development of primary infrastructure—the network of trunk roads that transform greenfields into developable land. To maintain a responsive supply of developed land, municipalities must therefore finance and build the expansion of primary infrastructure into a city's periphery. With few exceptions, like the Texas Municipal Utility District bonds, many municipalities have no easy way to do that. Removing supply side constraints on housing will therefore require two types of government action: first, reforming what I will call the supply side (i.e., land use and building regulations), and second, creating easy to use mechanisms to finance and build infrastructure at the periphery of cities.

When the supply side is fully reformed and the real estate market functions satisfactorily, it is possible that a number of urban households might still be too poor to be able to afford a housing unit that meets the minimum socially acceptable standard. In this case, a direct addition to their income (i.e., a demand side subsidy program, such as housing vouchers) might be necessary. If demand side subsidy programs are started before the supply side reforms have been completed, it is likely that these subsidies will result in higher prices rather more housing. Indeed, demand side subsidies increase housing demand, and if housing supply is irresponsive because of regulatory barriers, we can only expect higher prices.

For a government rightly impatient "to do something" about high housing prices, waiting for supply side reform to take effect before providing direct assistance to low-income households through vouchers is particularly frustrating. The attempt at supply side regulatory reform in the United Kingdom described below is illustrative of the difficulties encountered when changing existing regulations, even when the sources of supply rigidity are extremely well analyzed and when feasible solutions are clearly proposed.

Reforming the Regulations That Constrain Housing Supply Is Very Difficult

Reforming existing land use regulations is not easy, precisely because of the impact of regulations on land prices. Current escalating land prices usually reflect constraints on land supply. Removing these constraints will reduce some land prices—which is precisely the objective. Obviously, owners of properties whose price will decrease because of the regulatory reforms will see a decrease in the capital value of their land assets. Banks that have used land as collateral for making equity loans might even be in jeopardy. While the overall welfare of society would improve (in particular the welfare of low-income households), land use reforms will create winners and losers. In the long run, there will be more winners than losers, but in the short run, the losers will be very vocal to prevent reforms, often in the name of saving the environment or preserving agricultural land. The recent attempt to reform land use in the United Kingdom provides a good example of the difficulty of reforming land use regulations.

In 2003, because of concerns that extremely high housing prices in the United Kingdom could create macroeconomic imbalances, the British government appointed Kate Barker, an economist and member of the Monetary Policy Committee of the Bank of England, to review housing supply in the country. In 2004, Kate Barker issued her report "Review of Housing Supply."[26] Her diagnostic was dramatic: "In 2001, the construction of new houses in the UK fell to its lowest level since the second world war. Over the ten years to 2002, output of new homes was 12.5 per cent lower than for the previous ten years." And "over the last 10–15 years, supply has become almost totally unresponsive, so as prices have risen, the supply of houses has not increased at all."

She found that the planning process was in large part responsible for this situation. Her extraordinary observation that *"One of the striking features of the local planning process is the lack of any reference to price signals"* could unfortunately apply to most planning process that I have known in affluent countries as well as in developing countries. The United Kingdom has been the birthplace of many world-renowned economists, from Adam Smith to John Maynard Keynes. It is striking to think that British urban planners and municipal managers have run cities without the help of urban economists who could have initiated them to supply and demand mechanisms.

In 2005, Kate Barker was asked to follow up on her first report and focus her recommendations on the planning process itself, as she had identified it as one of main bottlenecks in the housing supply. In 2006 she issued "Barker Review of Land Use Planning Final Report—Recommendations 2006."[27] Her findings and recommendations were more specific to the planning process but her main conclusion was: "The failure of planning to respond sufficiently to market and price signals, including the impact on land prices of restricted supply, needs to be addressed, particularly in the context of the likely contribution of land supply constraint to high occupation costs." She also mentioned the problem of financing and building new infrastructure to increase the supply of urban land: "there is particular concern that necessary infrastructure, including that which is environmentally desirable, is not being delivered quickly enough."

The report was well received and was commented on extensively in the press, academic circles, and Parliament. However, in 2014, 11 years after Kate Barker's initial report, three British economists, Paul Cheshire, Max Nathan, and Henry Overman, published the book *Urban Economics and Urban Policy: Challenging Conventional Policy Wisdom*, arguing that the urban planning bottlenecks identified by Kate Barker are still intact and are continuing to produce escalating housing prices. In a section of their book titled "Evidence of the Economic and Social Costs of the Current Planning System," they distinguish between direct and indirect costs of urban planning. The direct costs are limits put on construction and the transaction cost imposed by lengthy administrative processes; the indirect costs are the impact of planning restrictions on real estate market prices. The story of land use restrictions in the United Kingdom shows that the resilience of restrictive urban planning practices is extremely high, even when the issues and solutions has been very well described by respected and highly competent economists.

This sounds like a very pessimistic assessment of the possibility of regulatory reform, even in cities with a well-functioning local democracy, a free press, and a core of competent scholars and practitioners. It seems to confirm that in cities like San Francisco, London, or Mumbai that have set up very restrictive urban planning regulations, housing prices are bound to increase, and reforms that would bring them down are impossible to implement.

I have often compared very restrictive urban regulations to hard drugs and cities that practice them to drug addicts. Trying to suddenly remove their drug fix creates severe side effects, because their organism is used to the drug and needs it, even as they are being destroyed by it. My guess is that any serious reformer should approach urban regulatory reform in the same way as a doctor develops a treatment for a drug addict: a progressive withdrawal planned over the long term.

The main lesson to draw is that any city contemplating a drastic set of regulations to restrict floor supply and land development should carefully explore their possible negative side effects on housing prices before embarking on implementation. Kate Barker's two reports and Paul Cheshire's book should be compulsory reading for every urban planner concerned with housing price and housing affordability. In chapter 8, I will describe more in detail what, in my opinion, planners should do to improve their performance and their contribution to the management of cities.

7 Alternative Urban Shapes and Utopias

Could a city be designed and managed like a machine or a factory or around a social order different from markets? In the previous chapters I have expressed the view that cities grow mostly according to a self-organizing principle created by markets. I have recommended limiting the role of planners to fixing street rights-of-way and designing transport systems that serve the shape and densities created by markets. In this chapter, I explore the possible validity of an opposite view.

Can a rational argument be made for planners to deliberately modify through regulations the shape of cities that otherwise would be created by markets?

Should planners regulate land use to serve an objective that they set themselves? This objective could be aesthetic (like forcing the use of a traditional regional design style of architecture) or utilitarian (like setting by regulation a pattern of development and densities that would ensure the financial viability of a preferred public transport mode).

And finally, would it be desirable for a benevolent planner to design all aspects of a new city based on clearly expressed rational principles, the way machines or factories are designed?

The Search for an Objective Function That Could Guide Design

The main challenge in both cases—modifying existing cities or creating new ones—is to find the rational principle that will justify the shape modification or guide the design. While it is usually rather simple to define a rational objective to design an object that has a well-known and specific purpose, it is much more difficult to do so when designing a city whose objective is difficult to define.

Indeed, a city is very different from typical designed objects. Let us use a bridge as an example of a designed object. A bridge has a well-defined purpose that can be easily quantified. For instance, the span of the bridge will be 100 meters, it should handle four lanes of traffic, the vehicles will run at a maximum speed of 110 km/h, and the weight of each vehicle will not exceed 44 tons. A bridge engineer will be able to propose several designs that meet these clearly quantified objective criteria, with variances that minimize construction cost or make the design more aesthetically pleasing. The final design selected will respond to objective criteria that everybody agrees on. Differences in opinion will likely exist for variables not included in the objective criteria, for example, some may prefer a more elegant but costlier bridge over a cheaper but less pleasing design.

It would be difficult to apply an equivalent set of specifications to a city, because a city doesn't have a clear function that can be described by numbers, unlike a bridge, a washing machine, or a phone. Further, as discussed before, a city's main quality resides in its ability to evolve rapidly and to react to the outside world. A bridge, a washing machine, and a phone are not designed to evolve. When their design becomes obsolete, the bridge is demolished and the washing machine and phone are discarded and their materials hopefully recycled. The smartphones designed by Apple are famous for their design excellence, but nobody expects an iPhone 7 to evolve by itself into an iPhone 8. We just discard our old iPhones when an iPhone 8 appears on the market. The excellence of the design of iPhone 7 is only temporary, until a better design emerges that results in the abandonment of the previous model. History tells us that some cities have been discarded by their inhabitants: for example, Fatehpur Sikri in sixteenth-century India; more recently, 60 Russian cities abandoned by government fiat in the twenty-first century; or even a city like Detroit, so hopelessly mismanaged that it has been abandoned by its most mobile inhabitants. However, most of the time it is expected that cities will survive, even when they are tossed around by external shocks. "Fluctuat nec mergitur" is the motto of the City of Paris. It roughly translates as "it is tossed around but does not sink." This motto is the closest thing to an objective function for a city. However, this pseudoobjective function would certainly not be able to guide a designer of cities who is deciding the layout of streets and the height of buildings. A function that would be limited to requiring constant adaptation to external unpredictable forces is no longer an objective function. A city has to be submitted to a Darwinian evolutionary process, negating the very concept of design with a known finality.

In his book, *Antifragile*,[1] Nassim Nicholas Taleb introduces the concept of institutions and systems that can increase their resilience precisely when they are subjected to unpredictable random shocks. Taleb argues that by trying to protect systems from shocks, we fragilize them and eventually contribute to their destruction. Taleb's insight can be applied to cities. The failure of Mumbai's cotton mills, described in chapter 3, could be attributed to the government fragilizing the city— rather than taking measures to adapt to change and external shocks. Trying to protect a city (or a country) from external shocks by building a protective wall around it is a fool's errand. Cities are thriving by multiplying exchanges with the world: Cut them off from the world and they will waste away. Herbert Spencer illustrates this principle in a flippant way: "The ultimate result of shielding men from the effects of folly, is to fill the world with fools."[2]

Unfortunately, urban planners have not been discouraged by the extreme difficulty of defining a function that will guide city design. Attempts to codify these objective functions—and to justify attempts to design a city—are typically done through initial blueprints or ongoing regulations.

The Search for the Objective Function of a City

We have seen in chapter 3 that, in the 1950s, Chinese planners' attempts at using the angle of the sun over the horizon to define "rationally" the distance between buildings resulted in a silly outcome, with urban residential densities fixed solely by latitude rather than by the complex interaction of land prices, transport technology, topography, history, income, and cultural preferences.

Planners who choose to dismiss the market forces that have shaped cities for centuries must replace them with a credible objective function. It is not a simple task, as we will see. In this chapter, I identify the objective functions that are currently used or have been used in the past to modify or replace the city shape that would have resulted from market outcomes. I will concentrate on four kinds of objective functions currently used to justify planners' intervention in the spatial development of cities:

• aesthetics as the objective function (e.g., Paris historical preservation),
• limiting externalities or public interest as objective functions (e.g., New York zoning regulations),
• containing urban expansion as the objective function, and
• aspirations as objective functions (e.g., sustainability, livability, and resilience).

After identifying the design objective function and the way it is applied (whether through initial plans or ongoing regulations), I then test the outcome to compare it to the objective. To be of any use in guiding city design, an objective function must be expressed clearly, and the outcome has to be measurable.

Aesthetics as Objective Function: Paris Historical Preservation

Most of Paris's[3] land use regulations are explicitly aimed at preserving the aesthetic of historical Paris. The last large transformation of Paris started in 1854 with the urban surgery conducted by Baron Haussmann and ended during the Universal Exhibitions of the Fin de Siècle that gave Paris the Eiffel Tower (1889) and the Grand and Petit Palais (1900).

This period of rapid urban transformation was followed by a public consensus on the need for historical preservation of what had been built so far and an aversion to additional transformation of the Paris urban landscape. The only changes to the Paris skyline occurred during the last part of the twentieth century. These modern era changes were limited to the construction of four isolated state-sponsored "monuments" rather than large-scale urban development: the destruction and periodic redesign and rebuilding of les Halles (1971–2016), the Tour Montparnasse (1973; the only skyscraper in Paris), the Pompidou Museum (1977), and the Bibliothèque Nationale de France (1988). In addition, some increase in height and limited and very controlled development was tolerated in the Paris fringe, like part of the fifteenth arrondissement. These few minor changes to Paris skyline were generally received with scorn by public opinion and the press. A popular consensus seemed to have emerged supporting the maintenance of the status quo in the appearance of the Paris streetscape.

The Objective of Most of the Paris Land Use Regulations Is to Maintain a Fin de Siècle Landscape

To preserve the landscape of fin de siècle Paris, the municipality created a set of elaborate regulations that maintains the continuity of facade and perspectives of historical Paris even for buildings that are newly built and have no historical significance. However, contrary to many zoning regulations in other cities, the regulations are not so much concerned with preventing internal land use changes but are instead largely focused on the appearance and alignment of buildings facing the streets.

Since the beginning of the twentieth century, Parisians have decided that the main virtue and attraction of Paris was to stay identical through time. Regulations dictate the height of buildings, the alignment and material of roofs, traditional street facades, and anything that could change the appearance of Paris streets. In reality, Paris is changing continuously, but only within its historical facades as the use of a building or even part of a building easily can be changed from residential to commercial and back again. The building envelope is frozen, but within this envelope land use changes are often rapid. Paris is like a set of boxes; the boxes do not change but their content does. This immobility concerns only Paris municipality, limited by the extent of Paris Boulevard Peripherique, itself following the lines of fortifications during the siege of the city during the Franco-Prussian war of 1870. The population of Paris municipality represents only about 18 percent of the Paris metropolitan population.

The economic growth of Paris has been possible, in spite of the freezing of the built envelope of historical Paris, due to the rapid growth of suburban Paris.

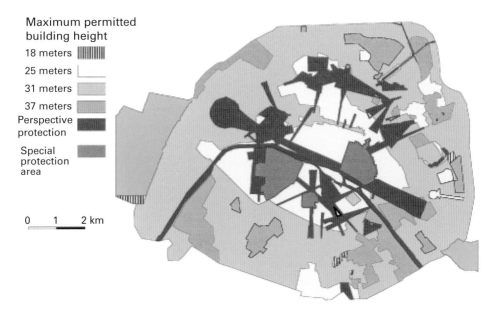

Maximum permitted building height

18 meters

25 meters

31 meters

37 meters

Perspective protection

Special protection area

0   1   2 km

Figure 7.1
Map of regulatory heights within Paris municipality.

Suburban Paris is much less regulated, and the government has actively promoted and subsidized some high-density developments, like La Defense business district and the five "new cities" within commuting distance of central Paris that are served by an elaborate system of rapid rail transit and highways.

Let us focus now on the height restrictions that have the most impact on the shape of Paris and on real estate prices. Figure 7.1 displays the permissible maximum heights of buildings in the Paris municipality.[4] The range of permissible heights varies from 18 meters to 37 meters. The highest permissible buildings therefore have about 10 floors and are mostly located in the periphery of the municipal area. The height regulations impose short buildings in the most ancient areas of Paris, like the Marais and the sixth arrondissement. These areas, where floor space is the most restricted by regulations, are also among the most accessible areas of Paris because of their centrality and the convergence of an elaborate system of public regional transport. In this sense, Paris regulations completely contradict expected market forces: They prevent the increase of floor space in areas of high demand and force densification in peripheral areas and outside the municipal limits where demand is low. However, Paris regulations do not pretend to alleviate traditional externalities like congestion or to increase economic growth. They are explicitly aimed at maintaining intact an aesthetic, historical, and prestigious cityscape. In that, they indisputably succeed.

Height restrictions are common to many cities. However, it is rare for a large capital city to restrict building to a maximum of 10 floors and even fewer floors in its most central area. What is even more uncommon is to have restrictions not only on building height measured from the street level but also in some areas measured from the sea level. This is the case in some areas of Paris shown in red in figure 7.1. These special regulatory areas, named "fuseaux de Protection" (perspective protection), are very specific to Paris and require some explanation.

These red areas are special protection areas where the altitude from sea level of the top of buildings is restricted as opposed to the height of buildings measured from the level of the streets in the yellow areas of figure 7.1. These special zones are established to protect the perspective view from different parts of the city toward landmark monuments (Hôtel des Invalides, Sacré-Coeur de Montmartre, Notre-Dame de Paris, Panthéon, etc.). In these special protection zones, the permissible height as measured from the street level varies continuously, depending on the location of the building in the zone and depending on the topography.

The example shown in figure 7.2 illustrates this point. Between A, on the edge of the Seine river, and B, the monument whose perspective view is to be protected, the maximum allowable height of buildings is determined by an oblique plane passing through A and B and shown as the line AB. The heights of A and B that define the line AB are not measured from local street levels but from altitude from sea level. The topography of Paris is hilly; consequently, the permissible height of buildings between A and B will vary as a function of street levels. On the graph, we see that because of the different altitudes of streets levels the height of buildings may vary from 17 to 25 meters. The enforcement of such rules requires an extremely detailed survey of the entire area. However, the regulations as formulated are highly effective at preserving perspective viewpoints for the main monuments of Paris.

This perspective protection constitutes an enormous constraint on the development of the central area of Paris. Imagine what midtown New York would look like if regulations required that St. Patrick Cathedral had to be visible from Central Park and from Washington Square!

The Objectives and Cost of Height Regulations in Paris

When evaluating regulations, two aspects should be investigated: first, whether the objectives of the regulation are met and, second, the benefits and costs to the city. Let us see how this applies to the control of building heights in Paris.

The objectives of Paris height regulations are very clear: they are purely based on aesthetic protection of historical Paris. The objectives are not limited to the protection of individual monuments but extend to the protection of monumental perspectives in the tradition of French classical seventeenth-century architecture.

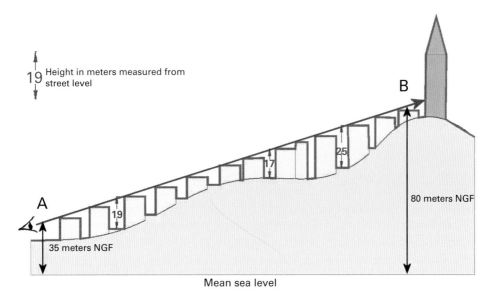

Figure 7.2
Regulation of altitudes of the tops of buildings in areas of protection. Meter NGF (Nivellement General de la France) measured from sea level.

The geometry, at time complicated to establish, is also clear and creates a regulatory envelope defined by an array of points whose Cartesian coordinates are well defined by their altitudes from sea level, as established by the general survey map of the country. Do the regulations achieve their declared objectives? Clearly, yes. The objective is the regulatory geometry itself. One could argue whether the perspective from a specific location of Paris adequately protects a monument like the Sacré Coeur of Montmartre, for instance, but these are only details. The objectives are certainly consistent with the formulation of the regulations.

What Are the Benefits of the Height Regulations?

The benefits of draconian heritage conservation are obvious; Paris is a city that attracts many visitors. In 2015, Paris was the most visited city in the world. The preservation of the perspective on the monuments and streets of Paris are certainly a part of the attraction. The well-preserved historical settings and carefully maintained extensive urban perspectives are an excellent background for the luxury goods for which Paris is famous: fashion, art, and gastronomy. In this sense, the benefits are much larger than the simple tourist revenue: They establish Paris as a desirable location for headquarters of luxury brands. The aesthetics of its large parks and avenues enhance the quality of life of the people who can afford to live and work there. The high benefits of maintaining Paris streets as they were at the time of the Impressionists implies that what modern architects could design to replace them would be inferior in aesthetic quality compared to what architects achieved in the nineteenth century. It is rather humbling for modern architects, but probably true.

And What Are the Costs?
What costs are implied by these regulations? Obviously, the regulatory heights create an envelope that severely limits the construction of new floor space in Paris, and they do so precisely in the area where there is most demand and where an extensive network of public transport converges. In addition, the quality of life enhancement provided by the regulations makes Paris even more attractive. The regulations clearly work against market forces: the floor area in the location generating the most demand for both firms and households is not allowed to grow. The supply of floor space limited by regulations pushes real estate prices higher as the economy of the city keeps growing. The obvious impact of the regulations is on real estate prices, resulting in a reduction in floor consumption per household—we have seen in chapter 4, that "apartments" of 9 square meters were renting for US$750 per month in 2014.

The scarcity, combined with the environmental quality, induced by regulations has created a continuous process of gentrification. Traditionally, the arrondissements[5] located in the western and southern parts of the city were considered bourgeois, while the arrondissements to the east and north were considered working class. In 2016, the entire area within Paris municipality is becoming bourgeois. The distinction is now between type of bourgeoisie: "old bourgeois" like the sixteenth arrondissement or "bourgeois-bohemian" like the nineteenth or twentieth. This massive gentrification is a direct result of the land use regulations that restrict the construction of additional floor space while making Paris more attractive. Middle- and low-income households who were traditionally living in the eastern and northern arrondissements are obliged to progressively move out toward the suburbs outside the municipal boundary, limiting their access to transportation and jobs in the city center. The municipality of Paris is attempting to slow down gentrification by purchasing apartments in old buildings and renting them below their market value to middle-income households. However, the impact of such rearguard action against gentrification is very limited because of its high cost.

The restrictions on building height in Paris have therefore contributed to shaping the city in a way that was not part of the regulations' objectives. Paradoxically, regulations, aimed at freezing the building envelope of the city as it was at the end of the nineteenth century, have resulted in two large spatial changes. The first one is an exile of the middle class and lower-middle class to outside the municipal boundary, and the second is a spread of many jobs toward the periphery. The population in Paris municipality peaked in 1921 at 2.9 million people. In 2014 it was 2.2 million. The number of jobs in Paris municipality has also decreased.

How Are the Regulations "Redesigning" the Paris Metropolitan Area?

How can a major world capital like Paris survive without the possibility of vertical expansion that has characterized other large cities, such as São Paulo, New York, London, Shanghai, and Seoul? The government has deliberately built a new CBD—La Defense—outside the Paris municipal boundary, 10 kilometers to the west of the traditional Paris CBD to absorb the demand for new office space that could not be accommodated in the center of Paris because of the height regulations. In addition, the government also created five new cities on the periphery to concentrate public facilities serving the suburbs and to attract commercial growth along public transport axes. All these new mini-CBDs have been linked by rapid transit to the capital subway network. Figure 7.3 shows the spatial trend in job location in the Paris metropolitan area, away from Paris municipality and around suburban transport nodes. Between 1996 and 2006 Paris municipality lost 1,700 jobs while 221,000 new jobs were created in the immediate periphery, most of them within 5 kilometers of the Paris municipal boundary, as shown in figure 7.3.

If there had been no limits to building heights, or rather if the height limits had been like the ones imposed on New York, London, Shanghai, or Seoul, there would have been more office and residential floor space built in Paris. While the free market creates a dispersion of jobs in the periphery and an increase in real estate value in the center in many large cities, the Paris height regulations accelerated and increased this market-driven trend.

It is ironic that Paris historical preservation regulations aim at preserving a type of land use that other regulations would forbid outside the historical Paris perimeter! For instance, local land use regulations would prevent any developer from reproducing the pattern of streets, building heights, and site coverage found in the most expensive neighborhoods of historical Paris, like Le Marais or the St Germain des Pres area.

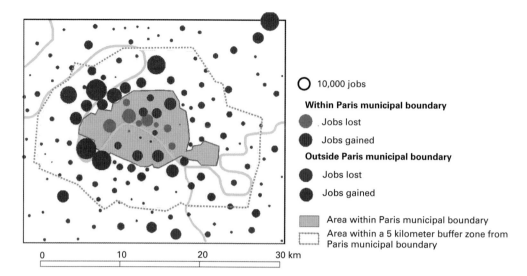

Figure 7.3
Jobs gained and lost in the Paris municipal area and immediate suburbs, between 1996 and 2006.
Source: Chambre régionale de commerce et d'industrie, Institut national de la statistique et des études économiques, Institut d'aménagement et d'urbanisme de d'Île-de-France, 2008.

A Final Assessment: Are the Regulations Protecting Historical Paris "Bad" or "Excessive"?

Paris is a special case, where land use regulations are mostly guided by the desire for historical preservation and special priority is given to monumental perspective effects that restrict the heights of buildings. For the development of the city, these are extreme constraints that are very costly for firms and for households. However, they create a quality of life that is unique and is reflected by the very high real estate prices.

To quote the American economist Steve Malpezzi, "regulations per se are neither good nor bad. What matters is the cost and benefit of a specific regulation under specific market conditions."[6] I will add another criterion to judge regulations: Do they meet their declared objectives? The worst regulations are those that have a high cost while not meeting their objectives.

The declared objectives of the Paris building heights regulations are extremely clear: maintaining Paris city center as it looked at the time of the Impressionists. There is no pretense, as in many other regulations, that preventing the transformation of existing buildings would prevent congestion or would protect the environment. There is a clear honesty in the regulations and their outcome. Parisians complain about the high cost of housing and the tiny size of apartments. However,

I believe that no mayor could ever be elected in Paris if she or he proposed to do away with the current height restrictions. In the case of Paris, it would be possible to calculate the cost of height regulations but much more complex to calculate the benefits that are mostly aesthetic. Every Parisian is aware of these nonquantifiable benefits and, so far, is willing to pay their costs. However, the gentrification that progressively will prevent low- and middle-income households from living in the municipal boundary is a much more serious social problem. No amount of social housing with below-market rents, as promoted by the municipality, could reverse meaningfully the gentrification trend.

In this book, I have often compared markets versus design. In Paris, the opposition between the two concepts is clear. There is a very large market demand for floor space in Paris municipality. Current regulations impose a design that prevents floor space supply to respond to this demand. But the regulatory tool used to design the city is transparent, and its objective clearly formulated.

My final conclusion on Paris building height regulations is that they are very costly, but they successfully do exactly what they are supposed to do. In this case therefore, there is no reason to pass a technical judgment on the regulations. The maintenance or relaxation of the regulations belongs to the political domain. Do Parisians feel that they are paying too high a price for these regulations or that the price they pay is well worth it? This can be expressed freely during municipal elections. The job of the planner is to explain the cost of regulations, not to approve or disapprove of them.

Limiting Externalities or Public Interest as Objective Functions: New York Zoning Regulations

New York built its first skyscraper in 1888, at about the time that Paris's golden construction age was about to end. While Paris was opting to freeze its historical skyline, New York, mostly in Manhattan, embarked on vertical expansion that continues today at an accelerating pace. The emergence of skyscrapers in New York was not due to the implementation of an inspired urban planner's vision, like the Plan Voisin that Le Corbusier proposed for Paris in 1920 (as discussed in chapter 3), but instead was the product of market forces. Although the individual builders and architects that built the skyscrapers were certainly creative, inspired, and talented, they only responded with great competence to their clients' demands for buildings that provided a high concentration of office space on a small lot.

The high price of land in the Wall Street area and the difficulty of expanding (except to the north) were powerful incentives to explore ways to stack large areas of office space vertically. The management of large companies needed many accountants and "scriveners," whose collated work would feed aggregated data to executives, enabling them to make timely business decisions. The circulation of information was done nearly entirely through ledgers and documents written on paper that had to be physically carried from the various departments to management and back. The high-rise building was particularly appropriate for facilitating this type of communication.

While the construction of skyscrapers was induced by market forces, changes in technology, like the invention of steel frame construction and elevators, allowed it to happen. In addition, no developer could have built a very tall building without the availability of generous credit from banks. All these preconditions, technological and financial, were met in New York at the end of the nineteenth century.

Skyscrapers were initially conceived exclusively for office buildings; it was only much later that the skyscraper was considered fit for residential use. Today in New York, out of 17 skyscrapers built or under construction between 2010 and 2016, eight are either mixed use or entirely residential. In addition, a few older skyscrapers in the Wall Street area recently have been converted to residential use.

The story and evolution of the skyscraper would constitute a book by itself, and no book written on the subject is as complete and interesting as Jason Barr's "*Building the Skyline*" published in 2016.[7] In his book, Barr, a professor of economics at Rutgers University, provides a comprehensive history of the emergence of skyscrapers in New York, the regulations that followed, and the dialectic that established itself among regulations, developers, economics, and skyscraper design. Although Barr's book focuses exclusively on Manhattan, it is one of the most comprehensive books on the interaction among design, markets, regulations, and technology in the development of cities. The sequence and content of New York land use regulations described in the following paragraphs is largely based on my interpretation of Jason Barr's insights, together with my own insights from working for the Urban Design Group of the New York City Planning Commission in 1968–1969 in the Mayor Lindsay administration.

The first skyscraper built, a modest 12 floors, caused wonderment but also worries. We would now call it a disruptive technology in that era. The negative effects on neighbors were evident: the skyscraper obstructed direct sunlight to adjacent buildings. At the end of the nineteenth century, artificial light was expensive. A tall new building casting a shadow on other shorter office buildings generated a cost that could be quickly evaluated in terms of an increase in artificial lighting costs. It was natural that citizens asked the local government to step in and regulate the dimensions of skyscrapers to decrease the clear negative externalities they caused on the neighborhood.

New York land use regulations concerning the buildings' "bulk"[8] started appearing at the beginning of the twentieth century because of the proliferation of ever taller skyscrapers. The comprehensive zoning plan of 1916 aimed to regulate the size of buildings by putting restrictions on buildings' bulk (i.e., altering the shapes of buildings to decrease their impact on neighbors). These restrictions varied, depending on the use of the zone where the buildings were located. The regulations were mostly entirely concerned with correcting the negative externalities created by the shadow of tall buildings, and to a lesser extent, sidewalk congestion. The regulations of 1916 related the heights of buildings to the width of street but gave height "bonuses" to developers providing setbacks from the street. However, many exceptions existed, such as if a skyscraper's footprint was no larger than 25 percent of the plot it occupied and if it was set back from the street, its height was not limited.

As observed by Jason Barr when commenting on the 1916 plan, "the plan represented the outcome of negotiations between the real estate industry, business owners, city planners, and government officials."[9] This is still the way new regulations are established in New York, as illustrated by the development of the Hudson Yard project on the west side of Manhattan in 2016. The success of New York as one of the major business centers of the world, maintained for more than a century, is based on this conversation between real estate developers and urban planners. However, as we will see, since 1964, complex regulation overlays and lengthy change approval processes have been applied in such a way that, to quote Jason Barr again, "large public buildings like new subways or new zoning regulations seem impossible today. A severe status quo bias has set in as we resist and fear large-scale changes that were embraced to build New York into the world's greatest metropolis."

The Turning Point in 1961: Planners Using Regulations to "Design" the City

The regulations of 1916 limiting the bulk of buildings were clearly aimed at decreasing obvious negative externalities caused by the shadows cast by tall buildings. Over the years, many amendments were made to the original regulations, but the objectives remained the same: reducing negative externalities caused by the height of buildings.

A turning point occurred in 1961 when a new zoning plan was published. The objectives of the new plan were explicitly aimed at modifying the shape of the city, and were no longer limited to decreasing negative externalities. Increasingly, planners used regulations to substitute their design for market forces in shaping cities. To be able to shape the city, the city's urban planners declared that they were acting in the public interest, which is far too vague a concept to be an objective for guiding human-made design. The notion of public interest is subjective and cannot be quantified as was possible when regulations aimed at reducing the impact of shadows cast by buildings.

Under the new 1961 zoning, planners were using regulations to achieve those new "design quality" objectives. The "shaping" objective is clearly acknowledged on the current New York City Urban Planning website with a topic named "Introduction & Shaping New York City through Zoning, 1961 to the Present."[10] The prime objective of zoning has become shaping the city, that is, "quality urban design" or possibly optimizing land use. It is an enormous departure from the original objective of zoning, but it seems that at the time nobody noticed the implications for the city.

In a democratically elected city administration, planners cannot simply impose the design they prefer on the developers of private buildings. However, in a very dynamic and innovative city like New York, where change is a constant necessity, it becomes possible to impose a city planners' design on a private developer by setting regulations that would allow an increase in floor area only on condition of modifying the design of a building and its use according to the wishes of the planners.

For instance, let us imagine that a city's planners think that a plaza open to the public but built on private land would make the city more pleasant and is therefore desirable. Expropriating the land required to create the plaza is out of the question. However, if a zoning regulation has been set to limit the floor area of the building, the city could then allow an increase in floor area above the current legal limit, on the condition that the new larger building meets the design requirement (a plaza open to the public) highly desired by planners. The developer is presented with a choice: be limited to the current floor space allowed by zoning, or build a plaza and be given a floor area "bonus" that will increase the buildable floor space of the land parcel.

If the developer thinks that the bonus is worth it (e.g., allows the developer to make additional profit), the regulations will then have created an open plaza, whose dimension and design can be decided by city planners and not by the developer. A new city amenity has been created at apparently no cost to the taxpayers. We will see below that it is not the case.

This system of design through regulation may provide leverage to planners only if two conditions are met: first, the building for which it is applied is in a location where there is a high demand for new commercial or residential floor space; second, the planners' design request may not be so extravagantly costly to the developer that no new building would be financially possible when the conditions are met. We are back to Jason Barr's remark that in New York, regulators and developers must consult each other so that the constraints imposed by the former do not bankrupt the latter. The more constraining the regulations are that limit the size of existing buildings, the more leverage the planners will have to design the city through regulations.

So planners who want to have regulatory leverage to impose their design on developers should have a clear strategy. First, limit the use and bulk of building as close as possible to the current one to prevent "free" addition of floor space; second, provide a generous increase in buildable floor area compared to the area allowed by regulations in exchange for land use change and any other design attribute that the planners might desire. Zoning regulations that would allow much more floor area than the area of existing buildings and flexibility in land use would provide no leverage for planners to request design features that the developers are unwilling to provide. By contrast, a regulatory-induced shortage of floor space increases the price of floor space and therefore increases the leverage of planners over developers.

Where draconian limits on floor space expansion in areas of high demand are imposed, planners have then the leverage to "design" the city by providing floor area bonuses in exchange for desired land use change. For instance, planners can impose the inclusion on private land of plaza and open spaces, whose design they may specify. They may also impose the addition of a certain type of land use, for instance, shops on the ground floor, or "affordable housing" whose characteristic and number they can specify, as described in chapter 6. Here we are very far from correcting the clear negative externalities that justified the first New York zoning regulations of 1916!

Planners' Attempts to Shape Private Buildings Have a Cost

Any modification in the design of a building has a cost, and potentially a benefit, although no money is exchanged. The design changes imposed by zoning would be justified if the benefits are higher than the costs.

Three cases are possible: the planners' imposed design increases the value of the building more than its cost; the design does not increase the value of the building but provides benefits to others; and finally, the design does not provide benefits for anyone. If the addition of a design feature, like a public plaza, would increase the market value of a building, it is most probable that the developer would have already included it in the initial design. If the plaza does not increase the value of a building but improves the street experience of passers-by, then the city is asking the building's users—households or firms—to pay through increased rents for a benefit accruing to the city's general population. It concentrates the cost of a public facility on a few citizens. The planners' imposed design therefore always increases the cost of new buildings and therefore most probably decreases the quantity of floor that would have been built if the design constraints did not exist.

By using FAR regulations to impose restrictions on the flow of additional floor area that can be built in a city, planners are de facto creating a new currency, consisting of bonus additional floor space that they will use to purchase from developers the urban design feature they desire—plazas, affordable housing, or

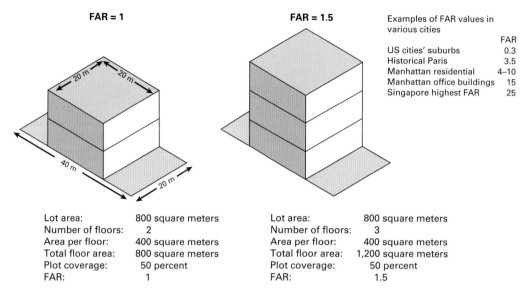

FAR = 1

FAR = 1.5

Examples of FAR values in
various cities

	FAR
US cities' suburbs	0.3
Historical Paris	3.5
Manhattan residential	4–10
Manhattan office buildings	15
Singapore highest FAR	25

Lot area:	800 square meters
Number of floors:	2
Area per floor:	400 square meters
Total floor area:	800 square meters
Plot coverage:	50 percent
FAR:	1

Lot area:	800 square meters
Number of floors:	3
Area per floor:	400 square meters
Total floor area:	1,200 square meters
Plot coverage:	50 percent
FAR:	1.5

Figure 7.4
How floor area ratio (FAR) is calculated.

anything else. The higher the scarcity of floor space, the higher is the value of the
bonus FAR currency, and therefore the higher the design variations planners can
purchase from developers (figure 7.4). The FAR bonus will have a high exchange
value only if the regulations are sufficiently restrictive to maintain a scarcity of
floor space. If the supply of floor space were completely elastic, then the value of
"bonus FAR currency" would lose its value, and eventually fall to zero. Planners
would then lose all leverage over developers. Thus the practice of incentive
bonus FARs requires maintaining a tight supply of floor space over an entire
city that increases the price of commercial and residential floor space for all firms
and households. As we have seen in chapter 6, the few so-called affordable housing units created by inclusive zoning FAR bonuses distributed through lottery
does not justify increasing the price of housing and commercial space for everybody else.

The Origin of Incentive Zoning: The Seagram Building in Manhattan
The Seagram Building was built in 1958 in New York, just before incentive zoning
of 1961 was invented. It was designed by the German-American architect Ludwig
Mies van der Rohe to meet his client's demand for a prestigious corporate headquarters representative of the International Style, the post-World War II offshoot
of the Bauhaus movement. The skyscraper of 38 floors included an open plaza,

facing Park Avenue at the center of midtown Manhattan. The quality of the design of the skyscraper and its plaza made the Seagram building an icon for good urban design and became a textbook example of enlightened corporate architecture. This was exactly what the owner of the Seagram building wanted to achieve and the reason they hired Mies van der Rohe as its architect.

By pure luck, my first job in the United States in January 1968 was located in the office of the architect Philip Johnson at the top floor of the Seagram Building, and I can testify that working in such a building and taking my lunch break on the plaza was an extraordinary experience. The Seagram had a well-deserved reputation of exemplary urban design. It also created a new category of land use: privately owned public space.

New York urban planners thought that by using clever regulations, they could replicate Mies van der Rohe's excellent design, and that it would be desirable to do so. Obviously, they could not mandate developers to replicate it, but they could create regulatory incentives to reproduce the plaza and create new privately owned public spaces at no cost to taxpayer money.

City planners decided to use the regulatory tool of FAR bonuses as an incentive to incite developers to build plazas similar to the one found in front of the Seagram Building. Originally, new regulations stipulated that for every square foot of urban plaza created, developers could get 10 square feet of saleable space in addition to the floor area they were entitled to under current zoning. The maximum floor area bonus obtainable, though, was limited to an additional 20 percent of the permissible floor area under current zoning.

The regulatory incentive set by planners did work. Several new skyscrapers were recessed from the street and provided public open space in front of the building. However, the attractiveness of the open space provided never matched the one offered by the Seagram building. For instance, on Sixth Avenue, between 47th and 50th streets, three consecutive plazas were built. But because they were next to each other on the same side of the avenue, they didn't provide the feeling of an open plaza but just a widening of the avenue. In addition, because the plazas were designed mostly to obtain an additional floor bonus, not to improve the quality of the building, the design of the plazas—streetscape, flowerbeds, and steps—seemed to be placed to discourage use rather than to serve as a pedestrian attraction. Indeed, privately owned public space has a number of considerations: it may be subject to lawsuits by users, and it must be privately maintained and policed, creating a potential liability and a sizable additional maintenance cost. Making the plaza unattractive to "vagrants" and even to passers-by somewhat decreases the potential for liability and the cost of maintenance. Subsequently, New York urban planners tried to tighten rules and expand the detailed specifications for the design of plazas in the pursuit of more effective privately owned public spaces. However, it is difficult to get good urban design just by regulation. The website of New York City Department of City Planning recognizes as much when it mentions that "the open spaces created by incentive zoning provisions have not always been useful or attractive."[11]

Do these "not always useful or attractive" plazas have a cost? After all, they were created by a few paragraphs added to the zoning code, clearly not a significant expense for the city budget. However, any architectural or urban design feature created through incentive zoning has a cost to the developer that is eventually passed on to the user. If the developers thought that these features would add to the value of a building, they would not have required an incentive to create them. For instance, the plaza of the Seagram building was built without incentive, because it added value to the building and its cost was considered less than the value it added. Commonly, developers add height to the lobby of prestigious office buildings and cover the walls with marble without requiring incentive. They do that because the additional cost is less than the value added. Incentive zoning adds two types of cost to the floor space built in a city. First, the capital cost and the recurring maintenance cost of the feature added because of the incentive, a cost borne mostly by the buildings' users, owners, or tenants. The second type of cost is borne by all the city's inhabitants and workers and results from the intentional shortage of floor space (due to restrictive regulations) that must be created for the incentive to work. Therefore, New Yorkers pay for the cost of these "not always useful or attractive" plazas. Let us not forget that incentive zoning can work only by creating a general shortage of floor space and releasing it slowly only for buildings that have features that planners would consider useful and attractive.

Did planners learn from this failure? Not really. In November 2011, to celebrate the fiftieth anniversary of the 1961 zoning resolution, the New York City Department of City Planning organized a conference "to cultivate new thinking about zoning as a governmental tool that may be used to address major economic, social, environmental, and physical challenges."[12] The various presentations described how zoning could make the city more "competitive, equitable, and sustainable." We are far from the use of regulations to correct tall buildings' negative externalities: shadows and sidewalk overcrowding. I challenge any planner to explain how severely restricting the bulk of buildings and releasing it piecemeal for some preferred usage and dimensions would make the city more competitive, equitable, and sustainable—even if quantitative indicators could be developed for these objectives. Adding new fuzzy objectives to zoning regulations will only add more complicated restrictions on the use of land and floor space.

Let us not forget that zoning can only restrict buildings' dimensions and types of use. When added to zoning, floor area bonuses act as a bribe to add building elements or usage that would not happen otherwise. By definition, the design through regulations promoted by floor area bonuses cannot be innovative, as they always promote the replication of an architectural feature or a usage from an existing building that particularly pleased urban planners. The Seagram Building plaza was innovative—it was built at the initiative of the architect. The plazas in front of the Sixth Avenue Midtown buildings were just bad copies of a past innovation. The practice of floor area ratio bonuses is to urban design innovation what a "paint by number" canvas is to painting by artists!

By contrast, architectural and urban design innovations can be only created by individuals working alone or in groups who do things in a new way, or even by some architects who break the rules and get away with it.

Do Additional Floor Bonuses Decrease the Credibility of FAR Regulations?

FAR bonuses—rewarding architectural features that urban planners value—negates the very justifications for regulations that restrict FARs. The restrictions put on FAR were originally aimed at limiting negative externalities created by the shadows of tall buildings.

Let us consider the case of several blocks where the FAR is fixed at 15 by the zoning plan—as it is the case in large areas of midtown Manhattan. In some blocks, the FAR may be increased to 18, for buildings having a feature that urban planners consider attractive, whether this feature is a plaza, a theater, or some affordable housing units. We cannot but conclude that the FAR value of 15 was arbitrary in the first place, as none of the added feature are likely to correct the negative externality caused by a higher building. The regulations restricting FAR to a level much below the demand for floor space in the area are therefore only an instrument of coercion, creating an artificial scarcity that will oblige developers to include features that planners deem to be an improvement on city quality.

One could still argue that an added plaza would provide much needed space for pedestrians, whose number would increase with the additional floor space built because of the bonus. This argument does not hold up to scrutiny. At the standard FAR of 15, the sidewalk of a building using the same lot area as the Seagram building will have an area of 913 square meters, or 1.12 square meters of sidewalk space for 100 square meters of office space. If the building gets a bonus and the FAR increases by 20 percent and a plaza similar to the Seagram is added, the area of total pedestrian space available—sidewalk and plaza—become 3.35 square meters per 100 square meters of office space. If we assume that the number of employees in an office building is proportional to its floor area, it means that an increase of 20 percent of the floor area would triple the area available to pedestrians at the street level. Clearly, if the concern is the space available to pedestrians around the building, the plaza is overdesigned.

No matter how pleasant the Seagram Plaza is, it is not costless. For a given floor area, leaving a large open plaza increases the number of floors and decreases the usable floor area on each floor. In the Seagram building, the area used for elevators and utility shafts occupies 31 percent of the area of a typical floor. If the Seagram had no plaza and occupied the entire site, like some neighborhood buildings do, the entire floor area could fit in 11 floors only, and the elevators and utility shaft would occupy only 7 percent of the total floor area, increasing significantly the saleable area. In other words, the plaza makes the construction of the floor space significantly more expensive.

The lavishness of the Seagram Building—use of travertine in corridors and lobby and bronze on the facade in addition to the vast plaza—was a deliberate decision made by its owner. For the Seagram Company, the prestige building sheltering its New York headquarters had a value for the brand beyond the potential market value of the building or the value of its rents. Planners who wanted to generalize this quality in all office buildings significantly increased the cost of office buildings in New York. FAR bonuses are therefore not innocent and costless.

We have seen that multiplying plazas does not necessarily increase the livability of the city. We cannot regulate good design. On the contrary, we should rely on private initiative and the imagination of individual architects to provide new types of Seagram buildings. The Rockefeller Center in New York is also a magnificent example of urban design and Art Deco building, but it would be absurd to draft regulations so that new buildings would get a bonus if they copy the layout of Rockefeller Center. New York is full of attractive buildings like the Woolworth or the Chrysler building, or the Flat Iron building; none of them was built because of regulatory incentives.

Micromanaging Land Use through Zoning

Since 1961, planners in New York City, in their enthusiasm for using zoning to make the city more "competitive, equitable, and sustainable," have engaged in micromanaging land use by superimposing layers of regulations that are going much further than designing plazas on private land. One of the most extreme cases of a zoning micromanagement rule I have ever seen is named the "Joint Living-Work Quarters for Artists." This rule is an overlay in the M1-5A and M1-5B zoning districts in SoHo/NoHo in New York City. While the current land use in the area is mostly commercial and residential, it is still zoned Manufacturing. Indeed, at the end of the nineteenth century, the neighborhood was used mostly by garment industry sweatshops. The "Joint Living-Work Quarters for Artists" rule stipulates that only artists may live in these areas zoned manufacturing but only if they occupy a joint living-work quarters. Here is the wording of this extraordinary zoning regulation: "Section 12-10 of the New York City Zoning Resolution refers to individual lofts in Soho and Noho as 'arranged and designed for use by … not more than four nonrelated artists," including "adequate working space reserved for [each] artist." An artist is further described "under Sections 275-6 of Article 7.B of the Multiple Dwelling Law, an 'artist' is defined—for the purpose of qualifying for joint living-working quarters." The text further defines the purpose of the zone: "The SoHo Zoning Resolution permits fine artists working on a professional level who demonstrate a need for a live/work loft to reside in specific lofts zoned for manufacturing. Artist certification provides the document that equates the person named therein with a light manufacturer."

To reside and work in the area zoned for manufacturing, an artist must obtain an "Artist Certification" that is issued by the Director of Artist Certification at the NYC Department of Cultural Affairs. If readers are interested, they can apply and fill in the form on the New York City Government website.[13]

As zoning was invented to protect citizens from negative externalities, one would assume that a special artist zoning category created in a manufacturing area would aim at isolating artists from the rest of the population, the way a tannery or a lead smelter would be put into a special zone. It could be argued that artists may create negative externalities because of the bohemian life they are assumed to lead. However, this not the case. The rule was created to protect artists' housing and working space against nonartists who would compete with them for renting or buying the same floor space. The argument of the planners is that art is a vital part of New York cultural and economic life and needs protection.

Indeed, originally, artists found it convenient to occupy illegally lofts abandoned long ago by the manufacturing sector in the Soho/NoHo area. The city regulators, made aware of this zoning violation, had the good sense to not expel the artists for zoning violations. But instead of amending the zoning by allowing a new type of mixed work/residential use that obviously did not create any nuisance to neighbors, the city planners created a new type of zoning rule that excluded nonartists.

An artist, however, usually does not have a city-issued license, like a barber, a plumber, or a mortician. To be able to enforce the new zoning resolution, the city therefore had to create an artist certification, not to restrict the exercise of the profession but to allow the zoning law to be enforced. The total area in SoHo/NoHo area zoned M1-5A and M1-5B that is restricted to artists is only 58 hectares (figure 7.5). Outside this area, New York artists must compete in the open market to find a work/living space area.

To have a legal lease or purchase a loft in the SoHo/NoHo manufacturing area where "Joint Living-Work Quarters for Artists" is authorized, artists must apply to the department of cultural affairs to obtain a certification as an artist, which

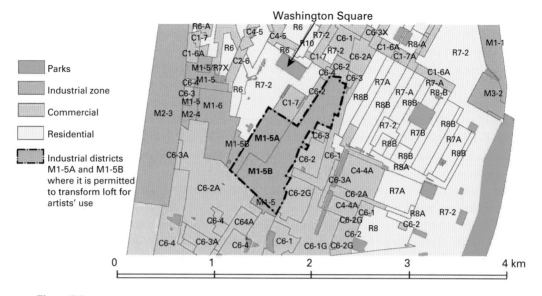

Figure 7.5
M1-5A and M1-5B manufacturing districts in SoHo/NoHo, Manhattan. *Source*: NYC Zoning District Map data containing the neighborhood south of Washington Square: M1-5A and M1-5B. Districts used with the permission of the New York City Department of City Planning. All rights reserved.

should include a portfolio for a visual artist, or scores and tapes for a musician! A municipal employee, after reviewing the portfolio or the musical score, will then decide whether the artist deserves a loft. One can imagine Jackson Pollock or Andy Warhol dutifully sending a portfolio, hoping for an approval by the Department of Cultural Affairs! And after being refused the qualification of artist by the city (apparently about 45 percent of applications are refused) moving to Omaha, Nebraska, to the loss of New York City.

I am telling this long story about this bizarre zoning category not to make fun of the NYC Planning Department but to show to what extreme zoning boards can err by excess of zeal in their desire to design city land use to its smallest detail. It is also an obvious example in which the zoning rule is unlikely to have any impact on the zoning objective of promoting art in New York City.

In addition, the "Joint Living-Work Quarters for Artists" zoning rule has a cost. The M1-5A and M1-5B zoning district in SoHo/NoHo is located in one of the most desirable retail and residential neighborhoods of New York, and there is high demand for residential quarters in these areas. Developers wanting to renovate buildings in the area must take into account the restriction that will limit the potential buyers or renters to registered artists. Furthermore, given the complex housing affordability problems faced by New York City, with around 60,000 homeless people living in shelters in 2016, it is astonishing to learn that municipal employees will spend time looking at artists' portfolios to decide whether they deserve to be able to rent a loft.

Abusive Separation of Functions Aimed at Slowing Down and Increasing the Cost of Land Use Changes

The new zoning plan of 1961 aimed at separating functions more thoroughly, and this separation has been increasing ever since. The three types of use districts—residential, commercial, and industrial—of the 1916 plan have been subdivided in the 1961 plan. Subsequent revisions created a multiplicity of new zones, each one subdivided into subzones with their own bulk requirements and potential for bonuses increasing the floor area. For example, the general commercial district is now subdivided into 72 specific zoning districts, themselves modified by overlays that further define what can be built. The multiplication of zoning types allowed closely reflects the existing land use of each block. A slight change in projected use by a developer would then require a variance or a zoning change, which could be exchanged for a new design feature requested from the developers.

For instance, the areas zoned commercial are subdivided into eight types of district named C1 to C8, each one limiting the type of commercial activity that could take place in them. However, each zone is divided into subdistricts, for instance district zone C4 is subdivided into 17 subcategories, each with different FAR limits and requirements and the possibility of additional FAR bonuses (figure 7.6). For a given land parcel, the amount of floor area that can be built is not completely apparent without calculations and assumptions about the possibility of FAR bonuses. For instance, a slight zoning change from C4-4 to C4-4A would increase FAR by 18 percent. District C4-6 would qualify for a 20 percent FAR bonus if a public plaza is built on the lot, but would lose this qualification if the district become a C4-6A district instead.

As the market price of urban land in Manhattan is established by the area of floor space that can be built on it, the value of a parcel of land is de facto dependent on the designation of its zoning. For instance, in New York, the price of a parcel of land is evaluated in dollar per allowed buildable square foot, not in dollar per square foot of land. Therefore, a slight zoning change could change the price of land instantly. This assumes that the FAR restrictions impose a limit below market demand. That seems to be the case in most of New York, and it is consistent with the incentive that planners have for restricting FAR below demand to maintain maximum leverage for incentive zoning.

Looking at the multiplication of zoning district designations, one cannot avoid thinking that the differences between two zones are often largely arbitrary and subject to change. Planners have the power to change the value of urban land at whim. This is precisely what gives power to zoning boards. Looking at the variations in FAR just for the C4 commercial districts (figure 7.6), it is difficult to perceive a clear objective in the differentiation, unless the objective is opacity.

One of the Objectives of New York Zoning Is to Slow Down Changes Caused by Markets

The distinctions between permitted commercial uses in different commercial zones are extremely detailed, and it is difficult to understand the reason for their complexity, except to maintain control or to slow down land use changes. Here is a partial declaration of objective from the New York City Department of City Planning:

Numerous zoning districts are mapped in the City's diverse neighborhoods to preserve their varying density and character. These limits help give shape to neighborhoods and predictability to their future. The City continues to adapt the Zoning Resolution as the land use patterns in the City change through private and public actions.[14]

The following example concerning a zoning change illustrates the high cost of maintaining regulatory fetters to prevent even small land use changes. A public hearing at the city planning commission in 2014 agreed to change the zoning of an existing shopping center in Queens from C2-2 to C4-1. Under C2-2, the shopping center was limited to such uses as hardware store or athletic goods store. But under the new C4-1 change, it became possible to allow shops selling furniture and appliances retail uses, which were not permitted previously! The city planning commission agreed unanimously to the change, while the land use lawyer that had argued the case in front of the commission declared that the change "would provide greater leasing flexibility and enhance the future economic viability of the shopping center." Indeed! It is difficult to understand the type of concern for the public good that incited planners to restrict the sale of appliances in a commercial area that allows hardware stores.

C4 Commercial districts

	C4-1	C4-2 / C4-3	C4-2A / C4-3A	C4-4A / C4-4 / C4-5	C4-4L / C4-5A	C4-4D	C4-5D	C4-5X	C4-6	C4-6A	C4-7	C4-7A
Commercial FAR	1.0	3.4	3.0	3.4	4.0	3.4	4.2	4.0	3.4	3.4	10.0 (5)	10.0
Residential FAR	1.25	0.78–2.43 (1), (4)	3.0 (4)	0.87–3.44 (4)	4.0 (4)	6.02 (4)	4.2 (4)	5.0 (4)	10.0 (4) (5)	10.0 (4)	10.0 (4) (5)	10.0 (4)
Residential district equivalent	R5	R6	R6A	R7	R7A	R8A	R7D	R7X	R10	R10A	R10	R10A

(1) 3.0 FAR permitted on wide streets outside the Manhattan Core under Quality Housing Program.
(2) 7.2 FAR permitted on wide streets outside the Manhattan Core under Quality Housing Program.
(3) 4.0 FAR permitted on wide streets outside the Manhattan Core under Quality Housing Program.
(4) Increase in FAR with Inclusionary Housing Program bonus.
(5) FAR bonus up to 20 percent for a public plaza.

Figure 7.6
FAR values for the commercial zone C4 and its subdivisions.

Complex Zoning and Land Price Formation

A specialized trade website relates that it took 16 years for a large New York developer to transform from industrial to residential the zoning category of a lot he had purchased on the East Side of Manhattan. In 2018, a new 140-meter-high residential tower has been built on the lot. This delay in adapting zoning to demand raises two issues. First, it increases the cost of building. During the 16 years, the capital used to purchase the land was frozen, and the buildings had obsolete land use. In addition, the legal overhead of obtaining the zoning change was certainly not negligible. Second, because the time and cost involved in getting a zoning change could not have been known with precision by either the developer or the land seller, it would have been difficult to establish a land price. Each side was taking a risk. The seller's risk was underpricing the land if the zoning change could have been obtained quickly. The buyer's risk was to overpay for the land in case the zoning change, if ever obtained, took longer than he thought. These risks and costs in holding underused properties are eventually reflected in New York real estate prices.

The ability to change land prices by slightly modifying zoning district categories creates a major problem when pricing land. Only a very specialized zoning lawyer would be able to evaluate the total area of floor space that could be built on a given parcel of land in New York City, given the many possibilities of zoning changes, development rights transfers, bonuses of all sorts, the potential of using 421-a (a property tax exemption), and so forth. This creates an asymmetry of information that is extremely detrimental to the good functioning of markets. Because of the complexity of the zoning code, a creative zoning lawyer is far more likely to increase the profitability of a future building than a creative architect or engineer. The incentive zoning paradigm that was supposed to improve urban design through clever regulations might in the long run have the opposite effect.

We should not forget that most of the beloved New York buildings still standing now, from the Woolworth building to the Seagram tower, were built without the "help" of modern zoning. A *New York Times*' article written in 2016 and relying on a detailed database notes that 40 percent of the existing buildings in Manhattan could not be built today because they contradict some land use zoning rules.[15] Many of these buildings are clustered together in the most expensive parts of Manhattan. Therefore, not meeting land use regulations does not seem to decrease their value, which would tend to demonstrate that zoning rules do not correct any perceivable negative externalities.

What advantages did the multiplicity of zoning categories and corresponding bulk add to the New York streetscape since 1961? One could compare the opacity of New York current zoning with the transparency established by the planners who conceived and surveyed the Manhattan grid in 1811. The existence of the grid and its survey markers immediately established clarity in the value of buildable land for the entire island of Manhattan. The value of land parcels facing avenues, on side streets, and at blocks corners could immediately be evaluated, with the same information available to the seller and the buyer clearly apparent on the plan. By contrast, the value of two adjacent land parcels, one zoned M1-5B and the other C6-2 on the zoning map of figure 7.5, is impossible to assess without the help of highly specialized zoning lawyers. I am sure that whoever established the distinction between the two zones had a rationale for doing so, but this rationale is not explicit, has a very high cost to New Yorkers, and is possibly as futile as the special zoning category for artists.

Urban Design Should Be Site Specific, Not Defined through Regulations
I am not suggesting here that planners should not impose any conditions on developers when significant land use changes are envisaged. But the modification required to the design of a building must be focused on the tangible negative externalities that it may generate. Shadows cast by buildings are not an important issue any more in high-density cities. Air conditioning and cheap artificial light have taken care of that. The demand for the transformation of office buildings into residential buildings in the Wall Street area demonstrates that fact. In high-demand areas, high FARs should be a right guaranteed to individuals.

However, tall buildings may generate urban design problems at their junction with the street. A redesign of the public space may be required because of the pedestrian traffic tall buildings may generate. For instance, the entrances of traditionally designed subway stations may obstruct sidewalks in high-density areas. Clearly, in such a case, design coordination between urban planners and the design of a very tall office building is to the advantage of all parties. The most creative urban design solutions are always site specific. No regulation can provide an optimum solution for every case. Instead of relying on bonus FAR to obtain a design change, it would be better if the city urban planners had a fund that could be used specifically to improve and adapt the design of streets and parks to the changing city land use. In a certain way, the use of FAR bonuses in incentive zoning is a barter system. It would be better to use a monetary instrument like an impact fee to replace this barter system. City urban planners would then be able to use the urban design fund that the impact fees would generate to redesign and adjust the design of public space. Location-specific design modifications could be required on the ground floor or mezzanine of buildings to link seamlessly with the new public realm features. This method is used routinely in Singapore and Hong Kong to increase the pedestrian areas to link private buildings with the street and with public transport.

The tendency today is in the opposite direction. The trend is to increasing the use of barter through incentive zoning, while decreasing the city's financial resources with the bizarre practice of providing the 421-a property tax exemption to large buildings[16] in addition to floor area bonuses. Tax exemption and floor area bonuses are given in exchange for something the city wants: plaza, arcades, or affordable housing. The use of tax exemptions reduces the city's resources. Consequently, the city has to resort to draconian zoning to barter zoning changes with developers in order to obtain a simple urban design feature like an underground connection to a subway station.

Some examples of site-specific design features have already been used in New York for large projects like Hudson Yards and the Vanderbilt Corridor, which address directly the issue of pedestrian access to transit close to large new buildings. New York has also a history of "transit bonuses"[17] that use FAR increases to induce private developers to pay for improvement to subway stations. These cases illustrate legitimate "design" dialogue between developers and urban planners to solve site-specific accessibility issues raised by increasing densities. I regret only that the currency used is always an increase to FAR rather than a site-specific impact fee on the increased office floor area that caused the negative externality.

New York Zoning Objectives: Slowing Down Unavoidable Change

As mentioned, New York's current zoning regulations have in fact two implicit objectives: shaping the city to the preference of urban planners and slowing down the land use changes that markets demand. Achieving these objectives through regulations has a cost that is paid by all New Yorkers in the form of higher rents and chronic housing shortages.

Because New York has a vibrant democratic government, the attempt to slow down land use change must have a constituency that represents a significant part of public opinion. Indeed, NIMBYism[18] is common to all large cities. People resist change. Any land use change, even if it is as benign as the disappearance of a corner grocery store, seems to be an unacceptable evolution to people who have lived in a neighborhood for a long time. In contrast, a city's mayor is well aware that citizens expect more jobs, housing, and the establishment of abundant retail and services, which require large and rapid land use changes. New York's planning department has managed this contradictory mandate by devising an extremely complex zoning system that has a well-oiled mechanism to permit change but makes change slow and costly. In this way, they satisfy both sides of their constituency, the side that wants no change and the one that wants new jobs and housing.

Containing Urban Expansion as an Objective Function

Paris and New York zoning plans illustrate how planners try to modify the shape of cities through regulations that constrain firm and household demands for floor space. Paris planners' zoning efforts resulted in the effective conservation of urban heritage and the acceleration of the dispersion of economic activity and population to the suburbs. In New York, planners successfully created new privately paid urban design features, some privately produced "affordable housing units," and a slowing down of the pace of land use change.

These two examples are very city specific and are not necessarily part of a general urban policy trend advocated by planners. By contrast, the policy variously called "containment," "compact cities," "smart growth," or "anti-sprawl," have been advocated in many cities around the world. I will use the word "containment" to characterize these policies. Containment policy advocates place physical restrictions on the expansion of cities, which is yet another attempt to design cities through regulations.

Containment Is a Recent Reversal of Two Centuries of Urban Expansion Policies

Containment is a policy that dates to the fin de siècle twentieth century and developed momentum at the beginning of the twenty-first century. Planners' support for containment has several origins. There was always a concern among planners that the gradual "encroachment" of urban areas on agricultural land would eventually result in food shortage—a concern currently embraced by the Chinese government. Hence, the necessity to slow down the spatial growth of urban areas by increasing the densities of cities.

The agricultural land shortage argument for containment was further reinforced by petroleum price volatility that occurred at the junction of the twentieth and twenty-first centuries. Households living in suburban developments relying on individual car transport cost were adversely affected by the unpredictability of gasoline prices. Households having shorter commuting trips or able to use public transport were much less vulnerable to these transport cost variations. The desirability of shorter commuting distances and therefore higher densities was added to the objective of saving agricultural land. Transport planners, involved in the development of public transport, joined the containment movement as public transport cannot operate efficiently in low-density suburbs. The large subsidies reducing the fare paid by public transport users have to become even larger when serving low-density areas.

At the beginning of the twenty-first century, the emergence of the gradual consensus on the serious threat caused by global warming gave an additional impetus to the containment movement, as urban transport is responsible for a large part of CO_2 emissions—about 20 percent of US GHG emissions in 2014.

All these concerns are based on real issues. My skepticism about the policy of urban containment does not reflect a rejection of the potential issues described above. I think that containment is simply the wrong solution for preserving food supply, improving mobility, and decreasing the production of GHGs. Not only is containment policy unable to solve these issues, but its systematic implementation can have serious consequences for housing affordability and for the welfare of urban households in general. I will argue these points in the following paragraphs.

Containment is a sharp reversal from urban planning doctrines of the nineteenth century and of most of the twentieth, when affluent cities were eager to expand and carefully planned their expansion. In the nineteenth century, large planned expansion of cities like Barcelona and New York were considered a sign of modernity and sophistication. Whether theoreticians advocated low-density suburban development like Ebenezer Howard's Garden Cities or the denser skyscrapers in the park of Le Corbusier, nobody doubted that the urbanized areas of cities had to expand. And expand they did. Levittown, a more modest version of the Howard design, together with its many imitators in the United States and Western Europe, provided a large part of the new urban housing stock affordable to a rapidly expanding middle class. These rapid suburban expansions lowered the high (and deadly) densities in the London of Dickens, the Paris of Zola, and the Chicago of Theodore Dreiser.

Distortion in Land Markets Could Result in Excessive Development of Urban Land

Containment policy assumes that land markets overallocate land to urban use at the expense of agricultural use or open space. Thus, cities use more land than what would be required, resulting in inefficient transport, pollution, and losses of valuable agricultural land. Planners in favor of containment advocate setting physical boundaries to prevent cities from expanding beyond what they deem is the right amount of land to be allocated to urban expansion. Greenbelts and urban growth boundaries set the physical limits of suburban expansion, ensuring that they do not exceed the preset "right amount" of land.

Eminent urban economists like Jan Brueckner and David Fansler, in a paper published in 1983,[19] already mentioned the "emotionally charged indictment of sprawl" (sprawl is the opposite of containment):

The economist's view of urban expansion stands in stark contrast to this emotionally-charged indictment of sprawl. Economists believe that urban spatial size is determined by an orderly market process which correctly allocates land between urban and agricultural uses. The model underlying this view ... suggests that urban spatial size is determined in a straightforward way by a number of exogenous variables.

Urban economists, however, do not deny that some of the exogenous variables, like the price of transport or of agricultural land might be at times distorted, and that these possible distortions may have an impact on the quantity of land used by cities. Urban economists have therefore identified the many factors that could distort urban land markets, such as the inability to price road congestion; the subsidies given to infrastructure and fuel prices; the abusive use of eminent domain underpricing rural land; and finally, the land use regulations that force households and firms to use more land than they need—minimum lot sizes, maximum densities, and maximum FARs.

These distortions could indeed result in an excessive expansion of urban land, and removing them would make expanding cities more efficient and the area they occupy closer to an economic optimum. For instance, Brueckner, in a paper titled "Urban Sprawl: Lessons from Urban Economics,"[20] provides an analysis of the possible causes for land market distortions and identifies practical remedies. For each possible cause of distortion, a theoretical model can be built that calculates the impact of the distortion on urban land consumption. For instance, in a country that subsidizes gasoline, an economist can calculate the impact of the subsidy on a city built-up area and the reduction in urbanized land that would result from removing the subsidy. The calculation would be part of a theoretical model that considers other parameters, such as population growth, household incomes, the cost of commuting time, and the price of agricultural land. The optimum equilibrium area of land for expansion depends on the value of many variables that are specific to the city studied.

For these reasons, economists never recommend an urban optimum density corresponding to a permanent equilibrium, as this density might change when model inputs like household incomes and transport price and speed change over time. However, by correcting distortions, such as removing fuel subsidies and pricing pollution and congestion, a city is more likely to get closer to an ever-changing optimum built-up area.

Brueckner argues that first correcting the distortions and then relying on markets to find a new equilibrium is a much more efficient way to improve urban land efficiency than trying to correct distortions by arbitrarily reducing the area of urban expansion through regulations like greenbelts and urban growth boundaries. He warns that reducing arbitrarily the urban area generated by distorted market forces might reduce urban welfare significantly, without addressing the negative effects created by the distortions.

Many urban economists have argued against containment policy, pointing to its social cost and its unconvincing environmental advantages. Edward L. Glaeser and Matthew E. Kahn write:[21]

Sprawl has been associated with significant improvements in quality of living, and the environmental impacts of sprawl have been offset by technological change. Finally, we suggest that the primary social problem associated with sprawl is the fact that some people are left behind because they do not earn enough to afford the cars that this form of living requires.

For Glaeser and Khan, the main problem caused by sprawl is the potential lack of mobility that it creates for households at the bottom of the income scale. Obviously, densification through containment will not alleviate the situation of the poor, as it would likely increase housing prices.

Other economists have analyzed the extent of the urban area of specific cities that have been constrained by greenbelts. For instance, Martial Echenique, a British economist, modeled three urban regions in England, including London and the Wider South East Region,[22] all constrained by green-belts. Echenique's model analyzed three options: containment (i.e., continuation of green-belt policy); dispersed development; and contiguous market-driven expansion. His conclusions are unambiguous:

The current planning policy strategies for land use and transport have virtually no impact on the major long-term increases in resource and energy consumption. They generally tend to increase costs and reduce economic competitiveness. The relatively small differences between options are overwhelmed by the impacts of socioeconomic change and population growth.

I have also quoted (in chapter 6) the work of Kate Barker and Paul Cheshire on the large social cost of London's greenbelt and its lack of evident environmental benefits.

Despite the overwhelming evidence that the preferred tools used by planners to constrain urban expansion are socially costly and do not provide any of the environmental and economic benefits expected, containment is still a widely advocated urban policy.

An Example of the Rationalization for Containment

More recently, containment policy seems to have been initiated and supported mostly by international institutions that gave a voice and designed a pseudotheoretical framework to better articulate the various antigrowth and NIMBY grassroots movements emerging from cities themselves. For instance, the World Bank, the Organisation for Economic Co-operation and Development (OECD), the

World Resource Institute, UN Habitat, and the Sierra Club have all advocated compact cities and containment with various degrees of stridency.

I am not arguing that these institutions should not be concerned with an uneconomic use of urban land, as this is indeed often a serious problem. I suggest that they should address market distortions by advocating the improvement of the pricing of what is poorly priced (like transport and parking) or is still mostly unpriced (e.g., congestion, pollution, emissions of GHGs). By skipping the economic analysis that should be carried out in each individual city and in essence implying that all cities overexpand and that higher densities are always better than lower densities, they are providing a terrible disservice to their urban audience. Their systematic advocacy for constraining urban land supply results in inflated land prices, exacerbated housing shortages that particularly affect the poor, and in general stalled creation of many social amenities that require affordable urban land.

Compact City Policies: A Comparative Assessment,[23] an OECD report published in 2012, best summarizes the institutional rationale for containment. This report is representative of arguments found in many documents issued by other institutions advocating containment. The main diagnosis developed in the report is that, first, urban population is growing rapidly in developing countries and, second, that in cities where the urban built-up area is growing faster than the urban population, action is required to limit urban extension to make cities more compact.

The diagnosis to determine whether a city is consuming too much land is therefore quite simple in this analysis. If the rate of growth of urban land is larger than the rate of growth of population, the city consumes too much land, and containment should become the main feature of its development policy.

The OECD report goes further in its recommendation for containment:

Throughout its long history, the compact city concept has evolved and enlarged its scope and policy objectives. From a simple urban containment policy **to protect the local natural environment or agricultural land from urban encroachment**, it has gradually acquired new policy objectives: **energy savings, quality of life and livability**, etc.

Containment—because of its many supposed side benefits—has become a quasireligious dogma. Planners continue to affiliate other benefits to the practice of containment, even when true causal links do not exist. The OECD report argues that the population of compact cities is closer to agricultural areas and therefore, "nearby farming encourages local food consumption and reduces the distance travelled by food, which also helps reduce CO_2 emissions."

We are getting farther and farther from the models developed by economists and closer to New Age mantras! It is ironic that Amsterdam, which is the iconic city for containment advocates, is located in a country that is the second largest

world agricultural exporter after the United States! Obviously, all the food produced around Amsterdam is not entirely consumed by its inhabitants.

There are many ways in which advocating for containment could be counterproductive, even in one of containment's biggest claims: that containment could
lower global warming. Two examples:

• One could imagine a city where photovoltaic panels on roofs linked to batteries
would provide most of the power needed for residential consumption and urban
transport. In such a city, high density and multistory housing should be forbidden
as they would be unable to produce the photovoltaic energy required per
household.

• Today urban transport might often be inefficient in using energy and consequently might be contributing excessively to global warming. However, the obvious solution is to follow Brueckner's advice, and to remove market distortions
through better pricing of transport (rather than add additional distortions through
containment). This in turn would stimulate technology change that would make
urban transport use more low carbon energy.

Do the Built-Up Areas of Most Cities Expand at a Faster Rate Than Their Populations?

We have seen that economically successful cities need space to expand. Their success attracts more households and firms, and each of the newcomers adds to the
floor space and land consumed by the city. In countries where the ratio between
urban and total population is still low, like China and India, the need for urban
spatial expansion is even higher than it is in countries where a large part of population is already urbanized, as in Latin America. As mentioned in the preceding
chapters, urban households' rising incomes create more demand for floor space
and land. The size of households decreases, but they consume more floor space
per capita. Higher-income households create a demand for more commercial and
cultural facilities, therefore more floor space and more urban land. The standard
urban model, described in chapter 4, suggests that cities with increasing incomes
and a low rate of urbanized population would need large areas to expand as the
quantity of urbanized land per capita is bound to increase. In chapter 4, we have
seen the example of Tianjin, China, where over 12 years the consumption of land
per person had increased by 34 percent, the population increased by 22 percent,
while the built-up area increased by 63 percent.

The recent work conducted by my NYU colleague Solly Angel with the Urban
Expansion Project[24] at the Marron Institute confirms the predictions of the standard urban model in most of the world's cities. As part of this work, Angel and
his team have published an *Atlas of Urban Expansion* showing how the populations

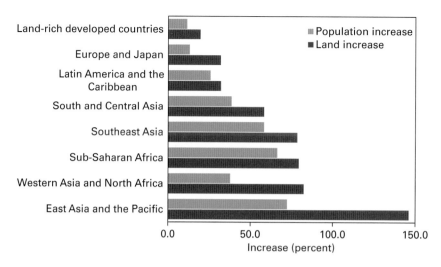

Figure 7.7
Average increase in population and built-up area in a sample of 200 cities between 2000 and 2013, by region. *Sources*: *Atlas of Urban Expansion 2016*, Marron Institute, New York University; UN Habitat, Lincoln Institute of Land Policy.

and built-up areas of a sample of cities of 100,000 people or more have grown during the past 25 years (1990–2014). The *Atlas of Urban Expansion—2016 Edition*[25] focuses on the land converted to urban use over the past 14 years in a global representative sample of 200 cities. The results by region provided by the Atlas are summarized in figure 7.7. In the cities of every region, on average the urban built-up area has grown faster than the population, resulting in an increase in the consumption of land per person over the period of study. In the East Asia region, where cities and income developed the fastest, the average increase in urban land has been twice as large as the increase in population, resulting in an average increase in land consumption per person of about 30 percent.

Implications of Containment Policy
Containment policy has only one measurable indicator: the difference between the rate of growth of the population and of the built-up area. If this difference is positive, containment is successful; if the difference is negative, it is not successful.

Containment policy, therefore, implies that as a city develops, its current built-up density should stay constant or increase—so that the population growth rate would be equal to or higher than the built-up area growth rate. In other words, a decrease in land consumption per person is always better than an increase.

This implies that the allocation of land for urban expansion is no longer related to income, cost of transport, and price of agricultural land, but simply mechanically linked to the rate of growth of the population.

Let us review where and when variations of average urban densities occur.

Is It Possible for Urban Populations to Grow at the Same Pace as the Built-Up Area?

The need for containment, according to its advocates, is demonstrated when the growth rate of a city's build-up area is growing faster than its population. Cities that adopt a containment policy should therefore try to limit the land area they use for expansion in a given period in such a way that within time interval t_1 to t_2 the ratio between the population and the built-up area remain equal to a constant K, as shown in equation 7.1.

So if the city's population grows by 10 percent in the interval between t_1 and t_2, then the built-up area also will be limited to growing by 10 percent or less.

However, the whole purpose of cities is to increase the welfare of the population. This welfare is expressed in terms of increased income, and therefore in increased residential floor space consumed. With increased income households consume more floor space used by community facilities like school and neighborhood parks and amenities like commerce and services.

Even in very affluent cities like New York, London, and Paris, planners are concerned about housing overcrowding, too few affordable dwelling units, too small schools with too large class sizes, and lack of community facilities and neighborhood open space. Most urban citizens consider that the creation of new libraries, museums, theaters, and concert halls is highly desirable. New services emerge, like indoor gyms. As incomes increase, firms also tend to consume more floor space per worker. Sweatshops are replaced by spacious factories. Office buildings include more meeting rooms and more office space per worker.

Consequently, as incomes increase, the consumption of total floor space per person also increases. This increase is not due to extravagant consumption but to

Equation 7.1

Containment policy often implies that the following condition be met:

$$\frac{P_2}{P_1} = \frac{A_2}{A_1} = K ,\tag{7.1}$$

where P_1 and P_2 are the population at times t_1 and t_2, respectively; and A_1 and A_2 are the built-up areas at time t_1 and t_2, respectively.

the very raison d'être of cities. Even the stricter containment advocates would agree with the desirability of increasing total urban floor space per person as population and incomes increase.

However, new increased floor areas need to be built over land. Evaluating the quantity of land that this new floor space will require is what separates containment planning from market-driven planning. Under containment, the built-up area of a city should not increase faster than its population. Under the market-driven approach that I advocated in the preceding chapter, it is the price of land that determines the amount of land consumed per person, and by extension how much land should be developed.

Market-driven land development allocates the new floor space to be built in new development zones (greenfields), or by adding new floor space to existing built-up areas, either by replacing existing buildings by taller ones or by using more intensively already developed land (for instance, by building "granny flats" in backyards). The allocation of new floor space between greenfields and existing built-up area is determined by land prices and construction costs. The height of a building is determined by land prices in various locations.

Containment-driven land development from the start puts an upper limit to the area of greenfield that can be developed. Putting a limit on greenfield development increases the price of land in the entire city, and therefore would tend to favor taller buildings in both the existing built-up areas and the greenfield development.

Let us explore the spatial consequences on the development of a city when containment planning, rather than market prices, is used to allocate land for urban extension. It is possible to calculate the change in building height, or rather in FAR that would be required to accommodate an increase if floor area consumption when the conditions of equation 7.1 are strictly met (equation 7.2).

Therefore, to satisfy a containment policy, where the built-up area is constrained to grow at the same rate as the population, the built-up floor area ratio between time t_1 and t_2 should grow at the same rate as floor area consumed per capita during the same period. For instance, if the floor area per person grows by 30 percent, then the average floor area ratio has also to grow by 30 percent to allow the built-up area to grow at the same rate as the population—as required by the containment policy. If the average floor area ratio grows at a slower pace than the floor area per capita, then the total built-up area will grow faster than the population and the goal of the containment policy will not be met.

The imposed parity between the rate of growth of the population and the built-up area has an unintended impact on the shape of the city and in particular on its density profile.

Equation 7.2

A city total built-up area A can be defined as a function of its population P, of the floor area consumed per capita Flc and of the built-up floor area ratio Far:

$$A = \frac{Flc}{Far}.$$

The built-up floor area ratio (A) is the ratio between the total floor area of a city (Far)—aggregating all floor area, residential, commercial and industrial—and the total built-up area (Flc)—including private lots, roads, and small parks, as defined in chapter 3.

To assess the impact of containment policy on a city shape, assume that the floor area per capita will increase between t_1 and t_2, reflecting improved housing and more amenities, but that the rate of increase of the built-up area will be strictly controlled by containment policy to be equal to the rate of increase of the population. We will then determine the gross floor area ratio of the city at time t_2 as the dependent variable.

Between t_1 and time t_2 then to satisfy equation 7.1, we should have

$$\frac{Far_{t1}}{Flc_{t1}} \cdot \frac{Flc_{t2}}{Far_{t2}} = 1,$$

and therefore,

$$\frac{Flc_{t1}}{Flc_{t2}} = \frac{Far_{t1}}{Far_{t2}}. \tag{7.2}$$

Imagine a city whose mayor decides to adopt a containment policy. The city's current built-up area is equal to S. The projected rate of growth of the population g will allow this area S to grow by an additional area $P = S \cdot g$.

Because the population density should remain constant to maintain the containment requirement, any increase in floor consumption should be provided by a proportional increase in the FAR.

The average floor area ratio within S will not be able to grow much, as it would require the demolition of existing buildings to replace them with taller ones. This is a slow process. The bulk of the new FAR will have therefore to be built within the perimeter of P using a FAR much higher than the one within S, as the area of P is fixed in advance by the policy. This would result in densities being higher in the periphery P than in the more central area S, contradicting all empirical and theoretical evidence we have discussed in chapters 3 and 4 for the standard urban model.

When containment policy is applied to a city, the main result is to increase both land and floor prices. The growth of floor space consumption envisaged in the scenario above would not really take place. With increasing land and floor prices, the increase in residential floor area per person will likely not happen; neither would the construction of pre-K schools or the new restaurants that increases in household incomes would have made possible.

Cities whose land supply is constrained by topography, like San Francisco, New York, Hong Kong, Vancouver, Sydney, and Auckland, all have high price—income ratios (as have we have seen in chapter 6). The containment policy, when it is enforced, has the same impact as topographic constraints.

This spatial outcome is not surprising. We have seen that the FAR of a building is not subject to design but is a real estate outcome. Buildings have high FARs where the unit price of land is expensive compared to the unit cost of construction, and it is low when the opposite is true. Proponents of containment, arbitrarily constraining the land area to be developed, are acting like planners in a command economy.

In market-driven cities, as we have seen in chapter 4, high densities and high land values are found in the highly accessible city center, while lower densities and lower land values are found in the periphery. Containment policy, if strictly applied, would result in a reverse density gradient compared to the standard urban model.

Cities with reverse density gradients do exist, for instance, Moscow in 1990 and Johannesburg under apartheid. All such cities were built without land markets. Interestingly, the density profile of Portland, Oregon (a city renowned for its "Urban Growth Boundary" containment strategy) that I measured in 1990, also shows an increase in density toward its periphery.

Is an Increase in Land Consumption a Sign of Wasteful Use?
Supporters of containment policy are concerned about an excessive use of urban land per person. However, to my knowledge, no containment policy advocate has ever defined what area per person would constitute an efficient consumption of land. Urban land consumption per person varies widely from one city to another, often by more than an order of magnitude. Figure 7.8 shows the change in average urban land consumption per person in cities grouped by regions between 2000 and 2014. In all regions, the consumption per person has increased significantly.

Other Objective Functions: Is Sustainability an Objective Function for a City?

Currently, the planning profession and the popular press are formulating guiding principles for the development of cities expressed as a single qualifier that is variously expressed as cities should be "sustainable," "resilient," and "livable." Practi-

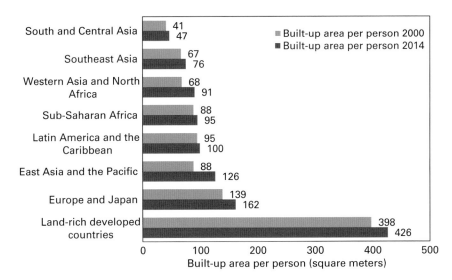

Figure 7.8
Urban land consumption per person between 2000 and 2014, by region. *Sources*: *Atlas of Urban Expansion 2016*, Marron Institute, New York University; UN Habitat, Lincoln Institute of Land Policy.

cally every urban planning department in universities all around the world has added "Sustainable" to their title. For instance, Oxford University offers a Master of Science in Sustainable Urban Development.

Is sustainable development different from just development? And could being sustainable guide the design of cities better than market mechanisms can?

In 2015, the United Nations proposed 17 Sustainable Development Goals, listed in figure 7.9, that must be achieved by 2030. It is difficult to disagree with any of these goals. Then, could they be used as the starting point to develop an objective function to design a city? The only goal mentioning cities explicitly is goal 11: Sustainable Cities and Communities. This Sustainable Development Goal seems to be an unfortunate kind of circular reference and is clearly unable to guide us. Let us then select two goals that might be applicable to cities, goal 1 (No Poverty) and goal 7 (Affordable and Clean Energy). Let us try to develop quantitative objectives to clarify these goals when applied to cities.

Countries with rapidly developing economies, like China and India, are running into the dilemma of choosing between the goals of No Poverty and Affordable and Clean Energy. So far it seems that they have opted to privilege No Poverty combined with Affordable Energy while postponing the Clean Energy component. Indeed, the available technology does not yet allow most poor countries with abundant coal resources to have affordable clean energy.

United Nations Sustainable Development Goals
1. No poverty
2. Zero hunger
3. Good health and well-being
4. Quality education
5. Gender equality
6. Clean water and sanitation
7. Affordable and clean energy
8. Decent work and economic growth
9. Industry, innovation, and infrastructure
10. Reduced inequalities
11. Sustainable cities and communities
12. Responsible consumption and production
13. Climate action
14. Life below water
15. Life on land
16. Peace, justice, and strong institutions
17. Partnership for the goals

Figure 7.9
UN Sustainable Development Goals.

Neither the Chinese or Indian government is willing to wait for affordable clean energy technology to start increasing their electricity production. Have they been right in their prioritization? Nobody knows. The environmental cost of their policy is obviously high, but keeping millions of people in poverty while waiting for cheaper renewable energy might have an even higher social cost. There is no objective function as there is for the design of bridges.

The choice between affordable and clean energy is purely political. Reducing poverty now using affordable polluting energy or waiting for the availability of affordable clean energy to reduce poverty in the future is a typical trade-off that politicians must make. There is no computable optimum, only choices.

Conclusions

The Problem with Designing New Cities
We may use science to predict what might happen. We are unable to scientifically define what should happen. This is the main problem with urban planners wanting to substitute their judgment for the self-organization of markets. They become messianic, like the proponents of containment. Their proposals are based on dogma: compact is better than not compact, bicycles are better than motorized transport. Planners, like economists, should just tell politicians "if you do this,

that will likely happen." They should provide several options. The choice among options is political or possibly ideological. It is not the place of planners to make this choice. Planners may have personal preferences for a type of city—personally, I prefer to live in dense cities like New York and Hong Kong—but my personal preferences are irrelevant when providing technical advice to a mayor. A quotation[26] from Yuval Harari should guide planners when giving technical advice to mayors:

Science can explain what exists in the world, how things work, and what might be in the future. By definition, it has no pretensions to knowing what should be in the future. Only religions and ideologies seek to answer such questions.

8   Urban Planners and Urban Economists Have an Important Role to Play If They Manage to Work Together

Mayors and Urban Planners Should Be Enablers and Facilitators, Not the Creators or Shapers of Cities

The productivity of cities comes from the proximity of households and firms. However, this close physical proximity, which is so essential to the creativity of cities, requires special rules, shared investments, and common services. Local governments are created specifically to set and enforce the rules that make proximity viable. In addition, local governments manage shared capital goods (e.g., infrastructure and public open space) and provide social services. Shared capital investment and services need to be paid for through local taxes, tolls, and user fees.

The role of mayors and their municipal staff, including urban planners and economists, is therefore rather like the role of a well-coordinated team of competent managers and janitors. The mayor, with his team of municipal managers, is not the city's ruler, nor is he the city's designer. A city is entirely created by its citizens' initiatives. These citizens are required to act within a set of "good neighbor" rules, and to be supported in their endeavors by a network of physical and social infrastructure managed by a mayor and a city council.

In a large city, the municipal budget is often much larger than the individual budgets of most of the city's firms and households. The political power provided by the large municipal budget to mayors, municipal councils, and their planning staff seems out of proportion with the modest role of managers and of competent janitors that the function would require. Hence the temptation to use this power in an abusive manner, as shown in the preceding chapters.

Some municipal governments conclude that the power provided by their large budget entitles them to "design" the city, and that their role should not be limited to competently providing the infrastructure and services required to support the activities of their citizens. We have seen an expression of municipal hubris in the preceding chapter. New York City zoning rules are no longer limited to establishing good-neighbor norms and to mitigating obvious negative externalities but are now aimed at designing the city through regulations. A municipality is fulfilling its proper role when it simply coordinates municipal public investments with the investments of private developers, as it has done, for instance, in the development of the Hudson Yard project in New York.

While they do not have to design the city, urban planners and economists have a very important role to play in managing their city's land assets, like streets and open space, and its infrastructure capital assets. In particular, planners have a major role to play in improving mobility and ensuring housing affordability. In this chapter, I describe the important role that urban planners should play in maintaining and hopefully increasing the welfare of the cities they work for. In doing so, I first have to describe the deviation from this role that has been prevalent during the past 50 years.

Do We Really Want Our Mayors and Planners to Have a Vision?

For about a quarter of century, many municipalities have been describing their development plans as a "vision." Calling a simple municipal action and investment program "a vision" is symptomatic of the grandiose misunderstanding that municipalities have concerning their role. *Merriam-Webster's Dictionary* defines vision as "the act or power of imagination." This is not what you would expect from your janitor! A vision is normally the outcome of a personal religious, artistic, or scientific insight, and should not be used to qualify a plan to extend a sewer network, to adjust a property tax, or to collect tolls on bridges. The use of the word "vision" to define a municipal works program has spread worldwide. A Google search of words "mayor vision" produces 50.2 million entries! A search in French and Spanish gives similar results. It seems that all over the world, mayors feel obliged to manage their cities through "vision."

Here are some of the results from the Internet search:

- "Hilton Head hires consultant to help jumpstart mayor's 'vision' process."
- "My Vision For Seattle—Mayor. seattle.gov."
- "Quezon City mayor's vision for an inclusive city."
- "Vision for London—Sadiq Khan Labour candidate for Mayor of London."

Does it matter if mayors use the word "vision" to describe their municipal program? I think it does. George Orwell wrote "but if thought corrupts language, language can also corrupt thought."[1]

A mayor convinced of the necessity of having a vision to manage a city would feel less inclined to respond in a supportive way to the changes brought by the activities and innovations of the city's population. A visionary mayor may feel compelled to impose her unique insights on the life of her Philistine citizens. The hubris of mayoral visions would be a clear example of what Orwell was thinking about when he wrote about the possibility of language corrupting thought. A mayor with a vision needs to be followed. She should not be questioned by people who lack vision. Visionary leadership implies a top-down approach. We have seen in the preceding chapters that a city is mostly created from the bottom up. However, a top-down approach is required to design infrastructure and services, but only as they are needed to support citizens' activities. The support role involved in this top-down design is not trivial and requires good data and outstanding technical and financial skills, but a personal vision is not a requirement. It might rather be a hindrance.

Where Did the Vision Come from in Silicon Valley?

Silicon Valley has been the world's most innovative urban concentration during the past half century. The creation of Silicon Valley is a perfect example of the advantages of a grassroots citizens' vision, as opposed to a top-down mayoral vision. Silicon Valley was not created by a visionary mayor but by a large group of brilliant tinkerers, at times collaborating, but certainly not coordinating, their actions by implementing a common plan. The tinkerers had visions. Hewlett Packard and Apple were started in garages, in violation of local zoning laws! The deans and provosts of Stanford University had vision, as they encouraged their students and researchers to start their own enterprises, and provided start-up incubator workspaces on land belonging to the university. But no visionary mayors or urban planners were involved in the creation of Silicon Valley.

Silicon Valley extends over about 18 municipalities. Maybe the limited size of the municipalities tempered the urban planners' ambition to control what the brilliant tinkerers were doing. The fragmentation of municipal power prevented planners from creating a special zone where anybody dealing with electronics would have to operate. One shudders at the thought that the municipal planners in Silicon Valley could have circumscribed the coders to a special coder zone, like the zone reserved for artists created in New York, as described in chapter 7! The planners of the various Silicon Valley municipalities deserve credit, though, for not having killed through land use regulations the activities of the emerging electronics industry. This industry, with its mix of coding, venture finance, and light manufacturing did not readily fit any traditional zoning district description.

I have worked in a few cities where "visionary planners" pretended to include the design of new "Silicon Valley" satellite towns in their Master Plans. These visions never took off. By contrast, where some of Silicon Valley conditions are met—a great university next to open land with flexible land use—similar creative activities may emerge. This has been the case in Beijing, for instance, in the area located between Peking University and Tsinghua University, and in some areas of the Pearl River Delta in southern China.

However, the role played by nonvisionary but competent planners was indispensable to the success of Silicon Valley. Indeed, its success depended on the municipal management teams being able to adjust to changing demand for urban services and infrastructure that were required by the sudden transformation of an area, originally largely residential, to a new type of land use. The competence of the municipal staff and their mayors was therefore indispensable for the successful growth of Silicon Valley. However, this role was not driven by a top-down "vision" but involved great professional competence in many sectors: land use and traffic management, transport, infrastructure building and maintenance, education, refuse disposal, security, taxation, and tariffs, among others. They did not need vision, but extreme competence.

In this chapter, I describe the important tasks that a municipal urban planning team has to fulfill, together with the type of working relationship between the municipal planning department and the other technical departments that form the staff of a municipality.

One of the major urban planners' tasks is to constantly monitor the city's welfare through quantitative indicators. The planners, detecting through data an impending deterioration in the quality of city life, warn the mayor, who decides what resources and priority to dedicate to the issue. Planners then propose strategies to address the mayor's priority objectives. The role of planners is therefore mostly technical and data driven. Although in the rest of this chapter, I will use the words "urban planners" to designate the professional staff in the municipal urban planning department, the term also covers urban economists working closely with the more traditional urban planners whose professional background includes architecture, physical planning, engineering, and urban geography. Urban economists able to understand the functioning of real estate and labor markets have to be integrated into the team of more traditional urban planners.

Urban planners' more important tasks can be divided into three major groups:

1. Monitoring important indicators and turning on blinking red lights when real estate prices, average commuting time, and other indicators point to an incoming crisis;

2. Developing and monitoring strategic projects to implement mayors' municipal objectives; and

3. Designing new land use regulations and extension plans, and auditing existing regulations.

The Role of Planners in Monitoring Indicators and Turning On Blinking Red Lights

Publicly traded companies are subject to elaborate and codified reporting requirements concerning their financial flows, their assets and liabilities. Municipalities maintain financial records about their operating budget but usually do not systematically maintain a database that monitors changes in the private and public assets on which their tax income and expenditures depend. The changes in a city's built environment largely determine its future income and expenditures. Of course, beyond being useful in projecting future municipal financial situations, the changes in the built environment and its value, determined by rents and real estate prices, are essential to be able to manage what I suggest is the main function of urban planners: maintaining mobility and housing affordability. In many cities, these essential databases concerning the built environment are either not maintained or are poorly maintained. And when they do exist, they are rarely analyzed and used to guide policy. I will repeat Angus Deaton's quotation that cited in chapter 6: "Without data, anyone who does anything is free to claim success."

In the past 20 years, many municipalities have developed spatial databases in GIS format that are open for public use. However, I doubt whether these databases are routinely analyzed for decision making. When downloading the data, it often happens that they are incomplete, that links are broken, and that many fields are just left empty. For instance, the city of Atlanta maintains a database called "Strategic Community Investment Report Data" (SCI, 2013). Recently, when one of my students tried to use the database, it appears that 18 percent of the original SCI parcel dataset had null values for the areas of buildings, and 22 percent of parcels had a lot size recorded as zero. The poor maintenance of the records suggests that the dataset has not been routinely used to identify urban issues and to develop urban policy. I had the same experience many times when trying to use the database of other cities in OECD countries.

The poor maintenance of municipal databases confirms my assertion that very few urban economists are involved in the daily policy making in cities. Urban economists are all data hungry, and if they were actively participating in policy making, they would make sure the city IT department properly maintains their databases. Traditional urban planners being more used to a qualitative approach to urban management—expressed by fuzzy words like "livable," "resilient," and "sustainable"—are likely to seldom use the municipal database.

The Master Plan Fallacy

Preparing a master plan—typically every 10 years—is a ritual that constitutes the "creative" part of the job of urban planners. In many cities, the urban planning department—with the help of consultants—prepares a master plan that includes two main parts: a large database and a set of maps, typically showing existing and future land use and urban extension. This would be a useful exercise if the database and maps were used as a permanent management tool and were periodically updated, say, every quarter. But this is seldom the case. After the master plan has been completed and approved by the local government, the team of consultants is disbanded, and the database is archived and is not updated. It is assumed that the data were only necessary for the preparation of the master plan, but once the master plan is completed, all that is needed is to implement it.

The decennial preparation of master plans is based on the false assumption that a city is like a very large building that needs to be periodically renovated and expanded. The master plan constitutes the renovation and expansion blueprint. Over the decade between master plans, it is assumed that the planners' role is to simply implement the features found in the blueprint. In reality, most master plans are only very partially implemented or not at all. This blunt negative assertion is based on my own experience during my 55 years as a practicing urban planner.[2]

Despite this poor record, every decade, master planning exercises are repeatedly initiated at great expense. Why? Municipalities feel that a master plan will help project an optimistic view of the future and is a great public relations exercise. It also shows that "they are doing something" to address municipal issues like traffic congestion and unaffordable housing. The master plan document usually includes many volumes of charts and data, providing gravitas to the final maps and drawings showing what the city will look like a decade later.

Most of the time, the master plan is a very costly public relations operation for the municipality. However, I have met a large number of people who sincerely thought that it was an indispensable document to ensure a brighter future. These people, invariably disappointed by the final decadal outcome, attribute its failure to a lack of political will on the part of the municipality to faithfully implement the plan. The failure of master plans is not due to the human imperfections of those in charge of implementing them but to a conceptual conceit: A city is not a large building requiring a detailed blueprint before being built. I will suggest below urban management tools that would be useful substitutes for master plans.

Maintaining a Database Generating Important Indicators
A large city must be managed on a day-to-day basis. It cannot be run on autopilot for 10 years, as the concept of a master plan seems to imply. A municipality's financial department maintains its accounts daily, updating constantly its income and expenditures, making projections and updating these projections regularly, and communicating to the mayor major changes to be expected in the budget

forecast. In contrast to the municipal budget, which is carefully updated by a team of accountants and bookkeepers, in many cities, the quantity and value of the assets on which the revenue of the municipality are based—its land under different uses, its buildings that provide rents and property tax, the income of households and firms that pay utility fees for municipal services—are not monitored on a regular basis, outside of the periodic master plan exercise.

Too often, the staff of the planning department fails to monitor the prices, rents, and land use changes that may anticipate a future crisis. Data essential to the welfare of citizens—such as the monthly number of building permits issued and the size, prices, and rents of the residential units built every month—are seldom published and analyzed on a regular basis, although the data are routinely collected and are available in a disaggregated form in ledgers dispersed in various municipal departments. In the same way, the data concerning the addition and demolition of commercial and industrial space, which is routinely entered in ledgers when registering buildings and occupation permits, is seldom entered in an accessible geographical database. Hence, crucial information about future housing affordability, traffic, and commuting patterns is lost.

Monitoring the changes of neighborhood real estate prices is extremely important for the management of the city. These prices show when and where the equilibrium between supply and demand might be shifting. Planners, de facto, control the supply of land and floor space through regulations and infrastructure investments; they can therefore act in advance to adjust the supply elasticity that would decrease real estate price volatility. This price volatility too often creates extreme hardships for low-income households and small enterprises.

A city planning department should therefore create, maintain, and monitor an extensive urban database. Simple models should link raw data to indicators. For instance, changes in a neighborhood population and floor space can be linked to population densities and rents, producing indicators whose changes in value would need interpretation but could lead to municipal action. In the same way as publicly owned firms are obliged to publish quarterly financial indicators to inform the public of the state of their finances, municipalities should publish quarterly a set of indicators that will inform the public about the welfare of its inhabitants. The local municipal democratic process would be greatly enhanced by such actions.

Turning On Blinking Light Indicators
At times, the value of some urban indicators may change rapidly. Often, the change is benign and just indicates the normal adjustment of a city land use to a changing economic environment. At other times, the changes may indicate a

deterioration of living conditions for the entire city or for some socioeconomic group. For instance, a rapid increase in density and decrease in floor space consumption in a specific neighborhood may indicate a decrease in the housing standards of the socioeconomic group living in this neighborhood. Urban planners should then warn the mayor about "indicators blinking red." They should provide an explanation for the change in density and propose alternative strategies to deal with it if in their opinion it may result in a loss of welfare in the future.

Just a few years before the housing finance collapse of 2007, I heard the words "blinking indicators" for the first time during a talk on mortgage risk and housing policy given by the late John M. Quigley, an American economist. Quigley, together with some of his colleagues, had assembled and regularly monitored a number of housing and financial indicators for the United States. At the conference, he used the expression "those indicators are all blinking red." His tone of urgency was striking. The mortgage crisis of 2008 followed his warning a year later.

I thought that the concept of blinking indicators could be applied to many city metrics, for instance, rent-to-income ratio, floor consumption per capita, and median commuting time. By maintaining a regularly updated urban database, well-trained urban planners and economists could detect changes as they are occurring and act before the problem becomes too acute. For instance, rapid increases in housing prices could signal an emerging constraint in the supply of floor space or developable land, or both. If a plan of action to remove a potential supply bottleneck is implemented quickly, it could prevent a further large increase in housing prices and a future affordability crisis that would have serious consequences for the welfare of the population and city productivity. The presence of blinking indicators by themselves does not suggest an automatic diagnosis, and they need to be interpreted in the local context. For instance, a rapid increase in housing prices could be caused by poorly formulated regulations, by land tenure issues, or by a lack of investment in primary infrastructure and transport. Or in a more benign way, by a large increase in households' income and in housing quality. Only after planners and urban economists have been able to establish a correct diagnosis will it be possible to design a strategy that will bring back the indicators to a value that would predict a return to smooth sailing.

The role of planners in monitoring databases could then be divided into three series of tasks shown schematically in figure 8.1. The series are:

• creating and monitoring a municipal database,

• identifying blinking indicators, and

• proposing strategies with relevant line agencies.

Those series are in turn divided into three main topics:

• spatial structural changes,

• mobility, and

• affordability.

The items in the database suggested in the left column in figure 8.1 are only indicative. Different cities will have different ways of measuring a city's spatial structure. There are useful papers proposing various sets of indicators. I recommend in particular those developed specifically for housing by Stephen Malpezzi and Stephen Mayo,[3] two urban economists, and those developed by Shlomo Angel,[4] an urban planner with a worldwide experience of cities.

Every year, the technology used to create and monitor urban databases is offering more information collected at a much lower cost. Each city should establish its database depending on the level of technology that is locally available and as a function of the city's priorities and morphology. In some cities, for instance, the locations where running water is available is limiting the expansion of the city. Obviously, in this case the area covered by the water supply network will be part of the spatial database. In other cities, areas vulnerable to flooding are a major hindrance to their development. Clearly, in these cities planners should include

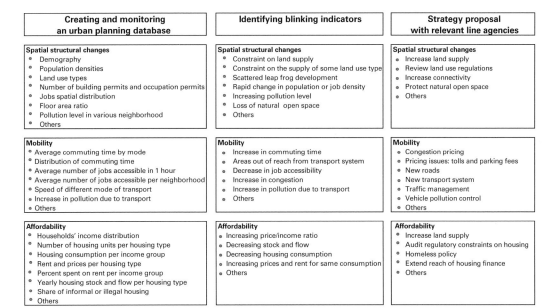

Creating and monitoring an urban planning database	Identifying blinking indicators	Strategy proposal with relevant line agencies
Spatial structural changes • Demography • Population densities • Land use types • Number of building permits and occupation permits • Jobs spatial distribution • Floor area ratio • Pollution level in various neighborhood • Others	**Spatial structural changes** • Constraint on land supply • Constraint on the supply of some land use type • Scattered leap frog development • Rapid change in population or job density • Increasing pollution level • Loss of natural open space • Others	**Spatial structural changes** • Increase land supply • Review land use regulations • Increase connectivity • Protect natural open space • Others
Mobility • Average commuting time by mode • Distribution of commuting time • Average number of jobs accessible in 1 hour • Average number of jobs accessible per neighborhood • Speed of different mode of transport • Increase in pollution due to transport • Others	**Mobility** • Increase in commuting time • Areas out of reach from transport system • Decrease in job accessibility • Increase in congestion • Increase in pollution due to transport • Others	**Mobility** • Congestion pricing • Pricing issues: tolls and parking fees • New roads • New transport system • Traffic management • Vehicle pollution control • Others
Affordability • Households' income distribution • Number of housing units per housing type • Housing consumption per income group • Rent and prices per housing type • Percent spent on rent per income group • Yearly housing stock and flow per housing type • Share of informal or illegal housing • Others	**Affordability** • Increasing price/income ratio • Decreasing stock and flow • Decreasing housing consumption • Increasing prices and rent for same consumption • Others	**Affordability** • Increase land supply • Audit regulatory constraints on housing • Homeless policy • Extend reach of housing finance • Others

Figure 8.1
Monitoring an urban database.

in the database a very detailed topographical study and modeling of potential flooding under various climatic assumptions.

The urban planning database should not duplicate the databases maintained by the line agencies in charge of transport, infrastructure, or social services. Line agencies are better at maintaining a detailed database for their sectors and have idiosyncrasies that should be respected. However, land use and demographic data, including projections, should be maintained exclusively by the urban planning department. I have seen too often line agencies making their own projections for land use and demography, simply in order to justify a technological choice made by them. I have seen sewer and storm drainage departments planning to use oxidation ponds for sewage treatment in areas where the trend in land prices suggested future high population densities. The sewer engineers were assuming a projected low density compatible with the use of oxidation ponds to justify their technology choice. This is again an area where an in-house urban economist would be better able to contribute to decision making—in this case the trade-offs between a land-intensive but low-cost hardware technology like oxidation ponds versus a traditional sewer system, much more capital intensive but with low-land requirements.

The Role of Planners in Developing and Monitoring Strategies to Implement a Mayor's Municipal Objectives

Municipal Policy Objectives, Alternative Strategies, and Impact Indicators

Mayors and city councils set up city policy objectives. These objectives are political, and rightly so. There is no scientific way to set up urban development objectives. However, while the priority objectives are political, the issues they aim to address can be resolved only through a technical approach expressed through a strategy. It is the role of planners to prepare alternative strategies to meet the mayor's objectives. Much too often, the strategies proposed are unfortunately limited to identifying government inputs and do not explore the potential impact, which will indicate whether the strategy is succeeding or failing in meeting its original objectives.

For instance, let us suppose that a mayor's objective is to improve public transport. The typical response will consist of announcing the financial inputs required to address the issue: how many million dollars from the municipal budget will be allocated to transport; some output indicators might be added, for instance, how many new buses or light rail lines will be added. However, what is important for the citizens is the impact of the municipal investment on their daily commute—how timely and less crowed buses will be and how much shorter the average commuting time might become.

If a quantified measure of the impact on commuting time has not been made explicit, there will be no way to measure whether the investment associated with the strategy has been successful in meeting the mayor's original objective. If success is measured solely by the amount of money spent and the number of buses procured, despite no measurable positive impact on urban transport, faulty strategies could be repeated at great expense without any results. It is impossible for citizens to evaluate a municipality's performance if the proper indicators of success—impact indicators—are not declared in advance.

The role of measurable indicators is not limited to monitoring progress and eventual success but is also part of the preparation of a properly formulated strategy. Indeed, the objective of a public transport strategy is not to buy new buses but to reduce travel times and to increase the commuting comfort of citizens. Unless this objective is clearly expressed and quantified as an impact indicator, there is no way to know whether the strategy succeeded or failed. Once the municipal council has declared an objective, finding the proper impact indicators is the first step in developing the strategy.

Strategies should include several types of indicators to

- identify the strategy,
- monitor whether the strategy has been successful, and
- eventually modify some element of the strategy to improve its performance.

The formulation of indicators while the strategy is being developed help focus on the desired result and not on the initial steps, like budget inputs, the purchase of equipment, or the construction of civil work. Many urban strategies have failed because the proper indicators were not initially imbedded in the strategy.

The design and implementation of a strategy requires identifying four types of indicators: impact, outcome, output, and input. I will illustrate the relationship between policy objectives, strategy, and indicators with an example summarized graphically in figure 8.2.[5] Obviously, during the strategy design phase, the indicators' sequence will have to be iterated several times. A desired impact when first formulated might prove to require inputs that are beyond the financial means or staffing capability of a municipality. The indicators will then have to be iterated until the inputs are found feasible while the expected impact is still worth pursuing.

During the strategy preparation phase, the indicators will be prepared in the following sequence: impact, outcome, outputs, inputs. During the various phases of strategy implementation, the indicators will be measured in the reverse order, reflecting the sequence of project implementation: inputs, outputs, outcome, impact. I have shown in figure 8.2 the indicators in the order that should be used during strategy preparation.

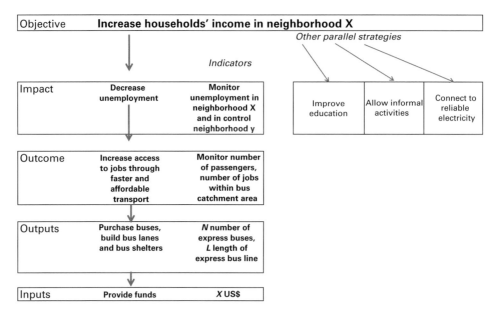

Figure 8.2
Objective tree: impact, outcome, output, and input. *Source*: Adapted from Roberto Mosse and Leigh Ellen Sontheimer, "Performance Monitoring Indicators Handbook," Technical Paper No 334, World Bank, Washington, DC, September 1996.

Using figure 8.2 and starting from a municipal objective, I will follow the sequence required to identify a strategy and the indicators that will allow quantification of the results expected during the different phases of a strategy.

Let us assume that a mayor and her city council have decided that alleviating poverty in a specific neighborhood X is a major policy objective as part of a city-wide development program.

Several alternative or concurrent strategies could be developed to alleviate poverty. One strategy could aim at increasing household incomes by improving employment opportunities, thus decreasing unemployment or underemployment. Other concurrent strategies could consist of transferring resources to the target population, or increasing the supply of social services, like health and education.

Let us select the first type of strategy aimed at increasing household incomes by improving employment opportunities in neighborhood X. Employment opportunities could increase in neighborhood X if workers had faster and cheaper access to the metropolitan labor market. Improving access to the labor markets usually decreases unemployment and increases salaries, as discussed in chapter 2. The values of the indicators, as discussed below, will be first projected during the design phase and then monitored during the implementation phase. The difference between the target numbers at the strategy design phase and those monitored during and after strategy implementation will indicate the degree of success of the strategy and help identify the elements that were crucial for the success or failure of the strategy.

Impact Indicators

The values of the impact indicators quantify the original municipal objective of the selected strategy. The objective is to decrease poverty in neighborhood X. The strategy selected to achieve the objective is to increase employment opportunities by providing faster and cheaper access to high-employment areas. The impact indicators during strategy design will fix a target decrease in both poverty and unemployment. For instance, if unemployment in neighborhood X is currently 25 percent, the strategy target will aim at decreasing this number to, say, 10 percent over 5 years, or adding a total number of newly employed workers[6] equal to N_1. If the number of commuters out of neighborhood X is currently N_2, the strategy implies that, every day, a target number of workers equal to $N_3 = N_1 + N_2$ should be able to use a faster and cheaper means of transport than is currently available. I assume here that new employment will be located outside the neighborhood. Creating new jobs within the neighborhood would be part of a different strategy.

During the strategy implementation phase, the impact indicator will monitor the rate of unemployment in neighborhood X every 6 months and compare it to unemployment in a neighborhood with similar socioeconomic conditions but without a transport project. The variations of the impact indicator over time will show whether providing better access to high-employment areas might decrease unemployment. It will indicate whether the strategy is likely to be effective. If the impact indicator shows that it is not, the strategy should be modified, or an entirely new alternative strategy should be tried.

Outcome Indicators

At this stage of strategy preparation, planners should find the more effective way to transport N_{3s} number of people at peak hour from location X to location Y and Z, where many jobs are located. Depending on the size of N_3 and the distance D between origin X and destinations Y and Z, alternative transport modes will be considered, from collective taxis to buses or urban rail. Individual means of transport like electric mopeds or motorcycles might also be considered. Let us assume that at this phase of preparation, it is found that an express bus line is the most effective commuting mode to transport N_3 passengers from X to locations Y and Z.

During the design phase of the strategy, the outcome indicators will set the target number of passengers using the buses, and then the schedule, frequency, and speed of the express buses from origin X to their destinations.

During the implementation phase, the outcome indicators will monitor and compare the occupancy rate of the buses, schedules, and speed to the target established during the design phase. During implementation, the outcome indicators might be used to modify the strategy if they are inferior to the target outcome indicators. For instance, if the new express bus line has a low occupancy rate and is underused, some alternative routes and different time schedules should be tried.

The outcome indicator is important to monitor, but the fact that a bus line is well used does not necessarily mean that the objective of the investment has been met. People may take the bus for other reasons than commuting to work. Or possibly, the passengers of the new bus line have shifted from a less convenient route that they were previously using to commute to work. A positive outcome indicator might only indicate that trips to and from the neighborhood are becoming more convenient, not necessarily that the poverty alleviation objective has been met. The outcome indicator is not a substitute for the impact indicator.

Output Indicators

During the strategy design phase, the output indicator will show the number of express buses that will be required to carry N_3 passengers to their destinations. The output indicators will then include the number of buses required to ensure the service, and the number and location of bus stations. The output indicators will also include the number of staff hours of surveyors, traffic engineers, and statisticians that will be required to monitor the implementation of the strategy and eventually to modify it.

During implementation, output indicators are used to measure potential cost overrun—fewer buses than originally planned for the money invested, for instance. The output indicator does not tell us whether anybody is using the buses, how frequent they are and even less if the new buses result in an increase in employment. The output indicators are important intermediary indicators but are not indicative of a successful strategy, even if they meet their targets.

Input Indicators

During the strategy design phase, the input indicators will include the total investment cost of the project: including design and supervision, the capital cost of the buses and of the construction of the bus stations, the operation and maintenance cost of the bus line and eventual subsidies, and the projected cash flow of the project, including fares and eventual operation subsidies. Some inputs, including operation and maintenance subsidies, might be recurring over time.

It is usual that during the design phase, the total inputs required to implement a strategy exceed the municipal budget or staff capacity. The planners will then have to iterate the four types of indicators until a consistency between expected impact and budget capacity is reached. Going through iterations during the design phase usually stimulates creativity and innovation.

During implementation, the input indicators will show whether budgetary and staff commitments have been met. Obviously, slowness in cost disbursement will have a negative effect on project performance and might cause a strategy failure. Ensuring that disbursements of project costs occur on schedule is a prerequisite for strategy success, but it does not guarantee it.

Indicators Have to Be Used to Weed Out Failing Strategies

It is normal that some strategies will fail. What is abnormal is to continue implementing a failing strategy. Designing and monitoring indicators is the only way to weed out failing strategies. The four types of indicators—impact, outcome, output, and input—are indispensable for designing and monitoring strategies, as well as for eliminating failing strategies.

Without calculating impact indicators, it is impossible to know whether the project investment contributed to the policy objective or not. In the example above, new buses may well be running on time, but they may have no impact at all on unemployment. The intermediary indicators—inputs, outputs, and outcome—provide us with important information about the design of the project, despite not telling us whether the strategy objective has been met. The intermediary indicators show how the performance of the project could be improved. For instance, if the buses are too slow and result in very long trips, corrective action could be taken, for instance, by improving the design of road intersections and the traffic management along the route.

Economic Rate of Return

By combining the results of the input and impact indicators, it is possible to calculate the internal economic rate of return of the project. The economic rate of return will calculate the present value of a discounted cash flow of the expenditures and the benefits (the additional flow of income coming to the neighborhood because of newly employed workers). For instance, in the example depicted in figure 8.2, in addition to the economic rate of return, it will be possible to calculate what the capital and yearly recurring cost of the strategy is per new employed worker. It may then be found that either the selected strategy provides a high economic return on the municipal investment, or possibly that the return is very low and alternative strategies should be explored that would increase the welfare of the citizens at a lower cost.

If we look at the way an industrial producer creates new products, we see a long list of trials and errors and eventually improvement in quality at a lower cost. Urban policies and strategies, by contrast, often do not follow this logic; they are often repeated even when it is well known that they failed. For instance, policies like rent control, greenbelts, new light rail transports, among others, are constantly repeated in spite of a near consensus on their failure to achieve their objectives. A quantitative evaluation of the failure of these policies is usually well documented through special reports or academic papers; it is seldom produced internally by cities, however, and the information does not seem to reach urban decision makers. Only a systematic analysis of data through indicators allows urban policies to be improved over time and failing policies to be abandoned. But as Angus Deaton wrote: "without data, anyone who does anything is free to claim success."[7]

Most Institutions, Cities, and Development Banks Monitor Mostly Input and Output

Unfortunately, most urban strategies tend to focus on input and output, seldom on outcome and almost never on impact. The output is often misunderstood to be the objective. Developing the four types of indicators when developing the strategy obliges us to think about the real long-term policy objective and avoid being solely focused on our immediate tasks, which are only intermediary phases to accomplish the real objective.

Robert McNamara, while he was the president of the World Bank, from 1968 to 1981, tried to impose this methodology during the appraisal of projects financed by the Bank. McNamara, who strongly reoriented the Bank toward fighting poverty, required the staff to quantify the number of direct project beneficiaries distributed by income percentile of the country or the city where a World Bank–financed project was located. That was the best way to evaluate the impact of projects financed by the World Bank whose objective was to decrease poverty.

In 1971, as a practicing urban planner working for the Government of Yemen under the United Nations Development Programme, I learned for the first time to use this quantitative approach for project evaluation, as I participated as "the local urban planner" in the appraisal of two urban World Bank projects. I was greatly impressed by this rigorous quantitative approach, which was completely new to me. It was in part because of this first very favorable professional impression that I decided to join the World Bank several years later when, with my family, we finally settled in Washington, DC.

In the post-McNamara period, unfortunately, there was a strong tendency in the World Bank to focus mainly on input and output indicators, as these indicators were directly under the control of Bank staff and affected directly the institution as it worked as a bank. A project was deemed successful if the funds were disbursed on time—input—and if there was no project cost overruns—output. This was apparent in World Bank statistics that presented the amount of loans disbursed per sector and per country. For instance, in transport projects the outputs were the number of buses that were purchased and the length of the bus lines built. The numbers measuring outcome and impact could not easily be aggregated into country statistics, because their nature varied so much between projects. Therefore, there was much less pressure to monitor carefully these numbers after projects were completed. While some projects included the full set of indicators during the project appraisal phase, it was rare that outcome and impact indicators were carefully quantified and monitored during the supervision phase of the project. By contrast, inputs and output indicators made or broke the reputation of professional staff.

The World Bank was aware of this problem. It had instituted an independent review of project performance by an Operations Evaluation Department (OED) and more recently by the Independent Evaluation Group. These departments, reporting directly to the president, tried to evaluate more systematically project outcomes and impacts for a selected numbers of completed projects. Inevitably, the results were published long after projects were completed. By the time the evaluation results were available, the team that originally prepared the projects had been dispersed to different countries and sometimes to different sectors. Usually, the OED reports constituted a very professional and detailed analysis of what went right or wrong during project conception and implementation. However, lessons were seldom learned, as new teams started new types of projects in different contexts in different cities, and the evaluation phase was seldom taken into account when designing new projects.

Can a City Avoid the Problem Encountered by the World Bank in Monitoring Strategies and Project Impact?

The problems inherent in monitoring and evaluating World Bank projects as I experienced them are unavoidable in centralized organization like the World Bank, which is physically remote from the location of the project. I think it is unavoidable that international organizations and central governments are likely to focus on the input and output performances of their strategies, as these are the only numbers that they can easily monitor and aggregate.

Development banks, such as the World Bank and its regional counterparts, like Asian Development Bank and Banco Interamericano de Desarrollo, are, first and foremost, banks. The speed of loan disbursement and the correct enforcement of procurement rules are likely to preoccupy bank staff, whose performance is largely judged by management mainly on these criteria, which directly affect banking viability. While the merits of different strategies and their impact on development are the objects of passionate intellectual debates, at the end of the day, the staff performance is judged through its ability to disburse a loan rapidly while following strict procurement rules. Disbursement and procurement are typically monitored through input and output indicators. Indicators linked to outcome and impact, while extensively discussed during project preparation, tend to be rapidly forgotten during project implementation.

Why then would I advocate a methodology to develop urban development strategies that I have seen fail repeatedly? I think that committed mayors and their planning staff are much more likely to follow through and be interested by impact if given the tools to do so. City-states, like Singapore and Hong Kong, manage independently their own finances and policy without interferences from a remote central government, and they are notoriously good at monitoring policies and taking rapid correcting steps as soon as they perceive that strategies are not performing as expected.

By contrast, a central organization cannot feel directly accountable for the details of projects implemented at the local level. Input and output are what they effectively control and therefore are likely to monitor carefully. For instance, a central government's ministry of Housing and Urban Development may commit itself to creating a target number of affordable housing units in a large number of cities. It has no way to aggregate at the national-level statistics on whether the units created are well located, or whether they result in increased welfare for the target population. The only things the ministry can usefully monitor and aggregate at the national level are the total capital outlays and the number of units created—input and output indicators. The staff of the ministry, if ever alerted that the dwelling units are not fulfilling the original objectives, will be unable to aggregate the different outcome and impact indicators if these are produced by the cities that benefit from the program. The ministry staff will face the same problem as the World Bank staff faced. By the time the indicator results arrive from the various cities, the ministry's staff that prepared the strategy might well have moved to other activities in other sectors. No lesson will ever be learned. By contrast, in a city administration, continuity is more likely. The issues arising during implementation of the strategies are more likely to be known in real time, and there will be a strong incentive to address the issues as they arise, if the mayor and the local staff have any control over the implementation of housing strategy even if it is financed at the national level. Maybe this is why city-states like Singapore and Hong Kong are more effective in managing their development than are equivalent cities that are part of large states.

For instance, let us look at the case of South Africa discussed in chapter 6. The policy objective was to provide as quickly as possible affordable housing to a very large segment of the urban population defined by its low income. The strategy adopted focused immediately on inputs and outputs: how many houses could be built each year, what should be their standards, and how large were the subsidies needed. The alternative strategies considered were only focused on the way to finance the program. The impact on the income of beneficiaries was never considered, although the main objective of the program was in reality to alleviate poverty. The output—the number of housing units built each year—was carefully monitored and because of their large number, the program was initially deemed successful. It was only after about 10 years of implementation that the serious shortcomings of the South African housing strategy were finally detected. The damage done in building large numbers of dwelling units in areas inaccessible to the metropolitan job markets is nearly irreversible.

Designing New Land Use Regulations and Auditing Existing Regulations

The necessity of living and working in close proximity requires rules that will minimize friction. Because the economic and technological environment is changing constantly, the rules have to be constantly adapted to the new environment. For instance, the introduction of self-driving cars in cities in the near future will require new regulations, just as new regulations were required when cars replaced horse carts as a main mode of urban transport.

Past regulations also have to be periodically reviewed for their relevance. As described in chapter 7, the shadows cast by very tall buildings were a major issue for the first part of the twentieth century, until indoor lighting and air conditioning became efficient and cheap. Being able to concentrate large areas of floor space where demand is very high increases the city welfare much more than restricting densities because of the need to ensure that every building receives direct sunlight and natural ventilation. The slender and very tall skyscrapers, residential and commercial, being built in New York's Wall Street area would have been extremely objectionable for their neighbors at the beginning of the twentieth century.

Urban planners should therefore constantly revise old land use regulations (or create new ones) to adapt them to the new economic and cultural realities of the time. Unfortunately, urban planning departments tend to prefer designing new regulations over reviewing existing ones for their relevance. As a result, a city's land use depends on layers of regulations that often contradict one another and whose objectives have been lost with time. Digging into urban regulations is often like digging into an archeological site; one often encounters elaborate artifacts whose original purpose baffles the mind.

This criticism of baffling regulations is not a new idea. In a book chapter published in 1979, Morris Hill and Rachelle Alterman wrote:[8]

Typically [planning standards] are handed down as "rule of thumb" from one situation to another, adapted by cumulated experience. Such norms are characteristically expressed as a simple inflexible per a given population, sometimes also including locational specifications. From the norms as usually expressed it is impossible to know the substantive justification—whether functional, economic, behavioral, social, psychological or environmental. Therefore, there is no easy way of modifying them to meet particular situations in a reasoned manner.

Planners Should Regularly Audit Land Use Regulations to Eliminate Those That Are Obsolete

The regulatory deadwood accumulated over the years constrains development and affects land prices and the supply of floor space, as these regulations limit what can be built. While nobody usually remembers the objectives of such regulations, planners and citizens assume that they were established as a result of lost wisdom and that it might be hazardous to remove them from the books.

I was confronted with such a situation some years ago in Malaysia,[9] when I was asked to find out why housing was so expensive in a country that is well endowed with developable land. I found that in residential areas, the regulations required extremely short blocks of 60 meters, resulting in an extremely high percentage of road areas that would not be normally required for horizontal housing (for example, a Manhattan block length averages about 240 meters). Additional land use regulations resulted in less than 44 percent of the land being developed for residential use in a housing project in Malaysia, compared to 60–65 percent in similar projects in other countries of the region.

Nobody in the Kuala Lumpur planning office knew why blocks had to be so short, but they assumed that there must be a good reason—drainage during the monsoon perhaps? I finally found a senior municipal engineer who told me that the practice was to locate fire hydrants at the end of a block and that the fire hose used by firemen was usually 30 meters long, hence the 60 meter length of a residential block. There was a great reluctance in changing the standard, in spite of firemen using different equipment and the possibility of locating fire hydrants differently.

The cost of these regulations to the housing sector and to the environment was extremely large while bringing no real benefits to citizens. Indeed, these regulations—by requiring more land for residential development artificially—extended the area of cities into the countryside while increasing the impermeable area of the development. In a monsoon country like Malaysia, this contributed to increased water run-off during the rainy season, requiring larger drains and, at times, causing erosion. The eventual revision of this set of land use regulations resulted in substantial savings in land development and environmental cost for the entire country.

The urban regulations of every city contain a number of what I would call "deadwood regulations." Regulations whose objectives have been forgotten and whose benefits can no longer be identified. It is therefore necessary to periodically audit all land use regulations to remove the ones that are obsolete and contribute to the high cost of urbanization.

Designing New Regulations

New technology and changes in the way cities develop may require planners to design new regulations. These should be designed with great care and tested before being imposed citywide. Land use regulations are very much like new medical drugs—they are supposed to provide benefits but they may also have serious negative side effects that may become apparent many years after they have been applied. All regulations should be submitted to a cost-benefit analysis. In addition, land use regulations that have a direct impact on housing and residential development should be tested for affordability for various income groups.

Regulations should be designed and tested with great caution, in the same way as what is required before a new drug is put on the market. Before imposing new regulations, urban planning departments should ask teams of independent urban economists to evaluate their impact on the spatial development of the city and on the cost of urban development.

The Role of the City Planning Department in a Municipality

Staff and Line Agencies

A municipality is a team composed of a political body, the mayor and the city council, and a technical core composed of "staff" and "line" agencies (figure 8.3). The staff agencies provide policy options to the mayor and policy objectives and support to the line agencies. The line agencies implement and maintain specialized services and infrastructure. The city planning department maintains a set of indicators to ensure that strategies meet the policy objectives of the mayor and the city council. The City Planning Department should be located among staff agencies. Unfortunately, this is seldom the case; most of the time City Planning is just one of the line agencies.

Why should the City Planning Department be among the staff agencies? Practically all line agencies are consuming land or have an impact on land prices. All line agencies' actions, from education to the fire department, are related to the number of people in a neighborhood and their incomes, usually linked to other socioeconomic indicators, such as household sizes, education, language spoken at home. The changes in the number and socioeconomic characteristics of a population are driven by the real estate market and the competitive demand for floor space coming from households and firms. Data on the use of land and on population changes should not be maintained in separate databases by each line agency but should be coordinated and centralized in the planning department, which should feed the data to the line agencies at regular interval.

The Planning Department Staff Should Include Economists

Instead of being exclusively focused on land use and regulatory issues, the planning department should be also involved in economic analysis on a day-to-day basis. Therefore, I suggest calling the city planning department "City Planning and Economics" (figure 8.3).

In many cities around the world, the city planning departments where I worked were staffed mostly by urban planners, architects, engineers, and lawyers. While economists, working as consultants, were occasionally asked to produce a report on a specific subject, I have never met an in-house economist providing inputs on a day-to-day basis on proposed land use regulations, monitoring changing of land prices, or warning other staff of the Planning Department of their policies' potential consequences. As we have seen in previous chapters, land use changes and population and job density changes are mostly driven by markets. Urban economists are uniquely trained to monitor and interpret market movements. The presence of an in-house economist would also help trigger ad hoc specialized economic analysis conducted by universities. This would have the double benefit of both tapping a wider and deep economic expertise as well as prodding academic economists into getting involved in "operational economics" at the city level.

The City Planning and Economics staff agency has three main functions:

• developing and maintaining an urban database that monitors among other things, land use, demographics, household incomes, and land prices and rents;

• identifying potential issues derived from observing variations in indicators; and

• working with line agencies to propose policy and strategic solutions to respond to identified issues and to respond to special requests from the mayor and the city council.

The alignment of the City Planning and Economics department as a staff agency is vital, because of its need to relate with all line agencies. Line agencies must develop their own detailed technical databases, but they should refer to the land use and demographic database from the planning department to develop policy. The consistency between the technical projects developed by the line agencies and the city development policy and the strategy developed in the City Planning Department is essential. It seems obvious, but it is not always the case.

Some years ago, I was working for the city planning department of the Jakarta metropolitan area (covering the area called Jabotabek). In liaison with the housing

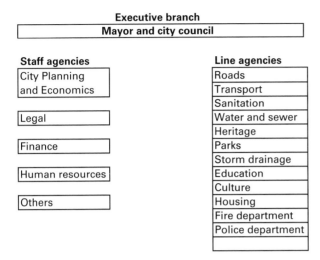

Executive branch
Mayor and city council

Staff agencies

| City Planning and Economics |
| Legal |
| Finance |
| Human resources |
| Others |

Line agencies

| Roads |
| Transport |
| Sanitation |
| Water and sewer |
| Heritage |
| Parks |
| Storm drainage |
| Education |
| Culture |
| Housing |
| Fire department |
| Police department |
| |

Figure 8.3
Urban planners and line agencies.

department and a major mortgage bank, we were developing land development standards that should be affordable to households between the fortieth and sixtieth percentiles of Jakarta's household income distribution. Our conclusion was that to be affordable, taking into account current market prices for land and construction, population densities in the housing projects financed by the mortgage bank would have to have between 300 and 400 people per hectare. Land use subdivision regulations were amended to allow these densities. However, the City Planning department did not amend density projections for the entire city to reflect these changes, as it was considered too far from the traditional planning approach based on design norms and perceived needs.

During the same period, some of my Indonesian colleagues were conducting a feasibility study for a regional sewer and wastewater disposal system for Jabotabek area. Their conclusion was that if the population density in the suburban area of Jakarta could be maintained below a maximum of 50 people per hectare, it would be possible to build a system of septic tanks, seepage pits, and oxidation ponds that would be much cheaper than building a reticulated sewer systems with traditional sewer treatment plants. They assumed that through adequately enforced land use regulations, the government would be able to keep the density below this maximum and as a consequence, they were proposing an investment budget for sewer and wastewater disposal based on this low-cost technology.

A third project, consisting of the planning and construction of a light rail urban transport system, was being developed by the urban transport department with the assistance of a bilateral donor. The light rail being developed consisted of one line crossing Jabotabek from east to west. The feasibility study assumed that the government would be able to regulate population densities in such a way that an east-west spine of high population density of about 300 people per hectare would be concentrated along the catchment area of the light rail line, while regulations would maintain low density in areas not served by the light rail. The financial projections were entirely based on this optimistic density scenario that would have ensured a high occupancy rate for the light rail.

The three projects were based on completely different and incompatible assumptions about the future spatial distribution of the population of Jabotabek. The feasibility of each project depended on different mutually exclusive spatial distributions of the population. The urban planning department maintained a map of projected densities and a map of zoning regulations, but there was no administrative links between the department of environment protection in charge of sewers and the department of transport. I found out about the three different density projections by accident, because I knew some of the engineers working on the two other projects.

This anecdote is not an isolated case. Looking at the municipal organization design of most cities, these types of inconsistencies happen all the time. I am not suggesting that to avoid these problems the Urban Planning and Economics Department supervise every sectoral project, but that any assumption about densities and in general on the spatial distribution of population be cleared with the Urban Planning and Economics Department to avoid these internal contradictions. In transport projects, the many occurrences of overestimation of projected passengers boarding are typical of self-serving projections of future urban densities along transport routes. It is possible to commit errors when projecting the spatial distribution of future populations, but it is inexcusable to maintain alternative projections within each line agency in the same municipality, especially when a centrally managed projection based on markets would invalidate the feasibility of a project.

Past and Future Growth Trends for Cities

Urban Growth Should Not Be Taken for Granted
The examples used in the preceding chapters concern urban issues that arose during the past 50 years. Should we expect different types of urban development challenges in the next 50 years?

I have always assumed that successful cities were magnets that attracted people eager to join their large labor markets. Most of my work as an urban planner has been focused on finding ways to manage urban growth by improving mobility and housing affordability as cities were expanding. The supply of new citizens born in, or immigrating to, cities seemed inexhaustible. Usually developing countries' cities were growing faster than those in rich countries, but the process of expansion was basically the same, and all were expanding.

At the beginning of the twenty-first century, I realized that the world population had crossed a demographic watershed and that the cities of the world were going to be divided between those who were growing and those who were shrinking. The cause of the shrinking ranges from internal causes like poor management—as has been the case for the decline of Detroit—to external causes like demographic reversal and rates of urbanization.

In 2010, during a work visit to Moscow, I learned that the government was planning to close 60 cities, whose populations were decreasing and aging to such an extent that maintaining their public services was no longer viable. Closing cities is an extreme case, but decreasing population has also affected many other cities. Among the 13 Russian cities with a population larger than a million people, only four were still growing; the others, including St. Petersburg as the second-largest city in the country, had declining populations. I was asked if I could give some advice on what to do in cities with decreasing populations. I declined and claimed incompetence; in 50 years of my international urban planning practice, I had never been confronted with the issues arising from decreasing urban populations.

More recently, during a visit to Toyama, a city of 1.2 million on the western coast of Japan, local urban planners described to me the problems faced by a city with an aging population, increasingly abandoned by its younger generation migrating to Tokyo to find work.

Japan and Russia are representative of countries with high income, low fertility, a high rate of urbanization, and a low rate of international immigration. Decreasing fertility in high-income countries that are already highly urbanized creates low urban growth, as the natural growth rate and the migration rate decrease simultaneously when the country's rural areas are not sending additional migrants to the cities.

Figure 8.4 shows the relationship between urban growth rates and rates of urbanization and income by region and type of income. We see clearly the correlation between high income, high rate of urbanization, and urban growth rate. Women in high-income countries tend to have a low fertility rate, reducing the natural growth rate caused by the difference between the number of births and deaths. The high urbanization rate in these high-income countries implies that there is not much excess labor left in rural areas to migrate toward cities and compensate for the low natural growth rate with immigrants from the countryside.

These cities of the rich world are eventually doomed to have a stagnating and eventually decreasing population, unless they deliberately open themselves to international migration and can draw migrants from countries with high fertility rates and low rates of urbanization.

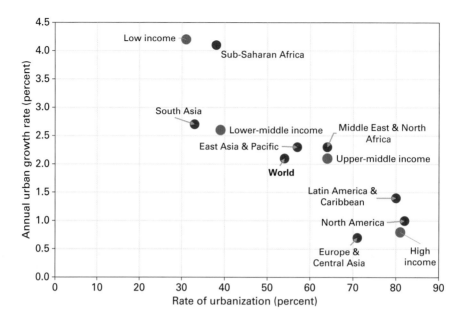

Figure 8.4
Rates of urbanization and urban growth rates by region, 2010–2015. *Source*: World Bank, "3.12 World
Development Indicators: Urbanization," Washington, DC, 2017.

Traditionally, large economically dynamic city-states like Singapore and the
cities of the Emirates, who could not draw migrants from a populous rural hinterland, have relied on controlled immigration to increase the labor force that keeps
their economy growing, thus increasing the income of their national population.
In Singapore, the foreign nonresident population represents 29 percent of the total
population. In Singapore as in the Emirates, most of the nonresident population
is not intended to eventually become citizens. They remain on short-term contracts. This allows the cities to target the skills they need for the development of
their economies. The nonresident emigrants are carefully selected among two
groups: highly skilled professionals and low-skilled labor force for services. These
city-states understand that the development of their economies, and therefore of
the welfare of their native citizens, depends on an expanding labor force and that
immigration is indispensable to their economies.

By contrast, countries of Western Europe and North America have a different
approach to immigration. In these countries, immigrants are assumed to eventually become citizens, but contrary to Singapore or the Emirates, the national
governments of Europe and North America do not explicitly link immigration
with urban economic self-interest.

While the United States and Canada have traditionally been dependent on immigration for developing their economies over the past two centuries, the economic self-interest argument for immigration is seldom explicitly made. The popular argument for welcoming immigrants from foreign countries rests more on a sense of generosity and hospitality than on self-interest. The verses engraved in bronze on the Statue of Liberty in New York express perfectly the generous feeling apparently allowing immigration to the American continent:

Give me your tired, your poor,
Your huddled masses yearning to breathe free,
The wretched refuse of your teeming shore.

While no successful immigration can occur without a minimum of generosity and benevolence, the economic benefits of immigrations are very large and should in themselves be the prime motivation of immigration policy. The economic case for immigration is often confused with the human rights case for refugees, which is of course a quite different argument.

While immigration is indispensable to fuel the economic growth of cities located in countries with low birth rates and with an already high urbanization rate, the pace of immigration should be controlled. To become fully economically effective, new immigrants must have time to adapt to the social norms and language of the host country, and this adaption takes resources that must be allocated in a national budget or at least by motivated NGOs. Without these resources and a minimum of assistance, the lowest-income immigrants might become an underclass separated from the host population by language and unfamiliarity with the social norms of the host country. In this case, the economic stagnation of the less-educated migrants reinforces the nativist anti-immigrant hostility, contributing to closing borders and to the decay of cities with aging populations.

The political upheaval of 2016, whose main outcomes were Brexit in Europe and the presidential election results in the United States, was caused in great part by two antagonistic perceptions of immigration. The populations of large cities were aware of the economic benefits of foreign immigration, while the populations of smaller cities and rural areas saw immigrants as job stealers rather than as contributors to the national economy. In New York in 2015 the foreign-born population represented 38 percent of the total city population. In London in 2011, 37 percent of the population was born outside the United Kingdom. No wonder that both cities voted against the anti-immigration parties in the 2016 vote!

Immigration is therefore a necessity for the economic survival of large cities in affluent countries with declining birth rates. However, because immigration policy is decided by national government and not by the cities themselves, it is quite possible that cities in affluent countries will see their economies decline, as the aging of their population will not be compensated by an influx of younger and more vigorous immigrants. Some large US cities, which include many foreign-born workers, are well aware of the problem and have declared themselves to be "sanctuary cities." Sanctuary cities like New York, San Francisco, and others have declared that their municipal police will not enforce emigration laws and will not cooperate with Federal departments to enforce them either. This demonstrates the differing interest between economically dynamic large cities and more stagnant smaller cities and rural areas.

Cities like London, Paris, Berlin, and possibly New York will soon be faced with the same problems encountered by Toyama. Looking at figure 8.4, it appears that it might take one or two decades before the cities of Latin America will face the same problems as European cities.

This book is about operational urban planning. It might be worthwhile therefore to explore what is likely to happen to the cohort of cities in affluent countries that will be starved of immigrants by their national government. We can use the example of Japan as a precursor of urban planning in cities with aging and shrinking populations.

Effect of Aging Populations on the Growth of Cities in Japan

The population of Japan peaked at 128 million in 2010. It is projected to decrease to 107 million, or 17 percent by 2040. Between 2010 and 2040, the active population[10] is projected to decrease from 64 percent to 53 percent and the dependency ratio (dependent population/active population) will increase from 57 percent in 2010 to 85 percent in 2040.[11] The decrease in population and the increase in the dependency ratio is more severe in smaller cities than in larger ones. In the three major metropolitan areas (Tokyo, Kyoto-Osaka, and Nagoya), the dependency ratio is less than the national ratio and is projected to increase more slowly from 49 percent in 2010 to 76 percent in 2040.

By comparison, in 2014, the dependency ratio of New York was 45 percent and that of the Singapore resident population (excluding foreigners) was 37 percent. Including foreigners, Singapore's dependency ratio would be even lower. The Japanese government, however, currently has no plan to encourage foreign immigration to compensate for the aging population. There were 2.1 million foreigners residing in Japan in 2014, much less than the 3.2 million foreign-born residents found the same year in New York alone. The way Japanese cities cope with declining populations will constitute an example for urban planners in cities of Europe and other places with an increasingly aging population not compensated for by an increase in foreign immigration. As we will see, the urban development problems encountered by cities with declining populations are very different from the ones described in the preceding chapters of this book.

Six of the eight Japanese cities of more than 5 million people had a positive population growth rate between 2005 and 2010 (figure 8.5). Tokyo, the largest city with 13 million people (Tokyo Prefecture), saw the largest population increase at 4.7 percent. By contrast, among the 39 cities between half a million and 5 million, the growth was negative for all but three of them. An aging population, apparently, does not prevent the larger cities from growing, although modestly, but it contributes to an accelerating decrease in population for smaller cities.

The mayor of Toyama, a city of 1.2 million with a loss of population of 1.7 percent between 2005 and 2010, considers that the population decrease is the major challenge faced by his municipality. Local planners explain that Toyama's young adults tend to emigrate toward larger cities like Tokyo or Osaka, where they are likely to find more new jobs than in a city like Toyama. This emigration of young people from smaller cities further decreases the size of their local labor market, making them even less attractive for new investment and creating a disinvestment spiral. The fiscal base of these cities and their budgets are also severely affected by the increasing pensions and social services they have to provide to the old while their tax base is shrinking.

What kind of urban projects become a priority in a city with a shrinking population? In Toyama in 2016, the major planning projects consisted of trying to regroup aged people from the suburbs to a more central location where they could be taken care of at a lesser cost. Some suburban areas are even demolished and citizens are given a subsidy to move toward more centralized locations. Public transports are redesigned to provide more mobility to the handicapped. Schools are reconverted to care centers for the aged. One of the major objectives of the municipality is to maintain the mobility of the elderly who can no longer drive, either by providing them with motorized wheelchairs and special wheelchair lanes on sidewalks or by organizing easy-to-board public transport in neighborhoods where the elderly have been regrouped.

At the same time, with tax subsidies, the municipality is trying to retain or create jobs outside the geriatric health sector, the only sector that is thriving. The municipality is also trying to make the city more culturally attractive to retain the young. These descriptions from Toyama are of course anecdotal evidence of what urban planning consists of in a city with a shrinking population. Most urban planners, including myself, are completely unprepared to manage cities who will be in a similar situation as Toyama and many other smaller Japanese towns. It is possible that technology, for which the Japanese have a demonstrated expertise, could partially solve the problem of an aging population. There is also a possibility

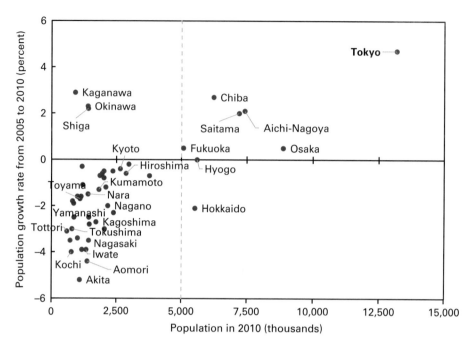

Figure 8.5
Population growth rates of Japanese cities above 500,000 people, between 2005 and 2010. *Source*:
Wendell Cox, "Japan's 2010 Census: Moving to Tokyo," New Geography, Grand Forks, ND, 2011,
http://www.newgeography.com/content/002227-japan%E2%80%99s-2010-census-moving-tokyo.

that in the future the Japanese birth rate will stabilize at a level that allows the
country to maintain a constant urban population and a corresponding stable
urban economy.

Growing and Shrinking Cities Will Not Be Randomly Geographically Distributed

Most cities of the world will not face the trials of Toyama. There are still many
countries with very young populations who are ready to move from rural areas
to urban areas, or to emigrate anywhere in the world toward the dynamic cities
that would welcome them. From the beginning of the twenty-first century we will
see a strong divergence between very dynamic megacities like the Pearl River
Delta cities, for instance, and shrinking cities in Europe and some parts of the
North American continent. Let us now look at the potential for dynamic cities.

In 2014 the United Nations published a report titled "World Urbanization Prospects 2014." I reproduce one of the major graphs from the report in figure 8.6. The

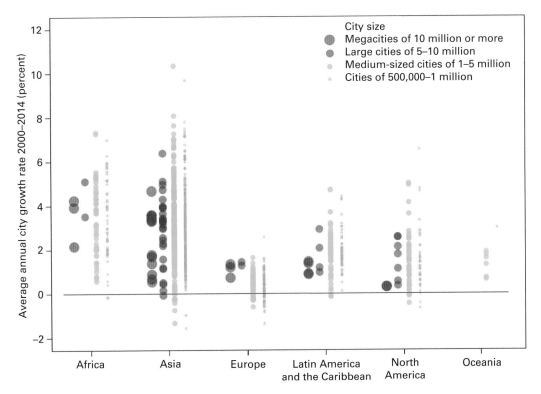

Figure 8.6
Urban growth rates by region and city size, between 2000 and 2014. *Sources*: Data are from United Nations, Department of Economic and Social Affairs, Population Division (2014). World Urbanization Prospects: The 2014 Revision, Highlights (ST/ESA/SER.A/352).

graph displays the growth rates between 2000 and 2014 for world cities sorted by continents and by size class. We see immediately a large dispersion of annual growth rates from 10 percent to –1.5 percent. The largest dispersion is on the Asian continent, where megacities of more than 10 million have been growing from about 0.5 percent to 5 percent.

The cities with negative growth rates are found mostly among medium-sized cities of one to five million people and smaller cities between half a million to one million. The negative growth of many cities below five million people is consistent with the Japanese experience.

The distribution of cities in figure 8.6 shows the preponderance of urban development in Africa and Asia, areas with the highest growth rates for megacities as well as for smaller cities. The shift in the economic center of gravity of the world, from North America and Western Europe toward Asia, which occurred at the beginning of the twenty-first century, is put in evidence on the graph; while some megacities in Asia are growing at more than 3 percent a year, megacities in Europe, Latin America, and North America are growing at less than 2 percent a year.

In Asia, the large investment in infrastructure that took place during the past 20 years has stimulated the growth of more cities by making trade easier and transport less costly. In 2013, the government of China announced an initiative called "The Silk Road Economic Belt and the Twenty-First Century Maritime Silk Road," usually abbreviated as "One Belt, One Road." This initiative will link the cities of central Asia with newly expanded port facilities in cities of South and Southeast Asia. This will create an enormous transcontinental trading zone of a scale never seen before. The planned infrastructure will provide access to the sea for central Asia countries, with their vast natural resources. The increased exchanges following the newly created maritime routes will further stimulate the growth of cities in the region and the migration of population toward large cities.

Some large cities of Asia, in particular in China and India, may already be affected by low birth rates linked to newly found affluence. However, these cities are in countries that still have a large reserve of surplus labor in rural areas. Their continuous growth for the medium term is therefore ensured. The possibility of extensive communication and cultural exchange between Asian countries with different and deep cultural traditions will certainly greatly stimulate the creativity and innovation of cities of the region.

African cities still have the largest unrealized potential. Their growth will benefit from a much younger population than the other continents possess. Their major challenge will be to develop in a timely fashion the infrastructure that is required for humans to live in close proximity in very large cities.

What Will Cities Look Like in the Middle of the Twenty-First Century?
As I have suggested, we will see two types of cities by the middle of the twenty-first century:

• First, cities that are growing fast and attracting immigrants from their own country and internationally.

• Second, cities that are losing populations and have increasingly high dependency ratios.

Both types of cities will pose serious urban planning challenges. The fast-growing cities will reach sizes that are unprecedented and for which current transport technologies are inadequate. The shrinking cities will require regrouping the population within a smaller perimeter as their fiscal resources will dwindle with their population.

Let us look first at the larger fast-growing cities of Asia. The recent Chinese policy of looking at the development of cities in clusters, instead of as one central city surrounded by its large suburbs, is a significant departure from past urban practices. City clusters already exist of course, like the Randstad in the Netherlands, which links Amsterdam, Rotterdam, The Hague, and Utrecht. The urban development around San Francisco Bay could also be considered a city cluster. What is different with the Chinese concept of cluster is their scale. The Randstad connects only 7 million people, while San Francisco Bay (including Silicon Valley) has only 6.2 million people. By contrast, the urban cluster of the Pearl River Delta already had 65 million people in 2010, larger than the entire population of the United Kingdom but concentrated on less than 10,000 square kilometers! The recent urban cluster including Beijing–Tianjin–Hebei links together more than 105 million people.

Will these gigantic urban agglomerations really constitute unified labor markets, with the capacity for innovation and productivity commensurate with their labor market sizes? For the moment, the urban transport technology that would allow these large labor markets to integrate does not exist. The existing urban clusters of Asia work well as supply chains, but their labor markets are still fragmented into several smaller overlapping ones. These overlapping but fragmented labor markets certainly provide a comparative productivity advantage over smaller ones like San Francisco Bay or the Randstad, but they do not allow the productivity that could be obtained by linking 100 million people in commuting trips of less than 1 hour.

The main challenge of urbanization in the future therefore rests on the development of urban transport technology. Very fast trains combined with individual means of transport that would provide fast door-to-door trips (or door-to-station and station-to-door trips) would allow the integration of these labor markets. The emerging self-driving technology and small vehicle sharing will probably be a major factor in unifying fragmented labor markets. The allocation of land and the standards used for housing will also constitute a major challenge, as a large movement of labor will be expected.

Cities that lose population will also pose serious challenges until they eventually stabilize. Can a city adapt to a stable population and a stable dependency ratio? We do not have models, as the last century was characterized by a general massive migrations from the rural areas to urban areas.

Whatever model of cities prevail, large urban clusters grouping 100 million people or cities of half a million losing population, urban planning in the middle of the twenty-first century will be very different from what we have known so far.

Notes

Chapter 1

1. Albert O. Hirschman, *Development Projects Observed* (Washington, DC: Brookings Institution Press, 1967), 296.

2. Edward Glaeser, "Reforming Land Use Regulations," in *Series on Market and Government Failures* (Washington, DC: Brookings Institution, Center on Regulation and Markets, March 2017), 2.

3. Alain Bertaud and Bertrand Renaud, "Socialist Cities without Land Markets," *Journal of Urban Economics* 41, no. 1 (1997): 137–151.

4. Kombinats in the Soviet Union and Eastern Europe were large vertical monopolies that usually spanned one industrial sector. For instance, the kombinat in this story operated sand quarries, cement factories, concrete panel factories, and housing construction for a region. Sometimes the kombinat also extended horizontally, operating farms to provide food to its workers.

5. Ronald Coase and Ning Wang, *How China Became Capitalist* (London: Palgrave Macmillan, 2012), 154.

6. *China Daily* (Beijing), November 16, 2013, "Decisions on Major Issues Concerning Comprehensively Deepening Reforms," adopted during the Third Plenary Session of the eighteenth meeting of the Communist Party of China Central Committee on November 12, 2013.

Chapter 2

1. Edward L. Glaeser, Jed Kolko, and Albert Saiz, "Consumer City," *Journal of Economic Geography* 1, no. 1 (2001): 27–50.

2. The Internet is certainly able to spread knowledge quickly without requiring spatial concentration. However, the impact of the Internet on disseminating knowledge might be similar to that of books: it makes knowledge available quickly and cheaply, but it doesn't replace the serendipity of a random meeting of people with similar interests.

3. Shlomo Angel, *Planet of Cities* (Cambridge, MA: Lincoln Institute of Land Policy, 2012).

4. Jane Jacobs, *The Economy of Cities* (New York: Random House, 1969). I do not wish to involve myself in the debate raised by Jane Jacobs, whether cities preceded agriculture. The existence of an obsidian industry in Çatalhöyük ca. 7000 B.C. is well established by archeologists.

5. Industrial Policy Resolution of the Government of India adopted in 1956 under the provisions of the Industrial Development and Regulation Act, 1951.

6. St. Petersburg was created by Peter the Great to open a port toward Western Europe in order to gain new technology through trade and cultural contact. Brasília, created by President Juscelino Kubitschek of Brazil, was part of an effort to develop the center of the country and to make the capital more politically independent from the large cities on the coast. Deng Xiaoping's main objective in creating Shenzhen was to graft and test within a limited perimeter some of the market institutions and technical knowhow used across the border by his Chinese compatriots in Hong Kong.

7. In Russian: "Gosudarstvennaya Planovaya Comissiya" [State Planning Committee], in charge of the Soviet economy.

8. Sam Staley and Adrian Moore, *Mobility First* (Lanham, MD: Rowman & Littlefield Publishers, Inc., 2009).

9. The OECD (Organisation for Economic Co-operation and Development) is a club of 34 rich countries each with a high human development index and committed to a market economy and democracy.

10. Rémy Prud'homme and Chang-Woon Lee, "Size, Sprawl, Speed and the Efficiency of Cities," *Observatoire de l'Économie et des Institutions Locales*, Université de Paris 13, 1998.

11. Patricia Melo, Daniel Graham, David Levinson, and Sarah Aarabi, "Agglomeration, Accessibility, and Productivity: Evidence for Urbanized Areas in the US," paper submitted to the Transportation Research Board, Washington, DC, 2013.

12. Not all CBDs are located at the center of the built-up area. Mumbai's CBD, for instance, is located at the Southern tip of a peninsula, while the centroid of the built up area is located more than 15 kilometers to the north. This situation is relatively rare, as market forces tend to re-center the CBD toward the center of gravity of a city's population.

13. The term "commuting routes" defines an itinerary from one place to another, which may have to follow minor roads in the absence of major roads linking the point of origin to the desired destination. Commuting routes are therefore independent from the existing design of major roads, which may often converge on a central point.

14. David Levinson, "Access across America," Center for Transportation Studies, University of Minnesota, Minneapolis, 2013.

15. Chang-Moo Lee and Kun-Hyuck Ahn, "Five New Towns in the Seoul Metropolitan Area and Their Attractions in Non-working Trips: Implications for Self-Containment of New Towns," *Habitat International* 29 (2005): 647–666.

16. Path dependency refers to situations in which options taken in the past limit the number of options available in the future. The concept is commonly used in history, evolutionary biology, and economics but is obviously applicable to urban development as well. For instance, in evolutionary biology a group of primitive living cells could possibly evolve in into a mammal or into a fish. But once the cells have evolved into a fish, they cannot possibly evolve into a mammal and vice versa.

17. Commuting trips include only trips between a residence and a workplace. Other trips, for shopping, social life, or leisure, are counted separately. Commuting trips are often a fraction of all trips, but they are the most important for proper functioning of the labor market. In addition, most commuting trips take place at rush hour and therefore test the capacity of the transport system.

18. In this case, I defined Seoul central city as the area within a circle of 10 km radius centered on Seoul City Hall. This area includes three distinct CBD-like areas with an intense spatial concentration of jobs.

19. Paanwalas sell paan, a mixture of betel leaf, areca nuts, and tobacco. They are small, informal, thriving retail businesses in the streets of Indian cities.

20. Chambres de bonnes or "maids' rooms" were independent rooms of about 9–12 square meters built under the roofs of opulent buildings in Paris and provincial towns, usually with common bathroom facilities on the same floor. When the households in these buildings could not afford maids anymore, the rooms became the cheapest rental rooms on the market. Their low cost has been maintained over the years in spite of their excellent location because they are often located on the fifth or sixth floors of buildings without elevators.

21. A Kampung, which means "village" in Bahasa Indonesian, is an informal but legal residential neighborhood in Indonesian cities. The lot sizes vary by income, with the smallest being around 10 square meters. Streets in a Kampung are usually 2 or 3 meters wide; some passages between houses are no wider than a half meter.

22. For instance, Stockholm urban regulations require a job–housing balance in each neighborhood, in spite of statistics showing that when this balance is achieved, it does not decrease trip length. Allowing mixed land use where firms and housing can be found in the same location is an excellent policy, but mandating it is illusory and only slows down the development process. In addition, the number of jobs per commercial structure can vary significantly over time.

Chapter 3

1. I differentiate "urban planning" from "design": planning involves various tasks, many of them being projections, for instance, demographic and traffic projections or projection of future demand for water or energy. Design is a more specific part of urban planning that involves imposing physical limits on the built environment. Design involves producing the plans of individual buildings but also drawing up zoning plans, limiting the height of buildings, separating land use, establishing urban growth boundaries, and similar activities.

2. Ebenezer Howard (1850–1928) was the founder of the garden city movement. He was a social reformer and utopian planner dedicated to improving the social conditions of workers in England in the latter part of the Industrial Revolution. His concept consisted of building clusters of self-sufficient cities of approximately 30,000 people surrounded by fields and forest and linked together by a network of railways. The goal was to escape the polluted and insalubrious environment of the large, dense industrial cities of his time. In a way he anticipated the creation of modern low-density suburbs, although modern suburbs are certainly not self-sufficient.

3. Maharashtra State government policy (DCR 58, 2001) allowed the mill owners to retain only one-third of their land for commercial purposes. The other two-thirds had to be given free of charge to the state for the development of low-income housing, open spaces, and social amenities.

4. Mumbai capital expenditure for the years 2014–2015 was about 73.5 billion Indian rupees or US$1.07 billion.

5. Designs created by artists do not need any rational justification but are by definition idiosyncratic. I am using here the other definition of design given by Webster's Dictionary: "to create, plan, or calculate for serving a predetermined end."

6. Many ancient cities of China were also planned along a square grid like Chang'an the capital of the Sui and Tang dynasties dating from the sixth century AD.

7. Land readjustment is a technique for converting agricultural land or low-density suboptimal land to urban land use without using eminent domain to provide areas for streets and open spaces. Landowners receive a parcel of developable land smaller than the original agricultural parcel but with a much higher value because of infrastructure. The agency, public or private, that manages land readjustment schemes pays for the infrastructure either by levying a fee from landowners or by taking a percentage of land from the original landowners.

8. Voisin was an airplane manufacturer who partly sponsored Le Corbusier's research work.

9. CIAM (Congrès Internationaux d'Architecture Moderne, or International Congresses of Modern Architecture) was created by a group of famous architects and artists in 1928 and met regularly until 1959. They were responsible for spreading the ideas of Le Corbusier, who was their main guide.

10. The regulation was national but was specified through local ordinances. In Shanghai it was specified in the "Code of Urban Residential Areas Planning and Design" (circular GB50180-93).

11. Five floors was the maximum number allowed for apartment blocks without requiring an elevator. Given the shortage of power in pre-reform China, practically all apartment blocks built were five stories high.

12. Urban population densities are typically measured in people per hectare. For instance, a density of 50 people per hectare corresponds implicitly to a land consumption of 200 square meters per person ($10,000/50 = 200$). Higher densities correspond to lower land consumption per person.

13. The built-up FAR is the ratio between the total floor area built in a city and the total land area developed, including roads but excluding large open spaces. It differs from the plot area ratio, which measures the ratio between the area of floor space built on a private plot and the area of the plot, excluding the roads around the plot.

14. Urban population density, d, is usually expressed in number of people per hectare. As a hectare is equal to 10,000 square meters, the consumption of land per person, c, is equal to $10,000/d$. For instance, a population density of 50 people per hectare is equivalent to a land consumption of 200 square meters per person.

15. The government of Singapore regularly rents or buys space in shopping malls for the greater convenience of its citizen. This practice allows the government of Singapore more transparency in its operating costs, as the rents of its real estate properties are valued at market rates.

16. Unfortunately, most governments consider their land assets to be inalienable. There is no reason to think so. South Africa and New Zealand are, to my knowledge, the only countries in the world that value government land assets at their market value and levy a municipal tax on them. Even if the tax is often underestimated, it is an excellent step forward in forcing government to value their land assets and, eventually, to sell them when not needed.

17. The labor participation rate is expressed as the percentage of people in the age group 16–65 years who are employed. The labor participation rate varies widely from country to country; from a low of 42 percent in Jordan to a high of 85 percent in Ethiopia. The world average in 2012 was 64 percent (World Bank http://data.worldbank.org/indicator/).

18. The average built-up FAR measures the ratio between the total floor area of an entire neighborhood or an entire city and divides it by the built-up area of the neighborhood or the city. The average built-up FAR therefore includes private plots as well as street areas and small open spaces in the built-up area. By contrast, FAR regulations measure only the ratio between floor space and private plots, and therefore they grossly underestimate the total area of land required for building one unit of floor space.

Chapter 4

1. The formulation of a vision to guide urban development is expressly recommended as one of the eight steps required to design an Urban Development Strategy by the World Bank and the Cities Alliance. See http://www.citiesalliance.org/sites/citiesalliance.org/files/CA_Docs/resources/cds/cds -guidelines/cds_guidelines_final.pdf.

2. Alex Anas and Yu Liu, "A Regional Economy, Land Use, and Transportation Model (RELU-TRAN): Formulation, Algorithm Design, and Testing," *Journal of Regional Science* 47, no. 3 (2007): 415–455.

3. See Alain Bertaud, "The Spatial Structures of Central and Eastern European Cities: More European Than Socialist?" Presented at the International Symposium on Post-Communist Cities, University of Illinois at Urbana-Champaign, June 2004, http://alainbertaud.com/wp-content/uploads/2013/08/AB_Central-European-Spatial-Structure_Figures_2.pdf.

4. Readers not familiar with the standard urban model and curious to learn how these equations were derived are referred to chapter 2 in Jan K. Brueckner, *Lectures on Urban Economics* (Cambridge, MA: MIT Press, 2011), and for a most complete discussion of the empirical data to chapter 8 in Arthur O'Sullivan, *Urban Economics* (Homewood, IL: Richard. D. Irwin, 1993).

5. The taxpayer who pays the gasoline subsidy pays the price for the misallocation of resource.

6. One of the few exceptions might be in Singapore, where the tolls for using central city roads are constantly adjusted to reflect the equilibrium between supply and demand.

7. Alain Bertaud and Jan K. Brueckner, "Analyzing Building-Height Restrictions: Predicted Impacts and Welfare Costs," *Regional Science and Urban Economics* 35 (2005): 109–125.

8. Jan Brueckner, "Welfare Gains from Removing Land-Use Distortions: An Analysis of Urban Change in Post-Apartheid South Africa," *Journal of Regional Science* 36, no. 1 (1996): 91–109.

9. See Alain Bertaud and Stephen Malpezzi, "The Spatial Distribution of Population in 52 World Cities: Recurrent Patterns and Some Implications for Public Policy," working paper, University of Wisconsin, Madison, 2007.

10. R^2 is a statistical measure of goodness of fit, i.e., how close the observed values are to the values predicted by a mathematical model. The range of possible values for R^2 varies from a minimum of 0, implying no fit at all, to a maximum of 1, indicating perfect fit.

11. Jeremy Atack and Robert A. Margo 1998, "Location, Location, Location!" The Price Gradient for Vacant Urban Land: New York, 1835 to 1900," *Journal of Real Estate Finance and Economics* 16, no. 2 (1998): 151–172.

12. Andrew Haughwout, James Orr, and David Bedroll, "The Price of Land in the New York Metropolitan Area," *Current Issues in Economics & Finance* 14, no. 3 (2008), Federal Reserve Bank of New York.

13. Arthur O'Sullivan, *Urban Economics* (Homewood, IL: Richard. D. Irwin, 1993), 282.

14. For a discussion of cities developed without land markets in command economies, see Alain Bertaud and Bertrand Renaud, "Socialist Cities without Land Markets," *Journal of Urban Economics* 41, no. 1 (1997): 137–151.

15. Shlomo Angel, Alejandro M. Blei, Jason Parent, Patrick Lamson-Hall, and Nicolás Galarza Sánchez, *Atlas of Urban Expansion*, vol. 1: *Areas and Densities* (New York: New York University, Nairobi: UN-Habitat, and Cambridge, MA: Lincoln Institute of Land Policy, 2016).

16. Alain Bertaud, "Mumbai FAR/FSI Conundrum: The Four Factors Restricting the Construction of New Floor Space in Mumbai," 2011, http://alainbertaud.com/wp-content/uploads/2013/06/AB-Mumbai-FSI-Conundrun-Revised_June-2013_kk-ab1.pdf.

17. A density of, say, 50 people per hectare is equivalent to a land consumption of 200 square meters per person (1 hectare = 10,000 square meters, 10,000/50 = 200).

18. *Merriam-Webster's Dictionary* defines sprawl as "to spread or develop irregularly or ungracefully" and gives an example: "the city sprawls without apparent logic or plan to the west, north, and south— American Guide Series: Rhode Island."

19. World Bank, "China's Next Transformation: Making Urbanization Efficient, Inclusive, and Sustainable," Supporting Report 2, "Planning and Connecting Cities for Greater Diversity and Livability" (New York: World Bank, 2014), 143, map 2.2.

20. The most damaging famines of Asia, in Bengal in 1943 and in China during the Great Leap Forward in 1961, were caused by government policy and subsequent inaction and had nothing to do with a decrease in agricultural land area.

21. I have assumed a uniform agricultural productivity in space, and therefore A is a horizontal line.

22. Among others, see http://en.wikipedia.org/wiki/General_Motors_streetcar_conspiracy.

23. In China, the discontentment of farmers with the price given by local government for their land is the source of numerous protests. In India in 2006, the government of West Bengal used eminent domain to expropriate about 4 square kilometers of farmland to allow a private company to build a car factory. Violent protest over the low price paid for the acquisition obliged the government of West Bengal to abandon the project, which was eventually relocated to another state.

24. Portland, Oregon, was one of the first cities in the United States to impose a UGB. It consists of a boundary, reviewed every 4 years, that limits the extension of the city to the area within the boundary. A large literature exists on the effect of the UGB on land and housing prices. The UGB concept applies to all larger cities in the state of Oregon.

25. Land subdivision regulations concern mostly new greenfield developments. They define (1) the geometry of development—e.g., minimum plot size, minimum street width, minimum areas to be left as public open space, parking requirements, and (2) the construction standards for, e.g., roads, storm water drains, water, and sewers. By contrast, land use and zoning regulations usually concern the restrictions on the type of use (e.g., commercial, residential) and intensity of use (e.g., maximum floor area ratio, maximum height, setbacks) of a specific lot.

26. The market price of an empty lot reflects what consumers are ready to pay for the flow of anticipated rent that the lot will generate over time. This price is usually higher than the original development cost + agricultural land cost, but not necessarily so. In South Africa, for instance, in large housing projects developed by the government for low-income households, some lots are selling on the free market for only one-third of the cost of developing them. I have found the same negative difference between market prices and costs in government-built housing projects in India and in Thailand.

27. Using equation 4.2: $(100 + 50)/0.6 = 250$.

28. Shlomo Angel, *Housing Policy Matters: A Global Analysis* (Oxford: Oxford University Press, 2000).

29. We are working here on a simplified version of reality. In real cities the distance from the center to the points x_1 and x_2 might varies depending on the geographic location.

30. As the population expands, incomes increase, and the price of transport relative to income decreases, both x_1 and x_2 will eventually shift to the right.

31. Patricia Clarke Annez, Alain Bertaud, Bimal Patel, and V. K. Phatak, "Working with the Market: Approach to Reducing Urban Slums in India," Policy Research Working Paper 5475, World Bank, Washington, DC, November 2010.

32. Robert Neuwirth, "New York's Housing Underground: A Refuge and a Resource," Pratt Center for Economic Development and Chhaya Community Development Corporation, New York, 2008.

33. This review is based on the report "Hanoi Capital Construction Master Plan to 2030 and Vision to 2050 (3rd report—comprehensive text report—11/2009)," PPJ and JIAP Consortium, Hanoi, 2009. The references to "scientific principles" are on pages 41, 54, 55, among others.

34. Annette Kim, *Learning to be Capitalists: Entrepreneurs in Vietnam's Transition Economy* (New York: Oxford University Press, 2008).

35. The original master plan land use map and this citation can be found at http://www.perkinseastman .com/project_3407114_hanoi_capital_master_plan_to_2030.

Chapter 5

1. Luis Bettencourt and Geoffrey West, "A Unified Theory of Urban Living," *Nature* 467 (2010): 912–913; and Luis Bettencourt, Horacio Samaniego, and Hyejin Youn, "Professional Diversity and the Productivity of Cities," *Scientific Reports*," June 2014, and http://newsoffice.mit.edu/2013/why -innovation-thrives-in-cities-0604.

2. A current New York City zoning regulations called "Joint Live-Work Quarters for Artists" or JLWQA is trying to match artists' residence, workshops, and art galleries within a few blocks of Soho by oblig- ing developers to offer a quota of loft-apartments with reduced rents for city-approved artists!

3. Steven E. Polzin and Alan E. Pisarski, "Commuting in America 2013: The National Report on Com- muting Patterns and Trends," American Association of State Highway and Transportation Officials, Washington, DC, 2013.

4. Shlomo Angel, Jason Parent, Daniel L. Civco, and Alejandro M. Blei, "The Persistent Decline in Urban Densities: Global and Historical Evidence of Sprawl," Working Paper WP10SA1, Lincoln Insti- tute, Cambridge, MA, 2011.

5. Cornelis Van Tilburg, *Traffic and Congestion in the Roman Empire* (Abingdon and New York: Rout- ledge, 2007).

6. Lee Chang-Moo and Kun-Hyuck Ahn, "Five New Towns in the Seoul Metropolitan Area and Their Attractions in Non-working Trips: Implications for Self-Containment of New Towns," *Habitat Interna- tional* 29 (2005): 647–666.

7. G. Giuliano, "Is Jobs-Housing Balance a Transportation Issue?" *Transportation Research Record: Jour- nal of the Transportation Research Board* 1305 (1991): 305–312, quote on 311.

8. Francisco Gallego, Juan-Pablo Montero, and Christian Salas, "The Effect of Transport Policies on Car Use: Theory and Evidence from Latin American Cities," Working Paper 407, Pontificia Universidad Catolica de Chile, Instituto de Economia, Santiago, December 2011.

9. David Schrank, Bill Eisele, Tim Lomax, Jim Bak, *2015 Urban Mobility Scorecard* (College Station: Texas A&M Transportation Institute and INRIX, Inc., 2015).

10. GTFS is a data standard format that allows developers to build apps providing accessibility data to transit users but also to business and real estate professionals. The GTFS formatted data can be used with disaggregated transport data to provide alternative travel times and accessibility between two urban locations.

11. Tatiana Peralta Quirós and Shomik Raj Mehndiratta, "Accessibility Analysis of Growth Patterns in Buenos Aires, Density, Employment and Spatial Form," World Bank Transportation Research Board, Washington, DC, 2015.

12. This interactive map of Buenos Aires can be accessed at http://wb-ba-analyst.dev.conveyal.com/. The interactive map allows one to test the job accessibility from any location in Buenos Aires using

four different modes of transport: walking, bicycling, transit, and individual cars. The map also provides the breakdown among types of jobs: commerce, services, manufacturing, etc.

13. In France, the Industrial Revolution started around 1815, roughly after the end of the Napoleonic wars, much later than in England, where it started around 1760.

14. Described in Presidency's National Planning Commission, "National Development Plan Vision 2030," Johannesburg, South Africa, November 2011.

15. Robert Cervero, *The Transit Metropolis; A Global Inquiry* (Washington, DC: Island Press, 1998), see pages 43, 327, and 435.

16. Free Flow Speeds calculated by Texas A&M Transportation Institute are derived from speed of vehicles traveling at night found in the INRIX speed database. These are observed speeds influenced by regulatory speed limits but also traffic lights coordination and other physical features of the street network.

17. Samuel Staley and Adrian Moore, *Mobility First: A New Vision for Transportation in a Globally Competitive Twenty-First Century* (Lanham, MD: Rowman & Littlefield, 2009).

18. Seven cities were in Western Europe, and six were on the American continents (five US cities plus Buenos Aires).

19. Andrew Haughwout, James Orr, and David Bedoll, "The Price of Land in the New York Metropolitan Area," *Current Issues* 14, no. 3 (April/May 2008), Federal Reserve Bank of New York.

20. Most countries' driving codes recommend a 3-second tip-to-tail interval between vehicles to allow drivers to react to vehicles in front of them slowing down drastically. Observation shows that most city drivers use a lower interval of about 2 seconds, thus reducing the area per vehicle at a given speed but increasing the risk of collision and therefore further congestion.

21. The inside area of a usable for passengers of city bus 12 meters long is about 19 square meters. When at full capacity, with 86 passengers, the inside density is 4.5 passengers per square meter, not quite as comfortable as riding in a car, but common at rush hour. It seems that in urban buses and subways, the absolute maximum capacity used by transport companies is 6.5 passengers per square meter of internal vehicle space. However, these numbers do not appear in congestion statistics.

22. See http://www.geo.sunysb.edu/bicycle-muenster/.

23. See http://www.toyota-global.com/innovation/smart_mobility_society/next_generation_urban _traffic_systems/.

24. US Census, American Community Survey 2010.

25. Robert Cervero, "Bus Rapid Transit (BRT): An Efficient and Competitive Mode of Public Transport," Working Paper 2013-01, Berkeley Institute of Urban and Regional Development, Berkeley, CA, August 2013.

26. Leroy W. Demery, Jr. "Bus Rapid Transit in Curitiba, Brazil—An Information Summary," public transit.us Special Report 1, Public Transit US, Vallejo, CA, December 11, 2004.

27. http://www3.epa.gov/airquality/peg_caa/carstrucks.html.

28. The first Toyota Mirai fuel cell electric vehicles started operating commercially in the United Kingdom in the fall of 2015.

29. CO_2-e account for the non-CO_2 GHG, such as methane, perfluorocarbons, and nitrous oxide, that a vehicle might emit together with CO_2. For each GHG, the mass of CO_2 that will create the same global warming effect is calculated and added to the total.

30. Leon Arundell, "Estimating Greenhouse Emissions from Australian Capital Territory Travel Modes," Working Paper 1.5, Leon Arundell, independent analyst publication, Canberra, 2012.

31. David Levinson, "Who Benefits from Other People's Transit Use?" *New Geography*, May 24, 2015, http://www.newgeography.com/content/004928-who-benefits-from-other-peoples-transit-use.

Chapter 6

1. Chang-Tai Hsieh and Enrico Moretti, "Why Do Cities Matter? Local Growth and Aggregate Growth," NBER Working Paper 21154, National Bureau of Economic Standards, Cambridge, MA, May 2015 (revised June 2015).

2. Angus Deaton, *The Great Escape: Health, Wealth, and the Origins of Inequality* (Princeton, NJ: Princeton University Press, 2013), 16.

3. The 12th Annual Demographia International Housing Affordability Survey covers 87 major metropolitan markets with populations of more than 1,000,000 in Australia, Canada, Hong Kong, Ireland, Japan, New Zealand, Singapore, the United Kingdom, and the United States: http://www.demographia .com/dhi.pdf.

4. The percentage of income spent on rent is calculated using the median income of renters, which is on average about 65 percent lower than the median income of the total population.

5. Solly Angel and Patrick Lamson-Hall, "The Rise and Fall of Manhattan's Densities, 1790–2010," Working Paper Series 18, Marron Institute of Urban Management, New York, December 2014.

6. Source Document: 19NYCRR 1226 - Property Maintenance Code of New York State (PMCNYS) Topic: Overcrowding (Occupancy Standards) January 1, 2003

7. Quoctrung Bui, Matt A.V. Chaban, and Jeremy White, "40 Percent of the Buildings in Manhattan Could Not Be Built Today," *New York Times*, May 20, 2016, from data compiled by Stephen Smith and Sandip Trivedi, Quantierra.

8. Robert Neuwirth and Chhaya Community Development Corporation, "New York's Housing Underground: A Refuge and a Resource," Pratt Center for Community Development, Chaya Community Development Corporation, New York, 2008.

9. This area includes staircases and corridors that are indispensable for multistory structures. The number assumes a living space of about 12 square meters.

10. The trickle-down affordability theory assumes that any increase in the housing stock, no matter at what unit price, will eventually improve the housing supply of every household, even the poorest. Households benefiting from the supply increase would move up to the new housing, thus freeing an equivalent number of units that will become affordable to households with income lower than that of the beneficiaries of new housing. Eventually, the cycle of moving up into better housing will repeat itself, and the benefits will "trickle down" to the lowest-income groups.

11. See http://www.inflation.eu/inflation-rates/china/historic-inflation/cpi-inflation-china-2000.aspx.

12. Albert O. Hirschman, *Exit, Voice and Loyalty: Responses to Decline in Firms, Organisations and States* (Cambridge, MA: Harvard University Press, 1970), 59.

13. See http://portal.hud.gov/hudportal/HUD?src=/program_offices/public_indian_housing/prog rams/hcv/about/fact_sheet.

14. See http://www.huduser.gov/portal/periodicals/cityscpe/vol16num2/ch15.pdf.

15. See http://www.sectioneightapplication.com/info/section_8_waiting_list.

16. Lawrence M. Hannah, Alain Bertaud, Stephen J. Malpezzi, and Stephen K. Mayo, "Malaysia—The Housing Sector: Getting the Incentives Right," World Bank Report 7292-MA, Infrastructure Division Country Department II, Asia Regional Office, World Bank, Washington, DC, April 10, 1989.

17. Gauteng is the name of the post-apartheid urban metropolitan area including Johannesburg, Pretoria, and some smaller municipalities.

18. See http://www.tradingeconomics.com/south-africa/unemployment-rate.

19. Mireya Navarro, "88,000 Applicants and Counting for 55 Units in 'Poor Door' Building," *New York Times*, April 20, 2015.

20. Richard K. Green and Stephen Malpezzi, *US Housing Markets and Housing Policy*, AREUEA monograph series 3 (Washington, DC: Urban Institute Press, 2003), 126.

21. Maxwell Austensen, Vicki Been, Luis Inaraja Vera, Gita Khun Jush, Katherine M. O'Regan, Stephanie Rosoff, Traci Sanders, Eric Stern, Michael Suher, Mark A. Willis, and Jessica Yager "State of New York City's Housing and Neighborhoods in 2015," Furman Center, New York University, New York, 2016.

22. See http://www.nytimes.com/2016/09/18/nyregion/donald-trump-tax-breaks-real-estate.html ?hp&action=click&pgtype=Homepage&clickSource=story-heading&module=first-column -region&region=top-news&WT.nav=top-news.

23. Chang-Tai Hsieh and Enrico Moretti, "Why Do Cities Matter? Local Growth and Aggregate Growth," NBER Working Paper 21154, National Bureau of Economic Research, Cambridge, MA, May 2015 (revised June 2015), 4.

24. See an analysis of kampung infrastructure issues and improvement in the World Bank document by Alcira Kreimer, Roy Gilbert, Claudio Volonte, and Gillie Brown, "Indonesia Impact Evaluation Report—Enhancing the Quality of Life in Urban Indonesia: The Legacy of Kampung Improvement Program," World Bank, Washington, DC, June 29, 1995. Available at http://www-wds.worldbank.org /external/default/WDSContentServer/WDSP/IB/1999/07/28/000009265_3961029220705 /Rendered/PDF/multi_page.pdf.

25. The autobiographical novel by Sheng Keyi, *Northern Girls* (New York: Viking, Penguin Books, 2012), gives a feel of what life was like for migrant workers in Shenzhen at the time of its creation.

26. Kate Barker, *Review of Housing Supply: Delivering Stability: Securing Our Future Housing Needs*, Final Report—Recommendations, March 2004, pages 3, 13, and 14, available at http://image.guardian.co.uk /sys-files/Guardian/documents/2004/03/17/Barker.pdf.

27. Kate Barker, *Barker Review of Land Use Planning*, Final Report—Recommendations, December 2006, page 4 and foreword, available at http://news.bbc.co.uk/2/shared/bsp/hi/pdfs/05_12_06_barker _finalreport.pdf.

Chapter 7

1. Nassim Nicholas Taleb, *Antifragile: Things That Gain from Disorder* (New York: Random House, 2014).

2. Herbert Spencer, "State-Tamperings with Money and Banks," in *Essays: Scientific, Political, & Speculative*, vol. 3 (London and Edinburgh: Williams and Norgate, 1891), 354.

3. In this section I use the word "Paris" to designate the 20 arrondissements that constitute the Paris municipality and have a population of 2.2 million people, compared to the 12 million corresponding to the Paris metropolitan area known as Île-de-France.

4. See http://pluenligne.paris.fr/plu/sites-plu/site_statique_37/pages/page_791.html.

5. Paris is divided into 20 arrondissements that are administrative boundaries, but they are also closely identified with type of lifestyle and real estate prices.

6. Alain Bertaud and Stephen Malpezzi, "Measuring the Costs and Benefits of Urban Land Use Regulation: A Simple Model with an Application to Malaysia," *Journal of Housing Economics* 10, no. 3 (2001): 393.

7. Jason M. Barr, *Building the Skyline: The Birth and Growth of Manhattan's Skyscrapers* (Oxford: Oxford University Press, 2016).

8. Bulk regulations, as defined by the NYC Department of City Planning, are the combination of controls (lot size, floor area ratio, lot coverage, open space, yards, height, and setback) that determine the maximum size and placement of a building on a zoning lot.

9. Barr, *Building the Skyline*, 163, 343.

10. See http://www1.nyc.gov/site/planning/about/city-planning-history.page?tab=2.

11. See http://www1.nyc.gov/site/planning/about/city-planning-history.page?tab=2.

12. NYC Department of City Planning, NYC Zoning History, Zoning the City—2011, Conference Description, https://www1.nyc.gov/site/planning/about/city-planning-history.page.

13. The website is http://www.nyc.gov/html/dcla/downloads/pdf/artist_certification.pdf.

14. See http://www1.nyc.gov/site/planning/zoning/about-zoning.page.

15. See http://www.nytimes.com/interactive/2016/05/19/upshot/forty-percent-of-manhattans-buildings-could-not-be-built-today.html.

16. The 421-a tax exemption reduces the property tax of developer to what it would have been before development for a period varying from 15 to 30 years. In exchange, the developer has to provide something the city would like, for instance 20 percent subsidized rental units, or a special urban design feature like a connection to a subway station. It is barter, and not a very transparent one.

17. See http://www1.nyc.gov/assets/planning/download/pdf/plans-studies/vanderbilt-corridor/history_of_transit_bonuses.pdf.

18. From NIMBY, "not in my backyard," an expression used by pressure groups to prevent development of any type, including indispensable public services like hospital and homeless shelters.

19. Jan K. Brueckner and David A. Fansler, "The Economics of Urban Sprawl: Theory and Evidence on the Spatial Sizes of Cities," *Review of Economics and Statistics* 65, no. 3 (1983): 479–482, quote on 479.

20. Jan K. Brueckner, "Urban Sprawl: Lessons from Urban Economics," Brookings-Wharton Papers on Urban Affairs, Brookings Institution, Washington, DC, 2001.

21. Edward L. Glaeser and Matthew E. Kahn, "Sprawl and Urban Growth," NBER Working Paper 9733, National Bureau of Economic Research, Cambridge, MA, May 2003.

22. Marcial H. Echenique, Anthony J. Hargreaves, Gordon Mitchell, and Anil Namdeo, "Growing Cities Sustainably," *Journal of the American Planning Association* 78, no. 2 (2012): 121–137. DOI: 10.1080/01944363.2012.666731.

23. OECD (2012), Compact City Policies: A Comparative Assessment, OECD Green Growth Studies, OECD Publishing, http://dx.doi.org/10A 787/9789264167865-en.

24. See http://marroninstitute.nyu.edu/programs/urban-expansion.

25. See http://www.atlasofurbanexpansion.org/. Shlomo Angel, Alejandro M. Blei, Jason Parent, Patrick Lamson-Hall, and Nicolás Galarza Sánchez, with Daniel L. Civco, Rachel Qian Lei, and Kevin Thom, *Atlas of Urban Expansion—2016 Edition*, vol. 1, *Areas and Densities* (Cambridge, MA: Lincoln Institute of Land Policy, 2016).

26. Yuval Noah Harari, *Sapiens: A Brief History of Humankind* (New York: HarpersCollins, 2016).

Chapter 8

1. George Orwell, *Politics and the English Language* (London: Horizon, 1946), 6.

2. I have directly participated as one of the main authors in the preparation of seven master plans in cities of North and Central America, the Caribbean, Europe, North Africa, and Asia. In addition, as a consultant, I have been asked to review countless master plans for cities located all over the world.

3. Stephen Malpezzi and Stephen Mayo, "Housing and Urban Development Indicators: A Good Idea Whose Time Has Returned," *Real Estate Economics* 25, no. 1 (1997): 1–12.

4. Shlomo Angel, "Housing Policy Matters," in *House Price, Rent, and Affordability* (Oxford: Oxford University Press, 2000), 232–249.

5. This graph is adapted from an evaluation manual produced by the World Bank in 1996. See http://siteresources.worldbank.org/BRAZILINPOREXTN/Resources/3817166-1185895645304/4044168.1186409169154/24pub_br217.pdf.

6. $N_1 = 0.15 \cdot P$, where P is the active population looking for jobs in neighborhood X.

7. Angus Deaton, *The Great Escape: Health, Wealth, and the Origins of Inequality* (Princeton, NJ: Princeton University Press, 2013), 16.

8. Morris Hill and Rachelle Alterman, "The Problem of Setting Flexible Norms for Land Allocation for Public Facilities," in *New Trends in Urban Planning*, ed. Dan Soen (Oxford: Pergamon Press, 1979), 94–102.

9. Lawrence Hannah, Alain Bertaud, Stephen Malpezzi, and Stephen Mayo, "Malaysia: The Housing Sector; Getting the Incentives Right," World Bank Sector Report 7292-MA, World Bank, Washington, DC, 1989.

10. Defined as population aged between 15 and 64 years.

11. Source: Table 1-1 Total population, population by the major three age groups (under 15, 15–64, and 65 and over), Population Projections for Japan (January 2012): 2011 to 2060, National Institute of Population and Social Security Research in Japan, Tokyo, Japan, 2012, http://www.ipss.go.jp/site-ad/index _english/esuikei/gh2401e.asp.

Index

Note: Figures and tables are indicated by "f" and "t" respectively, following page numbers.

Adequate housing, 269–270
Affordability
  in China, 230–231, 230f, 293–300, 297f
  demand side subsidies in, 260–263, 262f,
    267–268
  Demographia International Housing
    Affordability Survey for, 224–225, 225f
  for developing countries, 372–373
  economics of, 341–342
  in Gauteng (South Africa), 268–271, 270f, 272f,
    273–275, 275f
  government for, 220–221, 231–235, 232f–233f,
    301–302, 304–306
  household income in, 219–220, 222–224, 239,
    240f, 242–244, 243f, 247, 248f, 249–251, 251f,
    254–256, 255f
  housing policy and, 249–250, 252
  housing typology in, 244–247, 245f, 302–303
  incentives in, 283–284
  in Indonesia, 288–292, 291f
  informal housing for, 256–260, 258f
  in land use, 334
  minimum standards for, 235–236
  in New York, 275–281, 278f, 280f–281f
  PIR in, 224–230, 225f, 227f–228f, 231
  policy for, 267–268, 300–301, 328–329, 356–357,
    357f
  poverty and, 236–239, 238f, 287–288
  in South Africa, 366–367, 388n26
  subletting in, 282–283
  subsidies in, 303–304
  supply side subsidies in, 264–267, 265f
  tax incentives in, 284–285
  technology and, 345–346, 346f
  theory of, 49, 219, 301
  trickle-down theory for, 240–241, 391n10
  urban land supply in, 252–254, 253f
  zoning in, 281–282, 285–287
Affordable housing, 276–277, 281–282, 285–287
Agricultural land
  in Hanoi (Vietnam), 135–136
  land price and, 135–136
  land readjustment for, 385n7
  spatial distribution of, 114–116, 115t, 118, 119f,
    120–122, 121f–122f
  in urban economics, 122–124, 125f
  urban land compared to, 115–118, 117f, 119f,
    122f
Algeria, 4–6
Alonso, William, 95
Alterman, Rachelle, 367–368
Alternative urban shapes
  containment policy in, 334–335, 340–341
  demographic projection in, 341–344
  density and, 339–340, 340f
  economics of, 329–330, 330f
  government and, 332–333
  markets and, 335–337
  New York as, 317–326
  Paris as, 310–317, 311f, 316f
  politics of, 337–339, 346–347
  theory of, 307–310, 329–330, 333, 346–347
  zoning for, 326–332, 328f, 330f
Amsterdam, 338–339
Anas, Alex, 95
Angel, Shlomo, 21–22, 110, 116, 147–148, 339–340
Antifragile (Taleb), 308–309
Apple (company), 308, 351
Art Deco building (New York), 326
Asia. *See specific cities; specific countries*

Asian Development Bank, 365
Atlanta, 353
Atlas of Urban Expansion (Angel), 116, 339–340, 340f
Auckland (New Zealand), 228
Auditing, 365, 367–369

Banking
  Asian Development Bank, 365
  Banco Interamericano de Desarrollo, 365
  equity loans in, 305
  for land development, 364–367
  mortgages in, 226–227, 254–255, 255f, 356
  in urban economics, 318
Barcelona (Spain), 66–67
Barker, Kate, 18, 305–306, 337
Barr, Jason, 318–319
Beaune (France), 120–122, 121f–122f
Beijing (China)
  transit in, 173–175, 174f
  transport in, 162–165, 163f, 166–168, 167t
  urban planning in, 73–77, 74t, 75f–76f, 352
Bertaud, Marie-Agnes, 10–11, 101
Bibliothèque Nationale de France (Paris), 310
Blinking light indicators, 355–358, 357f
Brazil, 77–78, 77f
Brexit, 375
BRT. *See* Bus rapid transit
Brueckner, Jan, 18, 335–336, 339
Bruegmann, Robert, 116
Buenos Aires (Argentina), 156–158, 158f, 389n12
Building permits, 4–7
Building the Skyline (Barr, Jason), 318
Bulk regulations, 393n8
Bus rapid transit (BRT), 274–275. *See also* Transit
  congestion pricing and, 185, 212
  dwell time and, 186, 192, 195
  headways for, 191–197, 192f, 194f, 196f
  for mobility, 191–197, 192f, 194f, 196f
  urban planning for, 155, 160–162, 162f

Cairncross, Frances, 150–152
Canada, 375
Carbon Dioxide. *See* CO2 equivalent
Cars. *See* Transit; Transport
Çatalhöyük, 22
Central business districts (CBDs), 384n12
  congestion pricing in, 217
  data for, 42–45, 44f–45f, 195–196, 196f
  density and, 105–108, 106f–107f
  environment and, 80–81, 80f
  floor area consumption in, 52–53

for labor markets, 96–97
  for municipal governments, 315, 316f
  in Paris, 71–73, 72f
  as residential areas, 318, 327–328, 328f
  transit in, 311
  in urban planning, 36, 36f, 37–42, 38f–39f
Cerdà, Ildefons, 66–68
Cervero, Robert, 168
Chambres de bonnes (maids' rooms), 385n20
Cheshire, Paul, 18, 306, 337
Chicago, 335
Chile, 261
China. *See also* Beijing
  affordability in, 230–231, 230f, 293–300, 297f
  demographic projection in, 242–243, 243f, 295
  design in, 4
  economics and, 54, 295–296
  France compared to, 79–80
  government in, 82, 114–115, 246, 299–300
  growth in, 380
  Guangzhou in, 73–77, 74t, 75f–76f
  handshake buildings in, 296–300, 297f
  Hauxinzhou in, 54
  health in, 388n20
  household income in, 239, 240f, 242–244, 243f
  India compared to, 59–60, 339, 346
  Indonesia compared to, 288
  informal settlements in, 230–231, 230f
  Kaifeng in, 22
  Kowloon in, 296–297
  Land use in, 11–13, 15, 381
  low-income housing in, 294
  Ningbo in, 73–77, 74t, 75f–76f
  Pudong in, 54, 78–81, 78f, 80f, 386n10
  residential areas in, 73–77, 74t, 75f–76f
  Shenzhen in, 22, 295–300, 297f, 300
  South Africa compared to, 299
  technology in, 386n11
  Tianjin in, 114–115, 115t, 339
  urban planning in, 73–77, 74t, 75f–76f, 309
  US compared to, 189–190
  villages in, 293
Chrysler building (New York), 326
Cities, 28–32, 32f
  as labor markets, 19–27, 33–41, 35f–36f, 38f–39f, 48–49
  Planet of Cities (Henderson), 21–22
  "Size, Sprawl, Speed and the Efficiency of Cities" (Prud'homme/Lee), 33–34
City Planning Departments, 369–372, 371f
City-states, 366
Clean energy, 345–346

CO2 equivalent (CO2-e), 205–211, 206f–207f, 209f–210f, 390n29
Coase, Ronald, 15
Codes
  for congestion, 390n20
  for design, 5
  engineering in, 312–313, 313f
  for preservation, 312
  in Shanghai (China), 386n10
  for zoning, 324, 329
Command economies, 14
Commercial districts, 330, 330f
Communism, 4, 15–16, 26–27, 56, 73–74, 246
Communist Manifesto (Marx), 56
Commuting. See Transport; Travel time
Commuting routes, 384n13
Commuting trips, 384n17
Compact City Policies: A Comparative Assessment (OECD), 338
Complex zoning, 331–332
Composite model (transport), 39f, 40
Congestion
  codes for, 390n20
  data for, 168–175, 169f, 170t, 174f
  for environment, 148–149, 152–154
  GHG emissions from, 165
  mobility and, 172–175, 174f
  Mobility First (Staley/Moore), 176
  policy for, 154–158, 158f, 190–199, 192f, 194f, 196f, 198f
  theory of, 201
Congestion pricing, 191
  BRT and, 185, 212
  in CBDs, 217
  for government, 23–24, 30
  mobility and, 357f
  policy for, 170–172
  in Singapore, 184, 197–199, 198f
  tolls as, 23–24, 49, 201, 217
Containment policy
  in alternative urban shapes, 334–335, 340–341
  Compact City Policies: A Comparative Assessment (OECD), 338
  demographic projection in, 339–340, 340f
  for government, 337
  theory of, 337–339, 341–344
Cordoba (Spain), 22
Costa, Lúcio, 4
Culture
  cultural politics, 327–329
  of economics, 18

of household income, 282
housing typology and, 231
of informal subdivisions, 235–236
of Kampungs, 288–289, 385n21
of New York, 262
of NIMBY, 337–338
politics of, 5–6, 367–368
of poverty, 256–257, 296–300
preservation of, 326–327
technology and, 384n6
of urban planning, 18
of US, 335
of welfare, 284–285
Curitiba (Brazil), 191–196, 192f, 194f, 196f

Data. See also Spatial data
  for CBDs, 42–45, 44f–45f, 195–196, 196f
  for congestion, 168–175, 169f, 170t, 174f
  Demographia International Housing Affordability Survey for, 224–225, 225f
  for demographic projection, 178–180, 178t, 179f, 180t, 373–374, 374f
  for density, 13–15, 46t, 110–111, 111f, 245, 271, 272f, 273, 296–297, 297f, 386n12
  for economics, 12
  for FAR, 83, 84f, 85–86
  for floor area consumption, 252–253, 253f
  Free Flow Speeds, 390n16
  for GHG emissions, 159
  of growth, 378–380, 379f
  GTFS data, 156, 389n10
  for housing policy, 242
  income distribution as, 239, 240f
  income distribution curve for, 280–281, 281f
  for indicators, 354–355
  for informal subdivisions, 235
  for migration, 294
  for mobility, 152–158, 158f, 168–172, 169f, 170t, 185t, 186–190, 188f–189f
  for motorcycles, 162–164, 162f–163f
  PIR data, 225–228, 227f–228f
  quantitative models for, 94–95
  from Seoul (Korea), 45f, 46t
  spatial data, 11, 30, 39–45, 39f, 44f–45f, 46t, 212–216, 214f–215f, 216t
  Strategic Community Investment Report Data, 353
  technology for, 3, 101–102, 102f, 145, 156–158, 158f
  theory of, 146–147
  for transit, 361–362
  on transport, 31–33, 32f, 355

Data (cont.)
for transport modes, 157f, 161–162, 162f, 184t–185t, 188–191, 188f–189f
for travel time, 165–171, 166f, 167t, 168f–169f, 170t
for urban economics, 171–172, 229–230
for urban planning, 84f, 90, 305, 353, 355–358, 357f
Deadwood regulations, 368–369
The Death of Distance (Cairncross), 150
Deaton, Angus, 220, 277, 353, 364
La Defense (Paris), 315, 316f
Degentrification, 246–247
Demand-driven land use, 291
Demand side subsidies, 260–263, 262f, 267–268, 286, 303–304
Demographic projection, 24–25, 86, 370–373, 385n1. *See also* Density
in alternative urban shapes, 341–344
in China, 242–243, 243f, 295
in containment policy, 339–340, 340f
data for, 178–180, 178t, 179f, 180t, 373–374, 374f
Demographia International Housing Affordability Survey, 224–225, 225f
in design, 93
for government, 91–92, 262, 358
growth in, 372–376, 374f
infrastructure and, 137–138
for labor markets, 150–152, 151f
mobility and, 147–148
spatial distribution and, 110–111, 111f
theory of, 212–213
transport and, 169–170, 170t
for urban planning, 109–110, 160–161, 175–176
Demographics. *See* Density
Deng Xiaoping, 15, 26, 384n6
Density, 386n14
alternative urban shapes and, 339–340, 340f
CBDs and, 105–108, 106f–107f
data for, 13–15, 46t, 110–111, 111f, 245, 271, 272f, 273, 296–297, 297f, 386n12
density profiles, 102f, 104f, 106f, 109f, 111f, 342–343
FAR and, 84f, 88–90
in floor area consumption, 355
for Kampung Improvement Program (KIP), 292
labor markets and, 114–115, 115t
land price and, 140
land use and, 387n17
markets and, 242–244, 243f

in master plans, 105
maximum density, 235–236
policy for, 336
RDP for, 273–274
science of, 20–28
spatial data and, 46t
tax incentives and, 377–378
in theory, 108–109, 109f
topography, 84f
in urban economics, 356
in urban planning, 93–94, 100–101, 110–111, 111f, 372–376, 374f
in US, 59
vehicle density, 182–183, 182f–183f
Density gradients
reverse density gradients, 273, 344
theory of, 97–100, 98f–99f, 103t, 107–111, 111f
Department of Housing And Development (HUD), 18
Design. *See also* Alternative urban shapes
in China, 4
codes for, 5
demographic projection in, 93
economics in, 140–141
environment in, 312
of Garden Cities, 335
government and, 175–176, 315, 316f, 369
greenbelts in, 336–337
in Hanoi (Vietnam), 17
headways in, 186–190, 188f–189f
manufacturing and, 23–24
markets compared to, 1–2, 81–90, 84f
in New York, 319–321
objective functions for, 307–309
policy for, 223–224, 322–324, 346–347, 359–361, 360f
of Port-au-Prince, 4
in Russia, 4
of skylines, 78, 78f
theory of, 8–9
urban economics and, 61, 150–152, 151f
urban planning compared to, 385n1
for urban spatial structures, 71–78, 72f, 74t, 75f–77f
for urban village model, 297–300
zoning in, 321–322, 322f
Detroit, 373
Developing countries, 372–373
Development Projects Observed (Hirschman), 3–4
Dispersed model (transport), 39–40, 39f
Dreiser, Theodore, 335
Duvalier, Jean-Claude, 9–10

Dwell time, 186, 192, 195
Dynamic cities, 378–380, 379f

Echenique, Martial, 337
Economics. *See also* Poverty; Urban economics
  of affordability, 341–342
  of alternative urban shapes, 329–330, 330f
  China and, 54, 295–296
  command economies, 14
  of communism, 26–27
  of congestion pricing, 30
  culture of, 18
  data for, 12
  in design, 140–141
  economic rate of return, 363—364
  economies of scale, 20–21
  of engineering, 326
  of FAR, 84f, 86, 330, 330f
  of floor area consumption, 324
  of France, 47
  government and, 111–113, 112f
  growth and, 310–311, 311f
  of health, 376–378, 378f
  of height regulations, 313–315
  housing policy and, 260–263, 261f
  of housing supply, 302–303
  of Indonesia, 47
  of investments, 362–363
  of Kombinats, 383n4
  of labor markets, 155–156, 381
  of land development, 120–125, 125f, 283–284,
    302–303
  of land markets, 12–13
  of land price, 8–9
  of land use, 236–239, 238f, 329–330
  for London, 178–180, 178t, 179f, 180t
  market economies, 14
  mobility and, 45, 46t, 47–48, 158–160, 190–191,
    196–199, 198f, 201
  of mortgages, 226–227
  for New York, 178–180, 178t, 179f, 180t,
    284–285
  path dependency in, 384n16
  of PIR, 229, 244
  policy and, 25, 152–154, 287
  politics and, 375
  of Port-au-Prince, 8–9
  of poverty, 242–243
  in Pudong (China), 54
  of real estate, 27–28, 112f, 304, 331–332
  of rentals, 317, 391n4
  scale economy, 10

  of Shenzhen (China), 295–296
  of Singapore, 374, 376
  of spatial distribution, 93–97, 98f–99f, 99,
    109–110, 120–125, 134f
  of subsidies, 100–101
  technology and, 367–368
  theory in, 240–241, 253–254
  of transit, 158–160, 362
  of transport, 19–20
  trickle-down theory in, 240–241, 391n10
  Urban Economics and Urban Policy (Cheshire/
    Nathan/Overman), 306
  urban planning and, 1–4, 8–9, 16–18, 144–146
  of urban-rural boundaries, 118, 119f
  of urban spatial structures, 81–90, 84f
  in US, 338–339, 356
  World Bank for, 11–12
  World Trade Organization for, 132
Eiffel Tower, 309
Electric cars. *See* Technology
Emergency shelter, 302
Emirates, 374
Engineering
  clean energy in, 345–346
  in codes, 312–313, 313f
  economics of, 326
  FAR in, 342–343
  in France, 309–310
  theory of, 322–323
  urban planning compared to, 307–308, 354
Environment. *See also* Sustainability
  CBDs and, 80–81, 80f
  CO2-e for, 205–208, 206f–207f
  congestion for, 148–149, 152–154
  in design, 312
  GHG emissions and, 40, 204–205, 334–335, 338
  grid carbon content for, 207–209, 207f, 209f,
    212
  for Le Corbusier (architect), 298
  mobility and, 201–204, 204f, 206–208, 207f
  policy for, 222
  politics of, 337–339
  preservation of, 312
  technology and, 204–208, 206f–207f
  topography of, 202
  in US, 208–211, 209f–210f
  zoning and, 153–154
Environmental Protection Agency (EPA),
  203–206
Equity loans, 305
Europe. *See specific cities; specific countries*
Evans, Alan, 18

Externalities
  government and, 317–319
  negative externalities, 18, 55, 73, 86, 159–161,
    165, 171, 199, 284, 318–321, 324–327, 331–332,
    349
  traditional externalities, 311–312, 317–319

Facebook, 151
Fansler, David, 335–336
FAR. *See* Floor area ratio
Farmers, 135–137, 296
Ferguson, Adam, 1
Firms, 83–85, 84f
Fischel, William A., 18
Fixed capital, 28
Flat Iron building (New York), 326
Floor area consumption, 52–53, 342
  data for, 252–253, 253f
  density in, 355
  economics of, 324
  in Hanoi (Vietnam), 247, 248f, 249
  in incentives, 321–322, 325
  land supply and, 339–340, 340f
  land use and, 320
  policy for, 243
  in urban economics, 331–332, 341–342
Floor area ratio (FAR), 342, 386n13, 386n18
  data for, 83, 84f, 85–86
  density and, 84f, 88–90
  economics of, 84f, 86, 330, 330f
  in engineering, 342–343
  for government, 321–322, 322f, 325–326, 330f
  as incentives, 329, 332–333
  in land development, 276–277
  in land use, 84f, 88, 297–298
  minimum standards for, 256–260, 258f
  as policy, 323
  politics of, 283–284, 286
  poverty and, 284–285
  TOD and, 70–71
  in urban economics, 321–322, 322f
  in urban planning, 296–297, 297f
  in urban spatial structures, 54–56
France. *See also* Paris
  Beaune in, 120–122, 121f–122f
  Bibliothèque Nationale de France, 310
  China compared to, 79–80
  economics of, 47
  engineering in, 309–310
  transport in, 31–33, 32f
  urban economics in, 25
Free Flow Speeds, 390n16

Functions
  in markets, 329–330
  objective functions, 307–310, 317–319, 334,
    344–346, 345f–346f

Garden Cities, 335, 385n2
Gauteng (South Africa), 31–33, 32f, 392n17
  affordability in, 268–271, 270f, 272f, 273–275,
    275f
  government in, 300
GDP. *See* Gross domestic product
General Transit Feed Specification (GTFS), 156,
    389n10
Gentrification, 246–247
Germany, 203–204, 204f
GHG emissions. *See* Greenhouse gas emissions
Gibrat's law, 21–22
Giuliano, G., 152–153
Glaeser, Edward, 7, 18, 337
Global Warming. *See* Environment; Greenhouse
  gas emissions
Good neighbor rules, 349
Google, 151
Government, 276. *See also* Municipal
  governments
  for affordability, 220–221, 231–235, 232f–233f,
    301–302, 304–306
  in Algeria, 4–6
  alternative urban shapes and, 332–333
  auditing of, 367–368
  building permits and, 4–6
  in China, 82, 114–115, 246, 299–300
  congestion pricing for, 23–24, 30
  containment policy for, 337
  deadwood regulations for, 368–369
  demographic projection for, 91–92, 262, 358
  design and, 175–176, 315, 316f, 369
  economics and, 111–113, 112f
  for emergency shelter, 302
  externalities and, 317–319
  FAR for, 321–322, 322f, 325–326, 330f
  in Gauteng (South Africa), 300
  household income and, 219–220, 256–260, 258f,
    356–357
  housing consumption and, 256–260, 258f,
    366–367
  in housing policy, 301
  housing supply for, 302–306
  in India, 25–26, 241, 288
  in Indonesia, 300
  informal settlements and, 288, 290
  in land development, 285

land use and, 15–16, 146, 196–200, 198f, 318–319, 368–369, 388n25

markets and, 249–250, 252, 301–302, 316–317

master plans and, 47

mobility and, 64, 65f, 66–70, 69f

Monetary Policy Committee (UK), 305

in New York, 176, 230, 231–235, 232f–233f, 267, 283–284, 300, 376–377

in Paris, 315–317, 316f

for plot size, 256, 274

in policy, 9–11, 118–120, 138–139, 141, 162–163, 252–254, 253f, 255–256

politics of, 259–260, 314–315, 319–321

poverty for, 290–292, 291f

for public housing, 264–267, 265f

regulations and, 6–7

for rentals, 277–278, 278f

rent control by, 264–267, 265f

in Russia, 26–27

in Shenzhen (China), 300

in Singapore, 386n15

for social housing, 302

in South Africa, 222–223, 268–269, 274

in supply mechanisms, 325

supply mechanisms for, 302–304

tax credits from, 267

technology for, 369

transport modes and, 148, 152, 274–275

TTI for, 172–175, 174f

in UK, 18

urban economics for, 283–284, 312–313, 313f

for urban planning, 16–17, 319–321

in US, 18, 375

in voucher systems, 260–263, 261f

in zoning, 91–92, 235–236, 264–267, 265f, 310–312, 311f, 324–325

The Great Escape (Deaton), 220

Green, Richard, 280

Greenbelts, 335–337

Greenhouse gas (GHG) emissions, 207, 207f, 212, 390n29

from congestion, 165

data for, 159

mobility and, 204–206, 206f, 208–211, 209f–210f

theory of, 40, 201–202, 334–335, 338

urban economics and, 338–339

urban expansion and, 334–335

in urban planning, 202–204, 204f

Grid carbon content, 207–209, 207f, 209f, 212

Gross domestic product (GDP), 219, 290–291

Growth

in China, 380

data of, 378–380, 379f

in demographic projection, 372–376, 374f

economics and, 310–311. 311f

growth rates, 378–379, 379f

in Japan, 376–378, 378f

markets and, 314–315, 340–344

mobility and, 28–29

policy for, 113–114

science of, 21–22

in Shenzhen (China), 22

skylines and, 317–319

smart growth, 334

theory of, 27–28

transport and, 49

urban growth, 372–376, 374f

urban growth boundaries, 344

for urban planning, 24–27

GTFS. *See* General Transit Feed Specification

Guangzhou (China), 73–77, 74t, 75f–76f

Haiti. *See* Port-au-Prince

les Halles (Paris), 310

handshake buildings, 296–300, 297f

Hanoi (Vietnam)

agricultural land in, 134–135

design in, 17

floor area consumption in, 247, 248f, 249

housing typology for, 245–246, 245f

master plans for, 110, 130–136, 134f

plot size in, 246

politics of, 138–139

theory for, 138–139

transport in, 162–165, 163f

Harari, Yuval, 347

Haussmann, Georges-Eugène, 66–68, 175–177, 309

Hauxinzhou (China), 54

Hayek, Friedrich, 1

Headways

for BRT, 191–197, 192f, 194f, 196f

in design, 186–190, 188f–189f

Health, 360, 376–378, 378f, 388n20

Height regulations, 311–315, 311f, 313f

Henderson, Vernon, 21

Hewlett Packard, 351

Hill, Morris, 367–368

Hippodamus, 64–66

Hirschman, Albert, 3–4, 260

Historical preservation, 60–61

Homeless population, 302

Hong Kong, 59–60. *See also* China

Household income
  in affordability, 219–220, 222–224, 239, 240f,
    242–244, 243f, 247, 248f, 249–251, 251f,
    254–256, 255f
  in China, 239, 240f, 242–244, 243f
  culture of, 282
  government and, 219–220, 256–260, 258f,
    356–357
  mobility for, 285
  theory of, 221
Housing consumption
  government and, 256–260, 258f, 366–367
  housing consumption profiles, 261–262
  income distribution and, 247, 248f, 249,
    250–252, 251f
  land development and, 252–254, 253f
  minimum housing consumption, 256–260,
    258f
  mortgages for, 254–256, 255f
  policy for, 252
  theory of, 302–303
Housing flow, 240–241
Housing policy
  affordability and, 249–250, 252
  data for, 242
  economics and, 260–263, 261f
  government in, 301
  politics of, 262
  RDP as, 274
Housing pools, 281–282
Housing stock, 240–241, 246–247
Housing subdivisions, 230–231, 230f
Housing supply, 271, 272f, 273–274, 287,
    302–306. See also Housing consumption;
    Subsidies
Housing typology, 231, 244–247, 245f, 302–303
HOV lanes, 196–197
Howard, Ebenezer, 53, 298, 335, 385n2
Hsieh, Chang-Tai, 219
HUD. See Department of Housing And
    Development
Hudson Yards (New York), 333, 350
Hybrid cars. See Technology

Illegal settlements, 257–258, 258f
Immigration, 374–376, 374f
Impact indicators, 358–361, 360f, 361, 364–365
Incentives
  in affordability, 283–284
  FAR as, 329, 332–333
  floor area consumption in, 321–322, 325
  for land development, 320–321

  in New York, 282–283, 319
  property taxes in, 393n16
  tax incentives, 284–285, 377–378
  theory of, 328–329
  transit bonuses as, 333
Incentive zoning, 322–325, 329–330
Inclusionary zoning
  in New York, 275–276, 279–281, 281f
  theory of, 276–278, 278f, 282–287
Inclusive zoning, 264–267, 265f
Income-consumption relation, 249
Income distribution
  as data, 239, 240f
  housing consumption and, 247, 248f, 249,
    250–252, 251f
  income distribution curve, 280–281, 281f
  shelter consumption and, 244–247, 245f
India. See also Mumbai
  China compared to, 59–60, 339, 346
  government in, 25–26, 241, 288
  informal settlements in, 238f
  policy in, 383n5, 385n3
  urban economics in, 17, 237–239, 238f,
    308–309
  urban planning in, 77–78, 77f, 236
Indicators
  blinking light indicators, 355–358, 357f
  data for, 354–355
  impact indicators, 358–361, 360f, 364–365
  Input indicators, 362–365
  in low-income housing, 366–367
  monitoring of, 352–353
  outcome indicators, 361–362, 364–365
  output indicators, 362, 364–365
  for policy, 363
  for transport, 361
  for urban planning, 361–365
Indonesia
  affordability in, 288–292, 291f
  China compared to, 288
  economics of, 47
  government in, 300
  Kampungs in, 288–292, 291f
  KIP in, 267–268, 290–292, 291f
  road networks in, 292
  urban planning in, 128–129, 129f
Informal housing, 235–236, 256–260, 258f
Informal sector, 125–130, 127f, 129f
Informal settlements, 6, 16, 125
  in China, 230–231, 230f
  GDP and, 290
  government and, 288, 290

in India, 238f
poverty in, 257
theory of, 128–130, 129f, 288
urban planning for, 236–239, 238f
Informal subdivisions, 235–236
Infrastructure, 137–138, 260, 290–292, 291f
Input indicators, 362–365
Integration policy, 292
Internet, 383n2
Investments, in transit, 362–363

Jacobs, Jane, 22, 383n4
Japan
  growth in, 376–378, 378f
  Russia compared to, 373
  Toyama in, 373, 376–379, 378f
Jeanneret, Charles-Édouard. See Le Corbusier
Jobs. See Labor markets
Johnson, Philip, 323
Joint Living-Work Quarters for Artists rule,
  326–329, 328f

Kahn, Matthew E., 337
Kaifeng (China), 22
Kampung Improvement Program (KIP),
  267–268, 290–292, 291f
Kampungs, 288–292, 291f, 385n21, 392n24
Keyi, Sheng, 392n25
Keynes, John Maynard, 305
KIP. See Kampung Improvement Program
Kombinats, 383n4
Kowloon (China), 296–297
Kubitschek, Juscelino, 26, 384n6

Labor markets
  CBDs for, 96–97
  cities as, 19–27, 33–41, 35f–36f, 38f–39f,
    48–49
  commuting trips in, 384n17
  The Death of Distance (Cairncross), 150
  demographic projection for, 150–152, 151f
  density and, 114–115, 115t
  economics of, 155–156, 381
  for farmers, 134–135
  housing supply and, 271, 272f, 273–274, 287
  labor participation rates, 386n17
  metropolitan labor markets, 274–275, 275f
  in Seoul (Korea), 43
  spatial distribution and, 126
  theory of, 45, 46t, 47–48, 219–220, 314–315
  transport and, 34, 35f–36f, 36–41, 38f–39f
  in urban economics, 359–360, 360f

urban planning and, 11–15, 57–59, 58f, 84f, 85,
  106–107, 107f, 143, 220–221
in US, 42–43
Labor mobility, 30
Land development
  banking for, 364–367
  containment-driven planning in, 342
  economics of, 120–124, 125f, 283–284, 302–303
  FAR in, 276–277
  government in, 285
  housing consumption and, 252–254, 253f
  incentives for, 320–321
  market-driven planning in, 342
  markets for, 388n26
  municipal governments in, 358–361, 360f
  policy for, 233–234, 303–304, 365–367
  politics of, 364–365
  RDP for, 268–269
  technology for, 380–381
  theory of, 383n4
  urban economics of, 273
  of urban land, 335–337
  in US, 236–237
Land markets, 12–13, 96
Land price
  agricultural land and, 135–136
  complex zoning for, 331–332
  density and, 140
  economics of, 8–9
  land price gradients, 104, 104f
  profile for, 104f
  in spatial distribution, 100–101, 111–113, 112f
  theory of, 304–305
  tolls and, 97, 100
  for Wall Street, 317–318
Land readjustment, 385n7
Land supply, 305–306, 339–340, 340f, 344
Land use
  affordability in, 334
  in China, 11–13, 15, 381
  demand-driven land use, 291
  density and, 387n17
  economics of, 236–239, 238f, 329–330
  FAR in, 84f, 88, 297–298
  floor area consumption and, 320
  government and, 15–16, 146, 196–200, 198f,
    318–319, 368–369, 388n25
  in Hong Kong, 59–60
  markets for, 333
  in Paris, 310–312, 311f
  policy for, 304–306, 326–329, 328f, 330, 330f,
    344, 367–368

Land use (cont.)
 politics of, 337–338
 in Russia, 11, 13–15
 technology for, 10–11
 for urban economics, 336
 urban planning and, 48
 in US, 7, 59
Latin America. *See also specific cities; specific countries*
 Buenos Aires (Argentina), 156–158, 158f, 389n12
 Rio de Janeiro (Brazil), 102f, 103–104, 103t
 urban planning in, 339–340, 340f
Le Corbusier (architect), 4
 environment for, 298
 for Paris, 71–74, 72f, 74t, 335
 skylines for, 317
Lee, Chang-Woon, 28, 33, 38
L'Enfant, 66–68
Levittown, 335
Line agencies, 369–370
London, 335
 economics for, 178–180, 178t, 179f, 180t
 greenbelts in, 337
 markets in, 53
 transit in, 176–177
 transport modes in, 147–148
Los Angeles, 105–108, 106f–107f
Low-income housing, 249–250, 267, 294, 302–303, 366–367. *See also* Poverty
Luxury rentals, 279–281, 280f–281f, 282–283

Maids' rooms, 385n20
Malaysia, 263, 368
Malpezzi, Stephen, 18, 99, 101, 280, 316, 357
Manufacturing, 23–24
Maps, 353–354
Markets. *See also* Labor markets
 alternative urban shapes and, 335–337
 command economies, 14
 density and, 242–244, 243f
 design compared to, 1–2, 81–90, 84f
 functions in, 329–330
 government and, 249–250, 252, 301–302, 316–317
 growth and, 314–315, 340–344
 for land development, 388n26
 land markets, 12–13, 96
 for land use, 333
 in London, 53
 market-driven planning, 342
 market economies, 14

market equilibrium, 228
 in New York, 330, 330f
 parallel markets, 126–130, 127f, 129f
 policy for, 302
 "Size, Sprawl, Speed and the Efficiency of Cities" (Prud'homme/Lee), 33–34
 theory of, 303–304
 of urban economics, 369–370
 urban spatial structures in, 53, 56–57, 60–63, 91–92
Marx, Karl, 56
Marxism, 4, 56, 73–74
Master plans
 density in, 105
 government and, 47
 for Hanoi (Vietnam), 110, 130–136, 134f
 models for, 39–41, 39f, 108–109, 109f
 in Silicon Valley, 351–352
 spatial distribution in, 131–140, 134f
 theory of, 4, 8, 11, 394n2
 for transport, 28–30
 for urban planning, 353–354
Maximum density, 235–236
Mayo, Stephen, 357
Mayors. *See* Municipal governments
McNamara, Robert, 364–365
Mehndiratta, Shomik, 156
Merriam-Webster's Dictionary, 350, 388n18
Metropolitan labor markets, 274–275, 275f
Mexico City, 129–130, 129f, 162–165, 163f
Middle East, 22
Mies van der Rohe, Ludwig, 322–323
Migration, 289, 294
Miletus (Greece), 64–65
Mills, Edwin, 95
Minimum housing consumption, 256–260, 258f
Minimum standards
 for affordability, 235–236
 for FAR, 256–260, 258f
 for plot size, 274–276, 275f
 in standard urban model, 288–289
 theory of, 222–224
 in zoning, 231–235, 232f–233f
Mobility
 BRT for, 191–197, 192f, 194f, 196f
 commuting and, 146–147
 congestion and, 172–175, 174f
 congestion pricing and, 357f
 data for, 152–158, 158f, 168–172, 169f, 170t, 185t, 186–190, 188f–189f
 demographic projection and, 147–148

economics and, 45, 46t, 47–48, 158–160,
    190–191, 196–199, 198f, 201
environment and, 201–204, 204f, 206–208, 207f
GHG emissions and, 204–206, 206f, 208–211,
    209f–210f
government and, 64, 65f, 66–70, 69f
growth and, 28–29
for household income, 285
labor mobility, 30
parking and, 200
technology and, 149–152, 151f, 214–216, 215f,
    216t
theory of, 48–49
tolls and, 357f
transit and, 165–168, 166f–168f, 191–196, 192f,
    194f, 196f
transport and, 143–149, 160–165, 162f–163f,
    175–185, 178t, 179f, 180t, 182f–183f, 185t,
    211–214, 214f
transport modes and, 92, 143, 160–165,
    162f–163f
in urban planning, 48–49, 216–218, 217f, 337
Mobility First (Staley/Moore), 176
Models
    descriptive model, 101–105, 102f, 103t, 104f
    Los Angeles as, 105–108, 106f–107f
    for master plans, 39–41, 39f, 108–109, 109f
    quantitative models, 94–95
    standard urban model, 95–97, 98f–99f, 99, 101,
        113–114, 115–118, 117f, 129–130, 140–141,
        288–289
Monetary Policy Committee (UK), 305
Monitoring, of indicators, 352–353
Monocentric model (city). *See* Standard urban
    model
Monocentric model (transport), 39, 39f
Moore, Adrian, 176
Moretti, Enrico, 219
Mortgages, 226–227, 254–256, 255f, 356
Moses, Robert, 176
Motorcycles, 126, 135, 148, 190, 275
    data for, 162–165, 162f–163f
    policy for, 211
    travel time and, 167–168
Mumbai (India), 17, 57–59, 58f, 308–309, 384n12
Municipal governments, 276–277, 304
    CBDs for, 315, 316f
    in land development, 358–361, 360f
    policy for, 352, 364–365
    urban economics for, 314–315, 354–355
    in urban planning, 349–351, 369–372, 371f
Muth, Richard, 95

NASA, 3
Nathan, Max, 306
Negative externalities
    theory of, 18, 55, 73, 86, 159–161, 165, 171, 199,
        284
    in zoning, 318–321, 324–327, 331–332, 349
New York, 63f
    affordability in, 275–281, 278f, 280f–281f
    affordable housing in, 281–282, 285–287
    Art Deco building in, 326
    Chrysler building in, 326
    culture of, 262
    design in, 319–321
    economics for, 178–180, 178t, 179f, 180t,
        284–285
    Flat Iron building in, 326
    government in, 176, 230, 231–235, 232f–233f,
        267, 283–284, 300, 376–377
    height regulations in, 315
    historical preservation in, 60–61
    Hudson Yards in, 333, 350
    incentives in, 282–283, 319
    incentive zoning in, 322–325
    inclusionary zoning in, 275–276, 279–281,
        281f
    Independent Budge Office for, 284–285
    informal housing in, 235–236
    markets in, 330, 330f
    objective functions in, 317–319
    Paris compared to, 334
    policy in, 200, 208–209, 209f
    poverty in, 287–288
    private space in, 321–322, 322f
    Rockefeller Center in, 326
    Seagram building in, 322–326, 331
    Silicon Valley compared to, 351
    South Africa compared to, 275–276
    tolls in, 170–172
    transit in, 186–188, 188f
    transport modes in, 165–167, 166f, 167t
    urban planning in, 54–55, 144, 326–329, 328f,
        393n8
    Vanderbilt Corridor in, 333
    Wall Street in, 317–318
    Woolworth building in, 326, 331
    zoning in, 318–319, 326–329, 328f, 349–350,
        389n2
New Zealand, 228, 386n16
Niemeyer, Oscar, 4
NIMBY, 333, 337–338, 393n18
Ningbo (China), 73–77, 74t, 75f–76f
Nissan Leaf, 208–210, 209f

Northern Girls (Keyi), 392n25
Not In My Back Yard. *See* NIMBY

Objective functions, 307–310, 317–319, 334, 344–346, 345f–346f
OECD. *See* Organisation for Economic Co-operation and Development
OED. *See* Operations Evaluation Department
Old Law Tenements, 231–235, 232f–233f
Open spaces, 84f, 87–88
Operational applications, 140–141
Operations Evaluation Department (OED), 365
Organisation for Economic Co-operation and Development (OECD), 337–338, 353, 384n9
Outcome indicators, 361–362, 364–365
Output indicators, 362, 364–365
Overman, Henry, 306

Parallel markets, 126–130, 127f, 129f
Paris, 63f, 104f, 392n3, 393n5
    Bibliothèque Nationale de France in, 310
    CBDs in, 71–73, 72f
    Chambres de bonnes (maids' rooms) in, 385n20
    La Defense in, 315, 316f
    Eiffel Tower in, 309
    government in, 315–317, 316f
    les Halles in, 310
    height regulations in, 312–314, 313f
    land use in, 310–312, 311f
    Le Corbusier for, 71–74, 72f, 74t, 335
    New York compared to, 334
    objective functions in, 309–310
    Pompidou Museum in, 310
    Tour Montparnasse in, 310
    transit in, 176–177
    transport in, 44, 44f, 164–165
    transport modes in, 165–167, 166f, 167t
    urban economics in, 314–315
Parking, 200
Park spaces, 84f, 87–88
Path dependency, 384n16
People's Republic of China. *See* China
Permits. *See* Building permits
Phatak, V. K., 17
PIR. *See* Price income ratio
Pisarski, Alan, 28, 42–43
Planet of Cities (Angel), 21–22
Plot size, 246, 256, 274–276, 275f, 289

Policy. *See also* Containment policy
    for affordability, 267–268, 300–301, 328–329, 356–357, 357f
    bulk regulations as, 393n8
    Compact City Policies: A Comparative Assessment (OECD), 338
    for congestion, 154–158, 158f, 190–199, 192f, 194f, 196f, 198f
    for congestion pricing, 170–172
    deadwood regulations as, 368–369
    for density, 336
    for design, 223–224, 322–324, 346–347, 359–361, 360f
    economics and, 25, 152–154, 287
    for environment, 222
    FAR as, 323
    for floor area consumption, 243
    Good neighbor rules as, 349
    government in, 9–11, 118–120, 138–139, 141, 162–163, 252–254, 253f, 255–256
    for growth, 113–114
    for housing consumption, 252
    housing policy, 242, 249–250, 252, 260–263, 261f, 274, 301
    for housing pools, 281–282
    housing stock and, 246–247
    for immigration, 375–376
    income-consumption relation for, 249
    in India, 383n5, 385n3
    indicators for, 363
    integration policy, 292
    Joint Living-Work Quarters for Artists rule in, 326–329, 328f
    for land development, 233–234, 303–304, 365–367
    for land use, 304–306, 326–329, 328f, 330, 330f, 344, 367–368
    for markets, 302
    for motorcycles, 211
    for municipal governments, 352, 364–365
    in New York, 200, 208–209, 209f
    NIMBY as, 333
    OECD for, 337–338
    for poverty, 366–367
    real estate and, 229–230
    reform for, 304–306
    for road networks, 180–185, 182f–183f, 185t
    in Russia, 279
    Sierra Club for, 337–338
    subletting as, 266–267
    for taxes, 279–280, 280f

technology for, 97–198, 208–211, 209f–210f,
  214–218, 215f, 216t, 217f
theory of, 332–333
for transport modes, 211–213
travel time in, 363
by UN, 234
UN Habitat for, 337–338
for urban economics, 111–113, 112f
Urban Economics and Urban Policy (Cheshire/
  Nathan/Overman), 306
for urban planning, 358–361, 360f
World Bank for, 337–338, 364–365
for zoning, 277–278, 278f, 283–284
Politics
  of alternative urban shapes, 337–339, 346–347
  of building permits, 6–7
  of communism, 15–16, 246
  cultural politics, 327–329
  of culture, 5–6, 367–368
  economics and, 375
  of environment, 337–339
  of FAR, 283–284, 286
  of government, 259–260, 314–315, 319–321
  of Hanoi (Vietnam), 138–139
  of health, 360
  of housing policy, 262
  of Kampungs, 290–292, 291f
  of KIP, 290–291, 291f
  of land development, 364–365
  of land use, 337–338
  Marxism, 4
  of migration, 289
  of poverty, 220–221, 287–288, 301–302, 361
  of preservation, 316–317
  of public space, 1–2, 25–27, 323–324
  of South Africa, 101
  in UK, 375
  of urban economics, 303–304, 320–321
  of urban planning, 306
  in US, 350–351
  for world Bank, 365–367
Pompidou Museum (Paris), 310
Population. *See* Density
Port-au-Prince (Haiti), 4, 8–11
Portland (Oregon), 344, 388n24
Poverty
  affordability and, 236–239, 238f, 287–288
  culture of, 256–257, 296–300
  economics of, 242–243
  FAR and, 284–285
  gentrification and, 246–247
  for government, 290–292, 291f

homeless population in, 302
  in informal settlements, 257
  infrastructure and, 260
  in New York, 287–288
  plot size for, 289
  policy for, 366–367
  politics of, 220–221, 287–288, 301–302, 361
  rentals for, 279–281, 280f–281f
  section 8 for, 286
  in South Africa, 47–48
  subsidies and, 273
  theory of, 16
  in urban economics, 82, 141, 362
  urban planning for, 53, 223–224, 249–250
  welfare for, 284–285
  zoning for, 277
Preservation, 312, 313–314, 316–319, 326–327
Price/income ratio (PIR)
  in affordability, 224–230, 225f, 227f–228f, 231
  data from, 225–228, 227f–228f
  economics of, 229, 244
  theory of, 224–228, 225f, 227f–228f, 244
  topography in, 224–225, 225f
Private space, 63–64 63f, 321–322, 322f
Property taxes, 355, 393n16
Proportionate effect, 21–22
Prud'homme, Rémy, 28, 33, 38
Psychology, in urban planning, 367–368
Public housing, 250, 264–267, 265f
Public space
  politics of, 1–2, 25–27, 323–324
  for transport, 311–312
  in urban planning, 61–63, 332–333
  zoning for, 319–320
Pudong (China), 54, 78–81, 78f, 80f, 386n10

Quantitative models, 94–95
Quigley, John M., 356
Quirós, Tatiana, 156

RDP. *See* Reconstruction and Development
  Program
Real estate
  economics of, 27–28, 112f, 304, 331–332
  low-income housing and, 302–303
  policy and, 229–230
  urban planning and, 319
Reconstruction and Development Program
  (RDP), 268–271, 270f, 272f, 273–275, 275f
Reform, for policy, 304–306
Regulations. *See* Building permits; Codes;
  Government

Regulatory leverage, 320–321
RELU-TRAN (transportation model), 95
Rentals
  economics of, 317, 391n4
  for government, 277–278, 278f
  luxury rentals, 279–283, 280f–281f
  rent control, 264–267, 265f
  section 8 for, 286
  subletting of, 266–267, 282–283
  supply mechanisms for, 314
  taxes for, 283–284
Research, 21, 263
Residential areas
  CBDs as, 318, 327–328, 328f
  in China, 73–77, 74t, 75f–76f
Reverse density gradients, 273, 344
Rio de Janeiro (Brazil), 102f, 103–104, 103t
Road networks
  commuting routes and, 384n13
  in Indonesia, 292
  policy for, 180–185, 182f–183f, 185t
  topography and, 61
  urban economics of, 175–180, 178t, 179f, 180t
  urban spatial structures and, 63–64, 63f, 65f,
    66–70
  Vanderbilt Corridor (New York), 333
Rockefeller Center (New York), 326
Rural areas, 126–129, 127f, 129f, 134–135
Russia
  design in, 4
  government in, 26–27
  Japan compared to, 373
  Kombinats in, 383n4
  land use in, 11, 13–15
  policy in, 279

Sanctuary cities, 376
San Francisco, 227–228, 227f, 227f–228f
Scale economy, 10
Science, 2–3, 9, 13–15, 20–28, 40
Seagram building (New York), 322–326, 331
Section 8, 286
Seoul (Korea), 38, 43, 45f, 46t, 384n18
Shanghai (China). See China; Pudong
Shelter consumption, 244–247, 245f
Shenzhen (China), 22, 295–300, 297f, 392n25
Sierra Club, 337–338
Silicon Valley, 351–352
Singapore, 184, 197–198, 198f, 374, 376, 386n15,
  387n6
"Size, Sprawl, Speed and the Efficiency of
  Cities" (Prud'homme/Lee), 33–34

Skylines, 78, 78f, 317–319, 318
Smart growth, 334
Smith, Adam, 305
Social housing, 302
South Africa, 386n16. See also Gauteng
  affordability in, 366–367, 388n26
  China compared to, 299
  government in, 222–223, 268–269, 274
  New York compared to, 275–276
  politics of, 101
  poverty in, 47–48
  RDP in, 268–271, 270f, 272f, 273–275, 275f
  spatial distribution in, 271, 272f, 273
  supply side subsidies in, 268–269
  transit in, 274–275
  transport modes in, 167–168, 168f
Soviet Union (USSR). See Russia
Spatial data, 11, 46t
  theory of, 30, 39–45, 39f, 44f–45f
  for urban planning, 212–216, 214f–215f, 216t
Spatial distribution
  of agricultural land, 114–116, 115t, 118, 119f,
    120–122, 121f–122f
  density and, 110–111, 111f
  descriptive model for, 101–105, 102f, 103t, 104f
  economics of, 93–97, 98f–99f, 99, 109–110,
    120–124, 134f
  labor markets and, 126
  land price in, 100–101, 111–113, 112f
  in Los Angeles, 105–108, 106f–107f
  in master plans, 131–140, 134f
  in South Africa, 271, 272f, 273
  standard urban model for, 101, 113–114,
    115–118, 117f, 130–131, 140–141
  theory of, 126–130, 127f, 129f
  of urban land, 118–120
  for urban planning, 108–109, 109f
Sprawl. See Standard urban model
Sprawl (Bruegmann), 116
Staff agencies, 369–370
Staley, Samuel, 176
Standard of living, 290–291
Standard urban model, 388n18
  minimum standards in, 288–289
  for spatial distribution, 101, 113–114, 115–118,
    117f, 129–130, 140–141
  Sprawl (Bruegmann), 116
  theory of, 95–97, 98f–99f, 99, 335–336
  "Urban Sprawl: Lessons from Urban
    Economics" (Brueckner), 336
Stanford University, 351
Stockholm, 385n22

St. Petersburg (Russia), 373, 384n6
Strategic Community Investment Report Data,
   353
Streetscapes, 331–332
Street space. *See* Road networks
Subdivisions, 230–231, 230f
Subletting, 266–267, 282–283
Subsidies
   in affordability, 303–304
   demand side subsidies, 260–263, 262f, 267–268,
      286, 304
   economics of, 100–101
   for infrastructure, 290–292, 291f
   poverty and, 273
   supply side subsidies, 264–269, 265f, 285–286
Subways. *See* Transit; Transport
Supply mechanisms, 277–278, 278f, 302–304, 314,
   325, 391n10
Supply side subsidies, 264–269, 265f, 303–304
Surabaya. *See* Indonesia; Kampungs
Sustainability
   in Amsterdam, 338–339
   as objective functions, 344–346, 345f–346f
   sustainable cities for, 113–114, 131–133, 134f
   theory of, 326–329, 328f, 345–346, 345f–346f
Sustainable cities, 113–114, 131–133, 134f

Taleb, Nassim Nicholas, 308–309
Taxes
   congestion pricing, 23–24, 30
   policy for, 279–280, 280f
   property taxes, 355, 393n16
   for rentals, 283–284
   tax credits, 267
   tax incentives, 284–285, 377–378
   in urban economics, 349
Technology
   affordability and, 345–346, 346f
   in Buenos Aires (Argentina), 389n12
   in China, 386n11
   culture and, 384n6
   for data, 3, 101–102, 102f, 145, 156–158, 158f
   economics and, 367–368
   environment and, 204–208, 206f–207f
   for government, 369
   Internet as, 383n2
   for land development, 380–381
   for land use, 10–11
   microcomputers, 21
   mobility and, 149–152, 151f, 214–216, 215f,
      216t
   Nissan Leaf for, 208–210, 209f

   for policy, 97–198, 208–211, 209f–210f, 214–218,
      215f, 216t, 217f
   sustainable cities as, 113–114, 131–133, 134f
   for transport, 51–52, 161–162, 162f, 176
   in urban economics, 352
   in urban planning, 239–240, 380–381
   in US, 199–200
Telecommuting, 42
Thailand, 256
Theory
   of adequate housing, 269–270
   of affordability, 49, 219, 301
   of affordable housing, 276–277
   of alternative urban shapes, 307–310, 329–330,
      333, 346–347
   of city-states, 366
   of congestion, 201
   of containment policy, 337–339, 341–344
   of data, 146–147
   of demographic projection, 212–213
   of density gradients, 97–100, 98f–99f, 103t,
      107–111, 111f
   density in, 108–109, 109f
   of design, 8–9
   in economics, 240–241, 253–254
   of engineering, 322–323
   of GHG emissions, 40, 201–202, 334–335, 338
   Gibrat's law, 21–22
   of growth, 27–28
   for Hanoi (Vietnam), 138–139
   of height regulations, 311–312, 311f
   of household income, 221
   of housing consumption, 302–303
   of incentives, 328–329
   of incentive zoning, 329–330
   of inclusionary zoning, 276–278, 278f, 282–287
   of income-consumption relation, 249
   of informal settlements, 127–130, 129f, 288
   KIP, 267–268
   of labor markets, 45, 46t, 47–48, 219–220,
      314–315
   of land development, 383n4
   of land markets, 96
   of land price, 304–305
   of markets, 303–304
   of master plans, 4, 8, 11, 394n2
   of minimum standards, 222–224
   of mobility, 48–49
   of negative externalities, 18, 55, 73, 86, 159–161,
      165, 171, 199, 284
   of PIR, 224–228, 225f, 227f–228f, 244
   of policy, 332–333

Theory (cont.)
  of poverty, 16
  proportionate effect, 21–22
  of regulatory leverage, 320–321
  of sanctuary cities, 376
  science and, 2–3
  of smart growth, 334
  of spatial data, 30, 39–45, 39f, 44f–45f
  of spatial distribution, 126–130, 127f, 129f
  of standard urban model, 95–97, 98f–99f, 99,
    335–336
  of sustainability, 326–329, 328f, 345–346,
    345f–346f
  of telecommuting, 42
  for transport modes, 212–217, 216t
  trickle-down theory, 240–241, 391n10
  of urban economics, 2–3, 13, 17
  of urban planning, 27–33, 32f
  of urban spatial structures, 52–53
  of wasteful use, 344
Tianjin (China), 114–116, 115t, 339
TOD. See Transit-oriented development
Tolls, 387n6
  as congestion pricing, 23–24, 49, 201, 217
  land price and, 97, 100
  mobility and, 357f
  in New York, 170–172
  in Singapore, 387n6
  in urban planning, 61–62, 349–350
Topography
  density, 84f
  of environment, 202
  in land supply, 344
  in PIR, 224–225, 225f
  in Rio de Janeiro, 103–104
  road networks and, 61
  in urban planning, 43–44, 44f
  in zoning, 308, 312
Tourism, 313–314
Tour Montparnasse (Paris), 310
Toyama (Japan), 373, 376–379, 378f
Toyota, 216–217, 217f
Traditional externalities, 311–312, 317–319
Trains. See Transit; Transport
Transit, 390n21
  in Beijing (China), 173–175, 174f
  in CBDs, 311
  data for, 361–362
  economics of, 158–160, 362
  GTFS for, 156, 389n10
  investments in, 362–363
  in London, 176–177

mobility and, 165–168, 166f–168f, 191–196, 192f,
    194f, 196f
  in New York, 186–188, 188f
  in Paris, 176–177
  in South Africa, 274–275
  transit bonuses, 333
  transport modes and, 156, 158, 160–161, 209f,
    211–212
  travel time and, 358–359
Transit-oriented development (TOD), 70–71
Transport. See also Bus rapid transit
  in Beijing (China), 162–165, 163f, 166–168,
    167t
  CO2-e and, 208–211, 209f–210f
  composite model, 39f, 40
  data on, 31–33, 32f, 355
  demographic projection and, 169–170, 170t
  dispersed model for, 39–40, 39f
  economics of, 19–20
  in France, 31–33, 32f
  growth and, 49
  in Hanoi (Vietnam), 162–165, 163f
  indicators for, 361
  labor markets and, 34, 35f–36f, 36–41, 38f–39f
  master plan for, 28–30
  in Mexico City, 162–165, 163f
  mobility and, 143–149, 160–165, 162f–163f,
    175–185, 178f, 179f, 180t, 182f–183f, 185t,
    211–214, 214f
  monocentric model for, 39, 39f
  in Paris, 44, 44f, 164–165
  public space for, 311–312
  RELU-TRAN for, 95
  in Seoul (Korea), 38
  technology for, 51–52, 161–162, 162f, 176
  telecommuting and, 42
  travel time and, 184–185, 185t, 384n17
  urban village model for, 39f, 40–41
Transport modes
  BRT as, 191–196, 192f, 194f, 196f
  data for, 157f, 161–162, 162f, 184t–185t, 188–191,
    188f–189f
  government and, 148, 152, 274–275
  in London, 147–148
  mobility and, 92, 143, 160–165, 162f–163f
  in New York, 165–167, 166f, 167t
  in Paris, 165–167, 166f, 167t
  policy for, 211–213
  in South Africa, 167–168, 168f
  theory for, 212–217, 216t
  transit and, 156, 158, 160–161, 209f, 211–212
  urban economics of, 176–181, 178t, 179f, 180t

Travel time
  data for, 165–171, 166f, 167t, 168f–169f, 170t
  motorcycles and, 167–168
  in policy, 363
  transit and, 358–359
  transport and, 184–185, 185t, 384n17
  urban planning for, 213–214, 214f
Travel time index (TTI), 172–175, 174f
Trickle-down theory, 240–241, 391n10
TTI. *See* Travel time index
Tunneling. *See* Road networks

UK. *See* United Kingdom
UN. *See* United Nations
United Kingdom (UK), 18, 305–306, 375. *See also*
  London
United Nations (UN)
  policy by, 234
  UN Habitat, 337–338
  United Nations Development Programme, 8–9,
    68–70, 69f
  in urban planning, 345–346, 346f
  for Yemen, 364
United States (US), 231. *See also specific cities*
  Canada compared to, 375
  China compared to, 189–190
  culture of, 335
  density in, 59
  economics in, 338–339, 356
  environment in, 208–211, 209f–210f
  EPA in, 203–206
  GDP in, 219
  government in, 18, 375
  HUD in, 18
  labor markets in, 42–43
  Land development in, 236–237
  land use in, 7, 59
  politics in, 350–351
  technology in, 199–200
  urban economics in, 238–239
  voucher system in, 261
Urban containment. *See* Containment policy
Urban economics. *See also* Price/income ratio
  agricultural land in, 122–124, 125f
  banking in, 318
  data for, 171–172, 229–230
  density in, 356
  design and, 61, 150–152, 151f
  economic rate of return for, 363—364
  FAR in, 321–322, 322f
  floor area consumption in, 331–332, 341–342
  in France, 25

GHG emissions and, 338–339
  for government, 283–284, 312–313, 313f
  in India, 17, 237–239, 238f
  labor markets in, 359–360, 360f
  of land development, 273
  land supply in, 305–306
  land use for, 336
  markets of, 369–370
  Marxism in, 56
  in Mumbai (India), 308–309
  for municipal governments, 314–315, 354–355
  in Paris, 314–315
  policy for, 111–113, 112f
  politics of, 303–304, 320–321
  in Port-au-Prince, 9–11
  poverty in, 82, 141, 362
  of road networks, 175–180, 178t, 179f, 180t
  in Singapore, 197–198, 198f
  supply mechanisms for, 391n10
  taxes in, 349
  technology in, 352
  theory of, 2–3, 13, 17
  of Toyama (Japan), 373, 376–379, 378f
  of transport modes, 176–181, 178t, 179f, 180t
  urban planning and, 354–355
  "Urban Sprawl: Lessons from Urban
    Economics" (Brueckner), 336
  in US, 238–239
  of villages, 294
  villages in, 126–130, 127f, 129f
Urban Economics and Urban Policy (Cheshire/
  Nathan/Overman), 306
Urban expansion, 334–335, 339–340
Urban growth, 372–376, 374f
Urban growth boundaries, 344
Urbanization. *See specific topics*
Urban land
  agricultural land compared to, 115–118, 117f,
    119f, 122f
  land development of, 335–337
  spatial distribution of, 118–120
  urban land supply, 252–254, 253f
Urban model. *See* Standard urban model
Urban planning
  Atlas of Urban Expansion (Angel), 116, 339–340,
    340f
  auditing for, 368–369
  in Beijing (China), 73–77, 74t, 75f–76f, 352
  in Brazil, 77–78, 77f
  for BRT, 155, 160–162, 162f
  CBDs in, 36, 36f, 37–42, 38f–39f
  in China, 73–77, 74t, 75f–76f, 309

Urban planning (cont.)
  City Planning Departments for, 369–372, 371f
  containment-driven planning, 342
  culture of, 18
  data for, 84f, 90, 305, 353, 355–358, 357f
  demographic projection for, 109–110, 160–161, 175–176
  density in, 93–94, 100–101, 110–111, 111f, 372–376, 374f
  density profiles in, 342–343
  design compared to, 385n1
  economics and, 1–4, 8–9, 16–18, 144–146
  engineering compared to, 307–308, 354
  FAR in, 296–297, 297f
  GHG emissions in, 202–204, 204f
  goods in, 83–87, 84f
  government for, 16–17, 319–321
  growth for, 24–27
  immigration in, 374–375, 374f
  in India, 77–78, 77f, 236
  indicators for, 361–365
  in Indonesia, 128–129, 129f
  informal housing in, 256–260, 258f
  for informal settlements, 236–239, 238f
  labor markets and, 11–15, 57–59, 58f, 84f, 85, 106–107, 107f, 143, 220–221
  land use and, 48
  in Latin America, 339–340, 340f
  maps for, 353–354
  market-driven planning, 342
  Marxism in, 73–74
  master plans for, 353–354
  mobility in, 48–49, 216–218, 217f, 337
  municipal governments in, 349–351, 369–372, 371f
  NASA for, 3
  in New York, 54–55, 144, 326–329, 328f, 393n8
  objective functions in, 309
  operational applications for, 140–141
  policy for, 358–361, 360f
  politics of, 306
  for poverty, 53, 223–224, 249–250
  preservation in, 317–319
  of private space, 321–322, 322f
  private space in, 63–64 63f
  psychology in, 367–368
  public space in, 61–63, 332–333
  real estate and, 319
  Silicon Valley in, 351–352
  spatial data for, 212–216, 214f–215f, 216t
  spatial distribution for, 108–109, 109f
  for streetscapes, 331–332

  technology in, 239–240, 380–381
  theory of, 27–33, 32f
  tolls in, 61–62, 349–350
  topography in, 43–44, 44f
  for travel time, 213–214, 214f
  UN in, 345–346, 346f
  United Nations Development Programme for, 8–9
  urban economics and, 354–355
  Urban Economics and Urban Policy (Cheshire/Nathan/Overman), 306
  villages in, 126
  World Urbanization Prospects (2014) for, 378–380, 379f
Urban road standards, 84f, 87
Urban-rural boundaries, 118, 119f
Urban spatial structures
  design for, 71–78, 72f, 74t, 75f–77f
  economics of, 81–90, 84f
  FAR in, 54–56
  in markets, 53, 56–57, 60–63, 91–92
  in Mumbai, 57–59, 58f
  in Pudong, 78–81, 78f, 80f
  road networks and, 63–64, 63f, 65f, 66–70
  theory of, 52–53
"Urban Sprawl: Lessons from Urban Economics" (Brueckner), 336
Urban village model, 39f, 40–41, 296–300, 297f
US. *See* United States
USSR. *See* Russia
Utopias. *See* Alternative urban shapes

Vanderbilt Corridor (New York), 333
Vehicle density, 182–183, 182f–183f
Vietnam. *See* Hanoi
Villages, 293–294
  as rural areas, 126–130, 127f, 129f
  urban village model, 39f, 40–41, 296–300, 297f
Voucher systems, 260–263, 261f

Wall Street, 317–318
Wang, Ning, 15
Washington, D.C., 66–67
Wasteful use, 344
Welfare, 284–285
Wheaton, William, 95
Woolworth building (New York), 326, 331
Workers. *See* Labor markets
World Bank, 11–12, 21, 263, 337, 364–367
World Trade Organization (WTO), 132

World Urbanization Prospects (2014), 378–380, 379f
Wright, Jim, 8–11, 18
WTO. *See* World Trade Organization

Yemen, 68–70, 69f, 364

Zoning. *See also* Inclusionary zoning
  in affordability, 281–282, 285–287
  for alternative urban shapes, 326–332, 328f, 330f
  codes for, 324, 329
  for commercial districts, 330, 330f
  complex zoning, 331–332
  in design, 321–322, 322f
  environment and, 153–154
  government in, 91–92, 235–236, 264–267, 265f, 310–312, 311f, 324–325
  incentive zoning, 322–325, 329–330
  inclusive zoning, 264–267, 265f
  minimum standards in, 231–235, 232f–233f
  negative externalities in, 318–321, 324–327, 331–332, 349
  in New York, 318–319, 326–329, 328f, 349–350, 389n2
  policy for, 277–278, 278f, 283–284
  for poverty, 277
  for public space, 319–320
  for rural areas, 133–135
  supply mechanisms for, 277–278, 278f
  topography in, 308, 312